THE SOCIETY FOR
POST-MEDIEVAL ARCHAEOLOGY
MONOGRAPH 11

THE COLONIAL LANDSCAPE OF THE BRITISH CARIBBEAN

THE COLONIAL LANDSCAPE OF THE BRITISH CARIBBEAN

Edited by

Roger Leech and Pamela Leech

THE BOYDELL PRESS

Details of previously published titles are available from the Society

First published 2021
The Boydell Press, Woodbridge

ISBN 978 1 78327 565 6

The Boydell Press is an imprint of Boydell & Brewer Ltd
PO Box 9, Woodbridge, Suffolk IP12 3DF, UK
and of Boydell & Brewer Inc.
668 Mt Hope Avenue, Rochester, NY 14620–2731, USA
website: www.boydellandbrewer.com

A CIP catalogue record for this book is available
from the British Library

This publication is printed on acid-free paper

FSC
www.fsc.org
MIX
Paper from
responsible sources
FSC® C013056

Printed and bound in Great Britain by TJ Books Limited, Padstow, Cornwall

The Society for Post-Medieval Archaeology
dedicates this volume to the memory of its
deceased members Jon Brett and Geoff Egan,
both contributors, and each sadly missed

CONTENTS

LIST OF ILLUSTRATIONS

Chapter 3

All drawings and photographs by author unless otherwise stated.

Chapter 4

Chapter 6

Chapter 7

Chapter 9

Chapter 10

All photographs by author.

Chapter 11

All drawings and photographs by author.

Chapter 12

All drawings and photographs by author unless otherwise stated.

TABLES

Chapter 6

The editors, contributors and publisher are grateful to all the institutions and persons listed for permission to reproduce the materials in which they hold copyright. Every effort has been made to trace the copyright holders; apologies are offered for any omission, and the publisher will be pleased to add any necessary acknowledgement in subsequent editions.

LIST OF CONTRIBUTORS

Todd M. Ahlman	Director of the Center for Archaeological Studies, Texas State University, San Marcos
David Barker	Independent scholar and consultant (formerly of Stoke on Trent Museums)
Jon Brett†	(formerly of Bristol City Council)
Phil Dunning	Parks Canada (retired)
Geoff Egan†	(formerly of Museum of London Archaeology)
William C. Found	Professor Emeritus, York University
David Higgins	Honorary Research Fellow, University of Liverpool, and Chairman of the Society for Clay Pipe Research
Carter L. Hudgins	Director Emeritus, Graduate Program in Historic Preservation, Clemson/College of Charleston
Gillian Hutchinson	Curator Emeritus at the National Maritime Museum, Greenwich, London, formerly Curator of Archaeology and Curator of the History of Cartography from 1980 to 2015.
Nigel Jeffries MCiFA FSA	Senior Specialist – Medieval and later pottery, glass and pipes, Museum of London Archaeology
Dr Eric Klingelhofer	Emeritus Professor of History, Mercer University
Dr Roger H. Leech	Visiting Professor of Archaeology, University of Southampton, former President of the Society for Post-Medieval Archaeology
Marco Meniketti	Professor, Department of Anthropology, San Jose State University
Louis P. Nelson	Assistant Professor of Architectural History, University of Virginia
Philippe Oszuścik	University of South Alabama (retired)
Dr Robert A. Philpott	Department of Archaeology, University of Liverpool, formerly Head of Archaeological Unit, National Museums Liverpool
Gerald F. Schroedl	Professor Emeritus, University of Tennessee, Knoxville

FOREWORD

The Black Lives Matter movement and protests, the challenging of the continued presence of statues to commemorate oppressive and exploitative individuals and practices from the recent past, and serious attempts to decolonize university curricula are all part of a dramatic and much-needed shake up to thinking about history and associated subjects, and how they have been dominated by western, white, often male and elite views. For those of us who are western, white and elite in terms of education, yet have research interests in regions outside Europe (and North America), there are major questions and challenges around how we undertake this research working in collaboration with local colleagues and communities. The 21st century has seen a growth in collaborative research projects between academic archaeologists, and in projects that work with different local communities. Being inclusive is a major driver for new archaeological projects, and we recognize that the 20th century model of western, white experts helicoptering into exotic locations to carry out research (supported by local infrastructure), and then taking the results back to western universities, and writing them up for the benefit of western scholars and academia is no longer fit for purpose, and is actively detrimental to local colleagues, communities and the archaeology itself.

This volume is based on original research in the Caribbean, focusing on the islands of Nevis and St Kitts. As the editor notes in his preface, it brings together work begun in 2001 and from a conference in 2005, organized in collaboration with the historical societies for St Kitts and Nevis, and it has taken many years to come to fruition. The monograph contains papers resulting from a project funded by the British Academy looking at the historical archaeology of the Atlantic rim, undertaken by the University of Southampton in collaboration principally with National Museums Liverpool and Bristol City Museum and Art Gallery. The Liverpool involvement was directly linked to its International Slavery Museum, devoted to relating untold stories of enslaved people, both historical and contemporary. The Bristol element was devoted to recruiting five young people of African or Caribbean heritage to be involved both in the archaeological project and in working alongside young people from Nevis, the results and their experiences being disseminated more widely through BBC Bristol Online's Black Echo (BBC 2001). We recognize that the contributors are from European and North American academic institutions and backgrounds, and that this does not reflect the reality of archaeological work in the Caribbean. There are many Caribbean scholars working in the region, carrying out original field projects and publishing their findings. This scholarship has a long history. Indeed, the International Association for Caribbean Archaeology has, since 1961, gathered together professional, avocational and student researchers from both inside and outside the region, and dedicated its last congress (Barbados 2019) to 'Re-Examining Self: Caribbean Archaeology in the 21st Century'. However, the majority of this work is not entering the Anglo-American sphere of academic publishing, due to a range of reasons and exclusionary barriers; within the Society for Post-Medieval Archaeology itself there has been a lack of a diversity policy for publications. Of course, this does not detract from the scholarly contributions of this volume to both historical archaeology and the archaeology of the Caribbean, and having recognized the issues around diversity and inclusivity, we see this publication is a catalyst for the Society to do things differently in the future. Part of 'doing things differently' includes efforts by the Society to expand both membership and the makeup of Council to better reflect those participating in global post-medieval archaeology.

The Council for the Society of Post-Medieval Archaeology
October 2020

Preface

ROGER H. LEECH

This study of post-medieval colonial landscape archaeology brings together two separate but linked strands of research. The first is a research project initiated in 2001, when the author was awarded a larger research grant by the British Academy to assess the archaeological evidence for the early colonial settlement and landscape of the two eastern Caribbean islands of Nevis and St Kitts, a pilot project for the historical archaeology of the Atlantic rim, to be undertaken in collaboration with Dr Mark Horton, then of the University of Bristol, and Bruce Williams, then manager of Bristol and Region Archaeological Services in Bristol City Museums. The second was the meeting held in conjunction with the research project and convened by the Society for Post-Medieval Archaeology on Nevis in 2005, and initiated by the author who was at that time its President. The meeting was to coincide with the research then being undertaken as a result of the British Academy grant and to provide, through discussion and subsequent networking, an input to the scholarly publications which would in due course emerge. This aspect of the meeting has been entirely successful, and many of the contributors now remain in contact as a result. Scholars who participated in the meeting have also been busy drawing on these experiences and contacts and producing their own publications in the interim, some of which should be highlighted here for their important contributions to Caribbean studies.[1]

THE BRITISH ACADEMY PILOT PROJECT

Background

The English Leeward Islands were colonized from the late 1620s onwards. By the end of the century the islands were densely settled and their wealth, shipped principally to Bristol and London, far outstripped that of the North American colonies in total. This is a remarkable story, explored by historians but scarcely at all through its archaeology. Much of what might be known of the early settlement of the islands still awaits telling. The archaeological examination of much of the colonial landscape, the plantations and fields of the 17th and 18th centuries, has still to be undertaken, enabling the material record to be considered alongside the meagre documentary sources, decimated by fire, hurricanes, earthquakes, tidal waves and other European powers.

In 2000 Southampton University undertook on Nevis a preliminary assessment of survey and evaluation techniques for investigating the early modern historical archaeology of the island. Following this Bristol University was invited to formulate a programme of archaeological research on St Kitts. In 2001 the two universities utilized their particular skills in developing a pilot project for landscape archaeology across the two islands, in addition working closely with Bristol City Museum, exploring the global context of its collections. From 2002 onwards Bristol University's involvement was succeeded by that of National Museums Liverpool.

The preliminary assessment

A preliminary assessment undertaken in 1999 and 2000 showed the potential for an archaeological perspective on the 17th- and early 18th-century colonization of the two islands. On Nevis sugar production had fallen dramatically before the mid 1940s. In the absence of post-war ploughing, archaeological deposits are often well preserved. On St Kitts sugar production had continued, and there had been much more destruction of archaeological remains. The early historic mapping and documentation for St Kitts was much better than that for Nevis. Also Nevis was settled from St Kitts, and St Kitts itself was for a period part French. There was considerable potential for comparative study, particularly looking at the construction of individual island identities.

Scholarly context

Current understanding of the colonization of the English and French Leeward Islands in the 17th century was seen to be based almost entirely on documentary research. General studies pointed to the need for an archaeological perspective. Dunn's single chapter on 'life in the tropics' highlighted the lack of archaeological data: 'nearly all the early houses on the islands have long since disappeared, victims of storms, fires and tropical rot'.[2]

Watts's study in historical geography again highlighted the need for an archaeological perspective, notably in his arguably simplistic mapping of the Mountravers/Pinney estate on Nevis.[3]

Archaeological research into the English settlement of the Leeward Islands had been undertaken on Barbados and Montserrat.[4] Much more research had been undertaken into the archaeology of slavery.[5] Most research had been focused on the 18th century onwards. On Barbados the widespread destruction of archaeology through modern ploughing highlighted the potential of Nevis and St Kitts for providing an archaeological perspective on the 17th century.

An archaeology of the early colonization of the Leeward Islands needed also to draw on work in Virginia.[6] The preliminary assessment on Nevis had already shown the absence of any evidence for early colonial impermanent architecture such as had been identified at many sites in Virginia and the east coast of North America.

Research Objectives

The overall objective of the pilot research project initiated in 2001 was to formulate a strategy and plan for a wider study, reconstructing the colonial landscapes of the two islands, using the field evidence in conjunction with documentary sources, to transform understanding of the 17th- and 18th-century colonization of the Leeward Islands. We intended from this to develop a methodology and an understanding of the field data potential in three principal areas.

First we aimed to reconstruct two samples of colonial landscape, from Nevis and St Kitts. These would enable a view and interpretation of the enclosed European landscape of the 1630s onwards. Within these landscapes we would identify/record roads and other routeways, plantation houses and works, villages, yards and allotments of enslaved Africans, water supply and other plantation infrastructure, and the relationships of these to the urban settlements.

Secondly from this data we would aim to begin to understand how European, African, and indigenous cultural identities were transformed in the economies of the 17th-century Caribbean and Atlantic. From the assessment we could already begin to see how English building techniques were combined with those from the Americas to create a new housing culture. We could also begin to see possibilities for identifying the earliest slave villages, of the mid to later 17th century, which in turn would enable us to provide new insights into the emergence of African-Caribbean cultural identities. In both these areas we would be looking for the archaeology of the indigenous Amerindian peoples, collaborating with colleagues researching the prehistoric settlement of Nevis (which formed a separate proposal to the British Academy).

Thirdly we would aim to begin to understand how to provide archaeological perspectives on the economic and social changes resulting from the 17th-century establishment of tobacco and then sugar production, and on who and what was involved in the Atlantic trade.

THE TWO SAMPLE LANDSCAPES

From the assessment, Mountravers on Nevis and Wingfield on St Kitts were selected as the two sample landscapes, each extending through scrub and rain forest from the sea to the mountain and each well documented from the early 18th century in the Pinney and Jeaffreson papers (in Bristol University and Hamilton College, NY, respectively).

The results of the survey of the Mountravers landscape survey are described and discussed in Chapter 12. During the project the Mountravers or Pinneys estate was acquired by the Newfound Corporation, to develop the 380 acres of the estate for two hotels, 265 villas or apartments, and an eighteen-hole golf course. Newfound then supplemented the British Academy funding in order to gain early access to the survey results and to enable recording of features exposed in the initial construction activities. The future of the redevelopment now appears to be uncertain.

On St Kitts, the Wingfield survey being undertaken by Bristol University under the direction of Dr Mark Horton commenced in 2002 with survey-based fieldwork in collaboration with the St Christopher Heritage Society. This was mostly undertaken by Mr Scott Cooper, who was based with the Society over a period of three months, developing their databases and site location information. The main targeted area of survey was the western end of the island, which had been designated for major redevelopment by the Whitegate Bay Development Corporation, where extensive hotels, golf courses and residential development were planned in the coming years. The archaeological survey revealed a number of unknown sites, including early sugar estates and a ruined Moravian church. These were recorded and mapped in detail, and a report was compiled on the results.

A major excavation and survey was planned for Spring–Summer 2003 at the Wingfield Estate and in the 17th-century urban settlement of Old Road, but following cancellation by Dr Horton owing to media commitments was replaced with a survey of the parishes of St Mary Cayon and Christchurch Nichola Town directed by Dr Robert Philpott of National Museums Liverpool, which then became a new partner in the project. This survey is described and discussed in Chapter 7.

THE SOCIETY FOR POST-MEDIEVAL ARCHAEOLOGY'S MEETING IN 2005

The papers presented to the Society for Post-Medieval Archaeology's meeting on Nevis in 2005 form the second strand to this volume. This meeting was deliberately sited

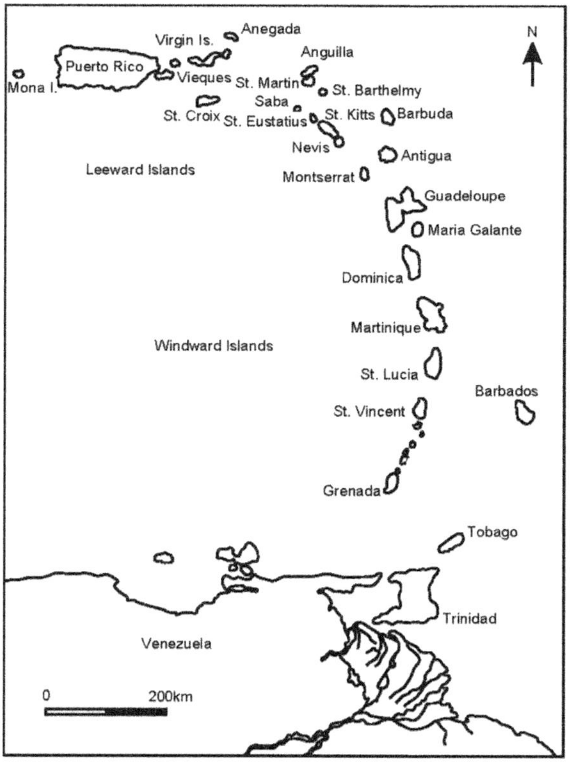

Fig. 0.1. Location of Nevis, St Kitts and St Eustatius in the Eastern Caribbean.

on Nevis so as to provide an input and discussion point for the survey projects then drawing to a close. This volume includes the most significant twelve of the 29 papers presented at the meeting. Site tours to Nevis, St Kitts, and St Eustatius (Fig. 0.1) were important for learning about sites surveyed specifically for the meeting and for networking and discussion (Figs 0.2–0.3). Following the meeting, some of the papers have been published elsewhere.[7] The planned survey of Wingfield was not presented at the meeting, but a report was given to the Society's meeting on Estate Landscapes in 2003 and published in the resulting monograph.[8]

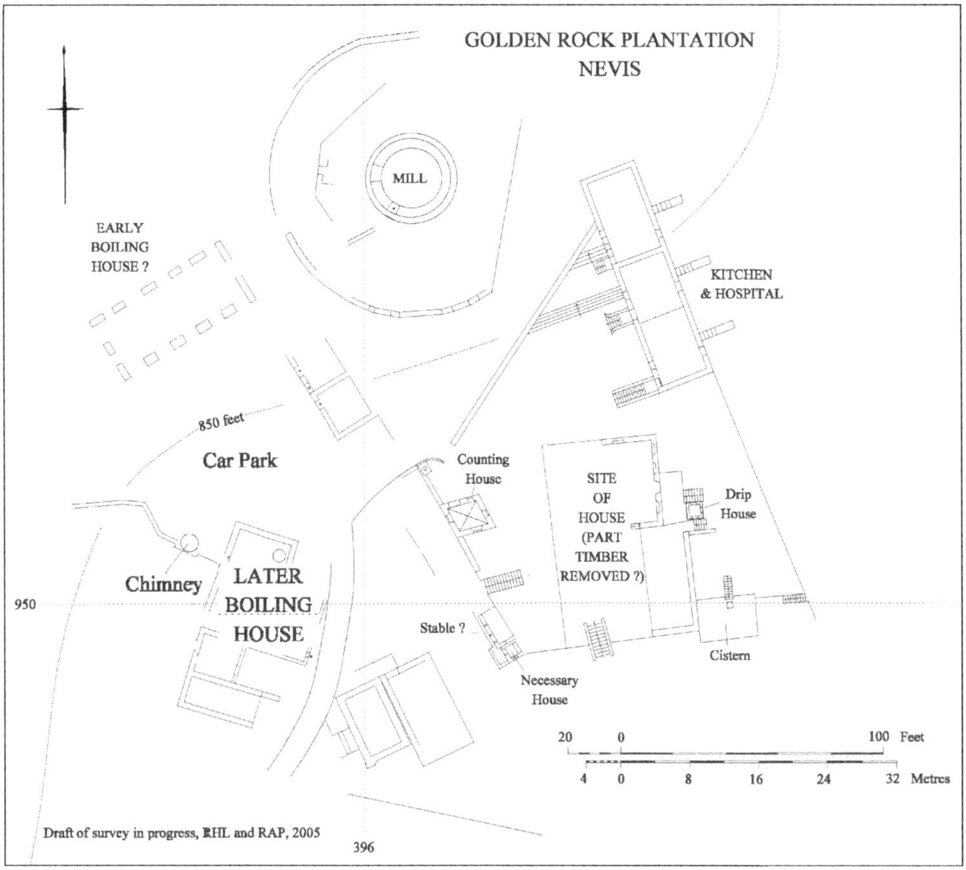

Fig. 0.2. Plan of the Golden Rock plantation, Nevis, visited on the meeting tour in July 2005.

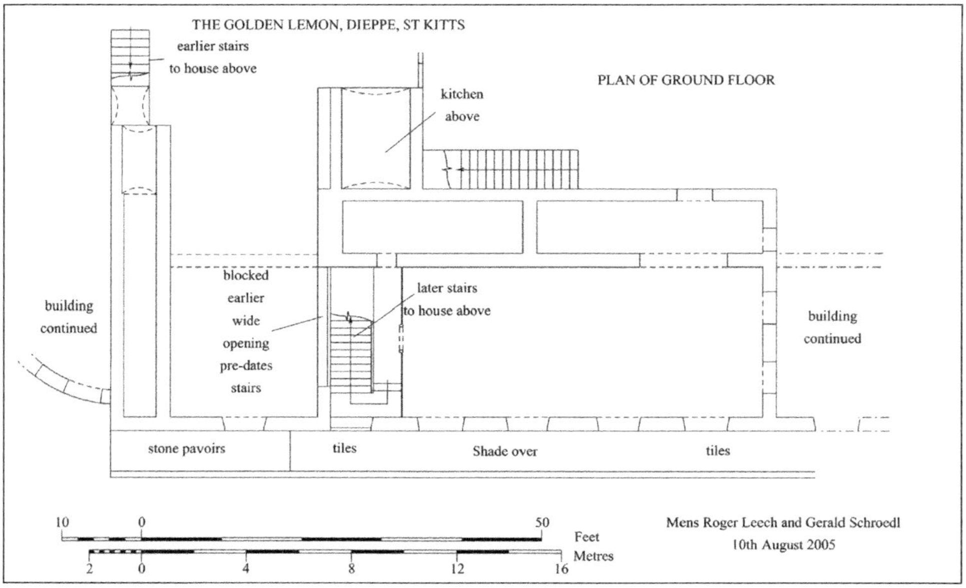

Fig. 0.3. Plan of the Golden Lemon Hotel, a former house and warehouse at Dieppe, St Kitts, visited on the meeting tour in July 2005.

MANAGING THE HISTORIC ENVIRONMENT

The fieldwork presented in this volume could undoubtedly make a contribution to the management of the historic environment of the two islands of St Kitts and Nevis. At present, Historic Environment Records such as exist in Europe and mainland North America for the protection of the archaeological heritage are largely lacking in the Caribbean. One outcome to this publication could be an attempt to construct such records for St Kitts and Nevis, both under considerable pressure from new development proposals.

One possible model is the record structure created for the management of the historic environment in Bristol, an Atlantic port closely associated with these two islands: there the Historic Environment Record (HER) is closely linked to a website directed at public interest in history and heritage, *Bristol Know Your Place*[9] (Figs 0.4–0.5). Highly relevant here are the recommendations recently made by ICOMOS in response to an unsuccessful application to designate Charlestown, Nevis, as a World Heritage Site. These are discussed further in the conclusion to Chapter 12, looking at the future of the colonial landscape of Nevis.

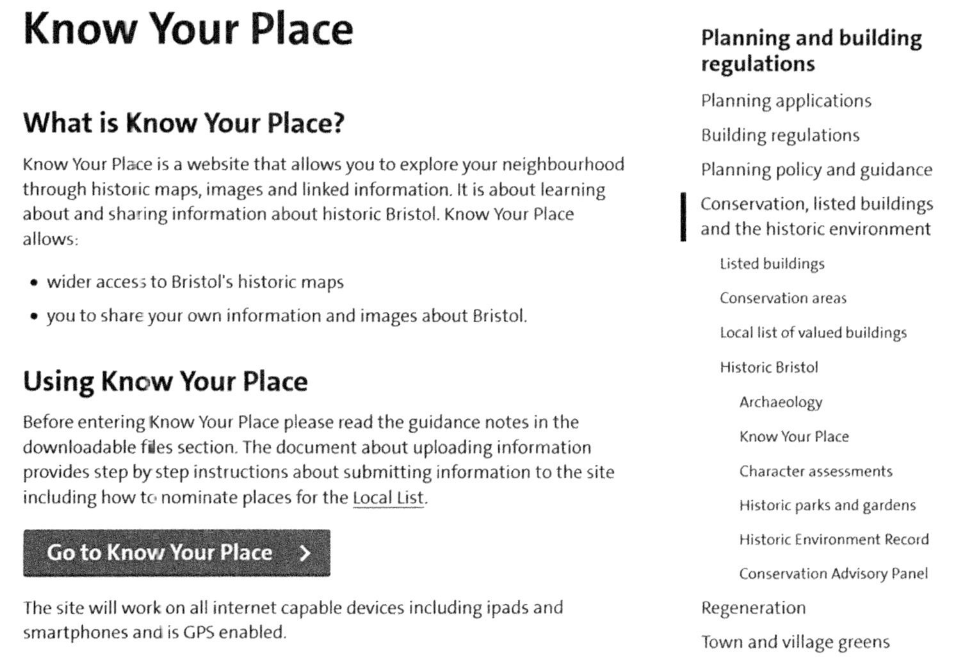

Fig. 0.4. *Bristol Know Your Place*, the home page.

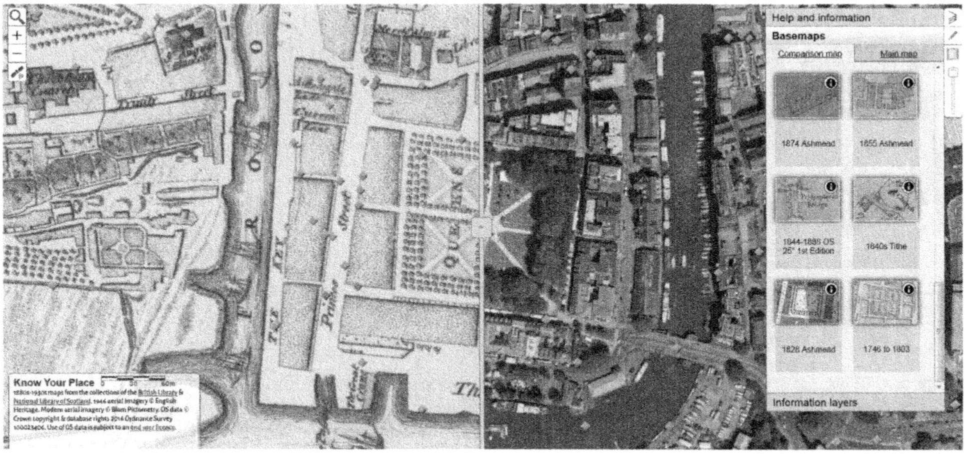

Fig. 0.5. *Bristol Know Your Place*, page presenting map options.

EDITORS' ACKNOWLEDGEMENTS

The Editors must first thank the contributors for their patience in waiting for this publication over a period of some ten years and for their willingness to assist rapidly with the many queries that arose once the manuscript was finally with the publishers. The catalyst for the production of this volume was the grant awarded by The British Academy to undertake a pilot project for assessing the potential of studying the landscape archaeology of the two islands of Nevis and St Kitts, already outlined above. The initial plan for the project and the planning of the 2005 Nevis meeting as an SPMA international conference owed much to the assistance of the Nevis Heritage Project and the Department of Archaeology at the University of Southampton, and Bristol and Region Archaeological Services, the former fieldwork section of Bristol City Museums and Art Gallery. Within these organisations the assistance of Dr Elaine Morris and Bruce Williams is gratefully acknowledged. On Nevis we owed much to the support received from the late Vince Hubbard, historian of Nevis and St Kitts, and Ernie Dover of Morning Star Holdings, and most especially from the Nevis Island Administration and the Hon. Vance Amory, Premier of Nevis 1992–2006. This work and the organisation of the 2005 conference could not have proceeded further without the help and support of the Nevis Historical and Conservation Society (Director Mr John Guilbert) and the St Christopher Heritage Society (Director Jacquie Armony). The meeting sessions were made possible through the help of the Four Seasons Hotel and the Mount Nevis Hotel on Nevis. The site visits to former plantation and other houses were made possible on Nevis through the kind assistance of the Golden Rock, Hermitage and Montpelier Hotels, and for Upper Rawlins with the enthusiastic support of Edward and Clarastine Herbert at Herbert Heights; the site visits on St Kitts received much help from Larry Armony at Brimstone Hill and from the Golden Lemon Inn at Dieppe. For the organisation of the site visit to St Eustatius we were similarly grateful to R. Grant Gilmore.

In its final gestation the volume was completed with the full support of the Council of the Society for Post-Medieval Archaeology. In preparing the text and illustrations for publication, the Editors would like to acknowledge especially the assistance of the Society's monographs editor Dr Ruth Young and the editorial staff of Boydell and Brewer, Dr Megan Milan, Emily Champion and Elizabeth Nichols.

Roger and Pamela Leech, August 2020

NOTES

1 Notably Ahlman & Schroedl 2020, Klingelhofer 2010, Meniketti 2015, and Nelson 2016.
2 Dunn 1972, 287.
3 Watts 1987, 335.
4 Handler & Lange 1978; Pulsipher 1987.
5 Summarized most recently in Haviser 1999 and Farnsworth 2001.
6 Carson *et al.* 1981; Deetz 1993.
7 This author's meeting contribution as Leech 2007 and 2008; John Triggs's paper in the Society's special issue on archaeology in Bermuda (Triggs 2011) and Elizabeth di Gangi in press currently for Post-Medieval Archaeology (DiGangi & McKeown in prep.).
8 Hicks 2007
9 Insole 2017.

BIBLIOGRAPHY

Ahlman, T.M. & Schroedl, G.F. (eds) 2020, *Contextualizing Sites through Colonialism, Capitalism, and Globalism*, Historical Archaeologies of the Caribbean, Tuscaloosa and London: University of Alabama Press.

Baugher, S., Appler, D. & Moss, W. (eds) 2017, *Urban Archaeology, Municipal Government and Local Planning*, Cham, Switzerland: Springer.

Carson, C., Barka, N.F., Kelso, W.M., Stone, G.W. & Upton, D. 1981, 'Impermanent Architecture in the Southern American Colonies', *Winterthur Portfolio* 16 (Summer/Autumn 1981).

Deetz, J. 1993, *Flowerdew Hundred. The Archaeology of a Virginia Plantation 1619–1864*, Charlottesville and London: University of Virginia Press.

DiGangi, E. & McKeown, A. (in prep), 'Skeletal Remains of British Soldiers Garrisoned at Brimstone Hill Fortress, St Kitts, West Indies, 1690–1853'.

Dunn, Richard S. 1972, *Sugar and Slaves. The Rise of the Planter Class in the English West Indies, 1624–1713*, Chapel Hill: University of North Carolina Press.

Farnsworth, P. (ed.) 2001, *Island Lives. Historical Archaeologies of the Caribbean*, Tuscaloosa and London: University of Alabama Press.

Finch, J. & Giles, K. (eds) 2007, *Estate Landscapes: Design, Improvement and Power in the Post-Medieval Landscape*, Soc. Post-Med. Archaeol. Monogr. 4, Woodbridge: Boydell and Brewer.

Handler, J.S. & Lange, F.W. 1978, *Plantation Slavery in Barbados: An Archaeological and Historical Investigation,* Cambridge, MA: Harvard University Press.

Haviser, J.B. (ed.) 1999, *African Sites Archaeology in the Caribbean*, Princeton: Markus Weiner.

Hicks, D. 2007, '"Material Improvements": The Archaeology of Estate Landscapes in the British Leeward Islands, 1713–1838', in Finch & Giles 2007, 205–7.

Insole, P. 2017, 'Crowdsourcing the Story of Bristol', in Baugher, Appler & Moss (eds), 2017, 53–67.

Klingelhofer, E. (ed.) 2010, *First Forts, Essays on the Archaeology of Proto-colonial Fortifications*, Leiden and Boston: Brill.

Leech, R.H. 2007, '"In What Manner Did They Devide the Land". The Early Colonial Estate Landscape of Nevis and St Kitts', in Finch & Giles 2007, 191–204.

Leech, R.H. 2008, 'Understanding Nevis – GPS and Archaeological Field Survey in a Post-Colonial Landscape', in Reid 2008, 127–36.

Meniketti, M.G. 2015, *Sugar Cane Capitalism and Environmental Transformation: An Archaeology of Colonial Nevis, West Indies*, Tuscaloosa: University of Alabama Press.

Nelson, L. 2016, *Architecture and Empire in Jamaica*, New Haven and London: Yale University Press.

Pares, R. 1950, *A West Indies Fortune*, London: Longmans.

Pulsipher, L.M. 1987, 'Assessing the Usefulness of a Cartographic Curiosity: The 1673 Map of a Sugar Island', *Annals of the Assoc. Am. Geogr.* 77:3, 408–22.

Reid, B.A. (ed.) 2008, *Archaeology and Geoinformatics: Case Studies from the Caribbean*, Tuscaloosa: University of Alabama Press.

Triggs, J. 2011, '"A Brave Cedar House": Landscape Archaeology at the Overplus House and Grove', *Post-Med. Arch.* 45:1, 144–82.

Watts, D. 1987, *The West Indies: Development, Culture and Environmental Change since 1492*, Cambridge: Cambridge University Press.

ABBREVIATIONS

BSH	Brimstone Hill
CSPAWI	Calendar of States Papers America and West Indies
DoS	Directorate of Overseas Surveys
EIC	East India Company
GMC	Guildhall Museum Catalogue
GR	Grid reference
ICOMOS	International Council on Monuments and Sites
JCTP	Journal of the Commissioners for Trade and Plantations
MoLAS	Museum of London Archaeology Services (after 2008, MOLA or Museum of London Archaeology)
n	number
N	Number
NCAP	National Collection of Air Photographs (curated by Historic Scotland in Edinburgh)
NCHCR	Nevis Court House Common Records
NISP	Number of Identified Specimens
NMM	National Maritime Museum, Greenwich, London
RCHME	The Royal Commission on the Historical Monuments of England (now part of English Heritage)
SCCLCM	St Christopher Council and Legislative Council Minutes
SSC	South Seas Company
TNA	The National Archives, formerly the Public Record Office, Kew, London
UEIC	United East India Company
UNESCO	United Nations Educational, Scientific and Cultural Organization

I

Colonial Landscapes of the Greater Caribbean

1

Caribbean Colonial Cartography: Exploring the Paper Landscape

GILLIAN HUTCHINSON

SUMMARY: This paper uses a variety of 18th-century examples of maps and sea charts of Caribbean colonies to explore how critical reading of cartography can contribute to archaeological investigation. It aims to show that maps and charts are sources of information not just about physical features and spatial relationships, or settlement processes and events. They also provide insights into human experience and interaction within the landscape.

INTRODUCTION

Bearing in mind J.B. Harley's proposition that 'maps are a discourse of the acquisition and dispossession that lie at the heart of colonialism',[1] this paper will consider cartography's limitations as an objective record of landscape, given that all maps were (and are) drawn to fulfil a particular purpose or agenda, explicit or implicit. I also want to draw attention to the role that cartography had in the creation of colonial landscape, how lines drawn on paper became physical features on the ground, and how the use of maps influenced estate acquisition.

CONTEXT AND COMMUNICATIONS

It is an obvious truth but so fundamentally important that it is worth restating, that the Caribbean was essentially a maritime landscape, consisting of dispersed colonies whose reason for existence was the production of sugar for export, completely dependent on sea transport. Transport by sea was hampered by wind patterns and by currents, which make departure from the Caribbean far more problematic than arrival, and by the great distances involved. As Jamaica is 1,000 nautical miles downwind of Barbados, export voyages to Britain took several weeks longer.[2] In consequence, shipping charges from Jamaica were higher and agricultural and refining processes had to be completed earlier in the year to enable the ships to beat the hurricane deadline. Because of the importance of shipping, the centres of population were the port towns, despite their inevitable location in the unhealthiest places. Bridgetown in Barbados, the capital of Britain's richest island colony, was built beside a pestilential swamp.

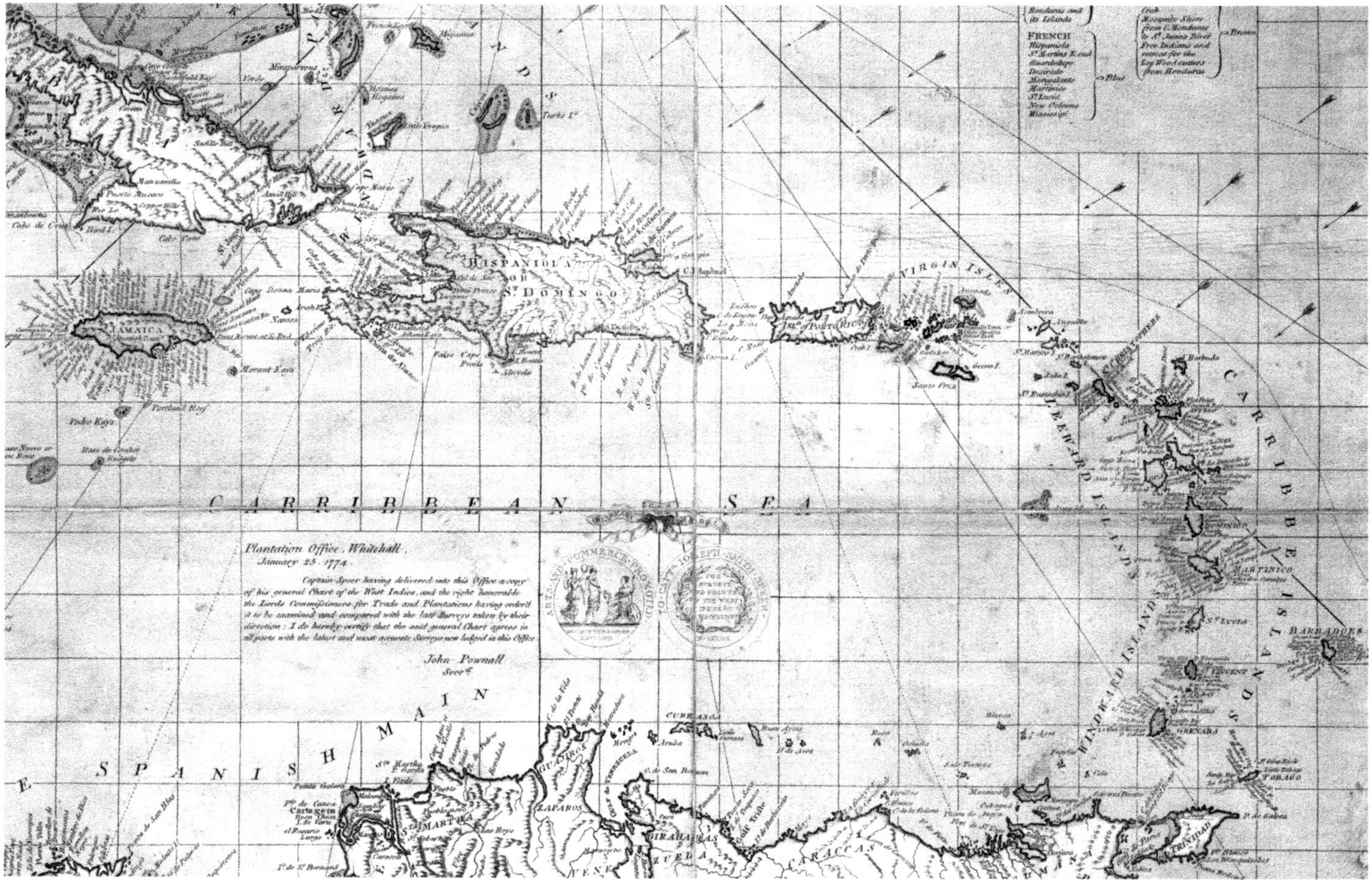

Fig. 1.1. Joseph Smith Speer, *Chart of the West Indies.* 1774 (NMM: Gren1B/3. Repro ID: K1019).

The map (Fig. 1.1) published by Speer in 1774[3] and endorsed by the Plantation Office, shows this geographical situation and adds the political dimension. The islands are coloured according to the nationality of their colonial masters. International rivalry ensured that the Caribbean was a fortified landscape and that some islands would have their settlement records complicated by sequential occupation by different European cultural groups. This map was drawn to inform a process of colonial reform intended to enforce the Navigation Acts, which demanded that British colonial produce had to be carried in British ships and channelled through Britain, to maximize the duty payable by the colonists.

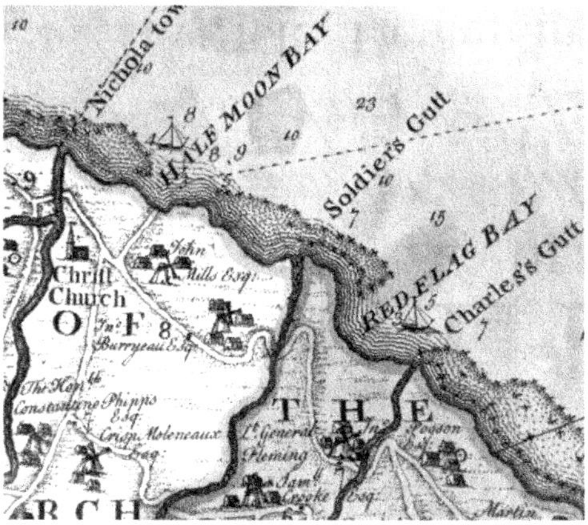

Fig. 1.2. Detail from Samuel Baker, *A new and exact map of the Island of St Christopher in America according to an actual and accurate survey made in the year 1753* (NMM: Gren79/3. Repro ID: K0943 & K0944).

For the British colonists in the Leeward Islands, the Dutch operating from the island of St Eustatius offered the opportunity to circumvent the Navigation Acts. Sugar could be bartered for goods imported from the Dutch maritime world and the island acted as a neutral freeport when the American Revolutionary War led to the prohibition of direct commerce between North America and the British islands. Jamaica was well placed for similar illicit trade with Spanish colonies.

Maps of individual islands reveal how difficult it would have been to control trade. Figure 1.2 is a small extract from the 1753 survey of St Christopher by Samuel Baker. Many roads and tracks are shown terminating at the shoreline, with anchorages marked in numerous places, even on the inhospitable Atlantic coast. While these might be used, in preference to overland carting, for coastwise transport of goods to the major out-ports where the transatlantic ships could moor, they also provided opportunities for clandestine trade with interlopers. Artefactual evidence from settlement sites may potentially reveal more about the nature and extent of these contacts than the written records can.

THE SELECTIVE VISION OF THE CARTOGRAPHER

While maps may offer scope for interpretation to challenge the documentary record, they must of course be treated with caution as representations of territory. Cartography is a highly selective process, not just as a result of the constraints of scale but because each map or chart was tailored to its intended purpose and market and was informed by cartographic conventions and cultural assumptions. Baker's list of what he chose to include on his map of St Christopher is extensive: 'the several parishes with their respective limits, contents, & churches; also the highways, the situation of every gentleman's plantations, mills and houses; with the rivers and gutts, likewise the buoys, roads, rocks, shoals and soundings that surround the whole'.[4] It could be used

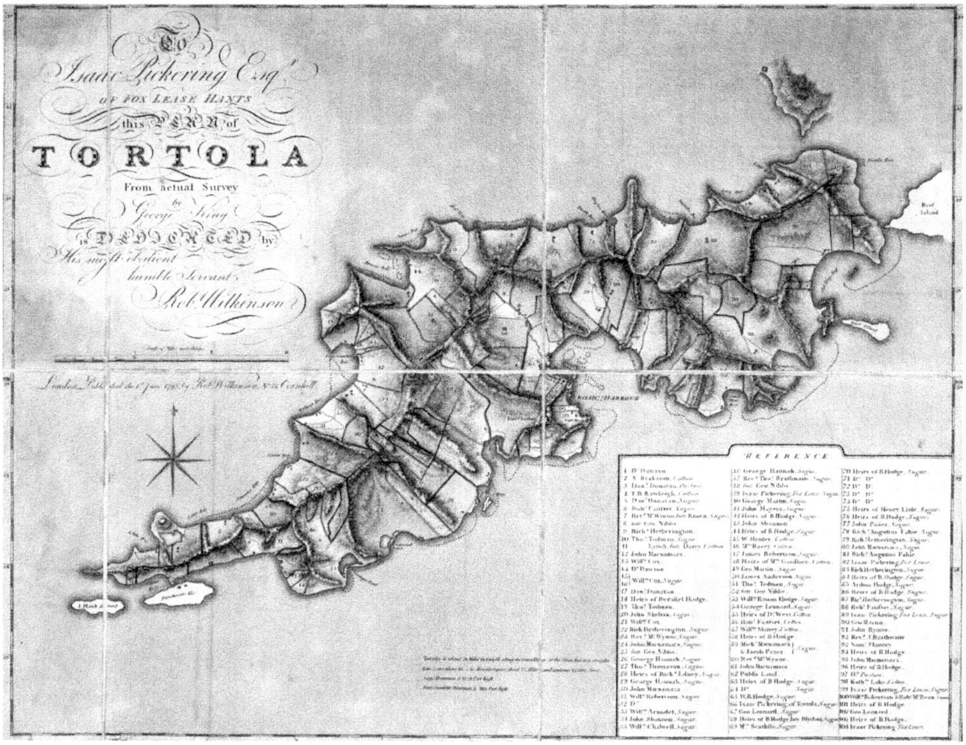

Fig. 1.3. *A plan of Tortola surveyed by George King for Isaac Pickering Esqr of Fox Lease Hants. 1798* (NMM: Gren80A/3. Repro ID: K1070).

to navigate the sea as well as to find the way around the country. The map serves the purposes of government and landed proprietors but there is a total absence of features or names which would reveal the existence of the enslaved people who made up the majority of the population and there is very little information about land use.

Detailed information about the land use of a whole island is presented in a map of Tortola, in the Virgin Islands (Fig. 1.3). This was drawn by George King in 1798 to show land ownership and specifically the extent and location of Isaac Pickering's lands. Tortola had been colonized by the English from the 1660s and by the time of this map at the end of the 18th century it was fully planted, displaying the features of sugar monoculture. The individual land-holdings generally ran down to the sea, and their other boundaries were more strongly influenced by topography than by rectilinear planning. This pattern is characteristic of mature 'organic' settlement rather than of suddenly imposed colonization.

The main harbour is centrally located on the south coast and at Road Town there was a thin strip of public land. All of the other 103 numbered plots were in private ownership, though in some cases their owners were noted as deceased. Sugar was the principal crop grown on 61 of the plots while the only other identified crop, cotton, was cultivated on only nine peripheral and dispersed plots. For 30 of the landholdings, no crop was listed in the table. Two plots were used for pasture, one at the extreme west of the island and the other at Fat Hog Bay at the east end.

Isaac Pickering of Fox Lease in Hampshire, England, who commissioned the map, held a large but discontinuous tract of land in the north-east of the island, and another well-placed plot in the centre separated by one plot from land held by Isaac Pickering

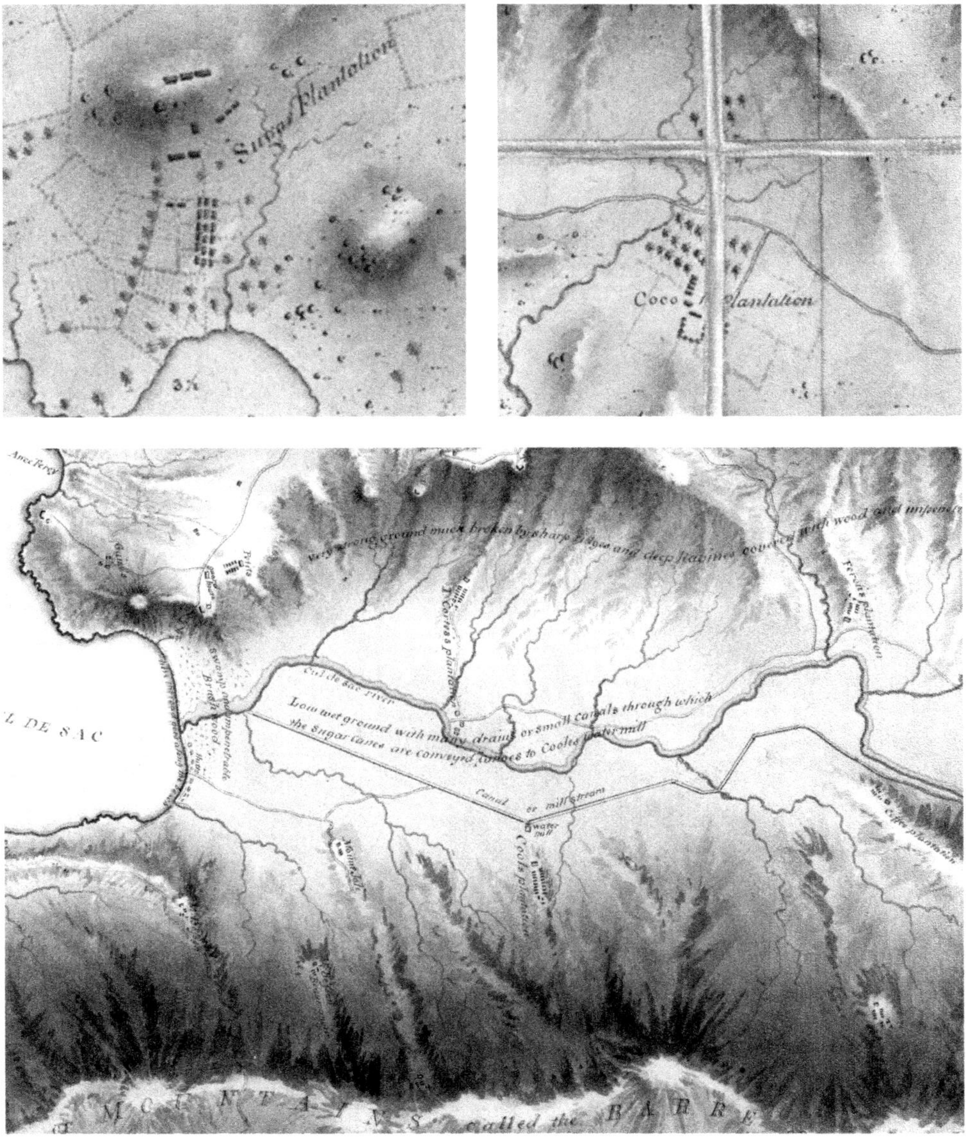

Fig. 1.4 a, b, c. (clockwise from top) Details from John Brown, *Military survey of that part of St Lucia occupied by the British forces from Decr 1778 to Jany 1784, when the island was restored to the French* (NMM: Gren80A/10. Repro ID: K1025).

of Tortola. By the mid 18th century the dominant planters had grown rich enough to become absentee landholders, perhaps using a junior family member to manage the estates. In the 1770s Isaac Pickering of Fox Lease used wealth from his plantations to enlarge his country house near Lyndhurst, an example of the linkage of Caribbean colonial and English rural landscapes. For absentee landholders the map did act as a substitute for the territory, as they made strategic decisions about estate consolidation and acquisition by reference to shapes on paper.

A different set of value judgements underpinned the mapping carried out by military engineers. For them the creation and display of commercial wealth and status was not a priority. They were gathering intelligence about how to defend territory or conduct operations within it. In consequence, anything that could present an obstacle or provide cover or be useful as a landmark might be included and considerable attention was paid to topography and vegetation. The 1784 map of part of St Lucia by Lieutenant John Brown was drawn at a scale of four inches to the mile and shows even such ephemeral features as the fishermen's huts opposite Pigeon Island. King's map of Tortola recorded the position of mills but gave no indication of other features of plantation layout such as the cane fields and the tracks or firebreaks which subdivided them. Brown is far more informative. Figure 1.4a, a detail from Brown's St Lucia map, plots the town plan of Gros Islet and a nearby sugar plantation and shows how cultivation was localized within the landscape. The structures depicted appear to include a group of slave houses set out in regular rows as well as larger buildings. Elsewhere there is a cocoa plantation (Fig. 1.4b) with its associated structures. Figure 1.4c is a detail of the canals in the valley leading down to Grand Cul de Sac Harbour: 'Low wet ground with many drains or small canals through which the sugar canes are conveyed by canoes to Cootes watermill'.

Brown also mapped English Harbour in Antigua, providing a record of the position and state of the fortifications, the layout of the dockyard and the hospital. A detail (Fig. 1.5) shows the huts of the dockyard artificers, a water-storage tank, and a bathing house nearby. Inland, Brown plotted the cultivated land and isolated structures in the landscape such as a sheep pen, a stone cattle pen, a pond, an 'old windmill' on a ridge and groups of huts.

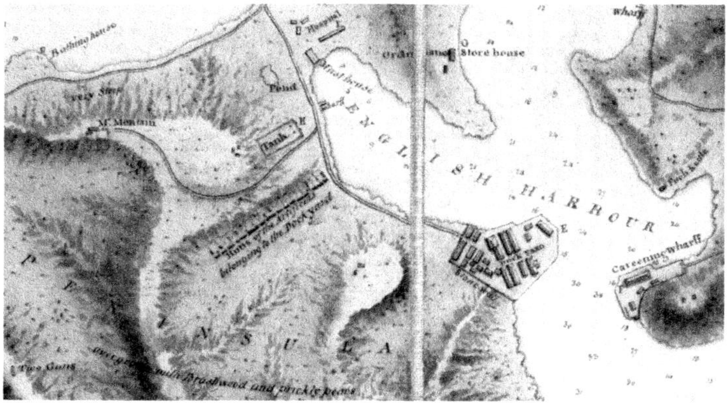

Fig. 1.5. Detail from John Brown, *Plan of the environs of English Harbour, Antigua* (NMM: Gren79/4. Repro ID: K0942).

CARTOGRAPHY'S ROLE IN CREATING COLONIAL LANDSCAPE

The settlement history of Tobago is exceptional in that the island was not colonized continuously and intensively from the 17th century onwards. In the 1740s Britain and France agreed to declare Tobago neutral territory. It was in this state that Captain Robert Duff found it during the Seven Years War when, in the hurricane months of 1760, he sailed there in the *Foudroyant* to reconnoitre for safe, sheltered anchorages where ships could replenish their supplies of wood and water.[5] Duff ordered surveys to be made and two manuscript sea charts of Tobago survive in his personal papers. One is a chart of the whole island while the other is a more detailed plan of Great Courland Bay by John Byrne (not to be confused with John Byres, the later surveyor of Tobago).

Consistently with its purpose, the island chart (Fig. 1.6) shows coastal features such as soundings, anchorage sites, and the seasonal encampments of French turtle hunters, with a detailed inset of Man of War Bay. There is a view providing guidance on how to approach by sea. Text notes comment that Tobago is not liable to hurricanes and that there is an abundance of excellent fish, turtles, and fresh water. The only inland feature marked is an 'Indian village'. The title cartouche depicts pineapples and palm trees, with a Carib hunting in the fruitful wilderness. The accompanying plan of Great Courland Bay notes the locations of good water and wooding places. This chart is unfinished but the cartouche (Fig. 1.7) depicts a man and woman, nearly naked and apparently European, beneath a quotation from Virgil extolling an uncomplicated and conflict-free life.

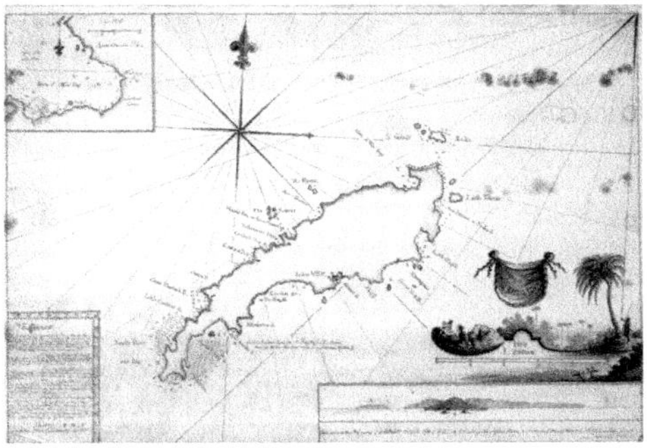

Fig. 1.6. John Byrne, *Tobago* (NMM: DUF245:17/2. Repro ID: F0348).

Tobago's potential as a new Garden of Eden was not to last long. Three years later under the terms of the 1763 Treaty of Paris which ended the Seven Years War, Tobago was one of the islands ceded to Britain, together with Grenada, the Grenadines, St Vincent, and Dominica. The ceded islands were to be planted to increase British sugar production.[6]

Fig. 1.7. John Byrne, *Great Courland Bay* (NMM: DUF247:17/4. Repro ID: F0367).

Thomas Jefferys' chart of Tobago[7] shows the barracks and guard house at the top of Great Courland Bay that the

British built as a first act of possession in 1764. French turtlers are still recorded at the south of Great Courland Bay and other notes refer to the rest of the population: 'The Indian King Rouselle with his wives and people about 30 in number lives here'; 'The Indian King Cardinal with his wives and about 80 people live on a hill hereabouts', and 'King Peter the Indian Chief with about 14 or 16 people lives hereabouts'. If these figures are to be believed, there were fewer than 130 indigenous inhabitants on Tobago at the time. Low numbers would of course be very convenient for the planters.

A surveyor named John Byres was employed by the Commissioners for the Sale of Lands in the Ceded Islands to draw up maps parcelling out the land for settlement. The series of maps was published in 1776 by which time most of the plots, except those which were 'very mountainous and uncultivable', had been bought or leased. Byres' map of Tobago is dedicated to the official responsible for 'settling differences and disputes with respect to the sale of lands'. The 'Indians' have apparently vanished. The territory itself was regarded as a blank piece of paper. Neat lines were drawn and these were converted into features imposed upon the landscape. Boundaries conferred rights and possession. Maps were not simply passive representations of landscape but were instrumental in creating it.

Very small plots of marginal ground at the south-west tip of the island were reserved for 'poor settlers' (Fig. 1.8). Larger plantations could be managed more efficiently but that resulted in a shortage of white males who were needed for defence. Tobago was particularly suitable for spice production which could be carried out on a small scale.[8] There is a space marked rather hopefully 'for a town', and 'land for a fort' is allocated in other places. A note beside this map states that a strip of land three chains wide round the island's perimeter is reserved for the government to use for defence, perhaps an example of the way that the tool of measurement, the chain, could be used as a tool of control. The land could be used by the contiguous planter but the government could claim it at any time without paying compensation. Tobago was transformed from a pre-colonial wild place to a fully squared-away plantation settlement in the space of a quarter of a century.

Fig. 1.8. Detail from John Byres, *Plan of the Island of Tobago, laid down by actual survey under the direction of the Honorable the Commissioners for the Sale of Lands in the Ceded Islands by Chief Surveyor 1776* (NMM: Gren81/1. Repro ID: K0918).

The map of St Vincent[9] in the ceded lands series, shows the 'land granted to the Charibs by the late Treaty in 1773'. Their population was estimated to be about 1,500 and the territory allocated to them was in the north part of the island, bounded by a river, except on the west side where Colonel Etherington, apparently unwilling to deny himself good plantation land, had an estate occupying both banks. In general the property boundaries on St Vincent are less rectilinear and conform more closely to natural features than on Tobago, reflecting the fact that St Vincent had earlier been planted through a gradual process of estate creation, by the French. The map gives an impression of great certainty, with land-holdings clearly defined. The Governor of St Vincent, petitioning for an increase to John Byres' salary to dissuade him from leaving the islands in search of a better-paid post elsewhere, intimated that he needed to keep the surveyor because the boundaries looked far less clear on the ground.[10]

In 1777 the Commissioner for settling disputes with respect to the sale of ceded lands referred a petition to the Treasury.[11] This provides some insight into the processes and pitfalls of estate acquisition 'off the map'. A consortium of five joint purchasers, including the Lieutenant Governor of Dominica and a former Governor of Senegambia, had bought nearly 2,000 acres of land in the parish of St David in Dominica. As there was no road to allow them to inspect the land 'they were under the necessity of making their purchases in the dark or rather to trust to the report of the Surveyors as to the surface and quality of the land'. Byres' map[12] shows an expanse of well-drained land between the mountains and Rosaly Bay. Although the consortium had managed to establish a sugar plantation on part of the land 'at very considerable expense and risk and with a great loss of slaves', a new survey had shown that more than 600 acres were 'wholly unfit for cultivation, consisting of broken mountains, deep valleys and inaccessible precipices'. They felt they had paid too high a price and sought compensation, including the grant of a plot of coastal land where they had already erected a crane and wharf.

MAPPING SOCIETAL LANDSCAPE

Maps may appear to depersonalize space, reducing landscape to abstract delineation, devoid of human presence. Observing the co-locations of settlements with each other and within parish boundaries, and their access to roads and religious and trading sites, gives some idea of the social, administrative, ecclesiastical, and commercial relations drawing in the population. The size and layout of landholdings, with their concomitant hierarchies of prosperity, varied significantly from island to island. Further ways in which cartography reveals societal landscape will be discussed with reference to a map of St Croix in the Virgin Islands, published in Copenhagen in 1799.

St Croix had been sold to Denmark by France in 1733 and by the 1770s, according to a text panel on Jefferys' map of the Virgin Islands, the inhabitants were 'chiefly English from Nevis and Antigua and Irish papists'.[13] They were small planters displaced from other islands by the process of estate consolidation into large units. St Croix was covered by a regular patchwork of similarly-sized and straight-edged plots, bounded by roads (Fig. 1.9). Place-names, such as 'Tipperare', reflect the ethnic origins of some of the planters. An example elsewhere is Irish Town in St Christopher. The naming

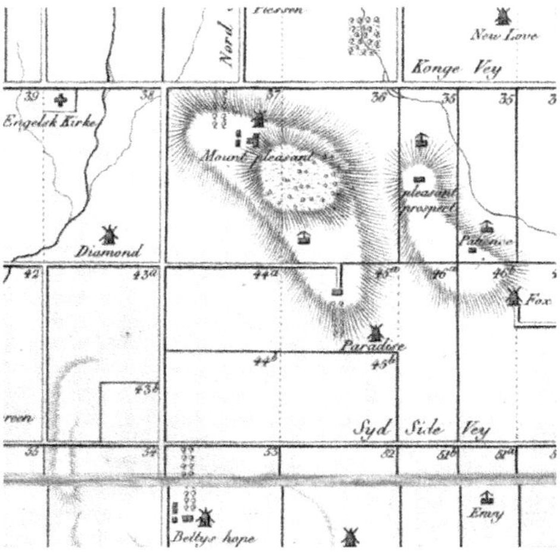

Fig. 1.9. Detail from P.L. Oxholm, 1799, *Charte over den Danske Oe St Croix i America* (NMM: Gren82/2. Repro ID: K0891 & K0892).

after home towns and counties is based on the desire to impose the familiar onto alien territory. That naming is part of the process of appropriation was clearly demonstrated when islands changed hands between colonial powers. So, for example, Byres' map of Grenada retains French names for rivers and points but was overlain by 'the addition of English names, alteration of property and other improvements'. Each of the ceded islands was divided into parishes, named after the homeland patron saints, St George, St Andrew, St David, and St Patrick, and if they were not enough to cover the ground, some apostles as well.

The names of individual estates on the map of St Croix reveal something of the attitudes, aspirations, and experience of the planter inhabitants. Ranging from the optimistic All for the Better, Mount Pleasant, Pleasant Prospect, Prosperity, Judith's Fancy, Sweet Bottom, New Love, Paradise; through the ambivalent Work and Rest, Wheel of Fortune, to the complaining Hard Labour and Little Profit. The place names on many Caribbean maps and charts preserve the memory and reaction of the inhabitants and those who brought their ships to the coasts. Jamaica has Hellshire and Starvegut Bay but also Healthy Cove. St Christopher has Mount Misery, Bloody Bay, and Shit Bay (this last may simply refer to the guano).

The people whose voices are preserved in the names were members of the dominant white population. Not only are most maps empty of any indications of where enslaved people lived and were buried, they are also silent about their experiences. The map of St Croix includes a table of statistical information about the population: 'Whites 2,223, coloured 1,164, negro 25,452'. This ratio of whites to enslaved Africans, approximately 1:13, is consistent with the late 18th-century statistics for the Leeward Islands and Antigua.

The St Croix map was drawn in 1799, in the interim between the issuing of the Danish royal edict prohibiting the slave trade and when it came into effect on 1 January 1803. In this context its agenda can be seen as polemic. The title cartouche (Fig. 1.10) depicts sugar plantation work, with slaves apparently eagerly subservient to the white overseer, and provision made for the welfare of women and children. The mapmaker is attempting to present the proposition that the system of slave labour is well-ordered and humane.

The preface to Jefferys' *West India Atlas*, which was written in 1775, reveals unease about slavery. 'This trade, to the disgrace of the age, has so deeply taken root, it is become so necessary to the present state of affairs, and our wants have justified it in a manner so absolute, that it is now almost a ridiculous common-place to cry out

Fig. 1.10. Title cartouche from P.L. Oxholm, 1799, *Charte over den Danske Oe St Croix i America* (NMM: Gren82/2. Repro ID: K0891 & K0892).

against the barbarity and cruelty of it'.[14] The atlas's title page presents a utopian fantasy. The scene is a sheltered cove, fringed by palm trees, with ships taking on cargoes of sugar. In the foreground a British sailor is keeping company with a relaxed and contented enslaved family, all sharing the enjoyment of paradise and the prosperity of the British Empire.

The maps discussed in this paper represent a view of the world from the vantage point of the powerful. Cartography can be defined as 'landscape with attitude', displaying the preoccupations of the map-makers and their clients along with the territory. The presence of the vast majority of the population, the enslaved people, who outnumbered the whites by about 13:1 at the end of the 18th century, is barely acknowledged. It can be conjectured that the mental maps enslaved people had of their localities bore little resemblance to those drawn by Europeans. There is a pressing need for archaeological investigation to reconstruct the missing layers of knowledge.

NOTES

1 Harley 2001, 195.

2 N, J. 1739. The author (John Crowley) described the two possible routes from Jamaica, via the Gulf of Florida or the windward passage through the Bahamas. The disadvantages of the Florida route were a long beat into the teeth of the trade winds, then dangerous currents and shoals in the Gulf. The hardest part of the windward passage was the first 50 miles west from Port Royal to the east point of Jamaica which could detain a ship for a month or more. Ships on both routes were harassed by Spanish Guarda Costas at this period.

3 Speer 1774.

4 Baker 1753.

5 Duff 1760–1; Duff 1760–2.

6 Campbell 1763 discusses the advantages and disadvantages of expanding Britain's Caribbean colonies, including the economic effects of increased emigration.

7 Jefferys n.d. (a).

8 Campbell 1763, 115. Nutmeg, cinnamon, ginger, sassafras, gum copal, dyestuffs, drugs and sweetmeats are listed as potential products.
9 Byres 1776 (a).
10 Morris 1776.
11 O'Hara 1777.
12 Byres 1776 (b).
13 Jefferys n.d. (b).
14 Jefferys 1775, 7.

BIBLIOGRAPHY

PUBLISHED SOURCES

Baker, S. 1753, *A new and exact map of the Island of St Christopher in America according to an actual and accurate survey made in the year 1753*, London: T. Bowles.
Byres, J. 1776 (a), *Plan of the Island of St Vincent, laid down by actual survey under the direction of the Honorable the Commissioners for the Sale of Lands in the Ceded Islands*, London: Hooper.
Byres, J. 1776 (b), *Plan of the Island of Dominica, laid down by actual survey under the direction of the Honorable the Commissioners for the Sale of Lands in the Ceded Islands by Chief Surveyor 1776*, London: Hooper.
Campbell, J. 1763, *Candid and impartial considerations on the nature of the sugar trade; the comparative importance of the British and French Islands in the West Indies: with the value and consequence of St Lucia and Granada, truly stated*, London: Baldwin.
Harley, J.B. 2001, *The New Nature of Maps: Essays in the History of Cartography*, Baltimore: Johns Hopkins University Press.
Jefferys, T. n.d. [1775] (a), *Tobago from actual surveys and observations*, London: Sayer & Bennett.
Jefferys, T. n.d. [1775] (b), *The Virgin Islands from English and Danish Surveys*, London: Sayer & Bennett.
Jefferys, T. 1775, *The West-India Atlas*, London: Sayer & Bennett.
King, G. 1798, *A plan of Tortola surveyed by George King for Isaac Pickering Esqr of Fox Lease Hants*, London: Wilkinson.
N, J. [John Crowley] 1739, *A description of the windward passage and Gulf of Florida with the course of the British trading-ships to and from the Island of Jamaica*, London: Applebee.
Oxholm, P.L. 1799, *Charte over den Danske Oe St Croix i America*, Copenhagen: Angelo.
Seller, J. 1764, *The English Pilot. The fourth book: the West-India navigation*, London: Mount & Page.
Speer, J.S. 1774, Joseph Smith, *Chart of the West Indies*, London: Bowen.
Speer, J.S. 1785, *The West India Pilot*, London: Hooper.

UNPUBLISHED SOURCES

Brown, J. n.d. (a). *Military survey of that part of St Lucia occupied by the British forces from Decr 1778 to Jany 1784, when the island was restored to the French*, NMM: Gren80A/10.
Brown, J. n.d. (b). *Plan of the environs of English Harbour, Antigua*, NMM: Gren79/4.
Byrne, J. n.d. (a). *Tobago*, NMM: DUF245:17/2.
Byrne, J. n.d. (b). *Great Courland Bay*. NMM: DUF247:17/4.
Duff, R. *Foudroyant* logbook 1760–1, NMM: DUF/2.
Duff, R. *Foudroyant* official instructions 1760–2, NMM: DUF/9.
Morris, V. 1776. Correspondence with St Vincent: Governor Morris to Treasury, TNA: T1/526/307-311.
O'Hara, C. 1777, Petition of Charles O'Hara and others, Dominica, TNA: T1/535/343 with estate map MPD 1/178.

2

Tropical Similarities Found in Military Barracks, Hospitals and Other Structures in the West Indies and British Florida Parishes

PHILIPPE OSZUŚCIK

SUMMARY: Although British Florida Parishes existed only between 1763 and 1781, the National Archives (TNA) for the UK Government and for England and Wales, formerly known as the Public Records Office (PRO) has surviving plans and drawings of military projects built and not built. This research project explored reasons for similarities in the use of tropical devises found in plans and on the surviving barracks and hospitals found in former Florida Parishes and the Caribbean. The TNA drawings are of interest because a project intended for one colony may be built in another instead or similar projects appear in several different colonies. British troops and colonists brought to the Florida Parishes from Jamaica may have actually resolved some of the heat complaints of troops brought over from Scotland and England. For example, piazzas became commonplace in the southeastern United States during and after the brief existence of the Florida Parishes but were rare before 1763. What influence did British engineers have on civilian houses by providing barracks, hospitals, and other military structures with shaded piazzas? When do tropical considerations appear in the Greater Caribbean at the same time or earlier? Lastly, why are similar plans and styles to be found in the Florida Parishes and the West Indies?

INTRODUCTION

Fortifications are among the earliest structures built by the English in the New World, beginning with Guayanilla Bay Fort in Puerto Rico, May 1585, Lanes Fort near Cape Rojo in Puerto Rico, late May 1585, and Fort Raleigh, Roanoke Island, North Carolina, August 1585. The plans of the first two forts were recorded by John Smith and were roughly square with timber curtain walls and bastions, wet ditches, and a water entrance.[1] These sea coast forts were large enough to defend the passengers and crew of their ship. In Puerto Rico the English defended themselves against the Spanish, but Native Americans were added to their defense plan at Roanoke Island.

Although the next attempt, Fort St George in Maine, August 1607, was abandoned in 1608. James Fort or the Southern Colony, also established in 1607, and became

Fig. 2.1. Corps of Royal Engineers, Brimstone Hill, St Kitts, West Indies, View of the 'Bowl', Barracks and Citadel, 1750/1783–1830.

the first permanent English settlement in the Americas. It was a triangular fort with corner bastions built of timber to protect the entire encampment. The colony quickly outgrew the protection of its walls and Jamestown was established outside the walls.[2]

Because of its location east of North Carolina and natural protection it had against gales in the Atlantic, Bermuda was settled in 1612. By 1615, eleven forts mostly of native stone were built, and were recorded by Captain John Smith on his 1624 map.[3] The fact that the English built eleven small forts rather than a large grand fortification is important. They were built by citizens who were scattered by land grants awarded to them and these lands were operated and maintained by their local militia. In contrast the Spanish began the practice of building large impregnable forts and walling their larger cities due to raids upon their towns by English, French, and Dutch privateers who all had Spain as their common enemy during the 17th century. In response the Spanish built several forts leading into their towns. The English found it important to fortify some coastal cities, such as Port Royal, Jamaica; and they built some large inaccessible fortifications to serve as a final defense on mountain ridges, such as Brimstone Hill, St Kitts (Fig. 2.1), Saddle Hill, Nevis, St Annes Castle, Barbados, to name but a few. However, these were mostly later forts following the establishment of the organized British Army in the West Indies that peaked between 1792 and 1815.[4] A small fort was more usual, such as the Newcastle Redoubt in Nevis, *c.* 1650. Its 6.7m square design is similar in design and shape to the small redoubts of Bermuda which established this tradition in the 1610s.[5]

FORTIFICATIONS FROM 1763

The first regular British soldiers in the West Indies were placed in Carlisle Bay, Barbados in 1652. A cluster of smaller forts was established at Carlisle Bay, Barbados, in the Bermudan tradition. By 1678, British forces were in Jamaica and the Leeward Islands. Few plans exist at the National Archives (TNA, formerly the PRO) from the 17th and early 18th centuries, and only for after 1750 are plans more numerous. Sugar was the main reason that British forces were based here.

Major changes occurred in 1763 when Great Britain acquired Florida, and briefly Cuba, at the conclusion of the Seven Years War. A vast territory extending from the Atlantic Ocean to the Mississippi River, Florida was divided by the British into the East and West Florida Parishes. St Augustine became the capital of East Florida and was easily established. San Miguel de Panzacola, a settlement founded in 1757, after an earlier city on Santa Rosa Island was destroyed by a hurricane, became the capital of West Florida. Pensacola was no more than a palisaded fort so the British had to plat a

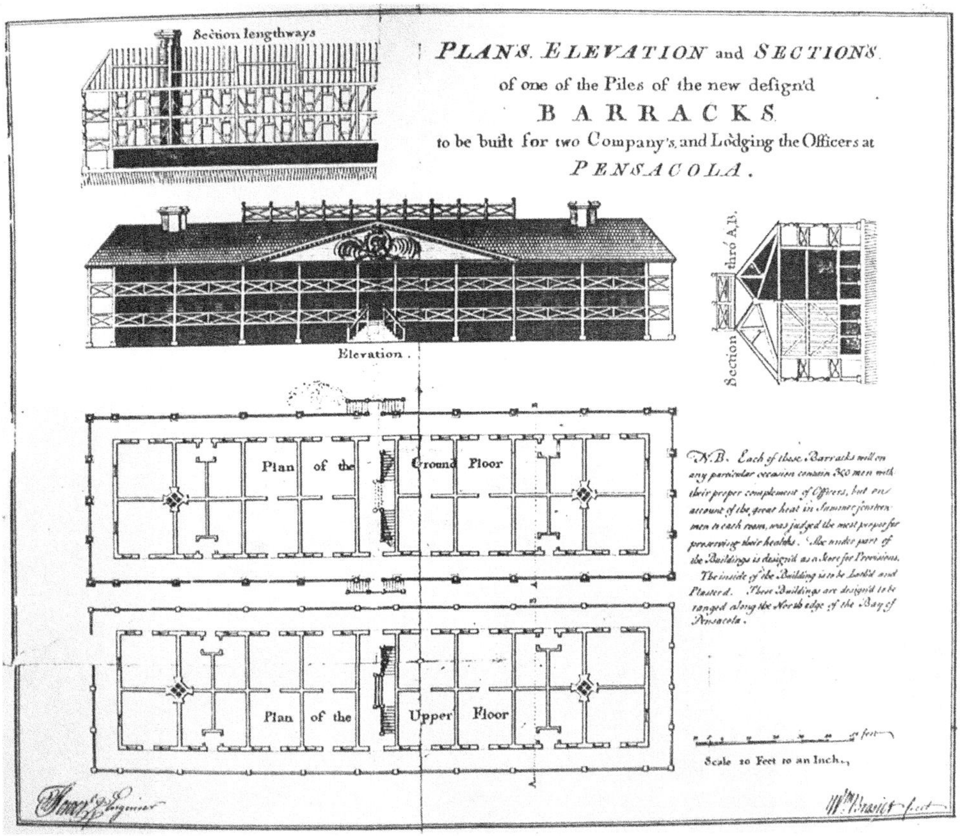

Fig. 2.2. T. Sowers, Engineer. Plan and Section for Barracks, Pensacola, FL, 1771, ink drawing. (TNA CO 5, MPG 1/10).

town and build this capital.[6] In 1763 Great Britain dominated North America with its acquisitions of Canada in the North and Florida in the South – a fourteenth colony, with two parishes that were larger than many of the original thirteen colonies. On the eve of the American Revolution this acquisition presented colonial authorities with an awesome sense of responsibility as Britain reinforced the parishes with army regiments to protect it against the Americans and the Spanish, who controlled Louisiana after 1763. With Loyalists moving into the Florida Parishes, when Patriots gained in number in the thirteen colonies, the Spanish sensed a need and opportunity to recapture the Florida Parishes, which was accomplished between 1781 and 1783, while the British were occupied with the Atlantic seaboard. The British were also busy strengthening Bermuda off the East Coast between 1783 and 1808. Edward Cecil Harris, author of *Bermuda Forts: 1612–1957,* observed that the colonial peace 'of the British overseas possessions was shattered (*sic*) …'. [7]

The British Florida Parishes existed for only two decades, yet ambitious architectural projects were undertaken by the military and colonial governments. New projects exhibited tropical, Caribbean elements, such as galleries (piazzas), louvered shutters, kitchen buildings, protective hip roofs, and raised plans for ventilation (Fig. 2.2).[8] While the thirteen East Coast colonies were distracted by political events, Loyalists in the Florida Parishes were busy introducing tropical elements with energetic application in their military and housing projects.

Research indicates that the reasons behind tropical similarities that exist between the Florida Parishes and the Caribbean are more complex than simple physical comparisons. First, Pensacola received military personnel from Jamaica as well as England and Scotland, allowing for the possibility that tropical elements were introduced after 1763 by reassigned West Indies garrisons. Secondly, the Florida environment had existing buildings with Caribbean elements from the Spanish and French which the British eagerly assimilated into their buildings. Thirdly, wealthier colonists bought the larger Spanish houses and the military received the Spanish fort intact along with its buildings (some with galleries), built with earthfast frames with *bousillage* fill as found in French colonial construction. Roofing material was palmetto leaves or bark as utilized by the French in Mobile since 1702.[9]

Colonial reports and letters sent home from English and Scottish troops shed some light as to why West Indies and Louisiana features found on buildings may have made a big impact on military and governmental housing at this time. English and Scottish troops, and officials complained bitterly of the stifling heat on the North Gulf Coast that caused more illness and personnel losses than in Jamaica. Other than notes found on plans referring to designs that meet the needs for healthy soldiers, one town plat had a note that its oblique layout would allow summer breezes to circulate through the streets. Military engineers, therefore, were consciously introducing details to make the buildings and projects as comfortable and healthy as possible.[10] They became confident and inventive with original designs. Citizens and military personnel from England were accustomed to its moderate climate, not the harsh, humid, hot climate of East and West Florida.[11]

Initially, colonies of the Spanish, British, and French in southeastern United States acquired tropical elements from their own earlier colonies in the Caribbean.

Fig. 2.3. Ignacio Daza, Engineer from Havana, Castillo de San Marcos, St Augustine, Florida, 1672 and later.

In military design, for example, one can easily see similarities between battered sides with *media naranja* (orange-shaped) domed bastion towers of the El Morro Castle in Havana (begun 1589),[12] the bastion towers on the walls of Havana,[13] San Juan's fortified battered walls and bartizans (1639),[14] and the battered walls and bartizans of Castillo de San Marcos (Fig. 2.3) in St Augustine, Florida (1672 and later).[15] The idea for St Augustine's wet moat, drawbridge, and barbican may have come from La Real Fuerza Castle, Havana (1558 and later).[16] As the coquina fortress in St Augustine was nearing completion, the Spanish constructed the small Fort Matanzas in 1740 to guard the two inlets to St Augustine 17 miles south of the town, repeating the San Marcos scheme in condensed form.[17]

When a visitor entered a colony of different ethnicity, he sometimes observed construction and design elements that might be adoptable in his own colony upon returning home. Tabby construction, for example, was introduced in St Augustine by the Spanish during the 17th century, an idea that came to Spain from North Africa. Tabby (the English derivation of *tapia* in Spanish) is a proto-concrete material made from oyster-shell cement with oyster shells as the aggregate. It offered cheap yet strong construction in coastal areas. After the British siege of St Augustine in 1702, a brick-faced tabby powder magazine was constructed in Charleston, South Carolina. General James Oglethorpe, founder of Savannah, Georgia in 1733, saw tabby construction in South Carolina and introduced and advocated tabby construction in permanent military and residential projects in Georgia.[18] An early example can be seen in the walls of the fortified Wormsloe Plantation house (Fig. 2.4), 1739, built outside Savannah, Georgia.[19] The small square plan with corner bastions was built on the scale of small Bermuda forts except that this fortification defended mostly the house and its inhabitants against Native Americans.

The most famous repeated fortification plan that was passed from one ethnicity to another in North America began with Fort Caroline, built by French near present-day Jacksonville, Florida in 1564. Triangular in layout to take advantage of the river to defend its elevation, only two wet ditches had to be dug on the banks of the St Johns

Fig. 2.4. Fortified Wormsloe Plantation House, near Savannah, Georgia, 1739.

River for defense against Native Americans or the Spanish. When the Spanish saw this fort in 1565 they built their fort 30 miles to the south, establishing the oldest surviving city in the United States, St Augustine. The Spanish used the same scheme for their fort, first on Anastasia Island and repeatedly from 1593 at the site of present St Augustine.[20] These plans were published in Europe with the outcome that James Fort was constructed with the same general plan in 1607 by the English. All were palisade structures with bastions and provided housing and military structures within the curtain walls. Edward Cecil Harris theorized that the unusual plan was a style of fortification adapted for the American wilderness.[21] A triangular plan is unusual for a fort with no common European precedent.

Elias Durnford (1739–94), British engineer and surveyor, designed the town plan of Pensacola in 1764, after arriving from Havana, Cuba, which briefly belonged to England before the Spanish ceded Florida to the British in the 1763 Treaty of Paris in return for Cuba.[22] The fact that Pensacola's layout resembles a Spanish Law of the West Indies town plan may be in part due to his stationing in Havana before being assigned to Pensacola. His painting, *Plaza Vieja*, 1762, strengthens the hypothesis that he was creating the ideal West Indies urban plan for the capital of West Florida Parish. This painting predicts the Caribbean elements of town planning that appear in his town plan for Pensacola. As chief engineer-architect of Pensacola, he was responsible for the layout of the British fort, town lots, barracks, and governor's residence.[23]

When Spanish colonies were ceded to the British by treaty, towns were emptied and some British colonists moved into existing, livable structures sold to them by exiting Spanish occupants,[24] providing housing with West Indies features. In Mobile, many of the French remained, providing the British with French Creole features. An amalgamation resulted, consisting of retained Spanish and French West Indies features but with preferred 'improvements' of British, such as glazed sash windows, clapboard siding, and the addition of British stylistic details to give the community a British nationalistic ambiance.[25] This practice was instigated in both St Augustine

Fig. 2.5. Juan Paredes House, 1803, and Rodriguez-Avero-Sanchez House, St George Street, 1760 (second story added 1768 during British period), St Augustine, Florida.

and Pensacola and was a common means by which British engineers from England acquired their knowledge of tropical, climatic elements on buildings.

Examples to quickly illustrate British modifications in St Augustine include the new wings in the Spanish Governor's house with two-story galleries, second stories added to the barracks in the Castillo, and wooden beds with wood pillows in these rooms. Many one-story tabby houses (Fig. 2.5) were enlarged by adding a half-story or second story with clapboard siding under gable roofs rather than retaining flat tabby roofs. Open grated windows were replaced by sash windows.

In Pensacola, Elias Durnford first drafted the plan of the 1757 Spanish fort with all buildings retained by the British while his enlarged, superimposed fortification was being constructed. Larger Spanish dwellings in good condition and mostly constructed

Fig. 2.6. Spanish Governor's House, detail of 'A View of Pensacola, in West Florida', watercolor by George Gauld, *c.* 1767.

in the French Creole cottage tradition were retained and used by officers.[26] The raised Spanish/French Creole cottages had integral galleries that served to cool the houses for the heat-sensitive British.

One example in Pensacola within the fort (Fig. 2.6) serves as a paradigm of this process: the 1757 Old Spanish Governor's house. It was sketched in 1767 from a ship by George Gauld, a British cartographer, as existing within the newly enlarged British fort.[27] Situated on higher ground, its two-and-a-half story façade appears above the wooden palisade. In this sketch, the house had not yet been improved, so its French Creole features are easy to perceive.[28] When Elias Durnford drew the plans for its renovation in 1770, the ground floor (Figs 2.7–2.8) still reflected the original French-like *salle/chambre* plan with large corner *cabinets* that framed a loggia in between. A full gallery was on the garden side with stairs to communicate between the stories, a common element in French and Spanish housing with raised plans. The principal floor was changed to have one large central room flanked by its cabinets, but its original two doors to the gallery were retained. The British changed the half-story within its steep hipped roof into a single room with full story height for use as a ballroom. Added to the ground level and primary floor rooms were fireplaces, a convenience not possessed by the Spanish Governor. The makeover for the façade was clearly British when seen from the harbor. The steep roof with dormers, were replaced by a full

Fig. 2.7. Elias Durnford, Plans, Elevation for the Governor's House Ground Floor, 1770, ink drawing. (TNA CO 5, MPG 1/611 Drawing 1–5, Pensacola).

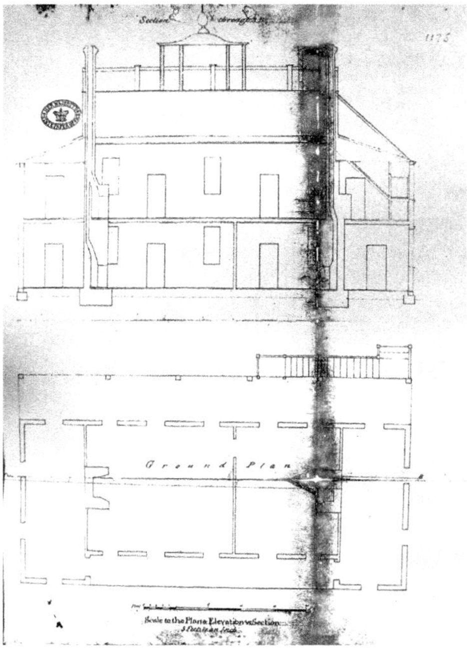

Fig. 2.8. Elias Durnford, Plans and Section for the Governor's House, 1770, ink drawing. (TNA CO 5, MPG 1/611 Drawing 1–3, Pensacola).

Fig. 2.9. St Francis Barracks, St Augustine, 1771 (transformed from the 1737 Priory Church), Florida.

second story that gained a central pedimented pavilion in the Middle Georgian (or Palladian Revival) style. Neo-Palladian balustrades were added to the main floor and the new third floor. The final nationalistic touch was a cupola provided with a classical finial, providing visitors entering Pensacola with a British identity.[29] In 1769 the newly appointed Governor Chester was to move in. However, Chester refused to live in the old house and ordered a new house to be drawn by Elias Durnford in 1770 (below, p. 27, Fig. 2.15).[30] The completed design of the Governor's house can be described as a Spanish/French/English amalgamation which can now be labeled British Creole.

A military project in British St Augustine involved a former Spanish church (St Francis of 1737) being converted into British barracks (Fig. 2.9) in 1771. A drawing, dating before 1863, and an old photograph taken in 1863 show a side gallery but the coquina (shell stone) façade was stuccoed and scored. The roof originally had a captain's walk and cupola. Today this building is the St Francis Barracks, the headquarters

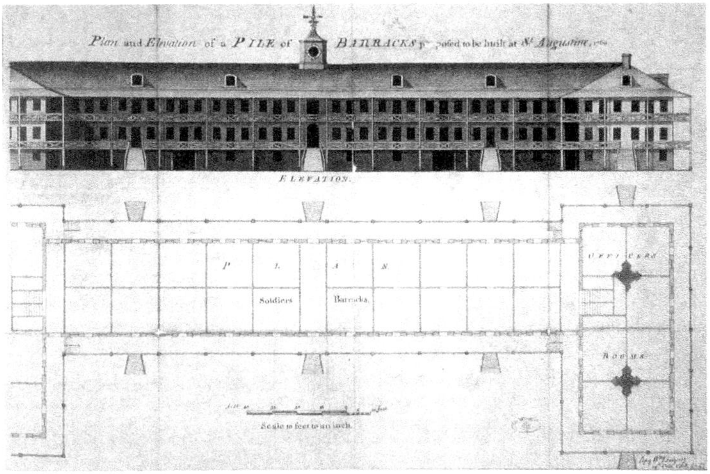

Fig. 2.10. William Brasier, 'Pile of Barracks Plan and Elevation Proposed to be Built at St Augustine', ink drawing, 1768 (TNA MPG 1/351).

of the Florida National Guard, so a military function is maintained.[31] The overall H plan with a captain's walk at the top of the building still exhibits a Neoclassical form derived from the 1771 Georgian scheme. U and H plans were repeated in military buildings in the Florida Parishes and the West Indies. A very ambitious three-story barracks (Fig. 2.10) was designed for St Augustine in 1768 by William Brasier, British engineer, and built in 1772 in a U-shaped plan, completely surrounded by verandas. Ten sets of exterior stairs led to the principal floor and stairs on the verandas served the next story although the wings which served officers had interior stair halls. With the surrounding galleries a double pitched, compound hipped roof provided the building with a West Indies character.[32] Like the governor's house at Pensacola, it had a Palladian Revival cupola with a classical finial and weather vane.

MILITARY INFLUENCES ON COLONIAL HOUSING

Florida colonists observed the construction of military projects with verandas, raised plans, and external stairs, and emulated these features on their houses for the same concerns cited by the military. Pensacola and St Augustine became the crucible of the Spanish/French/Anglo amalgamation cited to represent a British Creole style in East and West Florida. Active experimentation may have sprung when the Spanish Governor's house in Pensacola was remodeled and enlarged with Neoclassical details in 1767. Experimentation in plans and tropical details continued into the Second Spanish Period from 1783 to 1819. Loyalists who remained and newly arrived Americans who settled in East and West Florida continued to build Anglo-Creole cottages as evident by surviving 18th-century cottages in Pensacola, Louisiana, and Mississippi. Most British citizens, who did not want to remain under the Spanish, moved back to the Carolinas and other states, extending the new house form to the Carolinas who shared in common a plantation culture. Limited use of full piazzas had begun before 1763 in the Carolinas but now the new house tradition became common.

The cottage of Isaac Wright in Pensacola (Fig. 2.11), 1790, has an integral front gallery of French Creole heritage but also the hall-parlor plan and an exterior chimney, elements common to Carolina Tidewater cottages. During the Second Spanish Period, even the newly arrived Spanish adopted British contributions, such as sash windows and clapboard siding, as evident in the Wright cottage and in the Dorothy Walton cottage (Fig. 2.12), built by a Spanish citizen, G. Hernandez, in 1810. He amalgamated the central hallway idea of the Georgian plan into a great hall (or *salle*) with a fireplace. This room is flanked by two rooms on each side in the symmetrical Georgian manner. This plan variation became common between 1800 and the 1810s in the West Florida Parishes and spread up the Mississippi River as far as Cahokia, Illinois and beyond.[33] The center and original wood portion of 'Richmond' in Natchez, Mississippi was built in 1770 during the British Period, representing one of the earliest surviving Anglo-Creole raised cottages with a full gallery in the British West Florida Parish. It also features an external staircase leading to the primary floor gallery.

On the Gulf Coast, the new Anglo-Creole cottage is called the Gulf Coast Cottage. Few examples survive in the West Florida Parishes from the 18th century due to termites, fires, and hurricanes. Among the few built during the Spanish West Florida

Fig. 2.11. Wright Cottage, Hall/ Parlor Cottage, 1790, Pensacola, Florida.

Fig. 2.12. Hernandez-Walton Cottage, Pensacola, FL, 1810.

period are: Cottage Plantation, near St Francisville, Louisiana, 1790 and later, and Oakley Plantation house (Fig. 2.13), 1799, which was lived in by John James Audubon. These two houses are located outside St Francisville, West Feliciana Parish, Louisiana. Samuel Wilson, architect and a prolific writer of French colonial Louisiana, acknowledged that Oakley was one of the most significant surviving houses which reflected a British influence in West Florida.[34] Oakley rivalled in size the homes of the government officials in Pensacola. Jalousies installed below the ceiling of galleries gave extra protection against summer sunlight to the deep veranda.

Anglo-Creole cottages continued to be built into the American periods in the North Gulf Coast region. However the same or similar house form appears in the Carolina Tidewater basin, where the cottage became known as the Tidewater Cottage. Most were built after the 1770s but whether the new cottage began in Pensacola or in the Carolinas is not as important as the fact that builders in both locations recognized a new, healthier house type for the climate. Citizens in West Florida seem to have a slight edge in the development of the cottage since the incoming Florida colonists

Fig. 2.13. Oakley Plantation House, near St Francisville, LA, 1799.

were not used to the Gulf Coast humidity and heat while the Carolinas were occupied in a war for independence. An occasional raid into East Florida from Georgia may have also exposed Carolinians and Georgians to the house type but knowledge through trade during the Revolutionary War years would have been remote.

The earliest surviving examples in Mobile, Alabama date from the 1830s, such as on the Beal-Galliard cottage, 1836 (Fig. 2.14).[35] A country house at the time it was constructed,[36] it represents the type most likely built for the small plantation operations in the area as indicated on a plan of the eastern shore of Mobile Bay in 1770 or elsewhere, such as Cottage Plantation and Oakley Plantation.[37] The Beal-Gaillard cottage has a board wall façade while the other elevations are clapboard, a tradition that can be traced to French Creole cottages that placed clapboards over *bousillage* elevations not protected by galleries. Its extra wide central hall has French doors and French windows occupy the other gallery bays, indicating traditions surviving the Spanish West Florida period. Like Oakley, it has jalousies under the ceiling of the gallery. These 19th-century American period variations can be termed 'American Creole' cottages due to their perfect melding of French, Spanish, and Anglo traditions with Caribbean elements with the addition of Roman Revival and Greek Revival stylistic architectural decoration.[38] However, many architectural historians would simply call the American Creole cottage a Gulf Coast Cottage, a label used by habit.[39]

THE MATURE STAGE OF ANGLO-CREOLE MILITARY BUILDINGS

After the British became proficient with their use of Creole elements in not only military quarters and civilian housing, they began to create their own original designs as demonstrated with the 1768 barracks design for St Augustine (Fig. 2.10) and the perfected Gulf Coast Cottage (Fig. 2.14). These buildings demonstrate a complete understanding of tropical design elements without tentative experimentation, and could be considered a means by which the British expanded Creole architectural forms in military building projects. Moreover, the symmetrical aspects of Georgian

Fig. 2.14. Beal-Gaillard Cottage, 1836, Mobile, AL.

styles integrated easily and successfully with vernacular Creole values which accepted symmetrical plans by the mid 18th century. Successful building plans were passed from colony to colony, hence similarities between military projects of the Florida Parishes and the British Caribbean.

One of the earlier examples is Elias Durnford's drawing (Fig. 2.15) for a second Governor's Residence in Pensacola, 1770 (now razed). This was Governor Chester's 'dream house' which was to be a large Palladian Revival mansion of more than 7,200

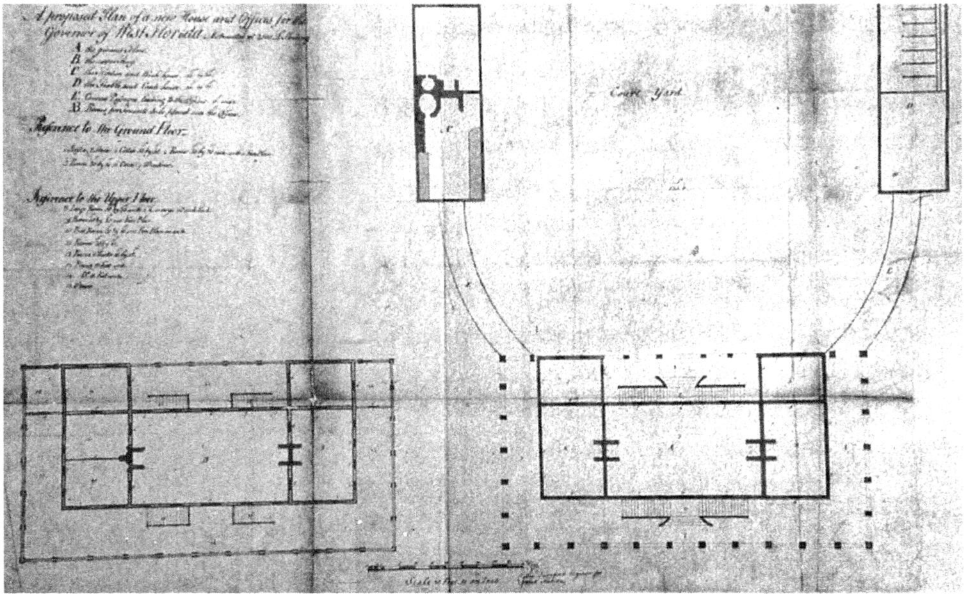

Fig. 2.15. Elias Durnford. 'A Proposed Plan of a New House and Offices for the Governor of West Florida', ink drawing, 1770 (TNA CO5, MPG 1/611, Pensacola).

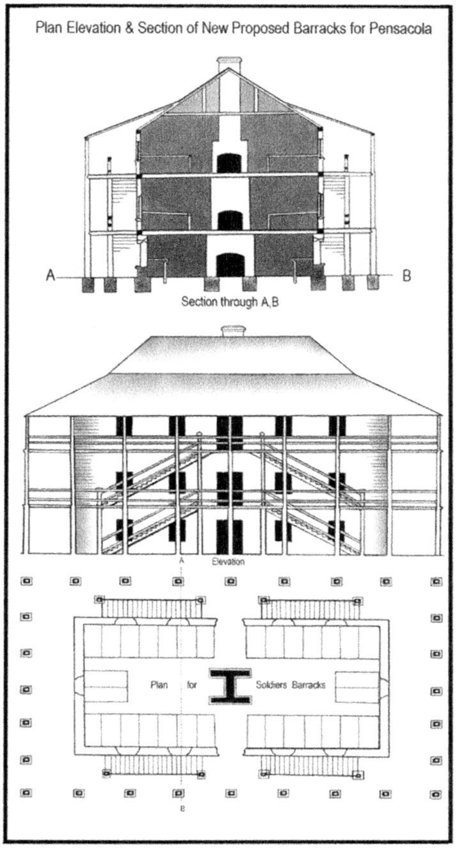

Fig. 2.16. Elias Durnford (Attrib.), 'Barracks', 1768, ink plan (TNA MPG 1/529 (1)).

square ft.[40] The main floors were about 3,600 square ft each, excluding galleries, the hyphen connections, and symmetrically placed outbuildings which together formed a U plan. Since an elevation drawing does not exist, the 'dream house' would have shared the Neo-Palladian details seen in James Gibbs's handbook, *A Book of Architecture*, 1728, which was used for many mansions in the colonies, such as the governor's house at New Bern, North Carolina. However, the Pensacola house was equally Creole in appearance with galleries on three sides plus a loggia on the garden elevation.[41]

While meeting the needs of the governor and commanding officers, concerted efforts to provide comfortable shelters to enlisted soldiers became the concern of the colonial government as evidenced in the designs of barracks and hospitals. Assimilated Georgian-Creole elements appear in the Pensacola, Soldier's Barracks (Fig. 2.16) drawn in 1768 most likely by Elias Durnford or an assistant.[42] The proposed design exhibits strict symmetry, surrounding galleries and bipartite roofs, features that became characteristic of many British designs in colonial Florida and West Indies. The enlisted men's room had no interior partitions, a central chimney and Durnford even arranged the wood beds placed against the window walls. The building was to measure 45ft by 65ft with galleries and would have four sets of stairs 8ft wide. Ceiling heights were to be 8ft for the ground floor, 11ft for the principal floor and 12ft for the top floor. The plan called for 81,400 bricks and 2,300 paving bricks to be made locally. Plentiful windows and doors to enhance air circulation were designed.[43] In comparison the officer's quarters of 1768 (Fig. 2.17) had a similar design but was thoroughly Georgian in plan with a central stair hall, and four rooms per floor. It had no gallery but had a Georgian hipped roof.[44] Without galleries, this brick structure would have been hotter and the hallway would have blocked effective lateral air circulation. These particular plans of barracks for soldiers and officers may not have been built in Pensacola; however, similar structures appear on some islands as will be discussed below.

Another set of barracks designs that were built (Fig. 2.2) that exhibit an understanding of the Gulf Coast climate are preserved in London. These were designed in 1771 by engineer T. Sowers.[45] Their dimensions were 65ft by 220ft each. However, the Pensacola fort plan of 1778 indicates that they were modified to 75ft by 175ft. Each structure was originally designed for 300 soldiers (two companies) plus officers.[46] The galleries for this Palladian inspired, symmetrical, double-pile design had X-shaped railing fretwork, a common feature in the West Indies. The barracks had fireplaces for eight rooms out of twenty rooms per floor, indicating that there was little concern for Pensacola winters. Exhibiting the concern for the summer humid heat, the plan itself has a legend that has written, 'On account of the great heat in summer, 14 (*sic*) men to each room was judged the most proper for preserving their healths.'[47] The 1778 plan of the fort shows that one of two barracks was built by that date.[48] A traveler in Pensacola in 1803 reported that the fort had two handsome barracks but one recently burned down.[49] Brick foundations recently discovered reveal that tabby mortar, the material first used in South Carolina and Georgia, was being utilized in Pensacola. In Pensacola the interior brick walls received a tabby coating and ground floors sometimes had floors of poured tabby although Sower's 1771 plan simply indicates that interior walls were to be lathed and plastered.

St Francis Barracks (Fig. 2.9) of St Augustine was mentioned earlier since it was a priory church before being converted to house troops in the town outside St Marks Fort. However, the one-story church required extensive modification to become a two-story structure of Georgian design with galleries. This design with verandas and pedimented end pavilions may have a Caribbean source. TNA holds a plan of the Fort at Musquito Point, Jamaica, dating to 1723

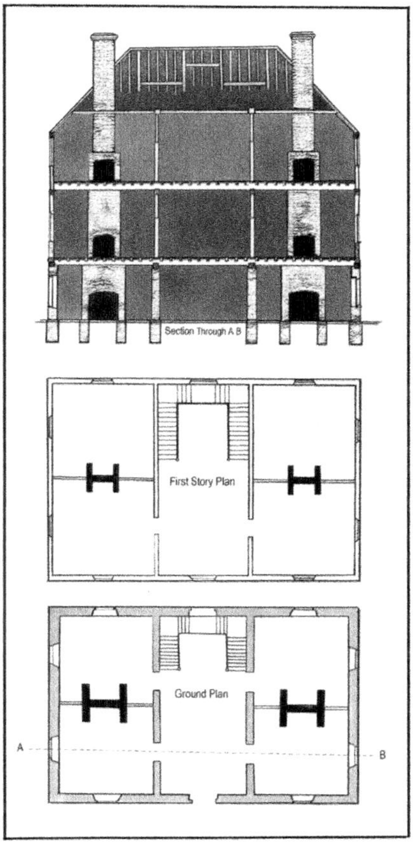

Fig. 2.17. Elias Durnford, 'Officer Barracks', 1768, ink plan (TNA MPG 1/529 (2)).

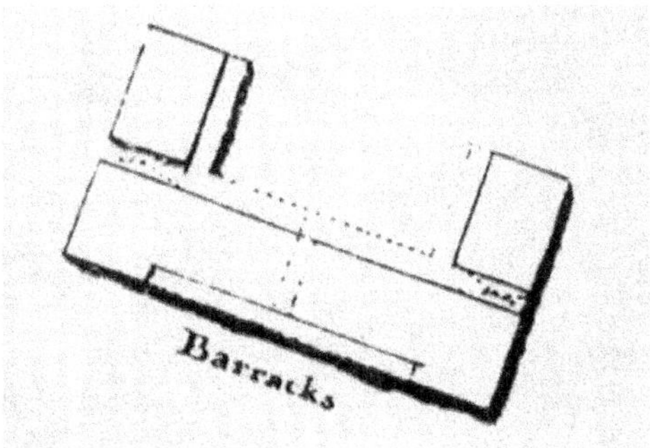

Fig. 2.18. Anon. Barracks Plan, Detail of 'A Plan of the Fort Building at Musquito Point in Iamaka (Jamaica)', 1723, ink drawing (TNA CO 700 Jamaica 9).

or 1725, with a galleried barracks (Fig. 2.18).[50] The front part is U-shaped similar to the St Augustine project of 1771. It too had a veranda flanked by the end pavilions but additionally, wings were added to the rear gallery to form an overall H-plan. Dotted lines indicate that an open central passage and 'dogtrot' passages on the rear elevation were constructed for ventilation and efficient circulation of soldiers.[51]

MILITARY PROJECTS FROM 1783 TO THE EARLY 19TH CENTURY IN THE WEST INDIES

Pensacola and St Augustine were evidently early centers for the development of military buildings and housing with galleries in the United States. Surprisingly the military buildings pre-date many of the surviving West Indies military projects utilizing the same features. Events leading to the American Revolution also made British East and West Florida attractive to Loyalist settlers, perpetuating English Neo-Palladianism in architecture. The mature British-Creole style, perfected between 1763 and 1783 in the Florida Parishes, was repeated in the military buildings from Bermuda and the Bahamas down to Barbados as the United Kingdom reinforced its garrisons in the islands through the War of 1812. The perpetuation of the Caribbean-Palladian style into the 19th century suggests that British Loyalists were content and associated the style with British colonial governments. It possessed geometric order and would have suggested stability to colonial inhabitants.

On the East Coast of the United States in the former thirteen colonies, a different spirit was kindled after 1783. Beginning with the 1785 Virginia State House by Thomas Jefferson, the United States associated the Roman Revival and Neoclassicism as symbolic of the new democratic republic. Thomas Jefferson even redesigned his house, Monticello, discarding many Palladian attributes in favor of Roman Revival stylistic elements to remove its design from its colonial association.

The British colonies in the West Indies, on the other hand, maintained the Palladian Revival and continued to draw from the Georgian Creole experiments that were perfected in the Florida Parishes. One building (Fig. 2.19), contemporary to the St

Fig. 2.19. Government Assembly Building, Spanish Town, Jamaica, 1762.

Fig. 2.20. Old Naval Hospital, Port Royal, Jamaica, 1819.

Fig. 2.21. Garrison Barracks, Hastings, Barbados, 1780.

Fig. 2.22. Garrison Hospital, Hastings, Barbados, 1806.

Fig. 2.23. Garrison Hospital, Hastings, Barbados, 1806–14.

Augustine and Pensacola military projects is the brick Government Assembly, Spanish Town, Jamaica. Built about 1762, it has an arcade and a louvered second-story veranda with alternating sash windows.[52] Its first story has a very deep arcade the length of the building and a complete city block. The second-story design, however, has louvered shutters flanking sash windows, a feature developed in the West Indies and not found existing in East or West Florida.

The Courthouse, added to the Spanish Town Square *after* 1800, continued to use the Palladian Revival rather than changing to a newer architectural fashion. The Old Courthouse in St Andrew Parish in Jamaica, 1807, is more vernacular. Jamaicans consider it to be a good example of Caribbean Palladian Revival and label it 'Jamaica Georgian'.[53]

The idea that verandas support a good healthy environment is evident in the Old Naval Hospital, 1819, Port Royal, Jamaica (Fig. 2.20).[54] Its hipped roof, central door or open 'dogtrot' on the principal floor is similar to the 1768 Barracks design proposal for Pensacola. Also close to that 1768 design are the barracks in St Lucia dating from 1890, including external stairs in the gallery. An early Garrison building (Fig. 2.21) in Hastings, Barbados, 1780, has a two-story arcaded veranda. The large Garrison hospital located in Hastings, Barbados (Fig. 2.22), dating *c.* 1806–14, can also be compared to the large 1771 barracks in Pensacola (Fig. 2.2) but it has doubled stairs as on the 1768 barracks. One of the hospital buildings in Hastings (Fig. 2.23) is U-shaped with corner pavilions on the street elevation and a long gallery on the rear elevation, bearing a likeness to the Florida barracks. Most of these island projects represent a late phase of Late Georgian design extending into the 19th century but modified with a strong Caribbean influence.[55]

CONCLUSION

Most literature on architecture in the United States emphasizes the development of the Creole house independently from military buildings. It is argued here that military engineers had an impact upon house development in the New World from the beginning, starting in Santo Domingo with the Diego Columbo Colón Palace, 1502 (Fig. 2.24). Engineers in the New World had recourse to Italian Renaissance handbooks that provided advice for ideal town planning, an input in turn to the Law of the West Indies, a Spanish-Colonial decree that described the manner of which to best construct buildings in the Americas, from housing for the rich (governor residences) to simple farm houses. As engineers designed housing for officers, governors, and enlisted men, colonial citizens were inspired by their example and built smaller houses or vernacular cottages with galleries that simplified the governmental models. In short time an assimilation of ideas of European, Amerindian, and African ethnicities evolved known as the Creole style. The five-part symmetrical design in the Columbus palace was simplified to the tri-partite plan of plantation houses and down to the simple West Indies cottage with a front gallery and hipped roof.

This research explored various means by which the British explored tropical features in military buildings with similar solutions in the southeastern United States and the West Indies. While rare examples of porches and other Caribbean elements can be found in the American English colonies before 1776, the military engineers and colonists in the Florida Parishes were actively exploring tropical devises from 1763 onwards. By 1770, sophisticated designs could be distinguished as Anglo-Creole or Georgian-Creole. The military were using West Indies elements on large structures to cool the quarters for hundreds of men per building. Citizens were equally seeking the means to build cooler homes for the Gulf Coast climate.

Buildings in the Florida Parishes differed mainly from many Caribbean buildings in that fireplaces were needed for about eight weeks of the year in Pensacola and St Augustine. Each locale relied on indigenous materials for construction which can be found in military projects. The Spanish explored buildings of tabby and coquina construction in East Florida; in West Florida builders relied mostly on timber – oak and pine for all projects from forts to cottages. The West Indies have limestone or volcanic stone, depending upon the island, resulting in massive masonry military construction.

Fig. 2.24. Diego Columbo Palace, Santa Domingo, 1502.

Arcades often replace the post-and-beam construction in West Florida. However, each area adopted the Neo-Palladian style of the Georgian Period for the local style which was adapted to the local vernacular building practices. Since colonists in East and West Florida Parishes remained Loyalist in their politics, as in the West Indies, there was no need to turn their backs to the British-Creole variation of the Georgian style that as associated with the mother country.

NOTES

1 Harris 1997, 30–1.
2 Morrison 1952, 135–7; Harris 1997, 32–3.
3 Harris 1997, 17, 47.
4 Buckley 1998, 15, 50–2, 63.
5 Morris *et al.* 1999.
6 Gordon 2002, 164–5.
7 Harris 1997, 129.
8 Sowers 1771; Oszuścik 1991, 33. A note on the barracks drawing calls attention to the rooms on the ground floor being used for stores, a similar function on ground floors of English and French colonial mansions in the states of the Southeast and Louisiana. The principal floors are raised above the ground with plentiful windows and with galleries for cool ventilation.
9 Gordon 2002, 165. French Creole *bousillage* is daubing that has the added material of Spanish moss for binding strength in addition to straw, animal fur, and dung.
10 Durnford, 10 July 1770; Reps 1969, 118, 121, 133–5. The unique town plan was known as 'New Town' and was drawn by Elias Durnford in 1770 for the eastern shore of Mobile Bay. The site chosen was adjacent to a British encampment that looked upon the bay from its 100ft bluff, called 'Red Cliffs'. The town was laid out with oblique parallelogram blocks and lots, orientated to take advantage of the southwestern breeze rising up from the bay and sweeping through 60ft wide streets to funnel the breeze to all citizens in each block. A normal north–south grid plan would have blocked this cooling breeze. Furthermore, the posed position of the town would have blocked cold fronts in the winter which normally come out of the Northwest. The only other time that the English laid out a colonial town with a grid not forming perpendicular angles was Marlborough, Virginia (1691) but that was due to the junction of a creek and river. 'New Town' in West Florida has a lengthy legend that acknowledged the concern for the healthfulness of the site and the consideration for cooling sea breezes. For more information see: Oszuścik 1989, 73–81; Durnford, July 1770 (TNA MPG 1/359).
11 Buckley 1998, 24, 33, 18, 35: British garrisons learned from experience that forts on the warmer side of Caribbean islands were hotter and soldiers were prone to illnesses, with yellow fever and malaria being the chief diseases. Medical records indicate that the death rate of soldiers at sea level was 178 per 1,000 in comparison to only 32.7 men per 1,000 living in barracks above 2,000ft in elevation. Only hurricanes disrupted more life in the West Indies.
12 Crain 1994, pl. 22.
13 Gordon 2002, 243, pl. 9.6.
14 Crain 1994, 32.
15 Gordon 2002, 242.
16 Crain 1994, 148.
17 Gordon 2002, 248–50. Coquina is a soft shell-rock loosely bonded by silica.
18 Sickels-Taves & Sheehan 1999, 5–9.
19 Sickels-Taves & Sheehan 1999, 155.
20 Gordon 2002, 236–8.
21 Harris 1997, 33. I believe that a triangle was chosen because it has the least number of sides among regular geometric shapes. If one elevation faces the water as was the case in all three, only the two land sides needed ditches which connected to the water to provide a wet moat. The ditches provided material for ramparts.
22 Rea 1974, 57–9. Elias Durnford also served as architect, and later Lt. Governor of West Florida. His younger brother, Andrew Durnford served as engineer and architect in Bermuda. See Harris 1997.
23 Gordon 2002, 167.
24 Oszuścik 1991, 39.
25 Elsbeth Gordon speaks of the amalgamation in St Augustine as converting Spanish

buildings to new uses, nurturing the Caribbean-style elements rather than tearing down St Augustine to remake it into an 'English' town (see note 6). However, since the British added second stories to houses of wood, replaced open grates of windows with sash windows, constructed new wood frame houses, and added a Palladian cupola to the Soldiers Barracks (a former Spanish mission building), the British were nationalizing the city. The new style, with the tropical elements is the same as described for Pensacola – a British Creole style.

26 Durnford 1768, TNA MPG 1/349. This plan shows the original Spanish structures retained by the English and it has a reference that lists the functions of the buildings plus new ones built by the British and a second reference listing future use of grounds outside the enlarged fortress. Another plan, 'Plan and Sections of the Fort at Pensacola, 1763' (TNA CO 700 Florida 5), represented the 1757 Spanish fort as it appeared in 1763. Using this plan for comparison, one can easily perceive which portions were kept by the British, which buildings were retained, added to, and torn down. Also, the new curtain walls and bastions doubled the size of the fortification and garden plots were drawn within the walls on land that was originally outside the fort.

27 Gauld *c.* 1767 (Library of Congress Print Collection), in Rea 1974, 57; George Gauld noted that the naval ships illustrated in the harbor were from Jamaica.

28 The Spanish in Pensacola used carpenters from French Mobile and a population of expatriate French colonists lived in Pensacola.

29 Durnford (Attrib) 1770, 1–3, TNA MPG 1/611; Osźuścik 1991, 26–8. The cupola served as a lookout, a light house and a base for a flagpole that displayed British colors.

30 Gordon 2002, 172–3.

31 Gordon 2002, 133–4.

32 For Brasier 1768 see Fig. 2.10; see also TNA MPG 1/351 in Gordon 2002, pl. 18.

33 Oszuścik 2004, 32–3. Since this article was written, I have discovered that the British may have provided the idea of a great hall doubling as a large hallway in Pensacola, such as in Fig. 2.19.

34 Wilson, Jr. 1987, 96.

35 Oszuścik 1992, 10–12.

36 Gould 1988, 96–7.

37 Durnford, 10 July 1770; TNA MPG 1/359.

38 Oszuścik 1991, 37–41; Oszuścik 1994, 28–9.

39 I continue to use the term Gulf Coast Cottage for the cottage type along the Gulf Coast since the local population recognizes this label.

40 Durnford 1770; TNA MPG 1/611 (Pensacola); Gordon 2002, 176.

41 Oszuścik 1991, 27–31.

42 Durnford (Attrib.), 1768; TNA MPG 1/529 (1).

43 Oszuścik 1991, 32–4.

44 Durnford (Attrib.), 1768; TNA MPG 1/529 (2); Oszuścik, 1991, 32–4.

45 Sowers 1771. Elias Durnford was appointed Lt. Governor of West Florida in 1769, perhaps the reason why Thomas Sowers, engineer, had been assigned to Pensacola at this time (Harris 1997, 129).

46 Oszuścik 1991, 33, 36.

47 Sowers 1771.

48 Durnford 1768, MPG 1/349; Durnford 1778; TNA MPG 1/358 (Pensacola).

49 Robins (Landry, transl.) 1966, 4.

50 Anon. 1723 or 1725; TNA CO 700 Jamaica 9.

51 Oszuścik 1991, 35–7. This plan is the earliest I have found to date that indicates ample galleries and loggia. I presume that more British barracks were provided with galleries, loggias, and piazzas between 1723 and 1768, but the 1723 plan is a rare finding. It was built since the plan was part of an overall fortification plan rather than as a proposed plan. The term, 'dogtrot', is used by vernacular architecture scholars in the United States to refer to the open space under the roof between the two rooms of a two-pen cottage.

52 Crain 1994, 156–7.

53 Crain 1994, 157.

54 Crain 1994, 135.

55 Crain 1994, 134–43; 157–8.

BIBLIOGRAPHY

Buckley, R.N. 1998, *The British Army in the West Indies: Society and the Military in the Revolutionary Age*, Gainesville, FL: University Press of Florida.

Crain, E.E. 1994, *Historic Architecture in the Caribbean Islands*, Gainesville, FL: University Press of Florida.

Gibbs, J. 1728, *A book of architecture, containing designs of buildings and ornaments*, London: W. Innys and R. Manby.

Gordon, E.K. 2002, *Florida's Colonial Architectural Heritage*, Gainesville, FL: University Press of Florida.

Gould, E.B. 1988, *From Fort to Port: An Architectural History of Mobile, Alabama, 1711–1918*, Tuscaloosa, AL: University of Alabama Press.

Harris, E.C. 1997, *Bermuda Forts: 1612–1957*, Bermuda: Bermuda Maritime Museum Press.

McGovern, J.R. (ed.), 1974, *Colonial Pensacola*, Pensacola, FL: Pensacola Escambia Development Commission.

Morris, E.L., Read, R., James, E. & Machling, T, 1999, '"The old stone fort at Newcastle ..." The Redoubt, Nevis, Eastern Caribbean', *Post-Med. Archaeol*, 33, 194–221.

Morrison, H. 1952, *Early American Architecture from the First Colonial Settlements to the National Period*, New York: Oxford University Press.

Oszuścik, P. 1989, 'Eighteenth Century British on the Eastern Shore of Mobile Bay', *Pioneer Am. Soc. Trans.* 12, 73–81.

Oszuścik, P. 1991, 'Government Projects in British Pensacola and Their Impact Upon the Southeast', *Arris: J. of the SE Chap. of The Soc. of Archit. Historians* 2, 20–41.

Oszuścik, P. 1992, 'Passage of the Gallery and Other Caribbean Elements from the French and Spanish to the British in the United States', *Pioneer America Soc. Trans.* 15, 1–14.

Oszuścik, P. 1994, 'Comparisons Between Rural and Urban French Creole Housing', *Material Culture* 26:3, 1–36.

Oszuścik, P. 2004, 'Two Houses with Caribbean Connections with French, Spanish, and Anglo-American Influences', *Pioneer America Soc. Trans.* 27, 30–42.

Rea, R.R. 1974, 'Pensacola Under the British (1763–1781)', in McGovern (ed.) 1974, 57–9.

Reps, J.W. 1969, *Town Planning in Frontier America*, Princeton: Princeton University Press.

Robins, C.C. (Landry, S.O., Jr., Transl.) 1966. *Voyage to Louisiana: 1803–1805*, New Orleans: Pelican.

Sickels-Taves, L.B. & Sheehan, M.S. 1999, *The Lost Art of Tabby Redefined: Preserving Oglethorpe's Architectural History*, Southfield, MI: Archit. Conservation Press.

Wilson, S., Jr. 1987, *The Architecture of Colonial Louisiana*, Lafayette, LA: Center for Louisiana Studies, University of Southwestern Louisiana.

PRIMARY SOURCES

Anon. 1723 or 1725, 'A Plan of the Fort Building at Musquito Point in Iamaka (Jamaica)', TNA CO 700 Jamaica 9.

Anon. 1763, 'Plan and Sections of the Fort at Pensacola', TNA CO 700 Florida 5.

Durnford, E. (Attrib.) 1768. 'Plan, Elevation and Section of New Proposed Barracks for Pensacola,' TNA MPG 1/529 (1).

Durnford, E. (Attrib.) 1768. 'Plan of a New Proposed Barracks for Pensacola' TNA MPG 1/529 (2).

Durnford, E. (Attrib.) 1770. 'Plans, Elevation of a House Occupied by the Governor,' TNA CO 5, MPG 1/611 – Pensacola (1–3).

Durnford, E. 1778, 'Plan of the Fort Showing Surrounding Streets and an Advanced Redoubt, Distinguishing Old Spanish Buildings and Showing Hurricane Damage', TNA CO 5 MPG 1/358 Pensacola.
Durnford, E. 1768, 'Plan of the Stockade Fort at Pensacola Representing it in its Present State with the Proposed Situation for New Barracks', TNA MPG 1/349, PFF/124175.
Durnford, E. 1770, 'A Proposed Plan of a New House and Offices for the Governor of West Florida', TNA CO 5 MPG 611-Pensacola.
Durnford, E. 10 July 1770, 'Plan of a New Town to be Traced Out on the East Side of the Bay of Mobile,' TNA: Co5 MPG 1/359.
Sowers, T. 1771, 'Plans, Elevations, and Sections for New Barracks in Pensacola,' TNA CO 5 MPG 10.

3

'Come Hell or High Water': Architectural Responses to Natural Disaster in the Early British Caribbean

LOUIS P. NELSON

SUMMARY: 'Come Hell or High Water' argues that the architecture erected by British colonials in the 18th-century Caribbean responded more to the region's natural disasters than to its heat. By surveying the architecture of four regions in the British Caribbean, including Barbados, the Leeward Islands, Jamaica, and South Carolina, this paper demonstrates that British builders in the Caribbean embraced at least three accommodations to these disasters, but that they did so unevenly. An explanation for such inconsistency across the region is found in the frequency of disasters. Quite logically, those colonies experiencing natural disaster with greater frequency integrated these three adaptations into their building stock much more consistently than did those where disaster struck only on rare occasion.

'COME HELL OR HIGH WATER'

In 1725, the vestry of St Peter's Anglican Church in Port Royal, Jamaica, began the *fourth* church erected by that parish in the course of only 50 years. The three earlier structures on the site had all suffered under a regular battery of natural disasters, including a devastating 1692 earthquake, a fire in 1702, and hurricanes in 1712 and 1722.[1] In an effort to erect a church that would better withstand the natural disasters that had beset their earlier buildings the parish erected a compact church on the plan of an extended Greek Cross measuring 80ft east–west and 72ft north–south (Fig. 3.1). With both an interior and exterior water table, the walls of the 1725 cruciform building are over 4½ft thick at ground level – far more than necessary to support the roof of a fairly small cruciform church that spans only 26ft. The thickness of the walls approximates to that used by builders of powder magazines rather than churches; in this, their fourth church, the vestry was determined to erect a structure that could withstand natural catastrophe. This vestry was not alone. Ten years before their counterparts in Port Royal, the vestry of the nearly adjacent parish of St Catherine's installed a plaque over their newly completed church:

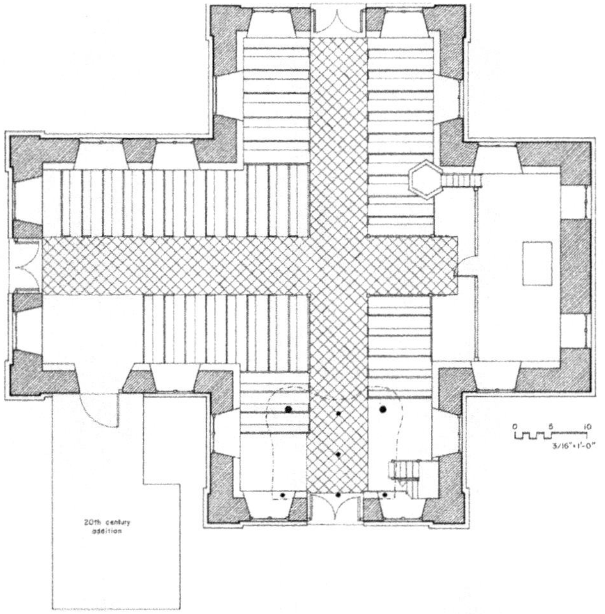

Fig. 3.1. Plan of St Peters, Port Royal, Jamaica, *c.* 1725.

> This Church dedicated to the service of Almighty God was thrown downe by the dreadfull Hurricane of August the 28th Anno Domini MDCCXII, and was by the Divine Assistance, through the Piety and at the expense of the Parishioners, more beautifully and substantially rebuilt.[2]

The Port Royal church was destroyed in the hurricane of 1712; St Catherine's succumbed to one of the two major hurricanes to strike the island in 1722. In rebuilding their large brick church on the plan of a Latin Cross, the vestry of St Catherine's supposed that their new church was not only more beautiful, but also better able to withstand the powerful dynamic forces of hurricane winds and earthquakes.

While the relationship between architecture and climate is a topic that has been often addressed by historians of architecture, these discussions usually center on accommodations to the region's intense heat.[3] The prevalence of galleries and open floor plans are often cited as architectural responses to physical comfort, providing shade from the sun and capturing any ocean breezes. Some historians, however, are beginning to question these seemingly obvious interpretations of Caribbean architecture. John Crowley, for example, has demonstrated that the emergence of galleries and piazzas in the 18th century had as much to do with healthfulness as with accommodation to heat.[4] Using a vast body of documentary evidence, Matthew Mulcahy has recently argued that British colonials in the Caribbean began to note the ways various buildings responded more or less successfully to the region's regular hurricanes by the late 17th century.[5] Building on Mulcahy's findings, this paper examines the surviving built environment for evidence of the extent to which British colonials actually implemented the architectural changes they discussed. An examination of the surviving

18th-century architecture in a variety of Caribbean locales suggests that not all British colonials were attentive to the architectural accommodations they themselves proscribed. Some builders preferred houses that limited the principal living chambers to a single floor under a broad hipped roof and set on a raised broad masonry foundation. When building substantial masonry buildings, they preferred structures with complex footprints, often cruciform, T-shaped, or rectilinear with corner towers or pavilions. And lastly, builders occasionally mixed building materials by resting a timber frame living story on a masonry ground floor. But these adaptations were not universally implemented across the Caribbean. While colonials in Jamaica and the Leeward Islands of Nevis, St Kitts, Antigua, and St Eustatius took these adaptations fairly seriously, those in Barbados and South Carolina largely ignored such precautions, challenging assertions of the rise of a distinctive architecture in the British West Indies in the 18th century.[6]

Clarence House, built in the 1780s as the commander's residence at the British naval installation at English Harbor on Antigua, typifies the rural house form common among elites in the Leeward Islands and on Jamaica (Figs 3.2, 3.3).[7] The single living floor of the elegant stone building is sheltered by thee adjacent hipped roofs, one covering each of the front, middle, and rear flanks of the building. In regions where there is obviously no concern for snow load, lower parallel hipped roofs – found throughout the Caribbean – offer less resistance to wind and include a much lighter roof-framing system than a single roof that must rise higher to span the full width of the building.[8] The building stands on a raised masonry foundation much broader than the main block of the house. In addition to providing the necessary floor for a gallery, the foundation established a well-anchored footing for the building.[9] The raised foundation also provided the added benefit of service spaces for house slaves. Single-story living, low, hipped roofs and broad, raised masonry foundations gave this house and many others a low horizontal profile and a strong, wide foundation.

Fig. 3.2. South elevation of Clarence House, English Harbour, Antigua, 1786–7.

Fig. 3.3. West elevation of Clarence House, English Harbour, Antigua, 1786–7.

Similar design features characterize 18th-century architecture elsewhere in the Leeward Islands. The building now called the Fairview Inn on St Kitts is a rare survival of an 18th-century plantation house on that island (Fig. 3.4). While the building has a Victorian piazza on the front and a two-story addition to one side, the 18th-century core of the building is a single living floor – in this

Fig. 3.4. West elevation of the Fairview Inn, St Kitts, late 18th century.

Fig. 3.5. Lopes House, Oranjestad, St Eustatius, 18th century.

Fig. 3.6. Minard Plantation House, St Ann's Parish, Jamaica, late 18th century.

Fig. 3.7. North elevation of John Tharpe Town House, Falmouth, Jamaica, 1790s.

case built of wood – standing on a raised masonry foundation and sheltered by a low hipped roof. These forms also characterize a remarkable collection of early frame houses in the town of Oranjestad on St Eustatius. Although founded by the Dutch and controlled by them since the early 19th century, this important trading center in the Leewards was governed and occupied by the British through much of the 18th century. The 18th-century Lopes House is typical of the earliest domestic building stock in the town (Fig. 3.5). Like Clarence House and the Fairview Inn, these buildings all restrict the living space to a single level under a hipped roof and they stand on a masonry foundation that often extends beyond the footprint of the house. As suggested by the wide, uncovered platforms of the Lopes House and others in Oranjestad, the masonry platform played a more important role than simply providing a floor for a gallery offering shelter from the sun. The absence of any evidence for a sheltering roof of a gallery or piazza on many of these buildings, in fact, suggests the possibility that these foundations preceded the gallery roofs that commonly shade the space they create.

While by no means the universal choice, such building traditions also characterize a substantial percentage of early plantation houses on Jamaica; Drax Hall, Minard, and Holland plantations, for example, all share these specific characteristics (Fig. 3.6). The large number of early plantation houses that survive in prints and as images on plantation plats suggest that the low, broad massing was far more common on early Jamaica.[10] With their single floor living, low hipped roof, and broad masonry foundation, the massing of these houses differ very little from Clarence House on Antigua. An urban example of this house form is John Tharpe's 1790s wharf-front house in Falmouth, Jamaica, a building with low, single-story living under a compartmentalized roofing system and resting on a raised masonry foundation (Fig. 3.7).

In his study of early British commentary on building in the Caribbean, Mulcahy has noted that colonials recognized that building low to the ground was one of the most common preventative measures against hurricanes. Mulcahy reports that colonials recognized the suitability of lower buildings as early as the late 17th century. In the 1660s, for example, one observer wrote that in the Caribbean,

> there are many very fair houses of Timber, Stone, and Brick, built after the same manner as those in their own Countries, save that for the most part they are but one or two Stories high at most, that they may the more easily resist the winds, which sometimes blow in those parts with extraordinary violence.[11]

Similarly, the late 17th-century governor of the Leeward Islands reported that in Charlestown, Nevis, there are 'good dwellings and storehouses, built with country timber, not exceeding 60 feet long and 20 broad, story and a half, the "Hurri-Canes" having taught people to build low'.[12] Inspection of extant early buildings suggests that the desire for low profiles often resulted in parallel hipped roofs covering adjacent flanks of a building. By the 18th century, colonials also began to appreciate the strength provided by a broad foundation. A Moravian missionary writing about the Leeward Islands in the 1760s, wrote that building on a broad foundation was 'not only to provide for the enjoyment of shade in the open air but also to give the buildings a bigger foundation and thereby make them more resistant to the winds of storms'.[13]

Even so, such climate-responsive massing was not universal throughout the Caribbean. The low broad houses found in the Leewards and on Jamaica are conspicuously absent from the plantation landscapes of Barbados and South Carolina. The most prominent early plantation houses on Barbados are the monumental late 17th-century Drax Hall and Nicholas Abbey (Fig. 3.8). With two stories of masonry with another behind the tall curvilinear gables of the roofline, the builder of Nicholas Abbey was apparently not concerned about accommodating the building to hurricane force winds. The prevalence of raised gables on the island through the 18th century is suggested by the commentary of one Barbadian planter after the hurricane of 1780. He noted that 'gables have since in a great measure been abolished in Barbados'.[14] Like their 17th-century counterparts, 18th-century buildings built by elite planters also embraced the standard two-story mass common throughout the British Atlantic world. Alleyndale Hall, in both its earliest and later 18th-century forms was a full two stories of masonry as was Dukes plantation house, Buttals, Halton, Sunbury, Harmony Hall, and others on Barbados.[15] The same can be said of most plantation houses from

Fig. 3.8. St Nicholas Abbey, St Peter's Parish, Barbados, late 17th century.

Fig. 3.9. Lewisfield Plantation House, Berkeley County, South Carolina, 1770s.

18th-century South Carolina.[16] More famous buildings, like Drayton Hall from the late 1730s, and less familiar buildings like Lewisfield plantation from the 1770s, all share the tendency in that colony to build to a full two stories (Fig. 3.9). As is the case at Lewisfield, galleries on these buildings are usually added in the early 19th century and are usually supported by piers independent of the foundation for the main house. The single-story buildings with low hipped roofs and broad foundations found commonly in Jamaica and the Leeward Islands are nowhere in evidence among the plantation architectures of these other Caribbean colonies.

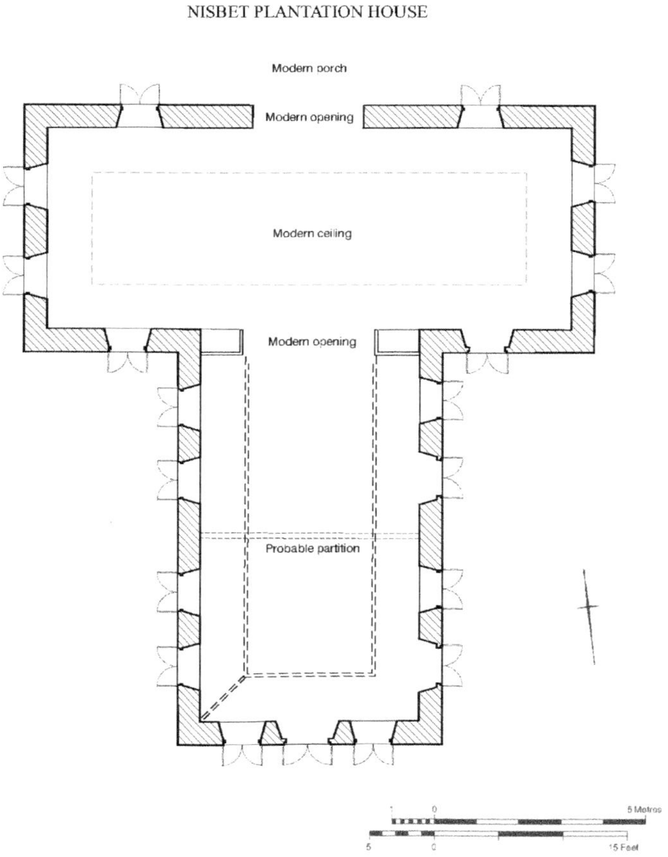

Fig. 3.10. Plan of Nisbet Plantation House, Nevis, *c.* 1778.

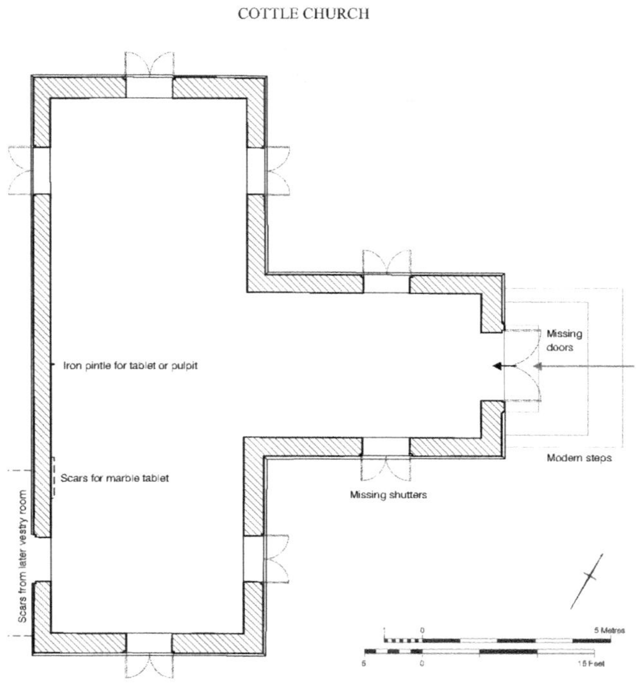

Fig. 3.11. Plan of Cottle Church, Nevis, *c.* 1824.

A second characteristic of 18th-century buildings on Jamaica and in the Leeward Islands is a preference for complex building footprints, often cruciform, T-shaped, or rectilinear with corner towers or pavilions. As I have argued elsewhere, the earliest Anglican churches on Jamaica show a notable tendency towards the cruciform plan, a form largely unfamiliar to Anglican church builders in late 17th- and 18th-century England.[17] In the two decades following the 1692 earthquake, Anglicans in Jamaica undertook the erection of three new substantial urban churches: St Andrew's Half-Way-Tree, begun in 1692, Kingston Parish Church, begun in 1701, and St Catherine's in Spanishtown, begun in 1712. All three were cruciform. Following these three churches, almost five out of every six churches newly built on the island in the 18th century were cruciform.[18] Cruciform churches, with their narrow roofs, shorter wall spans, and twelve mutually-buttressing 90-degree corners, may have seemed the more stable option than longitudinal plans with their long spans of unsupported walls or wide auditory churches with their broad, heavy roof systems.

Interestingly, many houses on both Jamaica and in the Leeward Islands seem to follow suit by abandoning the standard rectilinear formula for 18th-century Georgian houses by embracing more complex plans. Nisbet plantation house, erected on Nevis in the late 1770s, in fact, differs very little from the T-shaped plan of Cottle Church, an Anglican chapel erected on the same island some decades later (Figs 3.10, 3.11). A number of other Anglican churches on the island of Nevis are cruciform in

Fig. 3.12. Good Hope, Trelawney Parish, Jamaica, 1790s.

Fig. 3.13. Colbeck Castle, St Catherine's Parish, Jamaica, early 18th century.

Fig. 3.14. Evelyn Villa, outside Charlestown, Nevis, early 19th century.

plan, although in some cases these seem to be 19th-century expansions of simpler 18th-century buildings.[19] On Jamaica, a handful of 18th-century and early 19th-century houses were built with projecting wings to either end of the main house block, giving the house an H-plan. The most spectacular example of this type is Good Hope, John Tharpe's 1790s plantation counterpart to his town house discussed earlier (Fig. 3.12).[20] But among the more interesting house plans of this type is the rectilinear block cornered by pavilions or towers. The most spectacular example of a house in this plan is Colbeck Castle, erected near the south coast of Jamaica sometime in the early decades of the 18th century (Fig. 3.13). While the main block of the building is only two stories tall, the corner towers are a full three stories. The survival of a late 17th-century tower on the nearby Alley Church might have bestowed on the corner towers of Colbeck Castle a perceived sense of structural integrity. If this plan appears on a small handful of examples on Jamaica, it appears also on buildings in the Leeward Islands.[21] The suburban villa, now called the Evelyn Villa, erected in the early years of the 19th century in Charlestown on Nevis, shares this same footprint, if here the towers have become pavilions (Fig. 3.14). In either case, the numerous 90-degree corners of the plan might have lent structural stability to houses with such plans, at least in the minds of builders.

Unlike their counterparts in these regions of the Caribbean, planters in Barbados and South Carolina adhered largely to the simple rectilinear footprints built by their socio-economic counterparts across the British Empire. Not a single 18th-century plantation house with a complex footprint has yet surfaced in surveys of Barbados. In building churches, Barbadian Anglicans did erect one early church known to have taken a cruciform plan. In 1660, the vestry of St John's parish began the construction of a new stone church, probably replacing a wooden building. The church was designed with a western porch and a projecting

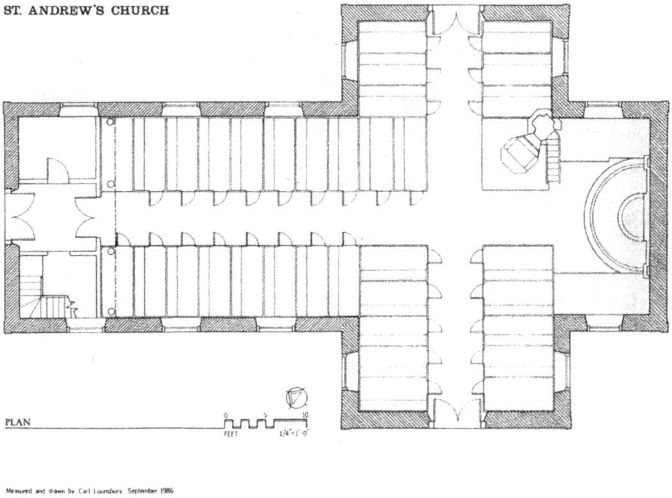

Fig. 3.15. Plan of St Andrew's Parish Church, Charleston County, South Carolina, 1707 and 1723.

chamber chancel to the east. In 1675, however, a devastating hurricane extensively damaged the body of the church. One of the only changes made to the building design in the ensuing reconstruction was the addition of two transverse wings, projecting to the north and south off the longitudinal building, wings that served to buttress the long side walls of the church.[22] Although the documentary records for most 18th-century Anglican parishes on Barbados do not survive, the body of 19th-century churches does not suggest that the cruciform plan came to define church design on the island.

The evidence in South Carolina is not quite so decisive. Anglicans in South Carolina built a number of cruciform churches, most prominently St Andrew's church after its reconstruction in 1723 (Fig. 3.15). The two other examples – neither of which survives – were similarly built in the opening decades of the 18th century. There is also some experimentation with unusual footprints in these same early 18th-century decades. Mulberry, erected in the 1710s with corner pavilions, and Exeter, built in the 1710s on an H-plan depart from the regional norm of the simple rectangle (Fig. 3.16). But neither plan has a later counterpart in the colony, suggesting that like the cruciform church plans in South Carolina, these early 18th-century experiments were eventually abandoned for more fashionable Georgian forms.

Fig. 3.16. Mulberry, Berkeley County, South Carolina, 1710s.

Another architectural tradition prevalent in both Jamaica and the Leeward Islands is the combination of wood framing and masonry technologies in buildings with a full two stories. The most extensive collections of these buildings survive in

Fig. 3.17. Moulton-Barrett House, Falmouth, Jamaica, 1795.

Fig. 3.18. Building at Market and Long Streets, St John's, Antigua, late 18th or early 19th century.

two towns, Falmouth on Jamaica and St John's on Antigua. The value of land in urban contexts, of course, put a premium on height and mitigated against the use of foundations wider than the main block of the house. The Moulton-Barrett House, built in Falmouth in the mid-1790s and the early 19th-century L-shaped building on the corner of Market and Long Streets in St John's, are among the best surviving examples of this type (Figs 3.17, 3.18). In a manner distinctive of this type, these buildings have a masonry ground floor dedicated to commercial use that extended to the lot lines on either side and butted up against the sidewalk. The upper floor, built of wood, extended over the sidewalk providing shade to the public space while simultaneously exploiting all available square footage for residential use. Although it has been removed in the case of the Falmouth example, access to these second floors was usually gained through a stair rising off the sidewalk. But such mixture of materials was not exclusive to urban buildings in these regions. As is demonstrated by buildings already addressed in this essay, especially the Fairview Inn on St Kitts, the Evelyn Villa on Nevis, and White Hall Estate on Jamaica, these building practices were widespread in the Leeward Islands and Jamaica in the 18th and early 19th century.

Why was the mixing of materials such a common choice among British colonials? The preference for brick seemed obvious in the face of hurricane force winds. As reported as early as the 1660s in an interesting commentary by César de Rochefort, masonry construction was recognized by both colonials and natives as the superior material in the Caribbean:

> The Indians, who had never seen such Structure of any such material [brick], look'd on it at first with a great astonishment, and having attempted to shake it, by the strength of their shoulders, but not stirring it, they were forc'd [to] acknowledg [sic], that if all the Houses were so built, the Tempest which they call the *Hurricane* would not prejudice them.[23]

But as many colonials came to realize, two- and three-story brick walls could be unstable in the face of the high winds of a hurricane or the vibrations of an earthquake. Taller brick buildings were more structurally sound when frequent mutually reinforcing 90-degree corners introduced by cruciform, T-shaped, or corner tower plans replaced the longer uninterrupted spans of simple rectangles.

Many builders in the Leeward Islands and on Jamaica preferred to avoid tall masonry walls by mounting a timber frame structure on a raised masonry foundation or ground floor. For everyday living, these builders recognized the fact that timber frame buildings were cooler and the elevated position of these upper floors gave occupants access to cooling breezes. But heat was not the only factor in considering this option. The masonry ground floor and frame upper story gave the building some of the resistance desirable in hurricane conditions without the fear of brick walls collapsing onto those taking refuge inside. The wood frame superstructure provided the building some flexibility in the face of hurricane winds and, even more importantly, during earthquakes. After the various earthquakes that rocked certain regions of the Caribbean in the late 17th and early 18th century, colonials recognized that frame construction fared far more successfully than masonry under the vibrations of an earthquake.[24] The integration of these two building materials has, in at least one pocket of the Leeward Islands, found its way to the lowest strata of the socio-economic spectrum. In the village of Old Road on Antigua, there survive a handful of small, two-room, single-story frame buildings that have a frame superstructure resting on and integrated into lower masonry walls (Fig. 3.19). In this construction, the corner posts of the building are set into the masonry construction of the building's foundation (Fig. 3.20). Like their elite counterparts, the builders of these small houses perceived some advantage to securing a flexible frame to a masonry foundation.

Fig. 3.19. House, Old Road, Antigua, 19th century.

Fig. 3.20. Detail of corner post on house, Old Road, Antigua.

Fig. 3.21. Nichols Building, Bridgetown, Barbados, 18th century.

Fig. 3.22. Undocumented building, Bridgetown, Barbados, 18th century.

Once again, however, these architectural choices are almost entirely absent from the building stock in Barbados and are evident in only a handful of very early buildings from South Carolina. While surviving 18th-century plantation houses on Barbados appear almost always to be erected a full two stories of masonry, their urban counterparts are the same or even higher. In Bridgetown, the Nichols building, with its elegant curvilinear gables, rises a full three stories as does another early house just near St Michael's Cathedral (Figs 3.21, 3.22). The buildings of Barbados' other major town, Speightstown, also rise two or three stories of masonry. Surveys of both towns suggest that even in the 19th century, such intermixture of materials was very rare. Similarly, the building stock of early 18th-century Charleston, South Carolina, is comprised largely of three-story masonry buildings (Fig. 3.23). Like the few buildings with complex floor plans, the one clear example of mixed-material construction from South Carolina, 8 and 10 Tradd Street, dates from the opening decades of the 18th century. In rural contexts of the same colony, the earliest surviving frame buildings are one-and-a-half or two stories tall and never supported by a substantial raised masonry foundation. If such intermixture was an option in early 18th-century South Carolina, it largely disappeared from the building stock by mid-century.

Field surveys of surviving 18th-century buildings demonstrate that British colonials transformed their buildings in at least three ways to better suit the hurricane and earthquake prone environment of the Caribbean. Buildings that best negotiated these conditions 1) had a low building mass, often supported by a wide and substantial foundation, 2) utilized complex plans that integrated a multiplicity of mutually reinforcing corners, and

3) incorporated both wood and masonry technologies in multiple story buildings. But as this survey demonstrates, these design features are common characteristics of early buildings in Jamaica and the Leeward Islands, only occasional characteristics of buildings in South Carolina, and almost entirely absent from Barbados. Since each of the locales finds its origins in 17th-century British culture, and since each of these colonies suffered under hurricanes in the period in question, what accounts for these variations in building practice? The answer lies in frequency.[25] As the Appendix demonstrates, Jamaica experienced on average one major natural disaster every six and a half years between 1650 and 1820. The Leeward Islands experienced such disasters once every nine years over the same period. South Carolina knew on average one disaster every eleven years between its founding in 1670 and 1820. The least disaster-prone colony of the four, however, was Barbados, with on average only one event every 21 years. Correlating the frequency of disasters with the characteristics of the built environment, it should come as no surprise that the most disaster-prone regions developed a building tradition that embraced more sustainable design while those with the lowest frequency of disasters largely ignored these precautions.

Fig. 3.23. 95 Broad Street, Charleston, South Carolina, 1770s.

The relationship between frequency of disaster and architectural responses in the built environment is probably best demonstrated by the architecture of regions that embraced those design traditions least consistently. The apparent rejection of disaster-response design in Barbados becomes less surprising when we recognize that Barbados experienced no major hurricane for almost the entirety of the 18th century, from 1694 to 1780. The paucity of disasters in Barbados through the 18th century might also suggest that these traditions became ensconced in the architecture of other regions in these very same years. But the second example is even more telling. Although South Carolina experienced hurricanes at a rate of one per eleven years over 150 years, those events are not evenly distributed; in the half-century between 1680 and 1730, the colony had hurricanes at a rate of one every seven years, a rate approximating that of Jamaica. Accordingly, the architecture of South Carolina appears to integrate more disaster resistant measures in their buildings in the earliest decades, largely dropping them from their lexicon of choices by mid-century. Between 1730 and 1820, conversely,

South Carolina experienced only one hurricane every fifteen years, a rate half that of earlier years and much closer to that of Barbados. While South Carolina experienced disaster more or less frequently, the built environment responded accordingly.

The architectural traditions of Jamaica and the Leeward Islands might also have been shaped by the fact that these two regions suffered not only from hurricanes, but earthquakes as well. Major quakes rocked the Leeward Islands in 1672 and 1690 and Jamaica in 1692, 1712, 1722, 1744, and 1812. But in addition to these, tremors shook the Leewards through the early 1740s and Jamaica between 1700 and 1707. By contrast, minor tremors shook South Carolina only in 1698; Barbados has never suffered from an earthquake. The complete absence of mixed-material construction on Barbados, then, suggests that this particular combination of materials was understood to respond more to the threat of earthquakes than hurricanes. Conversely, the high density of two- and three-story masonry buildings in South Carolina and Barbados – regions largely unthreatened by earthquakes and facing fewer hurricanes – reflects a general sense of confidence in the building stock by occupants of these colonies.

These initial findings have one last implication for our understanding of architecture in the Greater Caribbean. The most emblematic feature of Caribbean architecture – the piazza or gallery – might, ironically, have found earlier acceptance in those regions more prone to natural disaster. While the gallery would certainly have weathered hurricane winds quite poorly, the broad foundations common on buildings with low massing might have created an architectural precondition for the gallery. As a result, those colonies that built houses with broad elevated foundations – Jamaica and the Leeward Islands – might have embraced the gallery or piazza before those which did not.[26] Initial indications, in fact, suggest that galleries appear in these colonies by the 1760s or 1770s, some decades before they became common on Barbados or in South Carolina in the closing years of the century.

As suggested by this preliminary study of the relationship between climate and the built environment, architectural traditions in the British Caribbean might have been more responsive to the threat of natural disaster than to the drive to mitigate the heat. John Crowley is right to suggest that certain architectural traditions, such as the gallery or porch, might not have been motivated exclusively by the drive for physical comfort that so characterizes modern culture. Matthew Mulcahy's examination of the documentary record provides a useful context for understanding architectural accommodations to the disaster-prone Caribbean, but examination of the surviving buildings gives us a clearer picture of how these responses were implemented and how broadly they ranged across the region. Focusing on regional variations among real buildings demonstrates that the frequency of natural disasters played a critical role in shaping these architectural traditions. Those colonies situated within the broad path taken by most Atlantic hurricanes and sited closer to the Puerto Rico Trench (the natural fault line between the Caribbean and Atlantic plates) adopted certain architectural practices largely neglected by colonials in less disaster-prone regions of the Caribbean. It is the architecture of these colonies, Jamaica and the colonies comprising the Leeward Islands, that can be most readily characterized as 'Caribbean' in form.

The vestries of Jamaica's Anglican parishes were deeply concerned that their new buildings survive the onslaught of the next hurricane. The frequency of these storms meant that they expected such events to occur. They also recognized that another earthquake might shatter their world at any moment. By the middle of the 18th century, builders on Barbados were far less concerned about the structural resilience of their buildings; they had not had an earthquake in almost two generations and there had never been a report of an earthquake. It is only in this context that the Barbados hurricane of 1780, widely reported to be the worst suffered by that island in recorded history, had such a dramatic impact. The 1780 hurricane, followed by another six years later, would be only a brief season of concern about the implications of hurricanes on architecture; another would not arrive until the 1810s. While it seems that frequency, not the simple fact of an occasion, is the defining factor in determining architectural responses to hurricanes and earthquakes, only through far more extensive fieldwork and the careful examination of many more surviving early buildings can these preliminary suggestions be more completely substantiated.

APPENDIX:
NATURAL DISASTERS IN THE CARIBBEAN: 1650 TO 1820

Barbados:
Earthquakes: n/a
Hurricanes: 1653, 1674, 1675, 1694, 1780, 1786, 1813, 1817,

- on average, one natural disaster every 21 years between 1650 and 1820
- no natural disasters between 1694 and 1780

Jamaica:
Earthquakes: (tremors in 1688), 1692 (tremors from 1700 to 1707), 1712, 1722, 1744, 1812
Hurricanes: 1670, 1692, 1712, 1722 (2′), 1726, 1730, 1743, 1744, 1772, 1780, 1784, 1785, 1786, 1799, 1803, 1812, 1813, 1815, 1818 (2′)

- on average, approximately one natural disaster every 6.5 years between 1650 and 1820

Leeward Islands:
Earthquakes: 1672, 1690 (tremors from 1740 to 1745)
Hurricanes: 1650, 1652, 1667, 1669, 1681, 1689, 1707, 1733, 1747, 1751, 1758, 1766, 1772, 1780, 1804, 1809, 1817

- on average, approximately one natural disaster every 9 years between 1650 and 1820

South Carolina:
Earthquakes: (tremors in 1698)
Hurricanes: 1686, 1699, 1700, 1713, 1722 (2′), 1728, 1752 (2′), 1769, 1797, 1804, 1811, 1813

- on average, one natural disaster every 11 years between 1670 and 1820
- 1680 and 1730: on average one every 7 years
- 1730 to 1820: on average one very 15 years

Sources: Mulcahy 2005, Hall 1922, Sykes & Ewing 1965, Fraser 1989.

NOTES

1 'State of Churches in Jamaica', 1722, Fulham Palace Correspondence, 18:230; Pawson & Buisseret 1970, 1975.
2 While the 1714 church survives, the plaque has been moved to the front of the later 18th-century tower.
3 Buisseret 1980; Crain 1994; Gravette 2000.
4 Crowley 1997, 2001.
5 Mulcahy 2005.
6 Mulcahy 2005.
7 Nicholson 1994.
8 While the roofs on Clarence House are recent constructions, early examples of such roofs have been recorded on late 18th- and early 19th-century buildings in Falmouth, Jamaica. Specific examples include the roof of the Tharpe House, dated to the 1790s and the roof system sheltering 20 Duke Street, built in the 1810s.
9 A site inspection of the building suggests that the gallery only wrapped unbroken around three sides of the house; there may have been frame corner pavilions on the rear two corners of the house.
10 A number of early plantations, like Rose Hall, have the two-story Georgian masonry piles typical of elite housing throughout the 18th-century British world. Other two-story masonry piles include Annandale great house, Cardiff Hall, and the original great house at Seville. For examples of the lower form of great house, see James Hakewill's early 19th-century prints of Bryan Castle, Holland Estate, and others. See also the houses represented in plats as published in *Jamaica Surveyed*. See especially the images of White Hall Estate, Roaring Rover Estate, Orchard Plantation, and Golden Valley.
11 Rochefort 1666, 177.
12 'Answers to the Inquiries sent to Colonel Stapelton, Governor of the Leeward Islands', Nov 2, 1676, *CSPC*, 499. Quoted in Mulcahy 2005, 123.
13 Oldendorp 1770, 151; quoted in Chapman 1995, 153–5.
14 Anon 1935, quoted in Mulcahy.
15 Leech 2002; Fraser 1982.
16 Stoney 1938; Lane 1984; Poston 1998.
17 Nelson 2003.
18 This statistic is taken from the churches for which some information about the plan survives. Cruciform churches erected in 18th-century Jamaica include: St Andrew's Parish Church (1692–1705); Kingston Parish Church (1701–3); St Catherine's Parish Church (1712–14); Clarendon Parish Church (1722–40); Westmoreland Parish Church (before 1722); Port Royal Parish Church (1725); St Thomas-in-the-East Parish Church (*c.* 1750); St Anne's Parish Church (1765); St James Parish Church (1774); St George's Parish Church (before 1802); and Portland Parish Church (before 1804). Those that were not include Hanover Parish Church (before 1774) and Trelawney Parish Church in Falmouth (1796).
19 Examples include St Paul's parish church in Charlestown and the parish churches in St James, Windward and St Thomas, Lowland.
20 Another example is the house at Orange Valley, St Anne's Parish, Jamaica.
21 Another example of this plan on Jamaica includes Stokes Hall in St Thomas Parish.
22 'St John's Parish Minutes', Archives of Barbados, Bridgetown.
23 Rochefort 1666, 11.
24 Mulcahy 2005.
25 There is some recent research on the relationship between traditional Japanese domestic architecture and the frequency of earthquakes that I do not yet have access to but would have liked to cite here.
26 Edwards 1989; Oszuscik 1992.

BIBLIOGRAPHY

Anon, 1935, 'Autobiography of William Senhouse', *J. Barbados Mus. and Hist. Soc.* 3 (November 1935), 3–19, 87–99.

Buisseret, D. 1980, *Historic Architecture of the Caribbean, London:* Heineman.

Chapman, W. 1995, 'Irreconcilable Differences: Urban residences in the Danish West Indies, 1700–1900', *Winterthur Portfolio* 30, 129–72.

Crain, E.E. 1994, *Historic Architecture in the Caribbean Islands*, Gainsville: University of Florida.

Crowley, J. 1997, 'Inventing Comfort: The *Piazza*', in Martin & Garrison 1997, 277–315.

Crowley, J. 2001, *The Invention of Comfort: Sensibilities and Design in Early Modern Britain and Early America*, Baltimore: Johns Hopkins University Press.

Edwards, J. 1989, 'The Complex Origins of the American Domestic Piazza-Veranda-Gallery', *Mat. Cult.* 21, 3–58.

Fraser, H.S. 1982, *Historic Houses of Barbados: A Collection of Drawings*, Bridgetown: Barbados National Trust.

Gravette, A.G. 2000, *Architectural Heritage of the Caribbean: an A–Z of Historic Buildings*, Kingston: Ian Randle.

Hall, M. 1922, *Earthquakes in Jamaica from 1688 to 1919*, Kingston: Government Printing Office.

Higman, B.W. 1988, *Jamaica Surveyed: Plantation Maps and Plans of the Eighteenth and Nineteenth Centuries*, Kingston: University of the West Indies Press.

Lane, M. 1984, *Architecture of the Old South: South Carolina*, New York: Abbeville.

Leech, R. 2002, 'Alleynedale Hall, Barbados – A Plantation House of the Seventeenth Century', *J. Barbados Mus. and Hist. Soc.* 48, 123–41.

Martin A.S. & Garrison J.R. 1997, *American Material Culture: The Shape of the Field*, Winterthur: Henry Francis du Pont Winterthur Museum.

Mulcahy, M. 2005, *Hurricanes and Society in the British Greater Caribbean, 1624–1783*, Baltimore: Johns Hopkins University Press.

Nelson, L.P. 2003, '"Building Cross-wise": Reconstructing Jamaica's Eighteenth-Century Anglican Churches', *Jamaica Hist. Rev.* 22, 11–39.

Nicholson, D. 1994, *Heritage Landmarks of Antigua and Barbuda*, St. John's, Antigua: Carib Press.

Oldendorp, C.G.A. 1770, *C G A Oldendorp's History of the Mission of the Evangelical Brethren of the Caribbean islands of St. Thomas, St. Croix, and St. John*, reprint ed. Johann Jakob Bossard, trans. Arnold R. Highfield and Vladimir Barac, Ann Arbor: Karoma Press.

Oszuscik, P. 1992, 'Passage of the Gallery and Other Caribbean Elements from the French and Spanish to the British in the United States', *Mat. Cult.* 15, 1–14.

Pawson, M. & Buisseret, D. 1970, 'The Port Royal Project', *Jamaica J.* 4:2, 2–13.

Pawson, M. & Buisseret, D. 1975, *Port Royal, Jamaica*, Oxford: Clarendon.

Poston. J.H. 1998, *The Buildings of Charleston: a Guide to the City's Architecture*, Columbia: University of South Carolina Press.

Rochefort, César de, 1666. *The History of Barbados, St. Christopher, Nevis, St. Vincents, Antego, Martinico, Monserrat and the rest of the Caribby-Islands*, London.

Stoney, S.G. 1938, *Plantations of the Carolina Low Country*, Charleston: Carolina Art Association.

Sykes, L.R. & Ewing, M. 1965. 'The Seismicity of the Caribbean Region', *J. Geophysical Res.* 70:20, 5065–74.

4

London, Capital of Empire – Some Archaeological Reflections

GEOFF EGAN† *with a foreword by* NIGEL JEFFRIES

SUMMARY: The infrastructure of London during the era of developing empire reflected the dependence of the city and Britain on resources originating beyond Europe and something of this survives among the standing buildings and buried remains, though it is often the sheer scale of the latter that remains impressive. In contrast, the extensive archaeological assemblages of finds from post-medieval London, primarily up to the mid 18th century, furnish often surprisingly detailed evidence of specific aspects of the capital's role at this time. Various aspects of the excavated material culture are discussed from this perspective, and several themes for further study emerge.

FOREWORD

By Nigel Jeffries

The efforts and achievements of Geoff Egan (19 October 1951–24 December 2010), a leading UK specialist in medieval and later finds have been well documented.[1] Geoff was a well-travelled and popular figure. In 1976 he joined the Museum of London's Department of Urban Archaeology (DUA) and for 34 years played a central role in researching, cataloguing, and contextualizing the vast quantities of medieval and later 'small things' recovered either from archaeological excavations in London by the DUA and its successors the Museum of London Archaeology Service (1991–2008) and MoLA (2008–) or those which formed part of the collections of the Museum of London. In July 2010 he was appointed finds adviser for the Portable Antiquities Scheme based at the British Museum, a position he filled for only a short period until his untimely death.

For my part, my role in shaping this article began in late 2018 when Professor Roger Leech contacted me to ask, in my capacity as a former colleague of Geoff's at MoLA and having just completed work on the glass from the Nevis Heritage Project sites of Charlestown and Mountravers, if I might review the paper and suggest a pathway for its publication. Upon reading it I felt little point in revising or significantly rewriting it and so what you read below remains largely true to the first completed draft submitted by Geoff to Roger Leech in February 2010. Any subsequent changes by me or the monograph editor were largely to format the text to the SPMA style and amend the bibliography and footnotes to provide (for example) updated references for the cited articles and books which have been published since Geoff's article was submitted. The remaining part of this paper is substantially as written by Geoff.

INTRODUCTION

This paper is a first attempt to draw together some aspects of the capital's archaeology that relate to colonial expansion and the development of the British Empire. It looks briefly at some of the developments in London's infrastructure and concentrates on aspects of material culture, as evident in the archaeological record, over the centuries when the city became the capital of a gradually evolving world-wide empire.

At the end of the Middle Ages, London was the undisputed capital of an England that was on the north-western edge of Europe, with trade contacts (notably significant exports in cloth and pewter) into Central Europe and to a lesser extent into the Baltic and Mediterranean areas. Trade links beyond these areas were irregular incursions by bold individuals who were prepared to think beyond what most traders thought of as boundaries. By 1800 London had become the commercial capital of an empire of a scale previously unimagined, with dominant trade connections with four continents beyond Europe. England's location on the western fringe of the known world had been transformed into the pole position for vigorous trade with America, while a new, outward-looking entrepreneurship had transformed the formerly impossible distances between other lands outside Europe into regular commercial links.

While Roman and medieval London have produced occasional finds which themselves or the materials of which they were made originated beyond Europe, these were exceptional, often very prestigious high-value imports, like gems, glassware, and ivory.[2] With the post-medieval period's widening world view and the development of colonial expansion beyond the Mediterranean and the western-European seaboard great opportunities opened for the settlement of lands previously unknown to the English and for new trades in goods that were before only occasionally, if ever, brought into England. The sight of a very few people from beyond Europe living in London and plying their trades from the beginning of post-medieval period – a gradually increasing presence – would further have raised awareness of a wider world to explore.[3] The gradual establishment by the end of the 19th century of Britain's 'vaster empire than before' is still reflected in many of the most impressive private and corporate buildings across the country. Some of these edifices retain updated versions of their original purposes and former colonial connections, though with the passing of that empire, a significant proportion have lost their original purpose, together with the wide appreciation of this fundamental aspect of their origin. London's key role in the development of empire has never been in doubt, but the precise nature of that involvement is obscure in many aspects to which historians are only beginning to turn their attention, and its manifestation in archaeological investigations, which will doubtless become a recurrent theme in future work, has not been summarized before.[4]

As with much else in the post-medieval archaeological ambit, the richest material for this particular theme currently lies in the extensive 16th- and 17th-century assemblages recovered over the past half century, while the relative lack until recently of attention paid to field evidence for the later 18th to 20th centuries in the metropolitan centre is limited and further hampered by the lack of development of a more informed research framework for fruitful investigation.

BUILDINGS AND DOCKS TO CATER FOR A GROWING EMPIRE

A number of impressive buildings in central London were constructed directly to cater for the administration of the trade and regulation of other aspects of the developing colonies. Several relatively recent prestigious buildings for former colonies and dominions, from Gibraltar to India, Australia and South Africa, continue to be used in the era of the Commonwealth to promote tourism and trade as well as relations in other areas. They are all in a way descendants of East India House (Fig. 4.1), long vanished, and its site has never been investigated archaeologically. The most extensive buried witnesses to the development of empire in London that have been investigated are undoubtedly the widespread, massive foundations for warehouses, not least those of the East India Company (EIC: 1600–1834). Although such remains have loomed large on many sites, they have been accorded varying levels of attention during fieldwork. Most have been ignored as part of the background of 'Victorian' foundations unworthy of detailed recording, the 'overburden' of the recent past.[5] The 1982 excavation at the tellingly named Rangoon Street just north-east of the city core treated them with greater attention.[6] Here the foundations of an extensive warehouse built by the United East India Company (UEIC: 1708–1834) were revealed. Details of the brick-built drains and a large ice-house were recorded as well as the foundations themselves,

Fig. 4.1. East India House (Museum of London).

but only the ice-house really provided any specific insight into the nature of this impressive building, once the very obvious and fundamental point of the scale (immediately evident anyway from many surviving maps and plans) had been appreciated. Nothing recovered from the ground here gave away the specific trades represented by the wares that were once piled high within and there was not a single hint of the basic connection with the lands to the East. In short, the excavation illustrated vividly the scale of a major warehouse for international trade but it was entirely up to the documents to provide the specifics that enhance the interest. It is the objects that can really illuminate some of the most telling details for the present theme, as for others.

The early docks to the east of the City have increasingly been the focus of detailed investigations, particularly since the 1990s.[7] They include those of the East India Company at Millwall. The names alone of the Greenland Dock, with plant surviving from the whaling trade, and the Ivory, Spice, Tobacco, and other Docks named after specific exotic imports, are testimony to branches of the developing import trade. With a few exceptions, the goods that were the mainstay of incoming trade do not tend to be found in this working area so much as in or near the dwellings of the customers further into the urban centre (see below for some riverside concentrations of exotic items which obliquely reflect some of the trade links).

TRACES THAT SAILORS LEFT

The Thames-side homes of some of the sailors and ship captains who decided to live in the port have been uncovered. The excavation of two adjacent sites, respectively beside the Thames and one block inland – Victoria Wharf and Narrow Street, have together produced some of the most vivid finds relating to the expanding trade links for ships and sailors from the Port of London in the 17th and 18th centuries.[8] Together the finds assemblages illustrate the phenomenon of exotica being present in relative abundance on sites of buildings right on the river or sea frontage, but less so one block away, and virtually as infrequently as anywhere else in a given urban centre in the blocks still further from the waterfront (evident elsewhere, as for example in Portsmouth, though the phenomenon is by no means invariable).[9] As well as pottery from across Europe from west to east, and from Turkey, Persia, and China,[10] there are a series of colonial-Spanish coins with secondary stamps thought to indicate the city of Havana, a lump of coral from the Gulf of Mexico[11] and, most extraordinarily, what seems to be the only sherd of native-Caribbean pottery so far recorded in Britain (Fig. 4.2).[12] This distinct whiff of the Spanish Main must surely reflect the seafaring career of at least one of the inhabitants of the area – it is tempting to connect these exotic finds with a retired sea captain documented as living in one of the houses in the late 17th century.

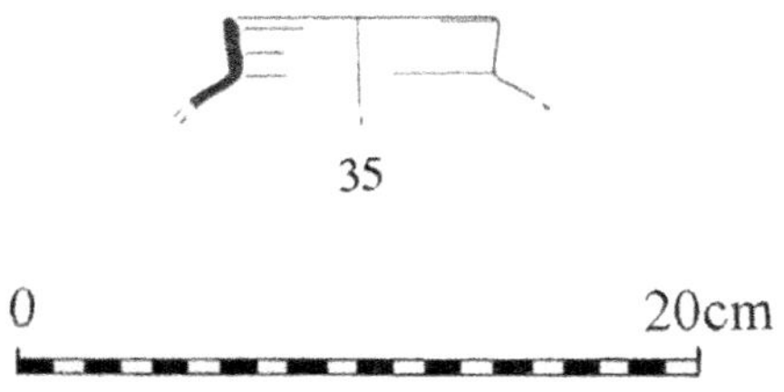

Fig. 4.2. Fragment of native Caribbean pottery excavated in Limehouse (Killock & Meddens 2005 PMA 39:1, 50, fig. 29, no. 35).

An extremely wide range of colonial and third-world, mainly 18th- and 19th-century coins, all apparently single losses, were recovered from the foreshore in Limekiln Dock prior to its redevelopment by private individuals but were made available for recording[13] – this group, covering the Americas, the Caribbean, the Indian sub-continent, and the Orient, and now dispersed, probably reflected the world-wide connections of London as immediately and broadly as the archaeological evidence from any single site.

GOODS AROUND THE WORLD

Imports and Exports

The large-scale import of goods from beyond Europe is an important aspect of the new age, but the new, far-flung links probably had an effect on how some of the more traditional European imports came to Britain. It has been suggested that 'conflict or trade in the Caribbean and Indian Ocean provided almost unlimited possibilities for privateers and merchants to acquire whatever they wished'.[14] Pewter 'plantation' tokens produced under James II and intended for circulation in Jamaica and other parts of the Caribbean have been found in the greatest numbers in London, where the presumption is that they had been diverted to local usage alongside the many local varieties of unofficial lead/tin tokens.[15] Coconut cups using the imported shells of the exotic fruit as the container were sometimes set with highly ornate, precious-metal mounts for the very rich in the 16th and early 17th centuries. A fragment of the base of a cup retaining a tiny sheet rove of silver recovered during excavation[16] is on one hand perhaps aesthetically the least impressive of these objects by far, but on the other it is the sole survivor of a lower grade of what has otherwise only survived from the top end of the market, a unique and valuable indicator of how far downmarket the range extended. The early trade with the East is obliquely reflected by many finds of early 17th-century tin-glazed vessels with Chinese-porcelain inspired Wan-Li designs, though actual oriental ceramics appear slightly later in London's archaeological record from the later 1600s.[17] At Spitalfields, just to the east of the City a lead seal with the East India Company's trademark was found in the cesspit that served a property occupied by a wealthy silk manufacturer, which had been put on a textile warehoused in that area, and intended for the trade to the East.[18] A series of similar seals, including some dated between 1801 and 1804, alongside those of clothiers in Devon and several London dyers, whose workshops are presumed to have been close to the findspot, were recovered from a contemporary drain at Bankside, just south of the River Thames. This assemblage is thought to represent some of the West Country cloths bought by the Company and brought white (undyed) to the capital for colouring prior to export, probably to China.[19] More widely, there are several finds of other cloth seals issued by the United East India Company (UEIC: 1708–1834) and its 17th-century predecessor the English East India Company (EIC: 1600–1834), as well as the South Seas Company (SSC: 1711–1838) trading to the Spanish-speaking parts of America and the Royal Africa Company (Fig. 4.3).[20] These riverside finds probably derive as unintentional losses from Thames-side dyehouses which coloured English cloths for the respective trading companies for export across much of the known world.

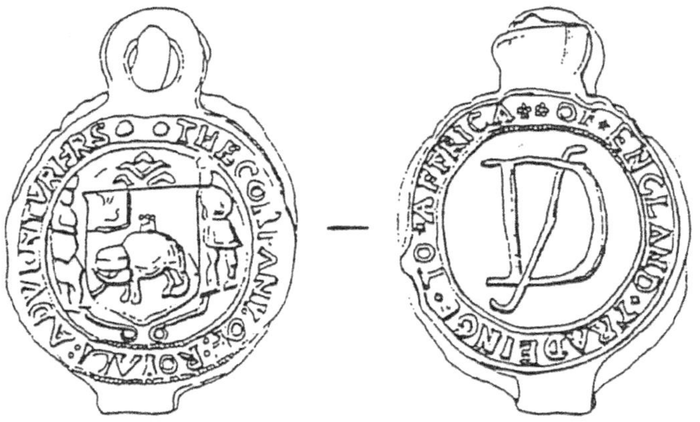

Fig. 4.3. Lead cloth seal of the Royal Africa Company (late 17th century) from Egan 1999, Fig. 8.1. Drawing by Jane Stone.

Corresponding finds of seals of the first two companies have occasionally been excavated in the lands to which they were traded – presumably archaeological evidence for cargoes of the single most significant English export commodity that reached (or were intended to reach) their destination. One early 17th-century clothier's seal excavated at Jamestown, Virginia is paralleled by one found at the Millennium Bridge site on the west of London's city waterfront, pinpointing the precise location of a dyehouse used by one of the earliest cloth exporters to the New World.[21]

NEW MANUFACTURES – IMPORTED RAW MATERIALS AND GOODS MADE FOR THE COLONIES

More widely across London, some common finds from the 16th century onwards reflect new, far-flung trade links. At the start of the 1500s the standard, two-sided combs for everyday personal grooming were almost exclusively made of boxwood. Versions made of elephant ivory came in slowly at first during the 16th century, until by *c.* 1620 they had come to dominate the market in the capital completely to judge by archaeological finds (Fig. 4.4).[22] This dominance continued for this purpose through the 18th and well into the 19th century. Cutlery handles, counters for games, and turned containers for needles, ink etc., too were regularly (though not nearly as exclusively as for combs) made of ivory. A large number of London sites at which deposits of this date survive produce evidence of manufacture in bone and ivory together, both by carving and

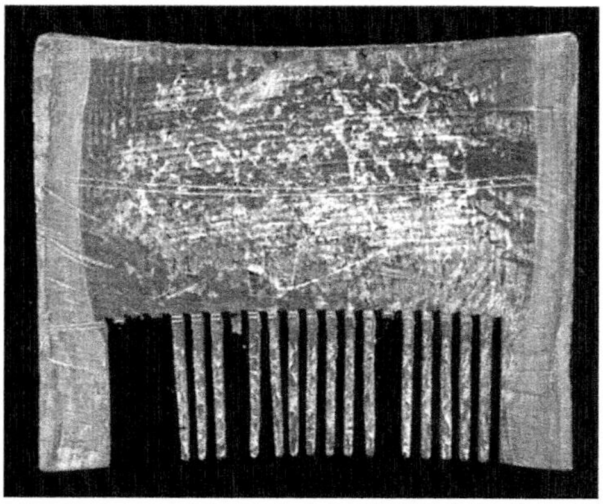

Fig. 4.4. An unfinished ivory comb, intended to be double sided (MoL ID: 97.42, digital image, Museum of London).

turning.[23] The near ubiquity of the latter on sites of this date initially comes as a surprise, since in more recent times it had come to be regarded as a luxury material.

A late 17th-century assemblage of waste from a fan-maker's workshop recovered from a pit near Ludgate[24] illustrates the greatly extended, world scale of the catchment area at this time for a small urban industry, admittedly one that pandered largely to a sophisticated, luxury lifestyle. Sticks that were discarded seemingly because they were cut to the wrong thickness or broke are made of bone, presumably home-grown, ivory from Africa or perhaps India, and turtle shell likely to be from the Caribbean – materials from at least three continents. The assemblage also includes some mussel shells containing traces of paint presumably for decorating the fans, as well as a bear's tooth which had been used as some kind of polisher. Turtles also appear in London's archaeological record in the form of bones resulting from the taste for exotic dishes like turtle soup.[25]

The ubiquitous clay pipe is, of course, a direct result of the trade in tobacco from the American colonies from the 1620s. It is present on virtually every later site in London and elsewhere in England. London was, inevitably, a major consumer and a major manufacturer of the pipes, the latter having seen a considerable amount of archaeological investigation. The expansion of the British Empire can, at this stage of investigation at least, probably most readily be illustrated archaeologically by finds across the colonial world of British-made clay pipes, not least ones from London manufacturers.[26]

A mid 16th-century sugar boiling house excavated at Ratcliff may be the earliest in England.[27] Ceramic moulds for refining molasses imported from the colonies in the Caribbean and elsewhere, sometimes found in huge numbers as at New Bridge Street, are also widespread across the City and in the suburbs.[28]

There is small but coherent focus of finds from London of manillas – the copper-alloy currency armlets (used in West Africa up to the 1920s) (Fig. 4.5). Some are from the site of a bank[29] – possibly exotica related to the company's business for display in the board room. A mould from a 17th-century foundry in Exeter shows they were being

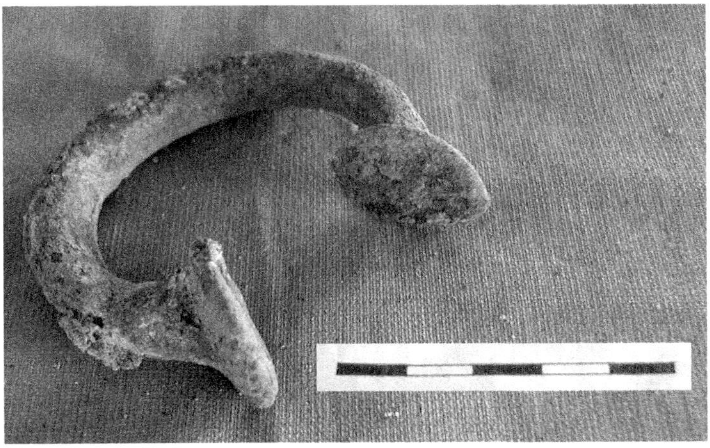

Fig. 4.5. Copper alloy manilla from excavations at Crosses Alley, Charlestown, Nevis.

Fig. 4.6. Glass beads and manufacturing waste from west London, second quarter of the 17th century © MOLA.

made as a side-line there,[30] and some of the London finds could be from similar production sites in the capital, though at present this is speculative.

The recent discovery at Hammersmith in west London within the grounds of the country estate of Sir Nicholas Crispe, entrepreneur, financier of the royalist cause in the Civil War, and wheeler-dealer with a finger in almost every major economic pie, of a kiln in which glass beads were being made probably during the 1630s (Fig. 4.6),[31] provides some of the most intriguing excavated material relating to the developing colonial trade, probably specifically the African slave to America and the Caribbean. Crispe held a patent for selling glass beads at this time (his involvement in their production comes entirely from the archaeological evidence) and he was on the board of more than one of the international trading companies based in London, including the Africa Company. Waste recovered at Hammersmith shows he was making beads both in 'European' style (relatively small, single colour or striped) and larger ones (*c.* 20mm and larger – striped, or long cylindrical ones in one colour) in fashions intended to appeal to the native peoples in the lands where colonies and trading stations were being established. Currently the few parallels known for the latter are from the Americas – probably because that is where the most developed archaeological connections have been made over the last generation from London. Comparanda have yet to be found in Africa, but the Fort of Akira, a key slave-trading centre with English connections at the time Crispe's kiln was in production, located by the sea in Ghana (the former Gold Coast), seems one likely location to anticipate they may come to light in view of the contemporaneity.

HINTS OF INTEREST IN THE WIDER WORLD – COLLECTED EXOTICA

Collecting, which can be seen as a personal expression of ownership of other cultures, began within Europe with Grand Tours by aristocrats interested in classical Rome and Greece, as exemplified by the Arundel Marbles, a few of which were found abandoned at the 17th-century Earl of Arundel's property on the Strand,[32] to become worldwide, sometimes with a specifically ethnographic focus. This may be archaeologically demonstrated by a Maori polished jadeite weapon excavated in Southwark,[33] a prestigious object, both in its original culture and as a collectable ethnographic trophy from one of the furthest corners of empire in 19th-century London. A porcelain pornographic figure of Chinese origin[34] is perhaps an expression of a more specialized interest, arguably a reflection of behavioural licence observed by unmarried men in many walks of life in the remote colonial/non-European world.

With some of these items the circle has come right round – they are at the same time a manifestation of the capturing and ownership of the exotic, which can be seen as an extension of colonialism, and an archaeology of archaeology.

CONCLUSION

The amount of excavated material from London that is directly pertinent to its role as principal base and eventually capital of a world-wide empire is perhaps initially surprising. Its extent and scope may on reflection be seen as a true reflection of the centrality of this status. Currently the archaeological evidence recovered for this is mainly from the 1600s and early 1700s centuries, but with the rapidly developing fashion for treating the investigation of features from the late 1700s to 1800s and occasionally the 1900s with the same attention as those from the earlier part of the post-medieval period, that is bound to change. Later features and finds will take a fuller place in any future study on the theme presented in this paper.

ACKNOWLEDGEMENTS

Thanks to John Allan, Tony Pilson, and Alex Werner for discussion of several finds noted here and for valuable information on them, and to David Higgins for providing references for London tobacco pipes found outside Europe. David Jamieson undertook the first researches on Sir Nicholas Crispe and his beads, on which the subsequent work presented here is based.

NOTES

1 Noël Hume *et al.* 2011.

2 Ward Perkins 1940, 293, pl. 84B – a piece of Near-Eastern glassware from Westminster; Egan & Pritchard 1991, 316–17 pl. 11C, 373 & 376 nos 1588, 1754 – a pearl from the Red Sea area and an elephant ivory comb (Ward Perkins 1940, 191, pl. 88.1 is part of another ivory comb, though it is described as bone and it is probably of post-medieval date); Egan 1998, 236–7, 272–4 nos 695, pl. 5C, 912 – a Near-Eastern glass lamp fragment. A lead/tin ampulla found in London is from the Holy Land, presumably a souvenir of pilgrimage (Spencer 1998, 305–6, fig. 214b – provenance not identified in text). See Crowfoot *et al.* 1992, for a fragment of Chinese textile – excavated in a London context assigned to the 14th century – that presumably came to Europe via the Silk Route, Egan 2004 for a potential find from medieval London of an inscribed (?) bell fragment that originated in Japan, and Pearce & Martin 2003, 100–1 fig. 1 for three fritware albarelli from Egypt or Syria, found in a late 15th-century pit, from Fenchurch Street in the City of London (Museum of London site code FER97). The Cheapside Hoard of late 16th-/early 17th-century jewellery illustrates from the origins of its exotic gems, including Russia, Arabia, Ceylon, and South America, a range of imports for London's elite from the known world at that time – Wheeler 1928; Forsyth 2003.

3 e.g. a trumpeter in the employment of Henry VIII in 1511 – Anglo 1968, 1, 85, 98; 2, pls 3, 18, membranes 3, 28 – 'John Blanke, the black trumpet', and a man who made 'Spanish' (steel) needles in a shop on Cheapside in the 1550s (he would not divulge the secret of their manufacture) – Holmes 1969, 23 (both writers refer to these individuals as negroes). By the 18th century several celebrated black individuals are known in a variety of roles in London society, including freed slaves.

So far, despite extensive examination of skeletons from post-medieval cemeteries in the capital, no human remains in London from before 1800 have yet been identified as non-European.

4 Figures of ships from English ports involved in Caribbean trade from the first, sparse and relatively unfocused but pertinent surviving records towards the very end of the 1600s given by Rawley (2003) leave little doubt that in the 17th century London was its national leader (and presumably the main originator), with Bristol and later Liverpool and other western ports overtaking the capital in the bulk of this trade at around the time the records become significantly more extensive and more detailed – a situation which previously helped mask London's leading involvement in the development of Britain's slave trade.

5 Lawrence 2006.

6 Museum of London RAG82 site code – a tea and drugs warehouse built for the United East India Company (UIEC) in 1796; Egan 1983, 189–90 fig. 1; cf. Evans 1990.

7 Divers 2004, 46–87; see Saxby & Goodburn 1998, and Heard & Goodburn 2003, 4–5, 20–1, 32–47.

8 Egan 2001; Egan & Keys 2005.

9 John Allan, pers. comm.

10 Stephenson 2001, 79–80, fig. 18 nos 2, 3; Jarrett 2005, 39–40 fig. 24 no. 7.

11 Egan 2001, 88 fig. 29; Tyler 2001, 64. Marrow/pumpkin seeds, an early archaeological manifestation of newly available foods imported from the Americas, were also recovered from early 17th-century contexts on the site – Tyler 2001, 65.

12 Jarrett 2005, 50–1 fig. 29 no. 35.

13 Found by Ian Smith and Tony Pilson, and photographed by Graham Kenlin for the Museum of London's archive (the images have not been traced).

14 Killock & Meddens 2005, 21.

15 Noël Hume 1956, 203; 1974, 159 fig. 60.26, 167; Tony Pilson estimates that at least a hundred of these have been found over the past 30 years in the Thames foreshore in central London.

16 Museum of London site code ASQ87, accession no. 483.

17 Pearce & Martin 2003; Barry 1994; by the end of the 17th century Chinese porcelain was the dominant import component of ceramic assemblages excavated in the capital – Pearce 2007, 93; the first commercially successful production of porcelain in England came famously in the mid 18th century from several London factories (despite John Dwight's experimental copying of Chinese porcelain and stoneware in the late 1600s at Fulham – Green 1999, 64–78, 90–2). Other exotic influences on the potters of Southwark were only occasionally evident – three late 17th-century ceramic salts discarded at biscuit stage at the Montague Close tin-glazed wares factory are in the form of seated Afro-Caribbean figures holding containers – Tyler *et al.* 2008, 24–5 fig. 16.

18 Harward *et al.* 2015, accession no. 605, 172; see Egan 1990; 1993, 99–100, 189 fig. 38 nos 292–5.

19 Egan 1993, nos 292–3 were found the drain. Other United East India Company (UEIC) seals in the group are dated between 1801 and 1804. The Devon clothiers' seals in the assemblage are thought to have fallen off textiles destined for the Far East, a loss-leader within the Company's trade, which kept Exeter's cloth exports going up to the 1830s.

20 South Seas Company (SSC) seals – Egan 1993, 138 & 199 fig. 48 no. M12 – see Gilmore 1973 for one found in Texas; Royal Africa Company seals – Egan 1993, 98–9, 138 & 189 fig. 38 nos 291, no. M11.

21 Ayre & Wroe Brown 2002, accession no. <26>, 62; this seal, like the majority of the material culture excavated in contexts from the first 20 years at Jamestown would probably have been shipped through London (including many items that were themselves Continental imports to London). This pattern of a 'London' material culture in the New World colonies prevailed to the 1620s, when the advantage of the quicker journeys from the significantly closer ports in the west of England, like Exeter and Bristol, became evident and the colonial consumer turned more to West Country ceramics, textiles etc.

22 Egan 2005, 64–5 no. 295; 2006, 61.

23 Sewart & Blackmore 1996 features a sizeable early 17th-century manufacturing assemblage.

24 Egan 2006, 61–2 fig. 10.

25 Armitage & McCarthy 1980. See note 11 for plant remains found in London representing foodstuff originally imported from America.

26 Recorded in Africa, the Americas, Australia, the Caribbean, New Zealand, Sri Lanka – e.g. Blakeman & Riordan 1978; Bradley 1983; Brassey 1991; Calvococoressi 1975; Davey 1989; Fernando 1993; Fox 1999; Higgins 2005; Higgins & Boxt 1990; Jack 1986; Marx 1968; Richie 1978; Rusden 1982; Walker 1983 (references kindly provided by David Higgins, India seems to be a notable gap so far).
27 Schwab & Nurse 1977.
28 Museum of London NBS84 site code; Jarrett 2004; 2005, 52; see Brooks 1983.
29 These could in some cases be travel souvenirs while others might be early local products of one or more London foundries. They include a group of six from the site of an 18th-century bank at Cornhill (GMC 1903, 385 no. 213), which could perhaps be from an apposite boardroom display, and Museum of London accession nos 85.59/44 from the Thames foreshore.
30 Blaylock 1996, 78; 2000, 45–6, pl. 17.
31 Egan 2006, 60 fig. 9, 63; Egan 2008.
32 Hammerson 1975.
33 Gathercole 1988.
34 Harward *et al.* 2015, fig. 169, 192.

BIBLIOGRAPHY

Anglo, S. 1968 (introduction), *The Great Tournament Roll of Westminster: A Collotype Reproduction of the Manuscripts* (4 vols), Oxford: Oxford University Press.

Armitage, P. & McCarthy, C. 1980, 'Turtle Remains from a Late 18th Century Well at Leadenhall Buildings', *London Archaeol* 4:1, 8–16.

Ayre, J. & Wroe-Brown, R. 2002, *The London Millennium Bridge Excavations of the Medieval and Later Waterfronts at St Peter's Hill, City of London, and Bankside, Southwark*, MoLAS Study Ser. 6.

Barry, J. 1994, 'Eighteenth Century Chinese Export Porcelain from Three London Sites', *London Archaeol.* 7:6, 150–6.

Blakeman, C.H. & Riordan, R.V. 1978, 'Clay Pipes from the Newton Plantation Excavation', in Handler & Lange 1978, 251–73.

Blaylock, S.R. 1996, 'Bell and Cauldron Founding in Exeter', *Hist. Metall.* 30:2, 72–82.

Blaylock, S.R. 2000, 'Excavation of an Early Post-Medieval Bronze Foundry at Cowick Street, Exeter, 1999–2000', *Devon Archaeol. Soc. Proc.* 58, 1–92.

Bradley, C.S. 1983, *Clay Tobacco Pipes from the Wreck of le Machault, 1760*, unpublished Parks Canada archive report.

Brassey, R. 1991, 'Clay Tobacco Pipes from the Site of the Victoria Hotel, Auckland, New Zealand', *Australian Hist. Archaeol.* 9, 27–30.

Brooks, C.M. 1983, 'Aspects of the Sugar Refining Industry from the 16th to the 19th Century', *Post-Med. Archaeol.* 17, 1–14.

Calvococoressi, D. 1975, 'European Trade Pipes in Ghana', *West African J. of Archaeol.* 5, 195–200.

Crowfoot, E., Pritchard, F. & Staniland, K. 1992, *Medieval Finds from Excavations in London* 4. *Textiles and Clothing c. 1150– c. 1450*, London: The Stationery Office.

Davey, P.J. (ed.) 1983, *The Archaeology of the Clay Tobacco Pipe*, 8, *America*, Brit. Archaeol. Rep. Int. Ser. 175.

Davey, P.J. 1989, *Clay Pipes from Recent Excavations in Buenos Aires*, Buenos Aires: Centro de Arqueologia Urbana, Facultad de Arquitectura, Diseño y Urbanismo.

Davey, P.J. (ed.). 1999, *The Archaeology of the Clay Tobacco Pipe*, 15, Brit. Archaeol. Rep. Int. Ser. 809.

de Silva, G.P.S.H. & Uragoda, G.C. (eds) 1993, *Sesquicentennial Commemorative Volume of the Royal Asiatic Society of Sri Lanka 1845–1995*, Colombo.

Divers, D. 2004, 'Excavations at Deptford on the Site of the East India Company Dockyards and the Trinity House Almshouses, London', *Post-Med. Archaeol.* 38:1, 17–132.
Egan, G. 1983, 'Post-Medieval Britain in 1982', *Post-Med. Archaeol.* 17, 185–204.
Egan, G. 1990, 'Leaden Seals – Evidence for East India Company Trade in Textiles', *Int. J. Naut. Archaeol. Underwater Explor.* 19, 87–9.
Egan, G. 1993, *Lead Cloth Seals and Related Items in the British Museum*, British Museum Occ. Pap. 93, London: British Museum.
Egan, G. 1998, *Medieval Finds from Excavations in London 6. The Medieval Household: Daily Living c. 1150 – c. 1450*, London: The Stationery Office.
Egan, G. 2001, 'The Non-Ceramic Finds', in Tyler 2001, 82–90.
Egan, G. 2004, 'A Japanese Bell from Medieval London?', in *Curiosa Archaeologica*, Jahrschrift der Hansestadt Lübeck 5 – festschrift for Alfred Falk.
Egan, G. 2005, *Material Culture in an Age of Transition: Tudor and Stuart Period Finds* c. *1450* – c. *1700 from Excavations at Riverside Sites in Southwark*, MoLAS Monogr. 19.
Egan, G. 2006, 'Archaeological Evidence for Craft Working in London, *c.* 1100–1800', in Gläser (ed.) 2006, 47–70.
Egan, G. 2008, 'Evidence for Early Seventeenth-Century Glass Bead-Making from Hammersmith, West London', *Post-Med. Archaeol.* 42:2, 332–3.
Egan, G. & Keys, L. 2005, 'The Non-Ceramic finds', in Killock & Meddens 2005, 62–75.
Egan, G. & Pritchard, F. 1991, *Medieval Finds from Excavations in London 3. Dress Accessories c. 1150–c. 1450*, London: The Stationery Office.
Evans, C. 1990, 'Power on Silt: Towards a History of the United East India Company', *Antiquity* 64:244, 643–61.
Fernando, M. 1993, 'Seventeenth to Nineteenth Century Clay Tobacco Smoking Pipes from the Seabed of the Galle Harbour', in de Silva and Uragoda (eds) 1993, 240–61.
Forsyth, H. 2003, *The Cheapside Hoard*, London: Museum of London.
Fox, G.L. 1999, *The Kaolin Clay Tobacco Pipe Collection from Port Royal, Jamaica* (*The Archaeology of the Clay Tobacco Pipe*, 15, ed. P.J. Davey), Brit. Archaeol. Rep. Int. Ser. 809.
Gathercole, R. 1988, 'A Maori Hand Weapon from Southwark', *London Archaeol.* 6:3, 70–1.
Gläser, M. (ed.) 2006, *Lübecker Kolloquium zur Stadtachäologie im Hanseraum 5: das Handwerk*, Lübeck: Verlag Beleke.
Gilmore, K. 1973, *The Keenan Site Texas Historic Commission, State Office Archaeol. Rep.* 24, Austin, Texas.
Green, C. 1999, *John Dwight's Fulham Pottery: Excavations 1971–79*, English Heritage Arch. Rep. 6, London.
Green, A. & Leech, R.H. (eds) 2006, *Cities in the World*, Soc. Post-Med. Archaeol. Monogr. 3.
GMC 1903: *Catalogue of the Collection of London Antiquities in the Guildhall Museum*, Library Committee of the Corporation of the City of London, London. (https://archive.org/details/catalogueofcolleooguiliala/page/384 accessed March 2019).
Handler, J.S. & Lange, F.W. 1978, *Plantation Slavery in Barbados: An Archaeological Investigation*, Cambridge, MA: Harvard University Press.
Hammerson, M.J. 1975, 'Excavations on the Site of Arundel House in the Strand, WC2, in 1972', *Trans. London Middlesex Archaeol. Soc.* 26, 209–51.
Harward, C., Holder, N. & Jeffries, N. 2015, *The Spitalfields Suburb 1539–c 1880 Excavations at Spitalfields Market, London E1, 1991–2007*, MoLA Monogr. 61.
Heard, K. & Goodburn, D. 2003, *Investigating the Maritime History of Rotherhithe: Excavations at Pacific Wharf 165 Rotherhithe Street, Southwark*, MoLAS Archaeol. Study Ser. 11.
Higgins, D. 2005, 'A London Pipe from the Caribbean', *Soc. for Clay Pipe Res. Newsl.* 68, 27–8.

Higgins, D.A. & Boxt, M.A. 1990, 'A Clay Tobacco Pipe Fragment Found in Northern Belize', *Soc. for Clay Pipe Res. Newsl.* 25, 10–13.
Holmes, M. 1969, *Elizabethan London*, London: The Stationery Office.
Hutchinson, M. 1996, 'Edward IV's Bulwark: Excavations at Tower Hill, London, 1985', *Trans. London Middlesex Archaeol. Soc.* 47, 103–44.
Jack, R.I. 1986, 'Clay Tobacco Pipes Exported from Scotland to Australia in the 19th Century: Some Preliminary Observations', in Sudbury (ed.) 1986, 125–9.
Jarrett, C. 2004, 'Sugar Cone Moulds', in Divers 2004, 105–10.
Jarrett, C. 2005, 'The Pottery', in Killock & Meddens 2005, 34–52.
Killock, D. & Meddens, F. 2005, 'Pottery as Plunder: A 17th-Century Maritime Site at Limehouse, London', *Post-Med. Archaeol.* 39:1, 1–91.
Lawrence, S. 2006, 'Overburden: The Importance of the Archaeology of the Modern Period in Britain', in Green & Leech (eds) 2006, 307–19.
Marx, R.F. 1968, *Clay Smoking Pipes Recovered from the Sunken City of Port Royal: May 1, 1966 to September 30, 1967*, Kingston, Jamaica: Jamaica National Trust Commission.
Noël Hume, I. 1956, *Treasure in the Thames*, London.
Noël Hume, I. 1974, *Guide to Artifacts of Colonial America*, London & New York.
Noël Hume, I., Straube, B., Cranstone, D., Gaimster, D., Willemsen, A. & Clayton, P. 2011, 'Geoff Egan: A Tribute', *Post-Med. Archaeol* 45:2, 337–49.
Pearce, J. 2007, 'An Assemblage of 17th-Century Pottery from Bombay Wharf, Rotherhithe, London SE16', *Post-Med. Archaeol.* 41:1, 80–99.
Pearce, J. & Martin, J. 2003, 'Oriental Blue and White Porcelain Found at Archaeological Excavations in London: Research in Progress', *Trans. Oriental Ceram. Soc.* 67, 99–109.
Rawley, J.A. 2003, *London, Metropolis of the Slave Trade*, Columbia, MO; London: University of Missouri Press.
Richie, C.F. 1978, *Clay Tobacco Pipes from the Baybulls Wreck, Newfoundland, 1696: A Report in Support of the Preliminary Excavations*, unpublished report for Parks Canada.
Rusden, K.G. 1982, *Clay Pipes: Their History and Varieties Found in New Zealand*, (privately published).
Saxby, D. & Goodburn, D. 1998, 'Seventeenth-Century Ships' Timbers and dock on the Thames Waterfront at Bellamy's Wharf, Rotherhithe, London SE16', *Mariners Mirror* 84:2, 173–92.
Schwab, I. & Nurse, B. 1977, 'Butcher Row, Ratcliff, E14', *Trans. London Middlesex Archaeol. Soc.* 28, 215–51.
Sewart, R. & Blackmore, L. 1996, 'The Waste Material ... The Worked Bone and Ivory', in Hutchinson (ed.) 1996, 134–42.
Spencer, B. 1998, *Pilgrim Souvenirs and Secular Badges Medieval Finds from Excavations in London*, London: Boydell Press.
Stephenson, R. 2001, 'The Ceramic Finds', in Tyler 2001, 77–82.
Sudbury, B (ed.). 1986, *Historic Clay Tobacco Pipe Studies* 3, Soc. for Clay Pipe Res.
Tyler, K. 2001, 'The Excavation of an Elizabethan/Stuart Waterfront Site on the North Bank of the River Thames at Victoria Wharf, Narrow Street, Limehouse, London E14', *Post-Med. Archaeol.* 35, 3–52.
Tyler, K., Betts, I. & Stephenson, R. 2008, *London's Delftware Industry*, MoLAS Monogr. 40, Museum of London.
Walker, I.C. 1983, 'Nineteenth-Century Tobacco Pipes in Canada', in Davey (ed.) 1983, 1–87.
Ward Perkins, B. 1940, *London Museum Medieval Catalogue*, London.
Wheeler, R.E.M. 1928, *The Cheapside Hoard of Elizabethan and Jacobean Jewellery* (London Museum Catalogue 2), London.

II

The Colonial Landscape of St Kitts

5

Changing Technology in the West Indian Sugar Industry, 1650–1920: A Visual Introduction

PHIL DUNNING

SUMMARY: This paper traces the technological changes in the manufacturing processes of the sugar industry in the West Indies from the 17th century into the 20th century. While the field work of planting and harvesting cane remained largely manual labour, the processing of cane into sugar changed dramatically over time. Power sources, equipment, and organization of the industry were part of a slow evolution, with different technologies existing concurrently. My examination of this evolution is based on period documentary sources, such as technical treatises, which provide an overview of the industry, and images, from early engravings to 20th-century photographs.

From the beginning of sugar production in the West Indies into the 20th century, work in the cane fields relied largely on the hoe for planting[1] (Fig. 5.1) and the machete ('cutlass') or the bill hook ('cane knife') for harvesting (Fig. 5.2). The cut cane was loaded onto carts or wagons (Fig. 5.3) and taken to the mill to be crushed, or 'ground'.

These mills employed one of three sources of power: animals, water, or wind. Animal, or 'cattle' powered mills were the simplest to construct (Fig. 5.4). Mules or horned cattle were harnessed to a central drive shaft which turned a set of vertical rollers to crush the cane. Although the initial capital outlay was less than required for other power sources, there was considerable expense involved in maintaining the necessary livestock.[2] Water power (Fig. 5.5) was popular on islands where streams were plentiful and reliable, such as Jamaica and St Lucia. The initial investment in equipment was substantial, but upkeep was lower.[3]

Wind power (Fig. 5.6) was common on many islands where breezes were fairly constant. Construction of a windmill required a bigger outlay of money than setting up either a cattle- or water-powered mill. However, in locations where water power was not available, wind was more efficient than cattle power. The major drawback to the windmill was that, even if breezes were reliable, they could not be guaranteed. Period books and articles on sugar production recommended that a windmill be augmented with a cattle mill in case the wind died.[4] As well, it was noted that the varying

Fig. 5.1. Workers planting cane, 1849. The top two feet of the cane stalk was placed on its side in a hole and lightly covered with soil. Planting stalks in individual square holes was called the 'Barbados' method; in trenches, the 'Jamaica' method. Planting was followed by months of weeding and fertilizing, also with the hoe. *The Illustrated London News*, June 9, 1849.

Fig. 5.2. Sugar Cane Cutters, Barbados, 1907–14. The workers are using bill hooks, or 'cane knives' to cut and harvest the cane. Machetes or 'cutlasses' were also common. Postcard, Bruce Weatherhead, Barbados.

Fig. 5.3. Cane Wagons, Barbados, 1907–12. Cane was brought from the fields to the mill in carts or wagons pulled by cattle or mules. Postcard, W.L. Johnson, Barbados.

Fig. 5.4. Cattle Mill, *c.* 1765. Cattle mills often had four sweeps rather than two. They were turned by mules or horned cattle (Croker *et al.* 1765).

Fig. 5.5. Water Wheel, *c.* 1765. Water wheels were an efficient power source and were popular where a steady water source was guaranteed (Croker *et al.* 1765).

Fig. 5.6. Windmill, Barbados, 1900–6. Wind power was common on many islands where breezes were reliable. Postcard, Barbados.

Fig. 5.7. Rollers and frame from a cattle mill, Romney Manor, St Kitts, W.I. This set of rollers is marked 'GOULDING/ LONDON'. Thomas Goulding is listed in various trade directories from 1792 to 1799 as a 'sugar mill maker and iron founder'.

Fig. 5.8. (above) Spanish train of boiling coppers, 1667. The train is made up of four coppers, each heated separately. Note the small still on the left. (Du Terte 1667). (below) Spanish train, Herbert Heights, Nevis, W.I. Second half of the 17th century. This base is for a train of four coppers.

strength of the wind caused the rollers to revolve at irregular speeds. This resulted in an inconsistency in the amount of juice extracted from the cane.[5]

All these mills used vertically mounted rollers. In the 17th and earlier 18th centuries they were built of wood with heavy iron sheathing on the grinding surfaces.[6] By the later 18th century rollers were often made completely of iron (Fig. 5.7).[7] The central roller drove the other two by means of cog wheels at the top. The rollers were sometimes grooved to help catch and feed the cane.

As the cane was crushed, the extracted juice ran through a trough or a pipe with a filtering screen or grate, to the largest of a row of boiling kettles (Fig. 5.8).[8] Originally these kettles were made of copper, and although cast-iron was later used, the term 'copper' is still used today. A row of these coppers was called a 'train'. The first 17th-century trains were protected from the elements by no more than a shed roof supported on poles. The individual coppers in the train were of descending size. Early trains typically had three or four kettles, each separately heated by individual wood fires. Such a train, with individual fires, is commonly called a 'Spanish train'. A small quantity of lime was added to the first, largest kettle to aid in the coagulation of impurities and neutralize acids in the juice. The impurities rose to the top in a scum, and were skimmed off. The skimmings from this and the other coppers were conveyed through a trough to the still-room, where they were used in making rum. The cane juice in the largest copper was boiled until some water evaporated. When the juice had boiled down to the desired consistency, it was ladled, or 'skipped', into the next copper. This process continued through all three or four coppers. The last, smallest, hottest copper was often known as the 'teache'. In this copper, the juice, by then a thick syrup, was boiled until it reached the stage of granulation. This was tested by taking a small amount of the syrup between the thumb and forefinger. The fingers were slowly drawn apart, and if the thread of syrup between them stretched to between a quarter and a half an inch before it broke, it was considered to be fully boiled.[9] From the teache the

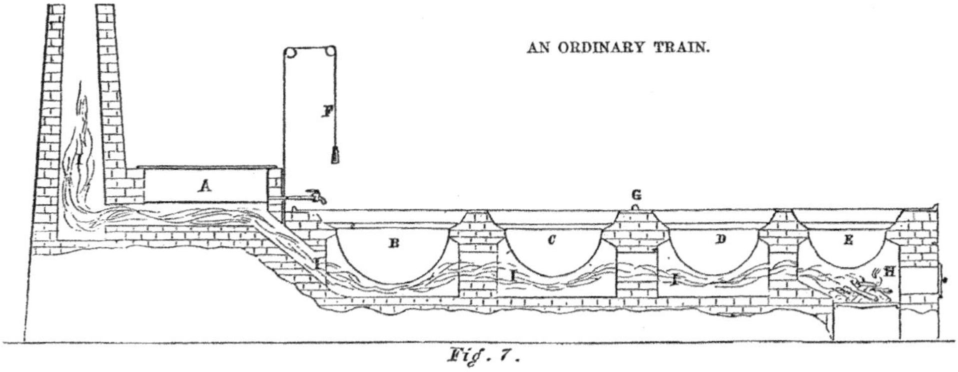

Fig. 5.9. Diagram of a 'Jamaica' train, 1857. The fire is built under the smallest kettle on the far right and is drawn through the flue under other kettles to the chimney on the far left. The heat for the clarifier, on the left, is controlled by raising or lowering a damper (Olcott 1857).

syrup was ladled into shallow wooden boxes or vats called 'coolers'. As it cooled, sugar crystals began to form in the syrup, which by now was termed 'molasses'.

By the 18th century, the boiling-down process had seen considerable innovations. The most important one was the introduction of one continuous fire chamber below the coppers, rather than individual fires (Fig. 5.9). The fire was built at the teache end of the train, and the heat was drawn through a flue until it reached a chimney on the other end.[10] This single-fire construction is commonly called a 'Jamaica' train. The fire was fueled by the waste material from the cane, gathered and dried after crushing. This waste was called 'trash', 'bagasse', or 'megass'.[11]

The juice was now piped, not to the first copper in the train, but to an additional kettle called a 'clarifier'. It was heated separately from the train, so that the temperature could be individually controlled. The lime was added here, and when the juice had been skimmed it was drained through a tap into the largest of the coppers. The coppers, by this time, were much larger than before, and during the 18th century, cast iron replaced copper. The entire process had grown in scale. The train was now made up of four or five coppers. Rather than a shed roof for cover, the clarifier, copper train (sometimes called a 'copper wall')[12] and multiple coolers were housed in a large 'boiling house' (Fig. 5.10). Some operations were so large as to require two copper trains

Fig. 5.10. (above) Boiling House Interior, 1854. Cane juice was piped to a central clarifier where it was fed into one of two copper trains. The sugary molasses was run off into coolers (on the left) through a movable trough (Tomlinson 1854). (below) Clarifier (foreground) and copper train (behind), New River Estate, Nevis, W.I. The clarifier is heated separately to control the temperature.

Fig. 5.11. (above) Curing house, 1853. Hogsheads of sugar are set on heavy joists above a sub-floor to catch the drained molasses. Two men bring a load of sugar from the boiling house.
(below) Hogsheads on joists above a catchbasin, 1900–7. Postcard, J.R.H. Seifert, Barbados.

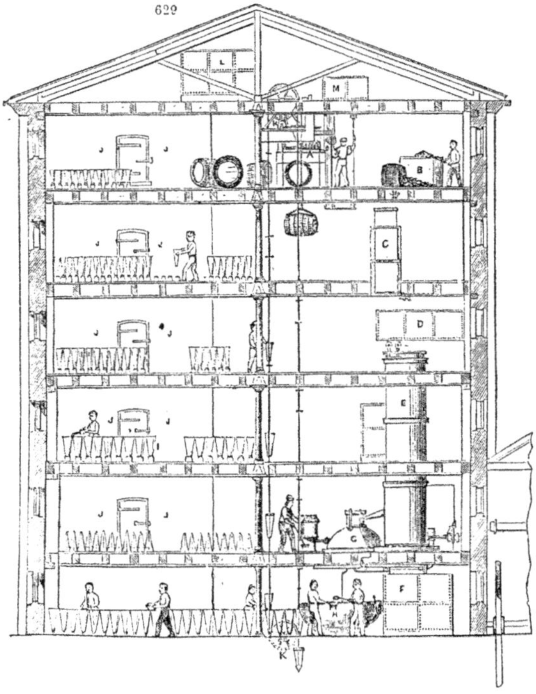

Fig. 5.12. Diagram of the interior of a sugar refinery, 1863. Sugar refineries used a complex series of operations and equipment (e.g., the vacuum pan labeled 'G', lower right) to convert the muscovado to white sugar. Note the sugar moulds draining in racks on the left (Hunt 1863).

feeding from a central clarifier or clarifiers.[13] The syrup from the teache was ladled into a long trough which could be swivelled from cooler to cooler. Each of the coolers contained about a hogshead of sugar (about 635kg to 770kg).

From the coolers, the sugar was taken to the 'curing-house', where molasses were drained from the sugar. The curing-house was a large room with a sloping sub-floor lined with mortar, lead or other impervious material.[14] Above this floor was a wood frame to hold barrels of hogshead capacity, called 'potting casks'. The top of each cask was open and the bottom was bored with a number of holes (Fig. 5.11). The syrupy sugar was poured into the casks, or 'potted'. Molasses drained from the sugar through the holes for three to six weeks and were collected from the reservoir formed by the floor. The molasses were used in the production of rum or exported separately in hogsheads.

The partially refined brown sugar that was left in the hogsheads was called 'muscovado'. This was the typical form of sugar exported from the British West Indies to England.[15] Further refinement was done by a process known as 'claying'. Little sugar was clayed on the British islands, as duties on refined sugar were much higher than on muscovado, and most planters found it more economical to ship muscovado sugar to refineries in England (Fig. 5.12).[16] In the process of claying, muscovado sugar was poured into cone-shaped moulds, usually made of unglazed ceramic. The mould, which had a hole at the tip, was placed in a frame and a plug set in the hole. The remaining molasses in the sugar would begin to settle to the bottom. After a time the plug was removed and the mould set in a jar, also ceramic, known as a 'syrup pot', 'treacle-jar', or 'drip' to collect the molasses (Fig. 5.13). The sugar in the mould was now ready for claying. A thick layer of water-saturated white clay was spread over the sugar at the larger end of the mould. The water was slowly released from the clay and as it percolated down it drew more molasses, which lightened the colour of the sugar. The process might be repeated several times, depending on the whiteness of the sugar desired.[17]

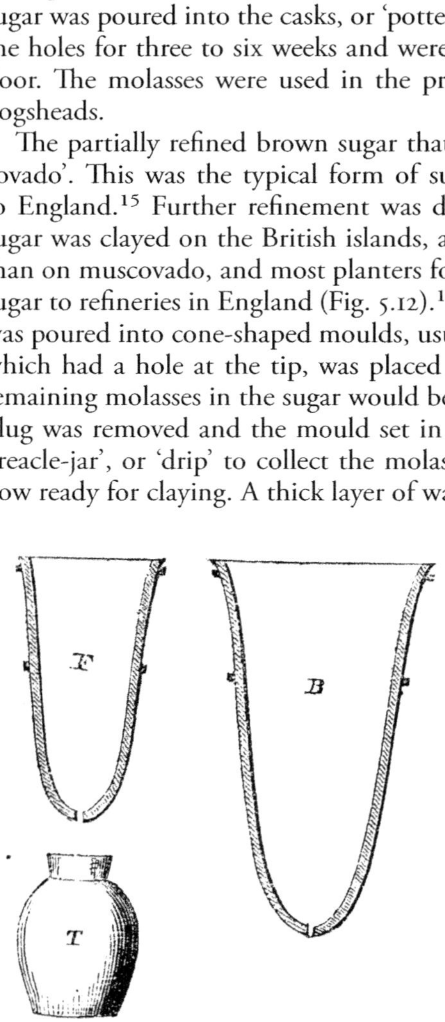

Fig. 2107. MOULDS AND TREACLE-JAR.

Fig. 5.13. Diagram, sugar mould and 'treacle jar', 'syrup pot' or 'drip' to catch the drained molasses (Tomlinson 1854).

On many sugar estates, there was little change in the processes of boiling-down and curing sugar throughout the 19th century, and indeed into the 20th century. An alternative source of power, the steam engine, introduced in the early 19th century, did, however, have an impact on the process of grinding the cane. The steam engine (Fig. 5.14) was a superior power source to water and wind because the planter could regulate the speed of grinding. As well, he was not at the mercy of changing winds, nor of a mill stream going dry.[18] Steam power, however, was slow to be accepted for a variety of reasons.[19] If a planter had an existing wind- or water-powered mill, the initial expense for the new equipment could be hard to justify, or it was simply beyond the capacity of many planters. A writer in 1851 said, 'I am aware that at present many West Indian proprietors are in such embarrassed circumstances, that they would find it difficult to make the requisite changes, being unable to command the necessary outlay'.[20] The machinery required regular maintenance by a trained machinist or engineer. A steam boiler required copious amounts of water, which was not necessarily available when needed on many islands. A boiler could be heated with bagasse, but it burned quickly, and the fire had to be fed continuously to maintain the temperature.[21] Coal or wood was recommended by technical writers.[22] Wood was scarce on most islands, and coal was an added expense for the planter. The availability of coal was not always guaranteed. A planter on St Kitts wrote in 1844 that he was awaiting the arrival of a coal ship, 'as we who have Steam Engines are anxious to grind and the supply of coals on the Island is very limited'.[23] The steam engine utilized horizontal, rather than vertical rollers (Fig. 5.15). The rollers were mounted in a heavy cast iron frame, one centred above and between the other two. These, like the engine, had been introduced around the turn of the 19th century. They were geared to a large flywheel to keep up momentum. Horizontal rollers were easier to feed cane into and were more efficient than vertical rollers in the extraction of juice. Vertical rollers were still preferred by many for wind and cattle mills, as in those instances they were attached directly to a vertical drive shaft.[24] Some windmills, however, were converted to horizontal rollers.

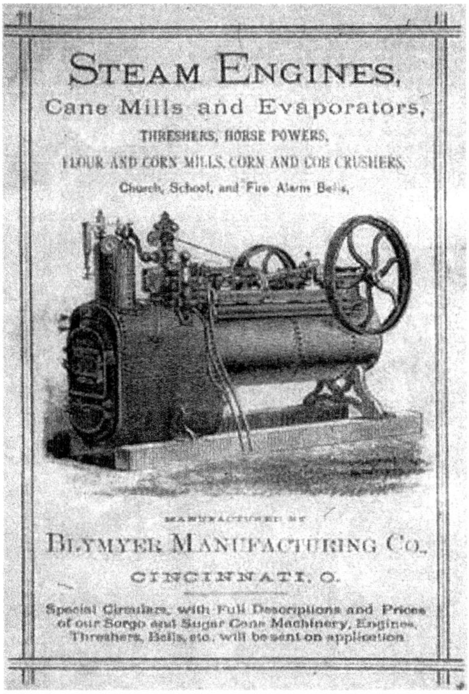

Fig. 5.14. Steam engine. n.d. (*c.* 1895). Catalogue for 'Steam Engines, Cane Mills and Evaporators'. The engine illustrated is typical of those found today on early sugar estates in the West Indies (Blymyer Manufacturing Co., Cincinnati, Ohio).

By the middle of the 19th century many technical writers advocated a multitude of competing technologies utilizing steam, for 'improving' the old system of evaporating the cane juice. Steam, it was argued, could be used for more than powering the mill. Some of these proposed technologies incorporated parts of the old system, while others completely replaced the clarifier and copper train with new equipment. For example, 'McCracken's Patent Evaporator' (Fig. 5.16) was intended to replace the final, smallest copper, or teache. The evaporator had an enclosed metal case surrounding open tubes in the bottom. Steam was introduced into this case and the heated juice

Fig. 5.15. (above) 'Double Geared Plantation Cane Mill' 1884. The flywheel and gears are in the foreground with the horizontal rollers behind (*The American Farmer*, 1884).
(below) Cane Mill, New River Estate, Nevis, W.I. The flywheel and gears on the left. The rollers are mounted in a heavy frame. Note the cast-iron feeder box for the cane attached to the roller frame.

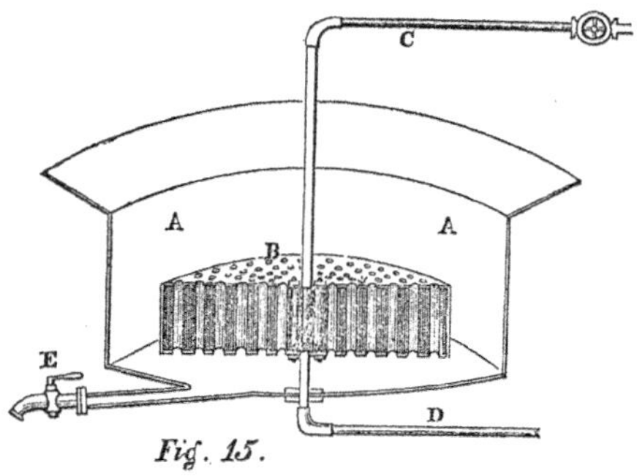

Fig. 5.16. (above) Diagram, 'McCracken's Patent Evaporator' 1857. It was intended to replace the teache in the copper train. The case in the bottom has open tubes through which the juice would circulate as it was heated (Olcott 1857).
(below) A similar evaporator at New River Estate, Nevis, W.I. Note the case in the bottom with open tubes.

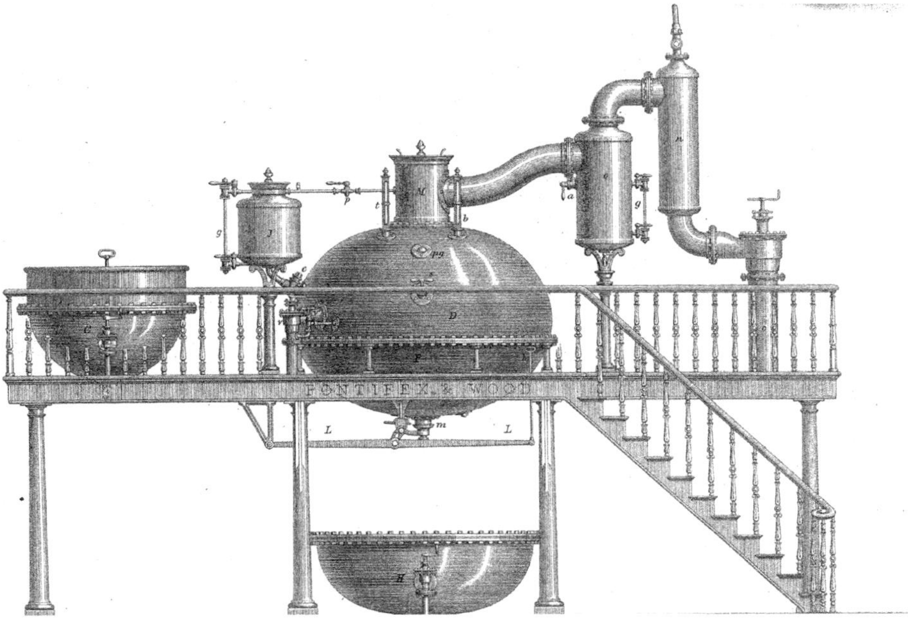

Fig. 5.17. Vacuum pan, 1854. The vacuum pan heated the molasses and evaporated water from it in a more controlled and efficient manner but was very expensive and required highly skilled maintenance (Tomlinson 1854).

circulated through the tubes. This process caused the juice to evaporate more evenly and rapidly than the teache, eliminating the possibility of overheating and caramelization. The most complex and expensive piece of equipment was the vacuum pan (Fig. 5.17). This apparatus, by boiling the sugar in a vacuum, allowed for more efficient crystallization.[25] Although such 'improvements' were taken up with enthusiasm by sugar refineries in Britain and the United States, these proposed modifications, as efficient as they may have been, found much less interest among most planters.[26] As with the engine itself, the new equipment required a large monetary investment and technically skilled labour to maintain and operate. A writer in 1853 commented that 'Machinery of the proper kind is difficult to obtain, and the almost human sensibility it displays in its liability to be deranged, causes disappointment and frequent loss, and satisfies the planter that complicated machinery can only be used with advantage in connection with an enormous outlay of capital'.[27] Steam power did not supplant wind, water or animal power. All four technologies existed concurrently. On the island of Montserrat in 1897, for instance, there were twelve steam-powered mills, 20 windmills, two water-powered mills, and '... some ... cattle mills'.[28] As well as the expense entailed in converting, there were practical reasons for the continuing use of other power sources. A mid 19th-century treatise on cane sugar advises that, even if a planter undertook the costly conversion to steam, if his estate was 'favourably situated with regard to wind' it should have an auxiliary windmill. When the wind was good, he would 'save a considerable amount of fuel', by not running the engine.[29]

Fig. 5.18. Central Sugar Factory, St Kitts 1912–16. Central sugar factories processed cane from multiple estates much more efficiently than individual estates could. Postcard, V.E. John, St Kitts, W.I.

Fig. 5.19. Interior, Central Sugar Factory, 1912–15. The key to efficient processing of cane by central factories was the use of up-to-date machinery on a large scale. Postcard, A. Moure Losada, St Kitts, W.I.

Fig. 5.20. Sugar cane train, 1907–14. An essential element in the quick and efficient processing of the cane was good transportation from the estates to the central factory. Many islands built railroads to facilitate this. Postcard, Leboullanger, Martinique.

The sugar industry has always been an erratic economy, with prices rising and falling depending on many variables, including weather, wars, politics and competition. The introduction of sugar beet in the 19th century, for instance, dealt a harsh blow to the producers of cane sugar.[30] Through the century, many planters struggled to survive, and many estates failed. In the second half of the 19th century, writers on the industry began to advocate the centralization of refining facilities, rather than individual estate-refining of sugar.[31] Centralized factories, or 'centrals', could make use of the most modern equipment, thereby increasing efficiency. The island of St Kitts presents a case study in the development of such a factory. In 1897 a merchant on the island wrote 'The present condition of the sugar industry is as bad as it could well be'.[32] A proposal was made at that time to erect a central factory, stating that '... central factories would pay ... provided modern labour-saving machinery was erected'.[33] In 1911 the island's legislature passed a bill facilitating private development of a central factory, which began production in 1912 (Fig. 5.18), using up-to-date methods of refining (Fig. 5.19). A railroad was built to bring the cane from the fields to the factory (Fig. 5.20), and a special pier constructed for shipping. The factory proved successful for a time, but the continuing volatility of prices took its toll on profitability. In a last attempt to save the industry, the government began taking over administration of the sugar estates in 1972. The central sugar factory was nationalized in 1976, and the state subsidized the industry.[34] This lasted until 2005, by which time the government had decided that it could no longer afford to absorb the continuing loss. The last cane harvest on the island was that year. Today St Kitts is concentrating on the development of its tourist industry, and a vestige of sugar production is part of it. The 'sugar train', which brought cane to the factory now serves to carry tourists on a scenic and informative tour of the island. Youtube: https://youtu.be/eSnMRCk-AMk.

ACKNOWLEDGEMENTS

I am grateful to Professor Roger Leech for his work on the 17th-century copper train at Upper Rawlins or Herbert Heights, Nevis, W.I. He has identified a significant example of early technology. David Rollinson, Heritage Consultant, shared his considerable knowledge and research on the equipment and works at New River Estate and Old Manor Estate, Nevis, W.I. Assistant Professor Frederick Smith, College of William and Mary, pointed out a major reference on 19th-century technology. Victoria O'Flaherty, Director of Archives, National Archives, St Kitts, identified an important report on the sugar industry in the British West Indies. And last, but certainly not least, thanks to Christina Bates, historian (retired), Canadian Museum of History (and my wife). She did her wizardry in making unwieldy sentences coherent, and muddled paragraphs clear.

NOTES

1 Edwards 1793, book V, 204–7; Kerr 1851, 38–9; Bell 1865, 15. Technical treatises throughout the 19th century repeatedly advocate the use of the plough, rather than hoeing. However, pictorial evidence (e.g. Fig. 5.1) and the continued repetition of the proposal in the prescriptive literature suggest that it was little taken up.

From the 1820s through the 1890s numerous publications on technology discuss the production of cane sugar. Overall, these descriptions are essentially the same. The various authors, however, emphasize different elements of the process, and have differing views on methodology. Comparison of these differences creates a more informed understanding of the industry.

2 Wray 1848, 294; Evans 1848, 109–10.

3 Wray 1848, 289.

4 Wray 1848, 292.

5 Kerr 1851, 80; Tomlinson 1854, II, 776.
6 Ligon 1673, 85; Sitwell 1888, 38. George Sitwell, ironfounder, records that he was making hollow cast-iron cylinders to sheath wood rollers by 1663.
7 Woodcraft 1855, 56. William Harding was given a British patent (No. 433) for all-iron rollers in 1721.
8 Ligon 1673, 90; Croker *et al.* 1765, III, n .p.; Ure 1849, 1208.
9 Anon. n.d. [Tomlinson 1850], 16; Niccol 1864, 14; Evans 1848, 174–5.
10 Anon. n.d. [Tomlinson 1850], 14–17; Ure 1849, 1208.
11 Ripley & Dana 1864, XV, 160; Niccol 1864, 13; Evans 1848, 106–7.
12 Tomlinson 1854, II, 778; Olcott 1857, 88–90.
13 Edwards 1793, V, 221; Ure 1849, 1208; Tomlinson 1854, II, 778.
14 Ure 1849, 1209; Niccol 1864, 14.
15 Niccol 1864, 14.
16 Anon. [Dodd] 1841, 161–8; Hunt 1863, 1019–33. *The Penny Magazine* [Anon. 1841] has a good basic description of the complex processes involved in the further refining of sugar. A more detailed and technical discussion is in Hunt 1863.
17 Ure 1849, 1210; Niccol 1864, 14–15.
18 Kerr 1851, 80–1.
19 Wray 1848, 308.
20 Kerr 1851, 59.
21 Leslie 1878, 426.
22 Tomlinson 1854, 777.
23 Davoren 1844.
24 Ure 1849, 1203.
25 Ure 1849, 1211–14; Hunt 1863, 1030–31; Tomlinson 1854, II, 781; Olcott 1857, 106–8.
26 Chamberlin *et al.* 1880, 3–29; Olcott 1857, 104; Evans 1848, 142–3.
27 Thorpe 1853, 766.
28 Norman 1898, 146.
29 Wray 1848, 292.
30 Hunt 1863, 1033–5; Tomlinson 1854, II, 789–95.
31 Biggs 1849, 67–84; Bell 1866, iv; Bolles 1889, 85.
32 Norman 1898, 241.
33 Norman 1898, 241.
34 Horsford 2004, 9.

BIBLIOGRAPHY

PUBLISHED SOURCES

Anon. 1841 [Dodd, G], 'A Day at the Sugar-Refinery', *The Penny Magazine of the Society for the Diffusion of Useful Knowledge*, London: Charles Knight. The chapters in this magazine that are on industries are titled, 'A Day at the …'. These chapters were published together as a separate book, *Days at the Factories*, in 1843 by Charles Knight & Co. In that publication the author is identified as George Dodd.

Anon. n.d. [Tomlinson, C. 1850], *The Useful Arts and Manufactures of Great Britain*, London: Society for Promoting Christian Knowledge. Although no author or date is listed on the title page of this book, Tomlinson states that he wrote it in a footnote, p. 276, Vol. I, of Tomlinson 1854.

Bell, F. 1866, *Hand-Book of Practical Directions for Sugar-Cane Planting, Sugar Making and the Distillation of Rum*, Sydney: J.J. Moore. Bell was an early advocate of sugar cane cultivation in Australia. Drawing on his experience in the West Indies, he describes several processes in detail that others ignore. He also presents a brief summary of the competing technologies available in 1866.

Biggs, J. 1849, 'On the Establishment of Central Sugar Works in the British Colonies', *The Colonial Magazine and East India Review* XVI, London: John Mortimer.

Bolles, A. 1889, *Industrial History of the United States,* Norwich, CT: Henry Bill.

Chamberlin, S.E., Abbot, H. J. & Endlich, F.M. 1880, *Report on the Methods of Manufacturing Sugar in West Indian Islands and British Guiana*, Washington: Government Printing Office. This report records the use of more sophisticated equipment on some estates on Barbados and British Guiana, while documenting less complicated machinery on islands elsewhere.

Croker, Rev. T.H., Williams, T. & Clark, S. 1765, *The Complete Dictionary of Arts and Sciences*, London & Cambridge: J. Coote.

Du Terte, Jean-Baptiste 1667, *Histoire Generale des Antilles par les Français*, Paris: T. Lolly.

Edwards, B. 1793, The History Civil and Commercial, of the British Colonies in the West Indies, Dublin: Luke White.

Evans, W.J. 1848, *The Sugar Planter's Manual*, Philadelphia: Lea and Blanchard.

Horsford, J. 2004, *From Sugar Cane to Scenic Train, The St. Kitts Railway*, St. Teath, Cornwall: Paul Catchpole.

Hunt, R. 1863, *A Supplement to Ure's Dictionary of Arts, Manufactures and Mines*, New York: D. Appleton.

Kerr, T. 1851, *A Practical Treatise on the Cultivation of the Sugar Cane, and the Manufacture of Sugar*, London: John J. Griffith.

Leslie, Mrs Frank 1878, 'Scenes in Sun-Lands, Cuba – A Visit to a Sugar Estate', *Frank Leslie's Popular Monthly*, VI, 417–26 (October 1878), New York: Frank Leslie Publishing House. Leslie gives a good description for the layman of the latest technology of the period, including conveyor belts to move the cane, charcoal filters, vacuum pans and centrifugals.

Ligon, R. 1673 (second edition), *A True and Exact History of the Island of Barbadoes*, London: Peter Parker.

Niccol, R. 1864, *Essay on Sugar and General Treatise on Sugar Refining*, Greenock, Scotland: A. MacKenzie.

Norman, H.W., Sir (Chair), 1898, *Royal Commission on Depression in Sugar Industry in W. Indian Colonies, and Their General Condition: Appendix* C., *Ill*, London: Her Majesty's Stationery Office

Olcott, H.S. 1857, *Sorgho and Imphee, The Chinese and African Sugar Canes*, New York: A.O. Moore. Although the title refers to sorghum sugar, the author has an extensive discussion of West Indian cane sugar production.

Ripley, G. & Dana, C. 1864, *The New American Cyclopaedia; A Popular Dictionary of General Knowledge*, New York: D. Appleton.

Sitwell, Sir G.R. 1888, 'A Picture of the Iron Trade (in the Seventeenth Century)', *J. Derbyshire Archaeol. and Nat. Hist. Soc.*, X, 28–46.

Thorpe, T.B. 1853, 'Sugar and the Sugar Region of Louisiana', *Harper's New Monthly Magazine*, November 1853. Although this article is on the sugar industry in Louisiana, the author discusses and compares practices with those in the West Indies and Cuba.

Tomlinson, C. 1854, *Cyclopaedia of Useful Arts, Mechanical and Chemical, Manufactures, Mining and Engineering*, London & New York: George Virtue.

Ure, A. 1849, *A Dictionary of Arts, Manufactures and Mines*, New York: D. Appleton.

Woodcraft, B. 1855, *Appendix to Reference Index of Patents of Invention*, London: Eyre and Spottiswoode.

Wray, L. 1848, *The Practical Sugar Planter; A Complete Account of the Cultivation and Manufacture of the Sugar-Cane, According to the Latest and Most Improved Methods*, London: Smith, Elder.

UNPUBLISHED SOURCES

Davoren, Dr R.G. 1844, Letter to John Rankin, Esq., London, dated Nov. 12, 1844 (author's collection).

6

Archaeological Evidence for Enslaved African Laborers from Two Locations at the Brimstone Hill Fortress, St Kitts, West Indies

GERALD F. SCHROEDL *and* TODD M. AHLMAN

SUMMARY: The Brimstone Hill Fortress, a British colonial period (1690–1854) site on the north-west coast of St Kitts, was constructed and maintained mostly by enslaved Africans. Laborers were acquired primarily from local plantations; others were procured by and permanently attached to military units. A 1791 map identifies buildings at five locations that African workers occupied. Excavations of three buildings at a limekiln complex and two structures in a habitation area confirm that enslaved Africans maintained their self-identity, utilized Afro-Caribbean and British-made wares in food preparation, and consumed salt beef and pork, local goats/sheep, and imported and local fish.

The Brimstone Hill Fortress sits atop a volcanic extrusion that towers over 230m above the Caribbean Sea on the north-west coast of St Kitts (Fig. 6.1). The British first fortified the hill with cannons in 1690 and continued to develop its military potential with numerous barracks, buildings, structures, and walls until its abandonment in 1853–4.[1] The only major military engagement at the fortress was the French siege and occupation of 1782–3. Brimstone Hill was maintained as a place of refuge for the island's population during times of foreign invasion until the mid 18th century after which its primary purpose shifted to military defense and a deterrent to slave revolts.[2] British military engineers designed the fort, with virtually all construction, renovation, and maintenance accomplished by enslaved Africans before emancipation and black as well as white laborers after

Fig. 6.1. St Kitts and the location of the Brimstone Hill Fortress.

1834.[3] At various times throughout its history, British army officers and enlisted men, members of the St Kitts militia, soldiers of the First, Second, Third, and Fourth West India Regiments, Africans from the 'Corps of Black Military Artificers and Pioneers' and from the 'Corps of Embodied Slaves,' as well as small numbers of civilians, military wives, and children occupied the Brimstone Hill Fortress.[4]

The archaeological potential of Brimstone Hill was recognized in the 1960s and clearing rubble from buildings and occasional small excavations were made through the 1980s.[5] In 1996 specific archaeological research goals were identified and the University of Tennessee initiated a long-term excavation program at the site. The research design conceptualizes Brimstone Hill as once being a highly structured and frequently oppressive multi-ethnic and multi-racial community where the number, organization, and relationship of people differed with changing social, political, economic, environmental, and cultural circumstances. The goals of the investigations are to (1) document the contribution that enslaved Africans made to the fort's construction, maintenance, military readiness, and social fabric; (2) excavate specific structures used or occupied by enslaved Africans, British officers, and enlisted men, and to describe their construction materials, floor plan, and architectural details; and (3) compare and contrast the associated archaeological assemblages. These studies are intended to (1) demonstrate that the heritage of Brimstone Hill is as much Afro-Caribbean as it is Colonial British; (2) generate better public interpretation of the site and provide information from which the people of St Kitts can better understand and appreciate their own cultural heritage; and (3) place the study of enslaved Africans and British soldiers at Brimstone Hill in the comparative context of Colonial Caribbean culture.

Much of the Brimstone Hill Fortress Archaeological project is focused on documenting and interpreting the role enslaved Africans had in the fort's history. For this reason, we have sought to determine how the St Kitts colonial government and British colonial and military officials planned and executed construction and renovation projects and how they arranged for the labor and materials to complete the work. We have looked particularly at the source of African laborers, when they were employed, how many carried out the work, where they were housed, how they were provisioned, the kinds of tasks required of them, how they were treated, and how they interacted with one another and with other people living and working at Brimstone Hill.[6] Translating these data to archaeology, we report here on the excavations of five buildings in two areas of Brimstone Hill where enslaved Africans lived and worked.[7] One of these (designated site BSH 1) is an industrial area at the base of the hill's north side where activities centered on the operation of a limekiln and associated buildings. The second site (designated BSH 2) is on the west slope of the hill below the curtain wall connecting the Orillon and Magazine Bastions (Fig. 6.2). Four buildings, two of which we excavated, were erected here to specifically house and service the needs of enslaved African workers. British Royal Engineers, in the 18th and 19th centuries, refer to structures that enslaved Africans occupied, presumably mainly as dwellings, as 'Negro huts.' We follow their usage here for the sake of consistency with these historic sources.

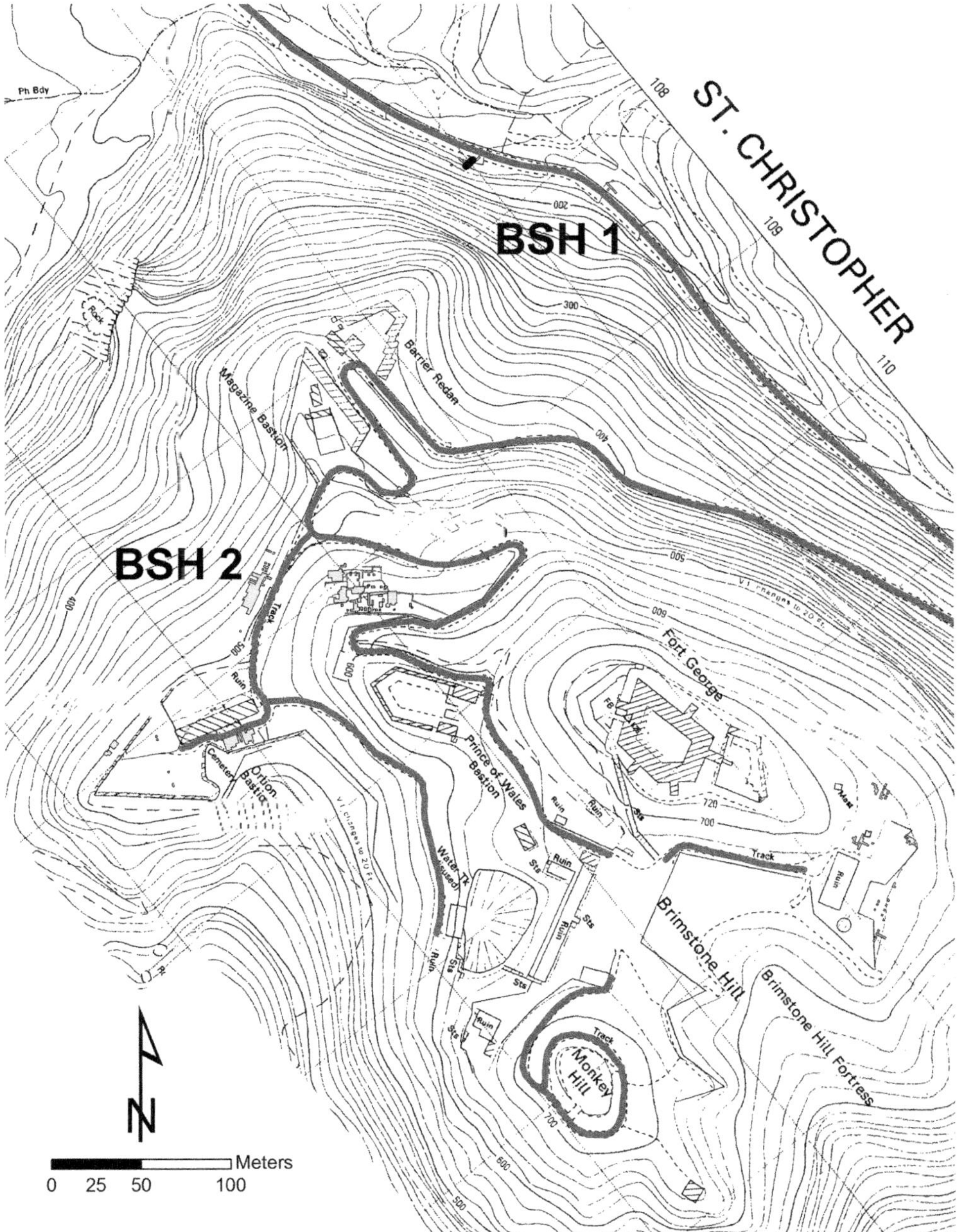

Fig. 6.2. Location of sites BSH 1 and BSH 2 at the Brimstone Hill Fortress.

ACQUISITION OF ENSLAVED AFRICANS

The first efforts to fortify Brimstone Hill in 1690 surely were accomplished with the labor of enslaved Africans but the earliest known report of such work is 1704.[8] There was frequent concern about the state of the island's defenses and by the 1720s the St Kitts Assembly and Council began to regularly identify enslaved Africans as the source of labor for improving their situation.[9] Not too surprisingly these concerns became magnified by real or rumored threats of foreign invasion and tended to dissipate after each threat had passed. In 1722, 1724, 1729, 1733, and at regular intervals thereafter, the St Kitts Assembly and Council taxed plantation owners to raise funds for the island's defenses;[10] they purchased slaves referred to as Public Negroes for these undertakings,[11] or they regularly passed legislation, that depending on the circumstances, compelled or requested plantation owners to temporarily send a portion of their slaves to work on various military projects.[12]

Plantation owners were required to send one or two slaves for every 80 or 100 that they owned. Because there were about 200 plantations on the island this usually generated an expected work force of 100 to 200 individuals.[13] Slave owners holding fewer than 80 slaves were not exempt from meeting this requirement. A supervisor, jointly appointed by the military and colonial government, was placed in charge of the slaves and was responsible for their management, for making sure that plantation owners complied with government mandates, and for filing monthly reports on his activities.[14] On occasion plantation owners were given the option to substitute a proportional number of horses, cattle, or mules in lieu of slaves.[15] For example, during the 1782–3 occupation of Brimstone Hill, the French permitted slave owners to send a horse, mule, or ox each day in place of six workers.[16]

At times the St Kitts Assembly and Council initiated the call for black laborers, but more often this was prompted by a recommendation or request of the British military, especially after the 1782 siege.[17] The chain of command in the 18th-century British military was complex, but most construction estimates and requests for laborers came from engineering officers at Brimstone Hill rather than regional commanders stationed elsewhere. Proposed work, however, almost always required the approval of senior officers in Antigua, Grenada, or Barbados, following the strategic plans of the British government in London.[18] This became more common during the Napoleonic era when much of the British military command structure in the Caribbean shifted to Barbados. In 1824 the Office of the Commissariat was put in charge of acquiring labor for the military and in 1829 these responsibilities were transferred to the Office of Ordnance.[19] At Brimstone Hill, however, the resident engineer continued to prefer hiring artificers and laborers directly rather than through a contractor.[20]

Generally, the military wanted more slaves than the St Kitts Assembly and Council could or was willing to supply. Because of these differences, absenteeism, and sickness, determining the actual number of African slaves employed at any one time is difficult and specific counts were seldom recorded. Large numbers of workers were needed for major construction, repair, and renovation projects, but smaller numbers of maintenance, sanitary, and service personnel probably resided there especially after the mid 18th century when there was a near continuous military presence at the fort.

In 1757, there were 230 enslaved Africans working at Brimstone Hill and from May to August 1789 the number increased from 120 to nearly 750 laborers.[21] Lewis Hay, commander of the Royal Engineers reported to the St Kitts Council in June 1793 that he was lacking 129 of the 600 laborers he had been promised, implying that 471 were employed at that time.[22]

During the period of greatest building activity, from about 1785 to 1810, the military made requests for as few as 20 and as many as 600 laborers. For example, in August 1785, the military sought 80 workers and the government provided 100.[23] In January 1792, a request was made for 120 slaves to work 36 days; colonial officials responded by sending all 120 for an additional 60 days.[24] The military sought 600 workers in April 1793 for four months work, but the colonial government could promise no more than 160 to 200,[25] and in October 1794, the Assembly and Council appropriated funds for 50 enslaved Africans to work six days at the fort.[26] Five months later, the military requested a workforce of 100 for 14 days and in September 1796 a request was made for 100 workers for eight to ten days.[27] As late as 1803, military engineers asked the colonial government to provide 15 workers for Brimstone Hill.[28] Overall between 1779 and 1796, military engineers, as recorded in the St Christopher Council and Legislative Council Minutes, made one to three annual requests totaling fourteen in all for enslaved African workers. Eight requests were for 100 to 130 individuals. One was for 600 workers, two were for 200 and three were for 80 or fewer laborers.[29] Recorded in the same documents for the period 1775 to 1795 the Assembly and Council on twelve occasions authorized sending between 50 and 600 laborers for as little as six days and for as long as two years.[30] These authorizations occurred one to three times a year. Four times the Assembly and Council approved a work force of 200 and on four other occasions they agreed to send 100 to 130 laborers. Once in 1790 the colonial government endorsed sending 300 workers and approved a request for 600 for four months work in 1793. In 1794 and 1795 the Assembly and Council agreed to send 50 to 60 workers to Brimstone Hill. The French had similar ambitions of strengthening the island's defenses during their 1782–3 occupation of Brimstone Hill, demanding, in addition to the conditions of the articles of capitulation, that the island send 200 enslaved African workers to the hill.[31]

Lists of laborers were requested or compiled as early as 1735 but this was apparently done only at irregular intervals.[32] The best surviving record is from January 1791 when the St Kitts Assembly and Council resolved to purchase and send 80 male and 40 female laborers to work at the fort for a period of two years; these individuals are listed by name, parish, the estate of origin, person responsible for sending them, and the slave's valuation.[33] All parishes are represented, as are 120 different estates. Valuations range from £60 to £100. Nine months later the Assembly and Council authorized another contingent of laborers for three months and compiled a second list.[34] Parishes and plantations are comparable to the first list, but most individuals differ from the first list and have lower valuations, ranging from £33 to £100.

Only one woman is clearly identified on either list, although the St Kitts Assembly and Council had authorized 40 female workers. This suggests that there were no restrictions against employing women, but that females were seldom utilized in constructing or renovating buildings and fortifications. The wives and children of some British soldiers and officers were permitted to live at the fort, and it seems probable, despite little historical documentation, that enslaved African women, some of whom were accompanied by their children, also lived with their husbands serving in black military units at Brimstone Hill.[35] In addition, enslaved African women were probably kept as servants, housekeepers, cooks, nurses, and mistresses at the fortress.[36]

WORKING CONDITIONS

As a stipulation of sending plantation laborers, estate owners and the military and civil government negotiated their condition of employment. This included compensation to the slave owner, specification of particular kinds of work, food and shelter, medical care, and life insurance.[37] Slave owners were compensated 1 to 4 shillings per day, and at times slaves also received a small payment for their work.[38] Enslaved laborers worked a six-day week with Sundays off when many would go back to their respective plantations, returning to Brimstone Hill Monday morning.[39] In one instance they received only a half day's salary if they arrived after 9:00 am but were credited a full day's work if they had traveled more than six miles and arrived before 11:00 am.[40] They received no pay if absent for three consecutive days.[41]

While military engineers or the Assembly and Council determined specific projects and work assignments, civilian overseers were hired to actually supervise the enslaved workers. Tasks were far ranging, including hauling materials and supplies, building stonework, carpentry, the manufacture of lime, clearing vegetation, and general labor.[42] Sometimes enslaved workers were required to bring their own tools as well as their own provisions from their respective plantations, but at other times the colonial government or more often the military provided their meals.[43] Meals often were salt beef, salt pork, or salted herring prepared from military stores or kept on hand by the colonial government.[44] Army or civilian doctors were compensated for treating on the job injuries, and upon several occasions plantation owners received payment for the injury or death of a slave.[45] This included, for example, the death of one African who apparently fell into a limekiln and another who broke his leg.[46] In the latter case the owner was compensated for 72 days lost time.

The colonial government at times complained that enslaved Africans were being used for unauthorized work and tried to restrict the jobs they could perform or threatened to withdraw them from the work. For example, the Assembly and Council directed that enslaved Africans should work only on the construction of Fort George in January 1791.[47] In May 1789 the Council argued that laborers should not be transporting materials up the hill, and in August 1791, it was prepared to withdraw the workforce because the military was not engaging in the kind of work that the slaves had been sent to perform.[48] In May of 1792, the government's work force had fulfilled a four-month obligation to the military and was withdrawn from service.[49] The St Kitts Assembly and Council once went so far as to specifically forbid slaves from doing quarry work, and another time refused to honor a request for 100 workers because the military had made previous assurances that a sufficient number of laborers had been provided to do the work.[50] Because of a disagreement within the British military in November 1790 over cost estimates, the enslaved Africans from plantations were temporarily sent home, although those that had been purchased by the government specifically for work at the fortress were kept on the job.[51] Neither the Assembly and Council nor the military always were satisfied with how well the work was progressing. So for example in 1791 the Assembly and Council was concerned about worker desertions and taking up new residences at the nearby town of Sandy Point,[52] while Robert Prescott, commander of troops in St Kitts, wrote to the Council in July 1779 that 'the Negroes hither to furnished have fallen far short of the numbers demanded that such as came were late and more attentive to pilfering provisions than to work for which reason I hope their overseers may be reprimanded for these reasons.'[53] Prescott was further annoyed that British soldiers might have to do some of the work.

MILITARY ARTIFICERS AND PIONEERS

The military also maintained its own attachments of African laborers that came to be known officially as the 'Corps of Black Military Artificers and Pioneers.'[54] This was done to reduce the costs of hiring military laborers and assure a reliable source of labor.[55] The British Army recruited pioneers throughout the Caribbean and managed to acquire over 3,000 in the 1790s.[56] Of these 110 and 112 individuals from St Kitts were conscripted for duty elsewhere in 1795 and 1796, and some of these were assigned to the West India Regiments, composed of black soldiers.[57] When not enough men could be acquired for pioneer duty from local sources, the British Army purchased them directly from Africa or conscripted them from captured foreign slave ships.[58] In 1797 two pioneers were allotted to each regimental company but by 1804 this was changed to one pioneer for every 30 white soldiers.[59]

Although at times ten or more British army companies from one or more regiments occupied Brimstone Hill, surprisingly few pioneers are reported at the fort until the early 19th century when they appear to have replaced at least a portion of the local enslaved African work force, perhaps assuming more regular or routine maintenance and custodial duties. Two pioneers were at the fort in 1797, one was there in 1804, and five were residing at the fort and in a nearby village in 1821.[60] One of these was a single free black named Paul, who was employed as a laborer and office keeper.[61] There are eight other reports recording between 3 and 70 pioneers on St Kitts between 1810 and 1844, most of whom were probably stationed at Brimstone Hill.[62] No specific living quarters have been identified for pioneers and little was recorded about the work they performed. Most pioneers presumably lived in barracks that also housed British and West India Regiment soldiers, but others, like Paul, probably were quartered near where they were employed as office workers, cooks, and servants. Regulations issued in 1830 permitted army officers to employ between one and eight black but no white servants. These individuals probably lived in rooms attached to the officers' quarters.[63]

Besides pioneer laborers, artificers, and servants, white as well as free black laborers were hired as carpenters, stone masons, armorers, and for other skilled and unskilled work at Brimstone Hill, and sometimes the civil government or military let cost reimbursable contracts, usually to local plantation owners, for specific renovation or construction work where the contractor was responsible for labor and materials.[64] This was especially true before the British army assumed control of the fort's development in 1778 but continued well after British Royal Engineers became responsible for construction and maintenance. For example, as early as 1734 Nathanial Crossley was paid £50 for constructing two sentry boxes, while Charles Farrell in 1781 and Andrew Gardner in 1786 respectively were paid £330 and £950 to build barracks.[65] Sometime the Council formed a committee to let contracts for construction or repairs and bids were solicited with advertisements in a local newspaper.[66] Contracts specified wages, working conditions, estimates of materials, housing, meals, medical benefits for accidents, and death benefits.[67] By the 1820s, despite implementation of detailed procurement procedures first by Office of the Commissariat and then the Office of Ordnance, military engineers at Brimstone Hill negotiated contracts directly with plantation owners, and shortly before emancipation the military began to bid work to black and white independent contractors and individual craftsman.[68] In 1841 and again in 1849 the military could not find civilian laborers or artificers to fill their contracts despite soliciting bids in public advertisements.[69]

LIVING QUARTERS FOR ENSLAVED AFRICANS

Few records reveal where African laborers, artificers, and pioneers or black militia and military units were housed at Brimstone Hill. Once Fort George was completed about 1805 most West India Regiment soldiers and probably some troops from the Corps of Embodied Slaves lived there.[70] No village or specific barracks for enslaved workers was maintained on the hill. In December 1785, Lieutenant James Lees, the station engineer, reports only that he was considering roofing 'the old store which would be an exceedingly good ... shelter for the public Negroes employed on the hill in bad weather.'[71] Rejecting a proposal to house workers at nearby Charles Fort, Lees' later plan, approved in 1789, was 'for preparing a more convenient situation [to house workers] on a flatt about halfway up the hill,'[72] and by this time workers were, 'Building huts on the Hill for the Negroes.'[73] Included among these structures are six buildings identified on a 1791 engineer's map of Brimstone Hill as 'Artificers and Negroe [*sic*] Huts.'[74] A further motivation to build them was the need to house the 120 African laborers that had been purchased by the St Kitts Assembly and Council and sent to work at Brimstone Hill for two years.[75]

Further corroboration comes from a list of buildings and their dimensions constructed in 1789 and 1790 that James Lees compiled in 1792 to defend himself against a variety of court martial charges stemming from his service at Brimstone Hill ranging from disobeying orders to embezzlement, misappropriating funds, and theft of government property.[76] Included on his list are four buildings, including two hospitals, a kitchen, and a Negro hut that are identified on the 1791 Royal Engineers map of the fortress as occupied by enslaved Africans and that are situated below the curtain wall connecting the Orillon and Magazine Bastions.[77] This area is designated BSH 2 where extensive excavations were made from 1996 to 1999 and again in 2004 (Fig. 6.3).

These buildings appear to correspond to a building shown on one of four watercolors of the fort attributed to Lees.[78] These paintings are also revealing because they show thatched huts at the base of the hill associated with the Commissariats Yard, where materials and supplies were landed for transport up the hill. The huts are identical to

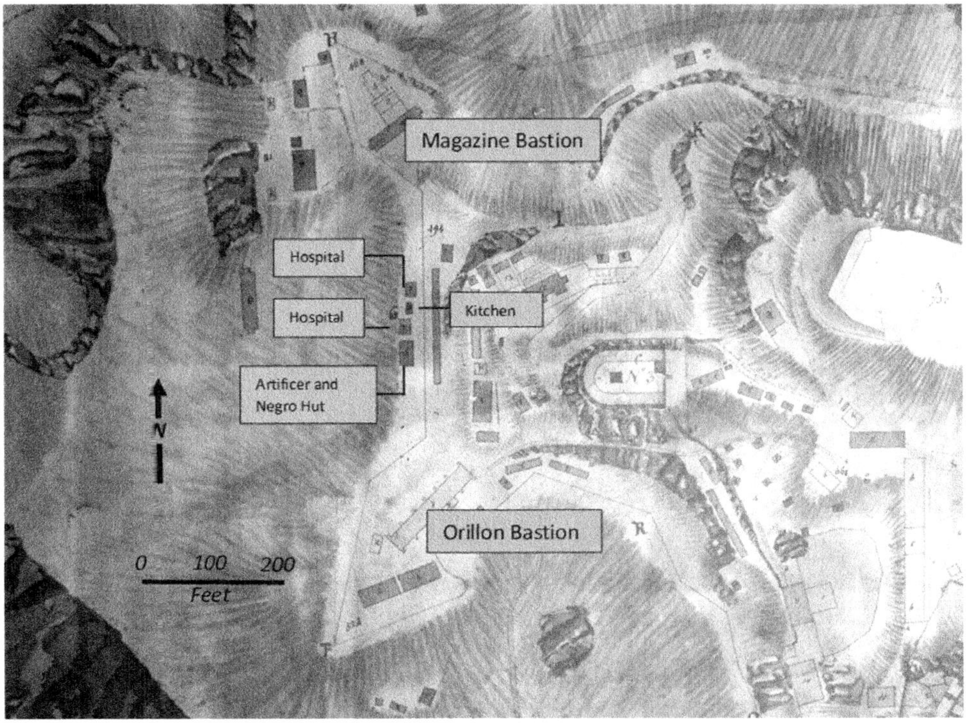

Fig. 6.3. Buildings occupied by enslaved Africans located between the Orillon and Magazine Bastions.

houses associated with slave villages shown in several other images, suggesting that they represent a village where enslaved Africans who worked at Brimstone resided. This would have been an ideal location for housing enslaved laborers, as it was well away from militarily sensitive areas, especially ordnance stores, and was immediately accessible for off-loading cargo and moving materials to nearby job sites. Except for the suggestion of Lees' images, there is no mention of slaves residing in this area.

Besides the buildings between the Orillon and Magazine Bastions, five other buildings utilized by slaves are among the structures designated on the 1791 Royal Engineers map. Two are situated at the foot of the hill and are associated with the limekiln industrial complex where archaeological investigations were made in 1996. The third occurs among the buildings and structures forming the Royal Engineers quarters, situated between the curtain wall connecting the Orillon and Magazine Bastions and the Prince of Wales Bastion. The fourth building is located south and down slope of the Orillon Bastion in association with the Clerk of Works and Deputy Storekeepers quarters, and a fifth structure is found at the north side of the parade ground. Lees, in 1792, also simply states that he built nine additional 'Negroe Hutts' each measuring 8ft by 8ft. It is undetermined where these might have been located and whether any are shown but not labeled on the 1791 map.[79]

THE LIMEKILN INDUSTRIAL COMPLEX – EXCAVATIONS

In 1996, archaeological studies were conducted in the limekiln industrial complex at the foot of the north side of the hill adjacent to the hill's primary access road.[80] This complex was built here because there is abundant limestone exposed at the base of the hill. A secondary road existed here early in the 18th century but the present road was not finished until the early 1790s.[81] One of the two buildings labeled as a Negro hut on the 1791 map was replaced about 1810–13 with a structure used for storing lime following its production in the nearby limekiln. The second building occupied by slaves is the first in a line of five structures adjacent to left side of the road ascending the hill. This building was probably destroyed in an 1813 flood that severely damaged the lime storage building and well house, so much so that both were demolished and rebuilt.[82] It is unknown whether or not the slave structure was in use at this time, but it was not rebuilt. The other four buildings include two masons' and carpenters' work sheds and two master artificers' and foremens' houses. The latter two dwellings were unoccupied in September 1799.[83] The BSH 1 site numbers designate the well (Structure 1), lime storage building (Structure 2), limekiln (Structure 3), and the ruins of two other buildings (Structures 4 and 5).

Structure 1 (well)

The well is located adjacent to the north or left side of the main entrance road to the fortress. The structure has an outside diameter of 3.4m and an inside diameter of 2.2m. The wall is *c.* 0.6m thick. The well's depth is undetermined. A stone platform measuring approximately 5.5m on a side and approximately 1.5m wide surrounds the well on the north and west sides. No excavations were conducted at this structure.

Structure 2 (lime storage building)

The lime storage building is located adjacent to the main entrance road approximately 50m from the well and approximately 30m down slope from Structure 3, the limekiln (Fig. 6.4). Structure 2 measures *c.* 9.9m long and 5.2m wide. The masonry walls are 0.60–0.65m thick and are 0.47m–2.32m high. The only opening is a doorway approximately 1m wide near the structure's north-east corner. Excavations show that the structure has a hard-packed mortar floor and that the building originally was roofed with slate shingles. Recovered wire nails suggest that the roof was replaced in the early 20th century with wood shingles or possibly tin sheet metal.

Excavations consisted of three trenches of contiguous one-meter squares or units. The first trench was excavated perpendicular to the west exterior wall and uncovered a cache of 38 cannonballs. The second trench, consisting of five units forming a transect across the structure's interior revealed the structure's floor and slate shingles representing roof collapse into the building's interior. The third trench was three units excavated perpendicular and exterior to the building's north wall. It revealed two superimposed hard-packed mortar floors. All the excavated sediments at BSH 1 were screened through quarter-inch mesh hardware clothe.

Fig. 6.4. Lime storage building, Structure 2, at BSH 1.

Structure 3 (limekiln)

The limekiln is located *c.* 4m higher on a comparatively level bench less than 30m east-southeast of Structure 2. The kiln is a large cylindrical open-topped structure with two supporting buttresses and two draw holes or eyes. A set of steps on the west side ascends to the top of the structure where it was loaded for firing. Rollinson was unable to determine if the structure is a draw or flare type kiln, both of which were used in the 18th century.[84] Rollinson indicates that a platform near the draw holes was where the fired-lime was crushed and sieved and that a slide or shoot must have been used to deliver the lime down the hill to the storage building.[85] A kiln was probably built at Brimstone Hill early in the history of the fort; the kiln at BSH 1 dates before 1778.

Structure 4

Structure 4 represents one of the work sheds or dwellings recorded at the site and consists of a stone foundation located adjacent to the left or north side of the road

Fig. 6.5. Workshop or dwelling, Structure 4, at BSH 1.

approximately 50m east and upslope from Structure 2 (Fig. 6.5). The north, south, and west foundation walls are visible at the surface. The building was 4.9m wide and more than 5.0m long; the walls are 0.60–0.75m thick and 0.70–0.85m high. Along each exterior wall are five notches each measuring approximately 0.11m square and spaced at 0.82–1.19m intervals. Vertical timbers were set in these recesses to form the building's walls. No doorway or window openings were detected, although recovered shutter hardware indicates their occurrence.

Structure 4 excavations consisted of individually placed one-meter squares exterior to the north-east corner and south walls and a trench of contiguous one-meter squares 7m long bisecting the structure's interior. The building has a mortared stone floor. Rubble was used to level the building's east end.

Structure 5

Structure 5 is located immediately adjacent to the road approximately 70m upslope from Structure 4. Most of it has been lost to erosion of the Sandy Point Ghut and encroachment of the fort's access road. Excavations consisted of four 1m by 1m units. Structure 5 consists of a corner portion of a north oriented foundation wall and two other disconnected wall remnants. The corner walls are 3.45m and 0.80m long. Hard packed mortar floors are evident interior and exterior to the walls and there is a mortar sill along one wall. Four notches in the wall comparable to those associated with Structure 4 indicate vertical post wall construction. Although poorly preserved, it too probably is one of the work sheds or dwellings recorded at the site in 1791.

THE LIMEKILN INDUSTRIAL COMPLEX – ASSOCIATED ARTIFACTS

Nails (n=356), metal (n=553), and construction material (pieces of slate and brick) (n=1,980) are the most frequently recovered materials from BSH 1. Most of the metal was recovered from Structure 2 (n=543) with only 9 metal artifacts from Structure 4 and 1 from Structure 5. The metal from Structure 2 was mostly thin pieces that could have been from tin roofing. Strap iron, probably from barrel hoops, building hardware, and unidentifiable iron were the next most frequently identified metal items. The construction material was primarily recovered from Structures 2 (n=1,237) and 4 (n=742). Only a brick fragment was found at Structure 5. Roofing slate is the most frequent construction material at both Structures 2 (n=1,233) and 4 (n=725). Both buildings had a slate roof while occupied in the 18th and 19th centuries.

The nails represent an interesting insight into the histories of Structures 2, 4, and 5. The recovered nails from Structures 4 (n=89) and 5 (n=9) are all wrought, which is consistent with the 18th- or early 19th-century construction of the buildings. This nail size is consistent with framing and interior finishing. The nails from Structure 2 (n=258) include 20th-century wire nails (n=163), 18th- and 19th-century wrought nails (n=84), 19th-century cut nails (n=2), and nails of unknown manufacturing (n=7). The wrought nails are mostly roofing and framing sized nails and are from the slate roof. The wire nails are primarily roofing nails and show that the roof of the lime storage building was replaced in the early 20th century and that the building was in use at that time.

A total of 91 ceramic sherds was recovered from the BSH 1 investigations of Structures 2 (n=39) and 4 (n=52). No ceramics were found at Structure 5. The 39 ceramic sherds from around Structure 2 are all non-local and include stoneware (n=10), porcelain (n=1), 19th-century whiteware (n=12), late 18th-century to early 19th-century creamware (n=6) and pearlware (n=7), and 18th-century earthenware (n=2) and Chinese Export Porcelain (n=1). Other than three sherds of redware that may date from the early to mid 18th century, 45 non-local ceramics sherds are creamware and pearlware that date to the late 18th to early 19th century. One sherd of Afro-Caribbean ware was recovered from Structure 4. Three whiteware sherds, dating to 1820 and after, were also recovered. For the most part, the ceramics date to the occupation and use of Structures 2 and 4 and are comparable to most areas of Brimstone Hill where excavations have been made (see below).[86] There is little to distinguish them as being used by enslaved Africans.

Glass is one of the most frequently recorded artifacts at Brimstone Hill, but comparatively few glass fragments (n=92) were recovered during the BSH 1 investigations.[87] Most of the glass was recovered from Structures 4 and 5 (Table 6.1). Most identifiable vessel forms are liquor related bottles (amber, dark green, and green colored glass) and colorless lamp chimney glass. The preponderance of liquor related vessel forms is consistent with other sites excavated at Brimstone Hill.

Table 6.1. Recovered glass from BSH 1.

Glass color	*Structure 2*	*Structure 4*	*Structure 5*	*Total*
Amber		1	1	2
Aqua			1	1
Blue/green			2	2
Colorless		12	8	20
Dark green	1	43	11	55
Green		8	4	12
Total	1	64	27	92

HOUSING FOR ENSLAVED AFRICANS

Situated a few meters from the defensive wall connecting the Orillon and Magazine Bastions are the four buildings, including two hospitals, a kitchen, and a Negro hut or dwelling that were occupied by enslaved Africans (Fig. 6.6). One hospital and the hut that also served as a work shed have been excavated.[88] There is no question that James Lees erected these structures in 1789–90 to house slaves that the St Kitts colonial government purchased to work at the site for two years. Except for a few artifacts, there is no evidence for any previous occupation or construction at this location. The

Fig. 6.6. Excavations of structures located between the Orillon and Magazine Bastions associated with enslaved Africans, view north toward the Magazine Bastion.

structures were demolished or abandoned certainly no later than 1810–15, and possibly as early as 1792–3 after the slaves' employment period expired and Lees had been recalled to England for his court martial. Both buildings, being wood construction on masonry foundations, would have deteriorated rapidly in the tropical climate.

Coincidental with the structures' abandonment was the establishment of the Non-Commissioned Officers cemetery in the Orillon Bastion, the bastion's progressively greater dedication to hospital facilities, the accumulation of refuse from the surrounding area, and the intentional deposit of a meter or more fill over the slave structures to accommodate expanded cemetery space for British soldiers.[89] Fill and refuse came from soldiers' barracks and officers' quarters situated above the defensive wall and from the ordnance yard and workshop in the Orillon Bastion as well as perhaps other areas of the fort. The number of soldiers interred between the Orillon Bastion and Magazine Bastions is unknown because with few exceptions the graves are unmarked. Excavations of the hospital and hut identified two north–south rows of graves. In some places the burial pits removed segments of the workshop's east wall, while others intrude the interior floor. There is no skeletal or cultural evidence that any of the graves represent enslaved Africans.[90]

HOSPITAL AND HUT EXCAVATIONS

From 1996 to 1999, and again in 2004, contiguous excavations of $132m^2$ in an area 7m by 25m uncovered nearly the entire footprint of the hut and work shed (Structure 2) and one hospital (Structure 1) (Fig. 6.7). Excavation of an additional eleven 1m by 1m units failed to locate the kitchen and second hospital. Erosion has damaged and removed most of the west walls of both excavated structures. The buildings are aligned north–south, parallel with and about 5m distance from the curtain wall connecting the Orillon and Magazine Bastions. This would have formed a convenient passage between the buildings and defensive wall and would have provided a shaded work or rest area throughout the day. The alignment of the buildings is off-set about 1m and

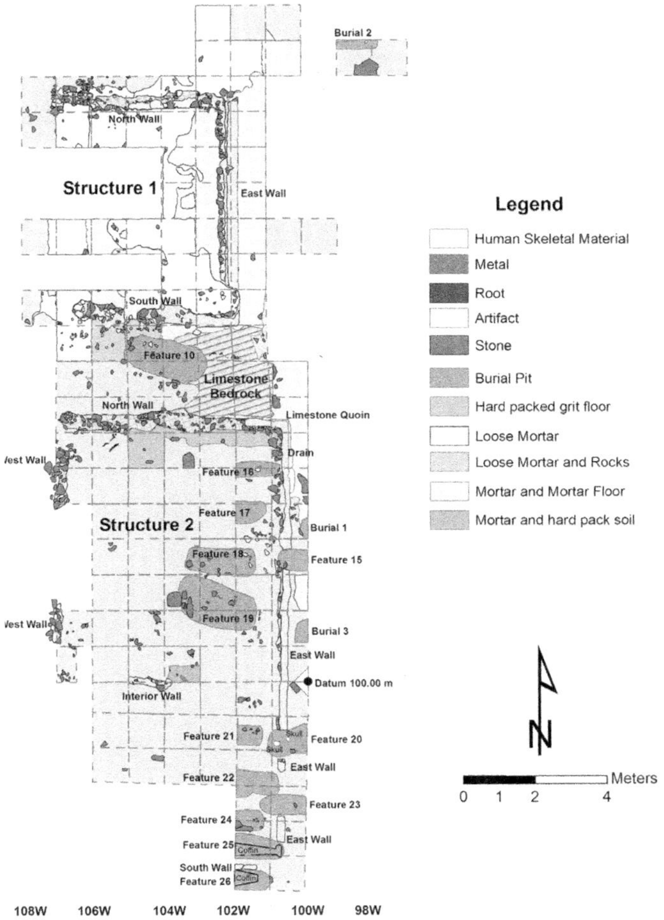

Fig. 6.7. Excavation plot of Structures 1 and 2 at BSH 2.

there is a limestone outcrop about 3m on a side that separates the two structures. All the sediments were removed in 0.1m levels and screened through quarter-inch mesh hardware clothe.

Structure 1 (hospital)

The hospital (Structure 1) is 6.5m long and approximately 5m wide (Fig. 6.8). These dimensions are the same as Lees recorded in 1792 (16ft by 20ft). The building consists of a narrow mortar and rubble stone foundation, 0.20m to 0.30m wide, and a 0.30m wide mortar sill running the length of the east wall and a segment of the south wall. No wall openings or interior partitions were detected in the excavated portion of the building. Most of the west half of the building's walls have been lost to erosion. The structure floor is hard-packed mortar and there is a 0.29m deep, square (0.40m by

Fig. 6.8. Hospital building, Structure 1, at BSH 2.

0.40m) post hole 0.65m from the mid-point of the east wall. The floor rests directly on a meter or more of hardened mortar and mortar rubble which served to level the area for construction. A mortar floor exterior to the structure's north, south, and east sides extends beyond the limits of the excavation.

Structure 2 (Negro hut and work shed)

The Negro hut or dwelling (Structure 2), located approximately 3m south of the hospital building, is approximately 6.3m wide and 12.6m long or 20ft by 40ft as Lees specified in 1792 (Fig. 6.9). The building's walls are stone rubble measuring approximately 0.60m thick and there is a mortar sill, similar to the one associated with the hospital building, on the east wall and portions of the south and north walls. A mortar floor

Fig. 6.9. Negro hut and work shed, Structure 2, at BSH 2.

occurs on the building's east exterior side, and there is a narrow open drain at the base of the foundation. The structure's floor is poorly defined, consisting of small, angular pebbles and mortar fragments. Excavations identified no interior posts, partitions, wall openings, or other structural features within the building. Twelve burial pits intrude the deposits that accumulated or were dumped within the structure's interior and penetrate through the building's floor. Six of the graves, in addition, were dug through and removed sections of the structure's foundation and mortar sill.

HOSPITAL AND NEGRO HUT ASSOCIATED ARTIFACTS

Artifacts attesting to the presence of enslaved Africans are: Afro-Caribbean ceramics, ceramic gaming discs, British made ceramics scratched with a variety of symbols and geometric patterns, and small numbers of cowry shells and glass beads. Faunal remains include cattle and pig, most of which was imported, and goat and sheep that were locally raised. Also found were skeletal remains of local and imported fish. Nearly 10,000 bone discs, and bone waste from their manufacture, were recovered adjacent to the exterior east walls of the two buildings. So much bone button manufacturing probably occurred here because this area was shaded most of the day, first by the fortress curtain wall early in the day and then by the building in the afternoon.

The discussion here focuses on materials that are directly related to Structures 1 and 2, pre-date the two structures, come from the disposal midden directly above Structures 1 and 2, north of the two structures, and from level 1 across the site where there may have been mixing between modern, disposal midden, and enslaved African context artifacts. A total of 96,485 artifacts were recovered from the BSH 2 excavations.[91]

Ceramics

A total of 32,337 ceramic sherds was recovered from the BSH 2 investigations included in this study (Table 6.2). The majority of the 191 sherds of Afro-Caribbean ware, a pottery made by enslaved and freed Africans throughout the Caribbean, probably was produced on nearby Nevis or St Kitts' south-east peninsula.[92] The occurrence of the pottery throughout the deposits suggests the ware was used from the mid 18th century to the early 19th century by a wide range of fort occupants. Compared to plantation contexts on St Kitts, the frequency of Afro-Caribbean ware from BSH 2 is relatively low suggesting that enslaved Africans at Brimstone Hill were not using and acquiring Afro-Caribbean wares at rates similar to enslaved Africans in plantation contexts.[93]

The vast majority (n=32,146) of the recovered ceramics are non-local wares from Britain/England, Holland, Germany, China, and possibly France. The most frequently occurring wares are British/English creamware (n=17,977, 55.9%), pearlware (n=9,146, 28.5%), and redware (n=1,549, 4.8%). Only 2,934 (9.1%) sherds of the non-local ceramics that date from the late 17th to mid-to-late 18th century were recovered. A third of these sherds (n=997, 33.3%) came from the disposal midden above Structures 1 and 2 and a little more than a quarter (n=766, 26.1%) came from around Structures 1 and 2. Only about 5% (n=143) of these earlier ceramics come from levels below Structures 1 and 2.

Table 6.2. Recovered non-local wares from BSH 2.

Time period	*Ware*	*Level 1*	*Midden above structures*	*Structures 1 and 2*	*Pre-date structures*	*Northern end of BSH 2*	*Total*
17th–20th century	Afro-Caribbean Ware	35	51	53	6	46	191
18th century	Black Basalt	4	15	14			33
	British Bone Porcelain	9	27	15	1	4	56
18th century	Chinese Export Porcelain	57	122	78	6	13	276
1762–1820	Creamware	3,791	7,637	4,982	720	847	17,977
18th century	Devonshire sand temper		2	1		1	4
18th–19th century	Earthenware	59	258	214	44	48	623
1814–1900	Ironstone	20	36	16			72
1765–1820	Pearlware	1,794	4,067	2,359	408	518	9,146
	Porcelain	20	33	12	3		68
18th–19th century	Redware	287	559	441	92	170	1,549
18th century	Refined redware	4	22	12			38
	Rhenish Stoneware	4	2	6			12
17th–19th century	Stoneware	377	682	359	62	63	1,543
1820–1900	Whiteware	133	195	15	3	4	350
18th–19th century	Yellowware	95	166	97	15	26	399
	Total	6,689	13,874	8,674	1,360	1,740	32,337

The vast majority of the non-local ceramics (n=27,548, 85.7 %) include creamware, pearlware, whiteware, and ironstone that date to the last quarter of the 18th century to the mid 19th century (Table 6.2). This increase in the disposal of non-local sherds in the last quarter of the 18th century corresponds with the increase of consumerism in the Caribbean[94] and, more importantly, the occupation of the structures in the 1790s, and subsequent use of the area for trash disposal and the intentional deposit of artifact laden fill.

Forty-three different vessel forms were identified in the ceramic assemblage (Table 6.3). There is an almost equal number of vessel forms from Structures 1 and 2 (n=34) and the disposal midden deposits (n=35) and far fewer forms (n=25) from the levels that pre-date the structures. This increase in the diversity of vessel forms probably reflects the increased consumerism from the late 18th century to the mid 19th century and the prevailing Georgian mindset that influenced patterns of domesticity and food service. From the early 18th century to the mid 19th century, the vessel forms are predominately serving vessels (around 84% of the recovered sherds). As elsewhere at Brimstone Hill, the infrequent occurrence of vessels relating to food storage and preparation reflect the communal nature of food preparation at military sites (Table 6.3). Sherds relating to the tea service (cups, saucers, and teapots) comprise from 13% to 15% of the recovered ceramic materials (Table 6.3). Even within the enslaved African contexts of Structures 1 and 2, tea service-related sherds make up 13% of the recovered ceramic sherds. This percentage is higher than that seen at some plantation contexts on St Kitts.

The ceramic sherds exhibit 48 interior and 48 exterior decorative techniques. Around 60% of the sherds are undecorated, which is lower than the overall Brimstone Hill ceramic assemblage.[95] Some of the most frequently occurring decorative techniques are hand painted (n=3,744), mocha/annular/dipped (n=1,903), Royal Pattern and Queens Shape (n=1,656), salt glazed (n=1,002), lead glazed (n=945), edge decorated (n=712), transfer printed (n=703), slip decorated (n=682), and tin glazed (n=384). These decorative techniques are fairly consistent across all the deposits, suggesting that enslaved Africans at BSH 2 had access to these materials equal to British soldiers and officers.

Ceramics scratched with a variety of different letters, geometric designs, and irregular patterns and shapes have been found at Brimstone Hill.[96] Most of the designs are geometric in nature with some letters, Xs, or crosses. From the contexts investigated at BSH 2, there were 157 sherds with some kind of scratched design on the exterior or interior surface. The greatest number of scratched sherds (n=83) came from the midden deposits above Structures 1 and 2 and probably originated from a variety of contexts around Brimstone Hill. About 36% of the scratched ceramic sherds (n=57) came from the vicinity of Structures 1 and 2. Five scratched sherds came from contexts below the structures and 12 came from north of the structures.

The marks only occur on creamware (n=158) and pearlware (n=19), suggesting that scratching ceramics was limited to about a 60-year period and quite possibly to the 1790s when the British government garrisoned more men at the fort and had the highest number of enslaved Africans working there. Most of the scratched sherds are undecorated (n=146), seven are blue hand painted, and four are mocha/dipped

Table 6.3. Ceramic vessel forms from BSH 2.

Vessel form	*Function*	*Level 1*	%	*Disposal midden above structures*	%	*Structures 1 and 2*	%	*Pre-dates structures*	%	*Northern end of BSH 2*	%	*Total*	%
Colander	Food preparation	1	0.01	3	0.02		0.00		0.00		0.00	4	0.01
Flat pan	Food preparation	1	0.01		0.00		0.00		0.00		0.00	1	0.00
Jug	Food preparation	13	0.19	90	0.65	37	0.43	7	0.51	8	0.46	155	0.48
Large bowl	Food preparation	36	0.54	93	0.67	79	0.91	15	1.10	17	0.98	240	0.74
Large pot	Food preparation		0.00	2	0.01	6	0.07		0.00		0.00	8	0.02
Pot	Food preparation	2	0.03	6	0.04	2	0.02	1	0.07	10	0.57	21	0.06
Crock	Food Storage	53	0.79	110	0.79	62	0.71	17	1.25	14	0.80	256	0.79
Cylindrical jar	Food Storage	1	0.01		0.00	2	0.02		0.00		0.00	3	0.01
Jar	Food Storage	22	0.33	99	0.71	80	0.92	2	0.15	27	1.55	230	0.71
Bowl	Serving	705	10.54	1570	11.33	1184	13.65	177	13.01	356	20.46	3992	12.34
Coffee pot	Serving	2	0.03	8	0.06	16	0.18		0.00		0.00	26	0.08
Creamer	Serving	7	0.10	9	0.06	8	0.09	2	0.15	5	0.29	31	0.10
Flatware	Serving	1381	20.65	2673	19.30	1599	18.43	267	19.63	274	15.75	6194	19.15
Goblet	Serving		0.00	2	0.01		0.00		0.00		0.00	2	0.01

Table 6.3 *continued*

Vessel form	*Function*	*Level 1*	%	*Disposal midden above structures*	%	*Structures 1 and 2*	%	*Pre-dates structures*	%	*Northern end of BSH 2*	%	*Total*	%
Hollowware	Serving	1081	16.16	2191	15.82	1420	16.37	216	15.88	263	15.11	5171	15.99
Muffin plate	Serving		0.00	3	0.02	12	0.14	3	0.22		0.00	18	0.06
Mug	Serving	134	2.00	239	1.73	297	3.42	20	1.47	52	2.99	742	2.29
Pitcher	Serving	174	2.60	312	2.25	282	3.25	44	3.24	156	8.97	968	2.99
Plate	Serving	596	8.91	1257	9.07	720	8.30	136	10.00	60	3.45	2769	8.56
Platter	Serving	25	0.37	55	0.40	21	0.24	6	0.44	3	0.17	110	0.34
Serving bowl	Serving	12	0.18	39	0.28	30	0.35	1	0.07	13	0.75	95	0.29
Small bowl	Serving	2	0.03	2	0.01		0.00		0.00	2	0.11	6	0.02
Small plate	Serving	6	0.09	12	0.09	7	0.08	1	0.07	7	0.40	33	0.10
Soup plate	Serving	42	0.63	291	2.10	204	2.35	31	2.28	43	2.47	611	1.89
Sugar bowl	Serving	14	0.21	32	0.23	4	0.05		0.00	1	0.06	51	0.16
Tankard	Serving	4	0.06		0.00	1	0.01	1	0.07	5	0.29	11	0.03
Tureen	Serving	1	0.01	7	0.05	11	0.13	5	0.37	1	0.06	25	0.08
Wastebowl	Serving		0.00		0.00		0.00		0.00	1	0.06	1	0.00
Crucible	Serving	2	0.03	7	0.05	36	0.42		0.00		0.00	45	0.14
Advertising lid	Storage		0.00	4	0.03		0.00		0.00		0.00	4	0.01
Bottle	Storage	74	1.11	162	1.17	150	1.73	15	1.10	27	1.55	428	1.32
Cup	Tea service	503	7.52	1055	7.62	656	7.56	131	9.63	171	9.83	2516	7.78
Saucer	Tea service	323	4.83	668	4.82	413	4.76	62	4.56	94	5.40	1560	4.82

Table 6.3 *continued*

Vessel form	*Function*	*Level 1*	%	*Disposal midden above structures*	%	*Structures 1 and 2*	%	*Pre-dates structures*	%	*Northern end of BSH 2*	%	*Total*	%
Teapot	Tea service	35	0.52	78	0.56	71	0.82	5	0.37	3	0.17	192	0.59
Chamber pot			0.00	1	0.01		0.00		0.00	1	0.06	2	0.01
Ink bottle		4	0.06	11	0.08	8	0.09	3	0.22	1	0.06	27	0.08
Inkwell			0.00	7	0.05	2	0.02		0.00		0.00	9	0.03
Lid		15	0.22	9	0.06	11	0.13		0.00	5	0.29	40	0.12
Salt shaker			0.00		0.00	1	0.01		0.00		0.00	1	0.00
Spout		1	0.01		0.00		0.00		0.00	1	0.06	2	0.01
Stopper		1	0.01		0.00	1	0.01		0.00		0.00	2	0.01
Swizzle stick		1	0.01		0.00		0.00		0.00		0.00	1	0.00
Unknown		1415	21.15	2767	19.98	1241	14.31	192	14.12	119	6.84	5734	17.73
Total		6689	100	13874	100	8674	100	1360	100	1740	100	32337	100

decorated. The lack of decoration is not surprising as the majority of the scratched sherds (n=133) come from the base portion of flatware vessels such as plates, platters, saucers, and soup plates. The hollowware vessel forms include bowls, serving bowls, and pitchers.

As Schroedl and Ahlman note, soldiers and enslaved Africans at Brimstone Hill lived in similar communal settings and probably scratched ceramics with markers of ownership and personal identity.[97] British soldiers and enslaved African used marks, such as letters, geometric designs, and/or religious symbols, that were most familiar and held significance to them but may not have had meaning to others. The idea of scratching ownership or identity markings on ceramics was rare as only 0.5% of the ceramic sherds were scratched. Even across Brimstone Hill, scratched ceramics are relatively scarce. Nevertheless, scratched ceramics are found in a variety of contexts throughout the Caribbean and around the world suggesting that this is a widespread practice, although restricted to a small number of vessels.[98]

As noted above, the relative frequency of ceramics greatly increases in the late 18th century and continues through the early 19th century. The decrease in the frequency of ceramic sherds dating to the mid 19th century (whiteware and ironstone in particular) represents both the occupational abandonment of BSH 2 and gradual reduction of troop strengths across the fortress at that time. Although the majority of ceramics are undecorated, there is a wide range of decorative techniques that suggest individuals were bringing some of the ceramics to the fortress throughout its occupation. It is probable that the British military supplied most of the undecorated or minimally decorated (for example edge decorated wares) vessels. Some soldiers and enslaved Africans were marking their individual vessels to distinguish them from what was supplied by the government. Officers may have purchased or brought their own ceramics such as porcelains, transfer printed and painted wares, and serving vessels like tureens.

Bottle glass

A total of 45,799 glass sherds was recovered from the BSH 2 excavations in this analysis and glass sherds are the most frequently recovered artifacts from the site (Table 6.4). Around 72.4% of the glass (n=33,163) was recovered from the disposal midden above Structures 1 and 2 and probably came from different contexts around Brimstone Hill. About 20.2% of the glass (n=9,211) came from direct association with Structures 1 and 2. Lower frequencies of glass came from deposits pre-dating Structures 1 and 2 (n=1,940, 4.2%) and north of the two structures (n=1,485, 3.2%).

As found elsewhere at Brimstone Hill, the bulk of the glass is dark green bottle glass from wine and liquor bottles (n=30,215, 66%) and represents the mass consumption of alcohol by soldiers and enslaved Africans.[99] The disposal midden above Structures 1 and 2 has the highest frequency of dark green bottle glass (n=21,346) and, compared to the other deposits, represents the lowest percentage (64.4%) of the glass from this context. The dark green glass from Structures 1 and 2 (n=6,196) represents 67.3% of the glass from these contexts. Below and to the north of Structures 1 and 2, dark green glass is 78.4% (n=1,521) and 77.6% (n=1,152) of the glass from these contexts. Of the identifiable vessel forms, most are from wine and liquor bottles (n=23,547) and case

Table 6.4. Recovered glass from BSH 2 by color.

Glass color	*Level 1*	*Disposal midden above structures*	*Structures 1 and 2*	*Pre-date structures*	*Northern end of BSH 2*	*Total*
Amber	31	545	76	13		665
Amethyst	4	4	4	7	1	20
Aqua	61	149	34	17	36	297
Black	5			2		7
Blue			1		2	3
Blue/green	1					1
Cobalt blue	2	5	1			8
Colorless	734	1,801	916	226	281	3,958
Dark green	7,243	14,103	6,196	1,521	1,152	30,215
Emerald	42	33	48		8	131
Green	25	51	4			80
Light Green	775	7,537	1,928	152	5	10,397
Milk glass	1	3	2	2		8
Purple		1				1
Unknown	2		1			3
Yellow	1	4				5
Total	8,927	24,236	9,211	1,940	1,485	45,799

bottles (n=4,700). From the disposal midden above Structures 1 and 2, 80% of the dark green glass comes from liquor and wine bottles and 13% comes from case bottles. The dark green glass from around Structures 1 and 2 is 74% liquor and wine bottle glass and 18% case bottle. From the deposits pre-dating the two structures, the dark green glass is 66% liquor and wine bottle glass and 25% from case bottles. Liquor consumption glass such as tumblers (n=2,082), stemware (n=69), and shot glasses (n=11) are relatively infrequent in the assemblage suggesting that alcoholic beverages were not always consumed from glassware.

The volume of glass relating to alcohol storage, serving, and consumption makes it clear that British soldiers and officers and enslaved Africans had easy access to wine, rum, and gin from the mid 18th century to the early 19th century. Rum and wine were provided by the British military to soldiers and locally made rum and moonshine (green rum) were often purchased by soldiers and enslaved Africans.[100] Officers purchased liquor and wine for their own consumption and may have shared with their servants or junior officers.[101]

Alcohol, such as gin and rum, was considered a form of medicine and was often given to soldiers and enslaved Africans for various ailments, which may explain the relatively higher percentage of case bottles from around Structures 1 (the hospital) and 2.[102] There are few sherds from medicine bottles (n=21) and vials (n=27) associated with either building. Although somewhat surprising, this is consistent with excavations of the soldiers' hospital and related structures in the nearby Orillon Bastion that have produced no medicine bottles.[103] Other glass sherds represent chimney glass, serving bowls, pitchers, soda bottles, and food storage jars. Overall, these sherds make up around 1.3% of the glass assemblage. An additional 6.2% of the glass assemblage was unidentifiable to vessel form.

Military, personal, and miscellaneous items

A total of 770 military (n=295), personal (n=154), and miscellaneous (n=321) items was recovered from BSH 2 (Table 6.5). The military items are mostly musket balls (n=143), military buttons (n=45), and gun flints (40). A surprising number of military buttons (n=11) and musket balls (n=51) were found in the Structures 1 and 2 deposits. Eleven gun flints, found in association with the structures, is not surprising as gun flints and other fire starters have been found in enslaved African contexts throughout the Caribbean.[104]

Items like buttons (n=108), ceramic gaming pieces (n=14), and buckles (n=10) are just some of the clothing, gaming, and jewelry pieces that represent non-military related personal items found at BSH 2. The gaming items (bone domino, ceramic gaming pieces, and marbles) suggest that British soldiers and enslaved Africans used a variety of items and games to pass the time and entertain themselves while at Brimstone Hill. The cowry shell is a direct indicator of the enslaved African presence at BSH 2 and the retention of an African cultural practice.

A variety of other items are not necessarily military or personal in nature and were grouped into a miscellaneous category. This category includes eating utensils (n=41), non-clothing buckles (n=23), straight pins (n=32), lithic flakes (n=23), and pebbles (n=16). Numerous pieces of brass, lead, and iron objects also were found, but were not identifiable to a specific function or use.

Smoking pipe fragments are a common artifact at BSH 2 and a total of 2,822 fragments were found. The majority (n=1,792) come from the disposal midden above Structures 1 and 2. About a quarter of the smoking pipe fragments (n=701) were recovered from around Structures 1 and 2, with the remaining examples derived from deposits below the structures (n=132) and the north end of the excavation (n=197). Most are stem fragments (n=1,607) and the rest are bowl fragments (n=1,215). Pipe stem bore diameters were recorded with drill bits to determine dates for the pipe stem fragments. The majority of the recovered pipe stems across all the contexts have a 5/64in bore diameter (Table 6.6), which is consistent with previous research at Brimstone Hill.[105] Using the Harrington Method for pipe stem dating, the pipes date between 1650 and 1780 with the majority dating to 1710–50.[106] As Hill and Schroedl found, pipe stem dating tends to be 50–75 years earlier than the expected occupation period of the sites at Brimstone Hill.[107]

Table 6.5. Military, personal, and miscellaneous items from BSH 2.

Description	*Level 1*	*Disposal midden above structures*	*Structures 1 and 2*	*Pre-date structures*	*Northern end of BSH 2*	*Total*
Military						
Bayonet Fragment			2			2
Button	8	19	11	1	6	45
Canister Shot	2	1	4	1		8
Cannonball		3	1	1		5
Grape Shot	4	7	1	1		13
Gun Flint	8	20	11	1		40
Gun Part	1	4				5
Lock Plate			1			1
Military Pin					1	1
Mortar	1	3	3			7
Musket Ball	24	54	51	5	9	143
Percussion Cap		4				4
Ram rod holder		1				1
Rifle Butt Plate			1			1
Shako Plate	3	9	2			14
Striking Plate		1				1
Trigger Guard			1	1		2
Uniform Braid Tip					2	2
Military Total	51	126	89	11	18	295
Personal						
Bead		2				2
Bone Domino	1					1
Buckle	2	4	1	1	2	10
Button	17	57	26	4	4	108
Coin		4	1			5
Cowry Shell			1			1

Table 6.5 *continued*

Description	*Level 1*	*Disposal midden above structures*	*Structures 1 and 2*	*Pre-date structures*	*Northern end of BSH 2*	*Total*
Cross		1		1		2
Cuff Link		2				2
Ceramic Gaming Piece	1	4	6		3	14
Jewelry		2			1	3
Marble		1	2			3
Ring	1					1
Thimble		1				1
Writing Slate	1					1
Personal Total	23	78	37	6	10	154
Miscellaneous						
Variety of Metal Objects	30	64	36	4	13	147
Brass Disk	3		2			5
Buckle	12	5	5		1	23
Drawer Pull	1	4				5
Eating Utensil	5	23	11	1	1	41
Fishhook		1	2			3
Fossil	3	5	4			12
Key	1	3	1		1	6
Lead Disk		2				2
Lithic Core	1	2	1			4
Lithic Flake	3	11	8	1		23
Lithic Pebble	3	7	4	2		16
Pin		10	22			32
Toothbrush	2					2
Miscellaneous Total	64	137	96	8	16	321
Grand Total	138	341	222	25	44	770

Table 6.6. Pipe stem bore diameters from BSH 2.

Bore diameter	*Temporal period*	*Level 1*	*Disposal midden above structures*	*Structures 1 and 2*	*Pre-date structures*	*Northern end of BSH 2*	*Total*
4/64	1750–80	6	22	20	2	2	52
5/64	1710–50	174	267	213	46	98	798
6/64	1680-1710	29	45	26	6	14	120
7/64	1650–80	1			1		2
Total		210	334	259	55	114	972

Most of the military, personal, smoking pipe, and miscellaneous items came from the midden deposits above Structures 1 and 2. About 30% of the military artifacts come from deposits around Structures 1 and 2 and could have been deposited immediately before or after the structures' occupations. These items may have been picked up or used by enslaved Africans throughout their stay at the fort. The relatively small number of personal items, especially buttons and other clothing related objects, suggests that enslaved Africans either did not stay long at the fortress or they were given little in the way of clothing, eating utensils, or items for hygiene, or had few opportunities to acquire them.

Metal and nails

Metal (n=6,745) and nails (n=8,008) from BSH 2 represent building construction and a variety of other construction and work-related activities. The metal includes items made from iron, lead, brass, and copper. The most frequently occurring metal pieces are unidentified iron fragments (n=2,657), sheet iron (n=1,910), and strap iron (n=1,335), which make up about 87% of the recovered metal. Most of the strap iron probably came from barrel hoops that were converted into other useable pieces for buildings hardware or tools, or possibly the discard of partially rotted barrels, some containing a variety of trash. Other building-related items include hinges, spikes, staples, washers, screws, pintles, shutter hooks, and lock plates. Work tools include files, an axe, and a pick head. The relative paucity of work-related metal from Structures 1 and 2 deposits is surprising as Structure 2 was also a work shed. The military may have kept tight control of the number and kinds of tools that enslaved Africans were allowed to use, and in addition, few tools of any kind, except for the manufacture of bone discs (see below), may have been employed in and around the structures.

Most of the recovered nails were wrought (n=5,553, 69%) or unidentifiable manufacture (n=2,342, 29%). The remaining nails were cut or tacks/brads. Most of the nails where condition (bent, clinched, or straight) could be identified were bent (n=1,286, 53%) and the rest were straight and clinched (n=1,136, 47%). When examining the contexts closer, most of the nails from the disposal midden above Structures 1 and 2 were clinched and straight (n=611, 76%), suggesting that lumber with nails in it was deposited here rather than nails removed from lumber. The frequency of bent nails (n=361) compared to clinched and straight nails (n=331) from the deposits in Structures 1 and 2 is similar suggesting that the buildings may have been torn down rather than allowed to degrade in place.

Bone discs

Abundant evidence for the manufacture of single hole bone discs, commonly interpreted as the cores for cloth covered buttons and found in colonial sites throughout the New World, came from BSH 2. These materials have been intensely studied and published elsewhere so only a brief summary of them is included here.[108] Disc, disc fragments, and removals on manufacturing debris total 9,422 discs, ranging from 8mm–32mm in diameter were identified (Table 6.7). Large numbers of discs and manufacturing debris were recovered along the exterior east wall of Structure 2, suggesting that individuals engaged in this activity took advantage of the shade provide by the structure and the nearby curtain wall. Most discs were manufactured from the ribs of both local and imported cattle and the costal bones of sea turtle, although two caprine mandible fragments and a parietal fragment from a horse or donkey are also represented in the sample. In preparation for disc extraction ribs were trimmed along the cranial border and the heads were removed and the resulting pieces were cut into two or more comparatively flat segments. These sections were then split longitudinally forming the blanks from which discs were cut using a brace and button bit. A considerable number of different diameter bits and multiple braces had to have been in use at any one time, although no evidence of these tools was recovered from the excavation. A greater proportion of discs measuring greater than 20mm are made from sea turtle bones because cattle bone blanks are too narrow to make larger sized discs.

Table 6.7. Summary of bone disc diameters from BSH 2 (modified from Klippel & Price 2007: table 2).

Disc diameter (mm)	*Reptile*	*Mammal*	*Unknown*	*Total*	*Percent*
8–11	86	649	5	740	7.8
12–15	2,126	4,361	57	6,544	69.5
16–19	195	708	2	905	9.6
20–3	461	407	1	869	9.2
24–7	99	69	0	168	1.8
28–32	110	83	3	196	2.1
Total	3,077	6,277	68	9,422	100.0

FAUNAL REMAINS

Analyses of animal bones are available only from the 1996 and 1997 excavations.[109] Their characteristics and analysis are presented elsewhere and are only briefly summarized here. Of 6,222 fragments, 1,230 were identified to a taxonomic level below class (Table 6.8). Pig, cattle, sheep/goats are the most abundant animals in the sample, although importantly small numbers of rabbit, chicken, tropical fish, and North Atlantic cod also were recovered. The frequencies of skeletal parts, an assessment of nutritional value (low and high meat utility), and stable carbon isotopes analysis indicate that most beef was introduced as barreled meat that came from Great Britain or North America and that sheep and goats were locally raised for consumption (Table 6.9). Nutritional assessment of pig bones indicates that 68% of the recovered bones represent high food utility, even though a typical suid skeleton is 67% low food utility in contrast to a bovid with a low/high food utility of about 50%. These data strongly suggest that pork was introduced as barreled meat and this included the animal's head.

Table 6.8. Vertebrate remains (NISP) from the 1996 and 1997 excavations at BSH 2 (after Klippel 2001, table 1).

Taxa	*Number*	*Percent*
Mammals		
Pig (Sus scrofa)	457	37.1
Cattle (Bos Taurus)	365	29.7
Sheep/Goat (Caprine)	142	11.5
Sheep (Ovis aries)	11	0.9
Goat (Capra hircus)	8	0.7
Other mammals[1]	57	4.6
Total Mammals	1,040	84.5
Bony Fish (Osteichthyes)[2]	90	7.3
Turtles/Snakes/Lizards (Reptilia)	88	7.2
Birds (Aves)[3]	12	1.0
Total specimens	1,230	100.0

[1] Includes black and brown rat, dog, cat, rabbit and horse or donkey
[2] Includes local tropical taxa and North Atlantic cod
[3] Primarily chicken

The faunal data show that enslaved Africans at BSH 2 were provisioned with barreled pork and beef, the same kinds of foods provided to British soldiers. Whether soldiers and slaves were allotted the same cuts of barreled meat is unknown. Enslaved Africans also had access to locally raised sheep and goats and it is conceivable that some, if not most, of these came from the plantations that sent workers to the fort. The fish bones indicate exploitation of reef and pelagic environments and demonstrate provisioning with preserved fish from North America.

Table 6.9. Combined skeletal parts frequencies and utility index for cattle, pig, and sheep/goats at BSH 2 (based on Klippel 1998, table 5, and figs 1, 2, 3).

Taxon/Portion	*Number*	*Percent*	*Utility Index*
Cattle (Bos taurus)			
head	28	7.7	Low
foot	9	2.5	Low
axial	283	77.5	High
upper limb	45	12.3	High
Total	365	100.0	
Caprines (Sheep/Goats)			
head	69	42.4	Low
foot	27	16.7	Low
axial	14	8.7	High
upper limb	53	32.2	High
Total	163	100.0	
Pig (Sus scrofa)			
head	134	29.3	Low
foot	15	3.3	Low
axial	179	39.2	High
upper limb	129	28.2	High
Total	457	100.0	

SUMMARY AND CONCLUSIONS

Beginning early in the 18th century, the St Kitts colonial government regularly employed large numbers of enslaved Africans to build, renovate, and maintain the Brimstone Hill Fortress. When the size and complexity of the fortress was expanded significantly in the late 18th and early 19th centuries, work forces under the direction of British military engineers reached their greatest size averaging about 100–200 laborers, but sometimes exceeding 600 workers. Plantation owners supplied these workers according to legislation enacted by the St Kitts Assembly and Council. Working conditions including specific tasks, particular building projects, compensation and wages, meals and shelter were negotiated between the colonial government, plantation owners, and military officials. The British military also engaged local contractors who supplied their own laborers as well as hiring free white and black local craftsman. This practice became more prevalent in the 19th century, especially after emancipation. The British army also maintained its own work force of enslaved African workers. While members of this 'Corps of Black Military Artificers and Pioneers' were present at Brimstone Hill, their numbers were never as large as found elsewhere in the Caribbean during the period of slavery. They became more common at the fort in the 19th century. Black military units at Brimstone Hill included contingents of the black militia or 'Corps of Embodied Slaves,' as well as the First, Second, Third, and Fourth West India Regiments. West India Regiment soldiers played a more prominent role in the fort's occupation from the time of emancipation until its closure in the 1850s.

Investigating archaeological deposits attributable to enslaved Africans at Brimstone Hill is an important research goal at the site and this effort has relied on the 1791 Royal Engineers' map of the fortress. Two such areas, shown on the map, are an industrial area at the base of the hill and a complex of four buildings situated between the Orillon and Magazine Bastions. Excavations in both areas have produced a wealth of architectural and artifact data relating to both the British Army and enslaved Africans at Brimstone Hill.

The industrial area (BSH 1) includes five structures, representing a well, lime storage building, limekiln, and two other buildings that were dwellings or work sheds. Two additional structures are no longer extant, and it is known that one of these, identified as a slave structure, was destroyed in an 1813 flood. A second slave structure was converted to the lime storage building probably around 1799 when other buildings in the complex were no longer in use. These data suggest that as the intensity of construction activities abated in the late 1790s and the access road to the hill was completed, the need to maintain resident personnel and dwellings for enslaved workers, masons, and carpenters at the limekiln was reduced or no longer warranted. Few artifacts accumulated in the excavated buildings because of their placement between the road on one side and the Sandy Point Ghut on the other side and because they had so few or no permanent residents. The late 18th- and early 19th-century ceramics from the excavations are consistent with the site's known occupation dates. The ceramics and other material culture from the site such as bottle glass, strap iron, and construction materials provide no distinct signature for the enslaved Africans known to have lived and worked there. Slate, tin sheet fragments, and nails show that the lime storage building was re-roofed several times, and was in use into the late 19th or early 20th century.

The four closely spaced structures (BSH 2) situated between the Orillon and Magazine Bastion were constructed by James Lees, the resident engineer, in 1789–90 specifically to house 120 enslaved Africans purchased by the St Kitts colonial government to work at the site for two years. Two are hospital buildings, both of which, as labeled on the 1791 military engineers' map of the site, were for artificers and colony laborers. The kitchen was placed between these two buildings. No known records indicate why Lees felt it necessary to erect two hospitals at the same location. The labels for the buildings alone, however, suggest that he recognized the need to segregate medical facilities for skilled and unskilled workers, even though both groups included enslaved

Africans. It is also probable that the second hospital was specifically intended for the 120 individuals housed in the adjacent Negro hut.

Excavations at BSH 2 uncovered the Negro hut (Structure 2) and the hospital (Structure 1) closest to it. The investigations were unable to find the other hospital or kitchen. The hospital and Negro hut conform to the dimensions reported by Lees. The structures have stone rubble foundations with mortar sills. The hospital had a mortar floor; the hut's interior floor was covered with angular pebbles and mortar fragments. The hut also served as a work shed for the manufacture of bone discs as thousands of these and the waste from their production were associated with an exterior open drain along the hut's east wall. Here the building's wall and nearby fortification wall would have provided a shady work area through most of the day. The buildings at BSH 2 may have been demolished or allowed to deteriorate shortly after the two-year work assignment was finished. They were then covered with over a meter of fill to allow for the expansion of the Non-Commissioned Officers' cemetery and consequently 12 burial pits intruded the fill, six of which damaged the hut's foundation and mortar sill. The fill undoubtedly came from a variety of occupational contexts, including areas where enslaved Africans lived and worked.

The site stratigraphy and intrusive relationships were used to establish and isolate in the artifact analysis the materials attributable to the enslaved Africans who occupied Structures 1 and 2 from the mixture of trash laden fill covering the buildings and the burials that intrude the deposits. There is little difference between the kinds of non-local ceramic wares and the kinds of vessels obtained by enslaved Africans at BSH 2 and other occupants of Brimstone Hill. Locally made Afro-Caribbean ceramics are found in the structures but their use is not unique to the African occupation. So too are ceramics scratched with a variety of letters, marks, and patterns, but Africans employed symbols to identify their individuality or group membership probably not used by British soldiers. Bottle glass from the excavations indicate that alcoholic drinks were universally available to the Brimstone Hill occupants. About a third of the numerous personal, military, and miscellaneous artifacts came from the excavations of Structures 1 and 2 and suggest that the enslaved occupants accessed ceramic gaming pieces, buttons, buckles, and a variety of other items, although perhaps not as often or in the same quantities as British soldiers. Faunal remains show that enslaved Africans were provisioned with barreled beef and pork and also obtained fresh goat and sheep. Additional, but much smaller numbers of bones indicate the consumption of chicken, rabbit, tropical fish, and North Atlantic cod. Importantly the local fish show that enslaved Africans had the ability to exploit or obtain fish from pelagic and reef environments. The BSH 2 excavations recovered a very large artifact sample representing a diversity of depositional contexts. The comparative study of these remains suggests only subtle differences in the material assemblages of enslaved Africans and British soldiers, indicating that African people living at Brimstone Hill obtained and used many of the same items.

BSH 1 and BSH 2 represent distinct episodes in the occupational history of enslaved Africans at Brimstone Hill. The limekiln industrial complex represents the ongoing need to generate large quantities of a product essential to the construction and maintenance of the fortress. The kiln probably became operational not long after the British re-occupied the site following the French occupation of 1782–3. It would have required a moderate sized work force dedicated to near uninterrupted removal of limestone, firing the kiln, processing the lime and hauling it to different construction projects throughout the fortress. By 1800 the need for an onsite work force was greatly diminished, although lime production continued even after the fort was closed.

The BSH 2 occupation is best regarded as a colonial government and British military experiment for meeting the labor requirements for rapid construction at a massive scale. Nearly all the labor at Brimstone Hill from about 1778 until the early 19th century came from plantations, and there were regular negotiations regarding the number of workers, the length of their service, and the conditions of their employment. The military was responsible for housing the 120 Africans purchased for them, and the structures at BSH 2 were built for this purpose. Expanding the Non-Commissioned Officers' cemetery clearly took priority over maintaining this area for housing African laborers. There is no indication that the St Kitts government made additional purchases of laborers, or that the military re-established similar quarters elsewhere at the fort once BSH 2 was re-purposed as a cemetery. Neither is it known what happen to the BSH 2 enslaved workers at the end of their two-year contract. They may have been returned to the St Kitts government for resale, or possibly absorbed into the military's corps of pioneers and laborers.

Brimstone Hill was a complex, highly structured, and often oppressive multi-ethnic and multi-cultural community. Historical research and archaeological investigations of the architecture and artifacts from the limekiln industrial buildings (BSH 1) and the hospital and hut between the Orillon and Magazine Bastions (BSH 2) have contributed greatly to discovering and interpreting some of these relationships. Much has been accomplished but much also remains to be done to reveal the complex history of African people at Brimstone Hill.

ACKNOWLEDGEMENTS

We thank Roger Leech for asking us to participate in the 2005 Post-Medieval meeting held on Nevis, and we thank Pam Leech for her editorial work. Archaeological and historical research at Brimstone Hill is made possible by the Brimstone Hill Fortress National Park Society, the University of Tennessee, the Center for Field Research and the National Geographic Society. We thank especially Mr Larry Armony (retired), General Manager for the Brimstone Hill Fortress National Park Society for his support of this research and for the support we received from the Society's Council of Management. We are also indebted to Dr Walter Klippel and his students for their contributions to the Brimstone Hill Fortress faunal analyses. Mr Victor Smith introduced us to the historical record of Brimstone Hill. His research and assistance with archival sources have added greatly to the Brimstone Hill archaeological investigations and our interpretations of the site. Ms Victoria O'Flaherty, Director of the St Kitts National Archives, generously granted access to the wealth of documents pertaining to Brimstone Hill housed in Basseterre. The 1791 Royal Engineers' map of Brimstone Hill, kept in the archives and showing the use of individual structures, has been the single most important document guiding the conduct of archaeological excavations at

Brimstone Hill. Lastly, we thank all the Earthwatch participants, University of Tennessee field school students, and St Kitts high school students for their work at the site.

NOTES

1 Smith 1994, 1995; Schroedl 2014, 2018.
2 Buisseret 1973, 46–7.
3 Smith 1994, 1995.
4 Smith 1994, 100; The National Archives, UK [hereafter TNA] WO44/354, 26 October 1818; TNA WO44/368, 26 February 1820.
5 Smith 1994, 101.
6 Buckley 1979, 1998; Voelz 1993.
7 Schroedl 2000, 2005, 2006.
8 Calendar of States Papers America and West Indies [hereafter CSPAWI] 1704–5, 622; TNA CO241/1, 19 October 1704.
9 Journal of the Commissioners for Trade and Plantations [hereafter JCTP] 1718–22, 383; St Christopher Council and Legislative Council Minutes [hereafter SCCLCM] 1732–4, 16 January 1732, 22 January 1733/4, 26 August 1734.
10 JCTP 1718–22, 383; JCTP 1722/3–28, 123; JCTP 1759–63, 233; CSPAWI 1728–9, 441; CSPAWI 1733, 148; CSPAWI 1734–5, 252 CSPAWI 1735–6, 81; SCCLCM 1732–4, 22 January 1733/4, 15 February 1733/4; SCCLCM 1755–62, 17 April 1756, 15 May 1759; SCCLCM 1770–83, 10 February 1780, 17 April 1781.
11 SCCLCM 1788–95, 21 January 1790.
12 SCCLCM 1732–4, 16 January 1732, An Act for continuing the works of the fortifications, forts and batteries of this island and for obliging all owners and proprietors of slaves to send a portion of their said slaves for such time as there is mentioned; SCCLCM 1734–40, 17 August 1743, 4 November 1740; SCCLCM 1778–83 27 October 1778, 9 November 1781; SCCLCM 1783–8 7 November 1785; SCCLCM 1788–95 28 June 1790; St Kitts Council and Assembly 1791.
13 SCCLCM 1734–40 3 October 1735; This legislation called for sending one worker for every 100 slaves; TNA CO240/14 3 August 1779, 'An Act to oblige all owners, renters, and possessors of slaves in this island to send a proportion thereof to work in the Forts and Fortifications of this island and for carrying on the public works and other services which may be deemed necessary for the public safety'; TNA CO240/14 5 December 1785; 'An Act to oblige all owners, renters, and possessors of slaves in this island to send a proportion of the same to be employed on Brimstone Hill and the work necessary for its defense.'
14 TNA CO240/14 5 September 1785.
15 SCCLCM 1782–5 21 February 1782, 27 October 1778; SCCLCM 1793–5 26 April 1793.
16 SCCLCM 1778–83 21 February 1782.
17 TNA CO241/18 4 March 1784, 16 August 1784, 2 March 1786; SCCLCM 1793–5 16 April 1793, 11 June 1793, 10 June 1794, 24 March 1795.
18 SCCLCM 1776–81 11 May 1780; TNA HO50/365 6 November 1790; TNA WO55/937, 13 April 1826; 10 December 1827, 5 March 1829, 12 January 1842, 11 November 1843.
19 TNA WO44/425, 16 October 1829; TNA WO44/408, 1 September 1829.
20 TNA WO44/425, 31 December 1829.
21 SCCLCM 1755–62 1 August 1757; SCCLCM 1788–95 25 May 1789, 6 January 1792; TNA CO101/29, 1 August 1789.
22 SCCLCM 1788–95 11 June 1793.
23 TNA CO241/18 16 August 1785, 22 August 1785.
24 SCCLCM 1788–95 1 January 1792, 6 January 1792.
25 SCCLCM 1788–95 16 April 1793.
26 SCCLCM 1788–95 6 October 1794.
27 SCCLCM 1788–95 24 March 1795; SCCLCM 1795–9 12 September 1796.
28 TNA WO55/937, 1 June 1803, 25 July 1803.
29 TNA CO241/18 19 July 1779; SCCLCM 1776–81 1 August 1779; TNA CO241/18 16 July 1785, 16 August 1785; SCCLCM 1788–95 6 January 1792, 16 April 1793.
30 TNA CO240/14 5 December 1775; TNA CO241/18 24 January 1785, 22 August 1785; SCCLCM 1782–5 8 March 1784; SCCLCM 1788–95 28 June 1790, 16 January 1791, 6 January 1792; SCCLCM 1793–5 16 April 1793, 6 October 1794, 24 April 1795.
31 SCCLCM 1782–5 21 February 1782.

32 SCCLCM 1734–40 3 October 1735, 30 September 1740; SCCLCM 1772–8 27 October 1778; SCCLCM 1793–5 4 July 1793.
33 SCCLCM 1788–95 31 January 1791, 144–5.
34 SCCLCM 1788–95 7 September 1791, 186–91.
35 Smith 1994, 100 suggests that 50 or more soldiers' wives and children may have resided at Brimstone Hill during the period of its greatest troop strength. Buckley 1998, 147, 155; see also TNA WO1/84 7 November 1795 that lists 8 to 40 women with each of 25 British regiments stationed in the West Indies. There are 30 to 40 women with regiments having troop strengths of 500 to 600. The regiments are not listed by island. See TNA WO57/56 20 November 1810 where the army in St Kitts reported feeding between 90 and 92 women and between 96 and 102 children. They also provided meals for 55 to 76 slaves. Dyde 1997, 44–5 suggests that very few wives or children accompanied black soldiers until after emancipation and that these men instead consorted with females on local plantations. Buckley 1998, 157, however, maintains that the ratio of black females to males was about the same as that for white soldiers.
36 Buckley 1998, 136–7, 160, 164, 342, 344–5.
37 TNA CO241/17 3 December 1781. For example, on this date the Council resolved: 'That every negro to be sent ought to carry one week's provisions in every week and that the owners of such negroes be allowed and paid out of the Public Treasury at the rate of four shillings and six pence per day for each negro for such time as negroes may be employed in the public service, such negro being an able bodied negro, and, that in case such negro so sent may be killed or receive any hurt when employed in the public service the owner of such negro to be paid out of the Public Treasury the damage he may sustain, such damage to be ascertained upon the oath of any two or three respectable inhabitants of the island.'
38 SCCLCM 1788–95 28 June 1790 16 January 1791, 7 September 1791, 8 June 1792.
39 SCCLCM 1788–95 1 January 1792.
40 SCCLCM 1788–95 16 February 1792.
41 SCCLCM 1788–95 16 February 1792.
42 TNA CO241/17 14 November 1780; TNA CO241/18 16 July 1785; TNA WO55/937 25 July 1803; SCCLCM 1788–95 1 January 1792; SCCLCM 1793–5 10 June 1794; SCCLCM 1795–9 12 September 1796.
43 SCCLCM 1788–95 29 April 1793; CO153/28 November 1794; TNA CO318/25 1804, 289; SCCLCM 1776–81 11 May 1780; SCCLCM 1734–40 5 February 1733/4; TNA CO241/17 3 December 1781; CO241/18 21 August 1785; SCCLCM 1776–81 27 October 1778.
44 TNA CO318/25, 3 July 1804, 289; SCCLCM 1734–40 5 February 1733/34, 22 September 1740; SCCLCM 1755–62 27 April 1756, 2 July 1756, 16 June 1757, 13 August 1757, 19 May 1758; SCCLCM 1770–82 20 August 1779; TNA CO241/17 20 January 1780, 28 June 1778; TNA CO153/28 November 1794.
45 SCCLCM 1734–40 10 January 1734; SCCLCM 1783–8 12 September 1788; TNA CO241/17 3 December 1781 SCCLCM 1788–95 16 January 1791, 16 April 1793.
46 SCCLCM 1732–34; 12 April 1733, 4 January 1734.
47 SCCLCM 1788–95 16 January 1791.
48 SCCLCM 1788–95 25 May 1789, 5 August 1791.
49 SCCLCM 1788–95 5 May 1792.
50 SCCLCM 1788–95 30 March 1789 SCCLCM 1793–95 13 April 1795.
51 TNA HO50/365 6 November 1790.
52 SCCLCM 1788–95 7 September 1791.
53 TNA CO241/17 17 July 1779.
54 Chartrand and Chappell 1996, 16.
55 Buckley 1979, 4–5; Buckley 1998, 128–37; Voelz 1993, 59–76.
56 Buckley 1979, 167, footnote 93; Buckley 1998, 132; TNA WO1/85 9 April 1796, 305–7. The available data, however, do not always distinguish between enslaved African pioneers owned by the military and those procured largely from plantations for temporary work through contracts or colonial assemblies.
57 TNA CO153/28 10 December 1795; TNA WO1/84 9 April 1796, 305–30. The St Kitts Council complained in 1796 and again in 1797 that they had not received payment for these individuals (SCCLCM 1795–9 1 June 1796 and 2 February 1797).
58 TNA CO318/25, 7 May 1804, 77–9; Buckley 1979, 53–5.
59 SCCLCM 1788–95 4 December 1790, 30 October 1795, 25 August 1795; TNA CO137/98, 20 January 1797.

60 TNA WO44/365 13 January 1821; TNA WO44/368 18 February 1821; TNA CO152/78, 30 April 1797; TNA WO1/626, 6 June 1804.
61 TNA WO44/365, 13 January 1821.
62 TNA WO44/405, 1 October 1823; TNA WO55/945, 31 August 1824; TNA WO334/6, 31 December 1830; TNA WO55/946 1830; TNA WO55/947, 13 August 1841. The eight individuals identified in 1830 appear on a printed list of about 400 names entitled 'List of Black Military Artificers and Labourers attached to the Engineer Department in the West Indies.'
63 TNA WO55/946, 22 July 1830.
64 SCCLCM 1732–4, 22 August 1733; SCCLCM 1734–40, 30 October 1741; SCCLCM 1755–62, 10 February 1757, 4 January 1760; SCCLCM 1772–8, 7 January 1774, 26 October 1780; TNA WO44/425, 30 October 1823.
65 SCCLCM 1734–40, 31 May 1734; CO241/17, 4 December 1781; CO241/18, 6 October 1786.
66 SCCLCM 1772–8, 7 January 1774; CO241/18, 22 July 1785.
67 CO241/18, 13 September 1785.
68 WO44/425, 22 September 1829, 16 October 1829, 31 December 1829; 1832.
69 WO44/461 9 June 1841; WO55/951 12 June 1849.
70 WO55/250 31 March 1827.
71 CO241/18 7 December 1785.
72 Royal Engineers Library, Grenada file, 22 November 1789.
73 TNA CO101/29, 1 September 1789.
74 Smith 1994, fig. 10; TNA WO78/2595, 8 June 1791 entitled 'Project for the defense of Brimstone Hill St Christopher referred to in the Report of the Board of Officers appointed to examine the Fortifications in the West Indies.' There are three nearly identical copies of this map. Two are in the National Archives of the United Kingdom, and the third is a framed copy in the St Kitts-Nevis National Archives, Basseterre. Only the copy in St Kitts labels and identifies the use of individual structures at Brimstone Hill.
75 TNA CO101/29, 20 May 1789; SCCLCM, 21 January 1790.
76 TNA WO71/32, 5–19 March 1792.
77 Smith 1994, fig. 10; TNA WO78/2595, 8 June 1791.
78 Scotia Bank, Basseterre. It is believed that the paintings, attributed to James Lees, although undated, were executed in the 1790s. These are watercolors that were purchased by the government of St Kitts and are now on display at the Scotia Bank, Basseterre, St Kitts. Slightly reduced images of two have been reproduced for sale at the Brimstone Hill Fortress National Park gift shop.
79 TNA WO71/32, 5–19 March 1792.
80 Schroedl 1997.
81 SCCLCM 1788–95, 1 January 1792.
82 TNA WO44/330, 21 August 1813.
83 TNA WO55/937, 6 December 1799.
84 Rollinson 1992.
85 David Rollinson, pers. comm. July 1996.
86 Ahlman & Schroedl 2019.
87 Ahlman & Schroedl 2019.
88 Schroedl 1998, 1999, 2000.
89 Smith 1994, 100–10; Schroedl 2019.
90 DiGangi 2005, 2006, 2007; McKeown 1997, 1998, 1999, 2000.
91 Ahlman & Schroedl 2019.
92 Ahlman *et al.* 2008, 2009, 2019.
93 Ahlman & McKeown 2018.
94 Ahlman & Schroedl 2019.
95 Ahlman & Schroedl 2019.
96 Schroedl & Ahlman 2002.
97 Schroedl & Ahlman 2002.
98 Dellino-Musgrove 2006; Lace *et al.* 2019; White & Beaudry 2009.
99 Ahlman & Schroedl 2019.
100 Buckley 1998.
101 Hawtrey 1903.
102 Smith 2005.
103 Schroedl 2019; Schroedl *et al.* 2019.
104 Ahlman *et al.* 2014.
105 Hill & Schroedl 2003.
106 Harrington 1978.
107 Hill & Schroedl 2003.
108 Klippel & Schroedl 1999; Klippel & Price 2007.
109 Klippel 1997, 1998, 2001, 2002; Patterson & Klippel 1999.

BIBLIOGRAPHY

Ahlman, T.M. & McKeown, A.H. 2018, 'Post Emancipation Material Culture and Housing on St. Kitts, West Indies', paper presented to the Annual Conference on Historical and Underwater Archaeology, Soc. Hist. Archaeol., New Orleans, Louisiana.

Ahlman, T.M. & Schroedl, G.F. 2019, 'Consumerism in the Caribbean: Examining Material Remains from the Brimstone Hill Fortress and Plantation Contexts, St. Kitts, West Indies', in Boyd (ed.) 2019, 319–35.

Ahlman, T.M., Braly, B.R. & Schroedl, G.F. 2014, 'Stone and Glass tools from St. Kitts' Southeast Peninsula', *J. African Diaspora Archaeol. and Herit.* 3:1, 1–26.

Ahlman, T.M., Schroedl, G.F., McKeown, A.H., Speakman, R.J. & Glascock, M.D. 2008, 'Ceramic Production and Exchange among Enslaved Africans on St. Kitts, West Indies', in Descantes *et al.* (eds) 2008, 109–22.

Ahlman, T.M., Schroedl, G.F. & McKeown, A.H. 2009, 'The Afro Caribbean Ware from Brimstone Hill Fortress, St. Kitts, West Indies: A Study in Ceramic Production', *Hist. Archaeol.* 43:4, 22–41.

Ahlman, T.M., Schroedl, G.F., Heath, B.J., Gilmore III, R.G., & Ferguson, J.R. 2019, 'Inter- and Intra-island Trade of Afro-Caribbean Ware in the Lesser Antilles', in Ahlman & Schroedl (eds) 2019, 68–89.

Ahlman, T.M. & Schroedl, G.F. (eds) 2019, *Historical Archaeologies of the Caribbean: Contextualizing Sites through Colonialism, Capitalism, and Globalism*, Tuscaloosa: University of Alabama.

Boyd, C.C. Jr. (ed.) 2019, *Change, Adaptation, and Accommodation: Archaeological Case Studies from the Southeastern U.S. and the Caribbean*, Knoxville: University of Tennessee Press.

Buckley, R.N. 1979, *Slaves in Red Coats*, New Haven: Yale University Press.

Buckley, R.N. 1998, *The British Army in the West Indies*, Gainesville: University Press of Florida.

Buisseret, D. 1973, 'The Elusive Deodand: A Study of the Fortified Refuges of the Lesser Antilles', *J. Caribbean Hist.* 6, 43–80.

Chartrand, R. & Chappell, P. 1996, *British Forces in the West Indies 1793–1815*, Men at Arms Series 294, London: Osprey.

DeCorse, C.R. & Beier, Z.J.M. (eds) 2018, *British Forts and Their Communities: Archaeological and Historical Perspectives*, Gainesville: University Press of Florida.

Dellino-Musgrave, V.E. 2006, *Maritime Archaeology and Social Relations: British Action in the Southern Hemisphere*, New York: Springer US.

Descantes, C., Speakman R.J., Glascock, M.D. & Boulanger, M.T. (eds) 2008, 'An Exploratory Study into the Chemical Characterization of Caribbean Ceramics', *J. Caribbean Archaeol. Special Public.* 2.

DiGangi, E.A. 2005, 'Human Skeletal Remains from Excavations at Brimstone Hill Fortress National Park, St. Kitts West Indies, July–August 2004', *Brimstone Hill Fortress Archaeol. Proj. Rep.* 25.

DiGangi, E.A. 2006, 'Human Skeletal Remains from Brimstone Hill Fortress National Park, St. Kitts West Indies, July–August 2005', *Brimstone Hill Fortress Archaeol. Proj. Rep.* 27.

DiGangi, E.A. 2007, 'Human Skeletal Remains from Brimstone Hill Fortress National Park, St. Kitts, West Indies, 2006', *Brimstone Hill Fortress Archaeol. Proj. Rep.* 30.

Dyde, B. 1997, *The Empty Sleeve: The Story of the West India Regiments of the British Army*, St. Johns (Antigua): Hansib Caribbean.

Gates St. Pierre, C. & Walker, R.B. (eds) 2007, *Current Methods and Interpretations in Worked Bone Studies*, Brit. Archaeol. Rep. Int. Ser. 1622, Oxford: Archaeopress.

Harrington, J.C. 1978, 'Dating Stem Fragments of Seventeenth- and Eighteenth-Century Clay Tobacco Pipes', in Schuyler (ed.) 1978, 63–5.
Hawtrey, F.M. 1903, *The History of the Hawtrey Family*, vol. 1, London: George Allen.
Hill, A.D. & Schroedl, G.F. 2003, 'Clay Tobacco Pipes from the Brimstone Hill Fortress, St. Kitts, West Indies', *Brimstone Hill Archeol. Proj. Rep.* 23.
Klippel, W.E. 1997, 'Faunal Remains from the 1996 Excavations at Brimstone Hill, St. Kitts, West Indies', *Brimstone Hill Archaeol. Proj. Rep.* 6.
Klippel, W.E. 1998. 'Faunal Remains from the 1997 Excavations at Brimstone Hill Fortress, St. Kitts, West Indies', *Brimstone Hill Archaeol. Proj. Rep.* 10.
Klippel, W.E. 2001, 'Sugar Monoculture, Bovid Skeletal Part Frequencies, and Stable Carbon Isotopes: Interpreting Enslaved African Diet at Brimstone Hill, St. Kitts, West Indies', *J. Archaeol. Sci.* 28, 1191–8.
Klippel, W.E. 2002, 'Provisioning Enslaved Africans in the British West Indies: The Animal Bones from Brimstone Hill Fortress, St. Kitts', *Brimstone Hill Archaeol. Proj. Rep.* 21.
Klippel, W.E. and Price, B.E. 2007, 'Bone Disc Manufacturing Debris from Newfoundland to Antigua during the Historic Period', in Gates St. Pierre & Walker (eds) 2007, 132–43.
Klippel, W.E. & Schroedl, G.F. 1999, 'African Slave Craftsmen and Single Hole Bone Discs from Brimstone Hill, St. Kitts, West Indies', *Post-Med. Archaeol.* 33, 222–32.
Lace, M.J., Albury, N.A., Samson, A.V.M., Cooper, J. & Ramos, R.R. 2019, 'Ship Graffiti on the Islands of the Bahamas, Turks and Caicos and Puerto Rico: A Comparative Analysis', *J. Marit. Archaeol.* 14, 239–71.
Majewski, T. & Gaimster, D. (eds) 2009, *International Handbook of Historical Archaeology*, New York: Springer US.
McKeown, A.H. 1997, 'Human Skeletal Remains from Excavations at Brimstone Hill Fortress National Park, St. Kitts, West Indies, July 1996', *Brimstone Hill Archaeol. Proj. Rep.* 5.
McKeown, A.H. 1998, 'Human Skeletal Remains from the 1997 Excavations at Site BSH 2, Brimstone Hill Fortress National Park, St. Kitts, West Indies', *Brimstone Hill Archaeol. Proj. Rep.* 8.
McKeown, A.H. 1999, 'Human Skeletal Remains from the 1998 Excavations at Site BSH 2, Brimstone Hill Fortress National Park, St. Kitts, West Indies', *Brimstone Hill Archaeol. Proj. Rep.* 13.
McKeown, A.H. 2000. 'Human Skeletal Remains from Excavations at Brimstone Hill Fortress National Park, St. Kitts, West Indies, June–July 1999', *Brimstone Hill Archaeol. Proj. Rep.* 20.
Patterson, J.A. & Klippel, W.E. 1999, 'African Slave Subsistence: The Faunal Remains from Brimstone Hill, St. Kitts', *Brimstone Hill Fortress Archaeol. Proj. Rep.* 14.
Reid, B.A. & Gilmore III, R.G. (eds) 2014, *Encyclopedia of Caribbean Archaeology*, Gainesville: University Press of Florida.
Rollinson, D. 1992, 'Lime Kiln – Brimstone Hill, St. Kitts', Basseterre (St. Kitts): Brimstone Hill National Park Society.
Schroedl, G.F. 1997, 'A Report on the July 1996 Archaeological Investigations at the Brimstone Hill National Park, St. Kitts, West Indies', *Brimstone Hill Archaeol. Proj. Rep.* 1.
Schroedl, G.F. 1998, 'A Report on the July 1997 Archaeological Investigations at the Brimstone Hill Fortress National Park, St. Kitts, West Indies', *Brimstone Hill Archaeol. Proj. Rep.* 7.
Schroedl, G.F. 1999, 'A Report on the 1998 Archaeological Investigations at the Brimstone Hill Fortress National Park, St. Kitts, West Indies', *Brimstone Hill Archaeol. Proj. Rep.* 12.
Schroedl, G.F. 2000, 'A Report on the 1999 Archaeological Investigations at the Brimstone Hill Fortress National Park, St. Kitts, West Indies', *Brimstone Hill Archaeol. Proj. Rep.* 17.
Schroedl, G.F. 2005, 'Current Archaeological Investigations at Brimstone Hill', *Cannonball, Newsletter of the Brimstone Hill Fortress National Park Society* 9:3, 1, 3–4, 6.

Schroedl, G.F. 2006, 'The 2006 Archaeological Excavations at Brimstone Hill', *Cannonball, Newsletter of the Brimstone Hill Fortress National Park Society* 10:2, 3, 8–9.

Schroedl, Gerald F. 2014, 'Brimstone Hill Fortress National Park (St. Kitts)', in Reid & Gilmore (eds) 2014, 78–80.

Schroedl, G.F. 2018, 'Enslaved Africans and the British Military at the Brimstone Hill Fortress, St. Kitts, West Indies', in DeCorse & Beier (eds) 2018, 178–205.

Schroedl, G.F. 2019, 'Archaeological and Historical Studies at the Orillon Bastion, Brimstone Hill Fortress, St. Kitts', in Boyd (ed.) 2019, 295–318.

Schroedl, G.F. & Ahlman, T.M. 2002, 'The Maintenance of Cultural and Personal Identities of Enslaved Africans and British Soldiers at the Brimstone Hill Fortress, St. Kitts, West Indies', *Hist. Archaeol.* 36:4, 38–52.

Schroedl, G.F., Ahlman T.M., & Taylor Bowden, T. 2019, 'Further Studies of Archaeological Deposits Impacted by the Collapse of a Segment of the Orillon Bastion Wall and Monitoring of the Wall's Restoration at the Brimstone Hill Fortress National Park, St. Kitts, West Indies', *Brimstone Hill Archaeol. Proj. Rep.* 33.

Schuyler, R.L. (ed.) 1978. *Historical Archaeology: A Guide to Substantive and Theoretical Contributions*, New York: Baywood.

Smith, F.H. 2005, *Caribbean Rum: A Social and Economic History*. Gainesville: University Press of Florida.

Smith, V.T.C. 1994, 'Brimstone Hill Fortress, St. Kitts, West Indies. Part One: History', *Post-Med. Archaeol.* 28, 73–109.

Smith, V.T.C. 1995, 'Brimstone Hill Fortress, St. Kitts, West Indies. Part Two: Description', *Post-Med. Archaeol.* 29, 77–106.

St Kitts Council and Assembly, 1791, *Laws of the Island of St. Christopher; From the Year 1711, to the Year 1791*, St Christopher: Edward Luther Low.

Voelz, P.M. 1993, *Slave and Soldier: The Military Impact of Blacks in the Colonial Americas*, New York: Garland.

White, C.L. & Beaudry, M.C. 2009, 'Artifacts and Personal Identity', in Majewski & Gaimster (eds) 2009, 209–25.

UNPUBLISHED SOURCES

St Kitts National Archives, St Kitts Sessional Papers, St Christopher Council and Legislative Council Minutes [SCCLCM]

1732–4

1734–40

1755–62

1770–83

1772–8

1776–81

1778–83

1782–5

1783–8

1788–95

1793–5

1795–9

St Kitts National Archives

Framed map entitled: General Plan of Brimstone Hill St Christopher, showing the Works and Buildings already erected in Red and the Works proposed for Completing the Defense in Yellow, 8 June 1791.

The National Archives of the United Kingdom [formerly the Public Record Office (PRO) now TNA],
CO101/29
CO137/98
CO152/78
CO153/28
CO318/25
CO240/14
CO241/1
CO241/17
CO241/18
HO50/365
WO1/84
WO1/85
WO1/626
WO44/330
WO44/354
WO44/365
WO44/368
WO44/405
WO44/408
WO44/425
WO44/461
WO55/250
WO55/937
WO55/945
WO55/946
WO55/947
WO55/951
WO57/56
WO71/32
WO78/2595
WO334/6
Calendar of States Papers America and West Indies
1704–5
1728–9
1733
1734–5
1735–6
Journal of the Commissioners for Trade and Plantations, Preserved in the Public Record Office
1718–22
1722/3–28
1759–63
Royal Engineers Library, Gillingham, Kent, England
1789 Folio, Grenada [?]
Scotia Bank Basseterre, St Kitts
Four undated watercolors of Brimstone Hill attributed to James Lees.

RECORD OF ARCHIVE DEPOSIT

The artifacts and archives from sites BSH 1 and BSH 2 are deposited at the Brimstone Hill Fortress National Park, Basseterre, St Kitts and at the Department of Anthropology, University of Tennessee, Knoxville, Tennessee, USA.

7

An Archaeological Survey of Sugar Plantations in St Kitts, 2004 and 2005

ROBERT A. PHILPOTT *and* JON BRETT†

SUMMARY: An archaeological field survey of just over 2600 hectares, within the parishes on St Kitts of St Mary Cayon and Christ Church Nichola Town, part of a British Academy funded project undertaken by the University of Southampton and National Museums Liverpool, focused especially on the survey of slave village sites. Uniquely for the British West Indies, McMahon's map records the position of all the slave villages in St Kitts in 1828 shortly before emancipation. Examination of the villages in the field has shown there are some recurrent elements in their location.

INTRODUCTION

In 2004 and 2005 a field survey was undertaken in two parishes on the north-east coast of St Christopher (St Kitts) by archaeologists led by Professor Roger Leech of the Department of Archaeology, University of Southampton, UK. The survey covered the northern part of St Mary Cayon and all the neighbouring parish of Christ Church Nichola Town with an overall study area of 2,600 hectares (Fig. 7.1). The survey formed part of the research project funded by the British Academy to assess the archaeological evidence for the early colonial settlement and landscape of the two Eastern Caribbean islands of Nevis and St Kitts described above (p. xix–xxii).

The project as undertaken on St Kitts had three main research objectives within the strategic objectives set out in the Preface (p. xxi–xxii), specifically here:

1 To undertake a reconnaissance survey of the 17th- and 18th-century colonial landscape of an area in the two parishes.
2 To identify the extent to which plantation centres have been abandoned or have changed through time, from the 17th to the 20th centuries.
3 To determine the archaeological and above ground remains of the slave villages for the plantations.

The survey area was defined by the major landscape features of the Cayon River to the south-east and St George's Ghut on the north-west. Historically, the Cayon River formed the boundary between the central, English, and the southern, French, divisions of the island. Chronologically, the survey concentrated on the period after

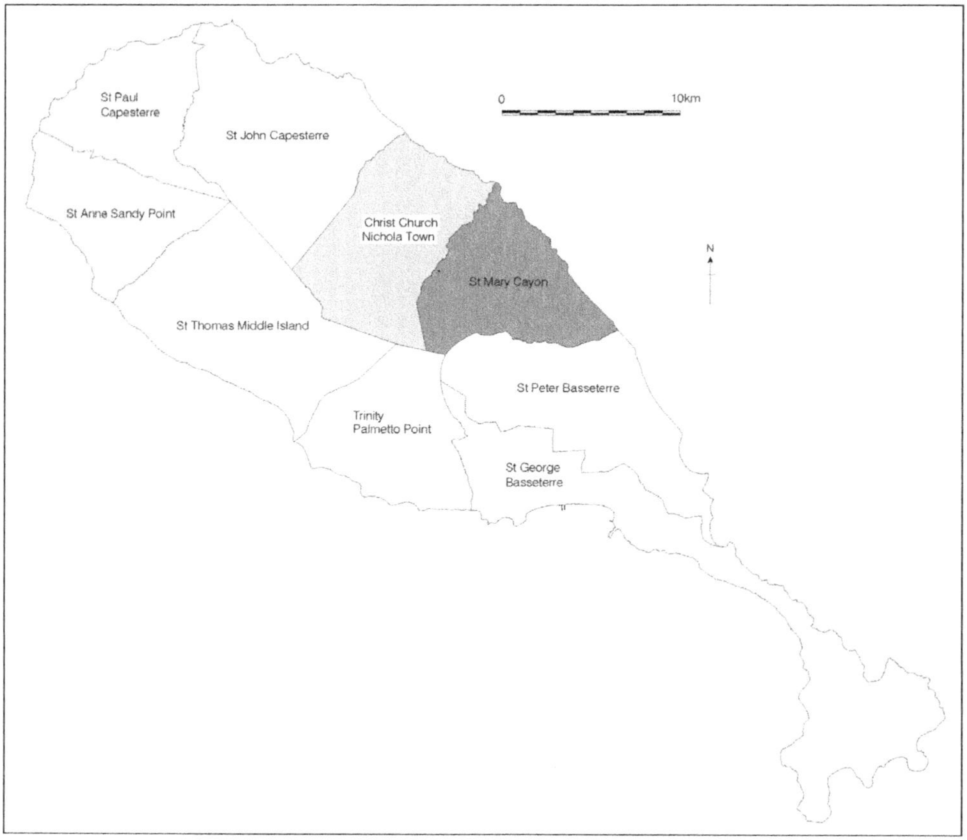

Fig. 7.1. Map showing the parishes of St Kitts, with the survey area in grey, with sites mentioned in the text. The French quarters, pre-1713, are in darker tone.

the introduction of sugar to St Kitts in the mid 17th century up to the introduction of steam technology for sugar processing in the 19th century.

FIELD SURVEY METHOD

Preliminary research identified a sequence of historic maps, in particular those by Pierre Buor dated *c.* 1711–13 (Fig. 7.2), Samuel Baker (1753) (Fig. 7.3), Anthony Ravell (surveyed 1765; Fig. 7.4) and the highly accurate large-scale plan by William McMahon (1828) (Fig. 7.5). By contrast with Jamaica where nearly 1,000 estate plans survive,[1] few individual plantation plans survive for St Kitts and only one was identified in the study area, for the Estridge estate, dated 1876.[2]

An initial assessment of the maps, particularly that of McMahon, enabled the plantations to be located on the ground. A reconnaissance visit was made to confirm the location of each site and assess the extent and survival of earthworks or structures. Field notes and an initial digital photographic record were followed by rapid

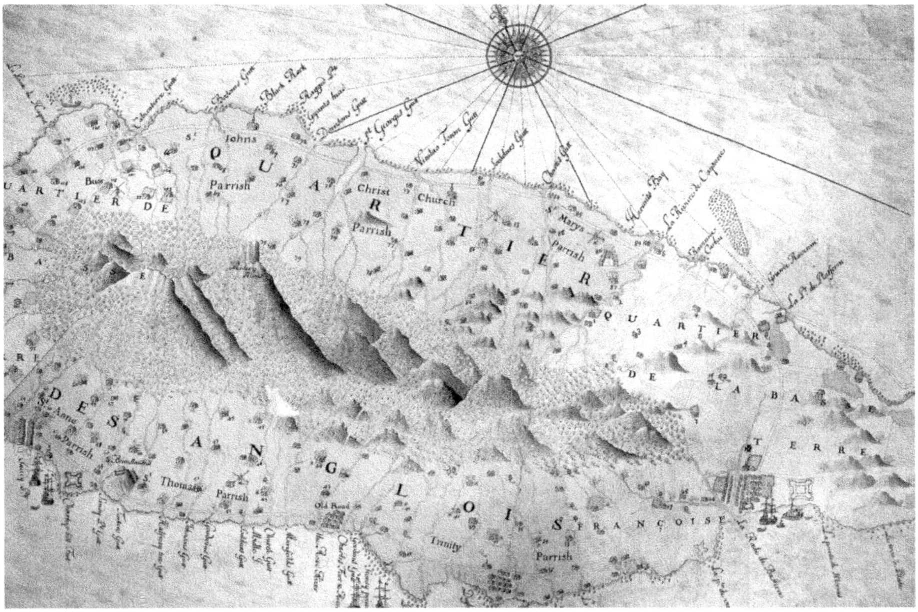

Fig. 7.2. Detail from Pierre Buor's map 'Plan Geometral de l'Isle de St Christophle', *c.* 1711–13 (British Library Maps K.Top.123.79.2).

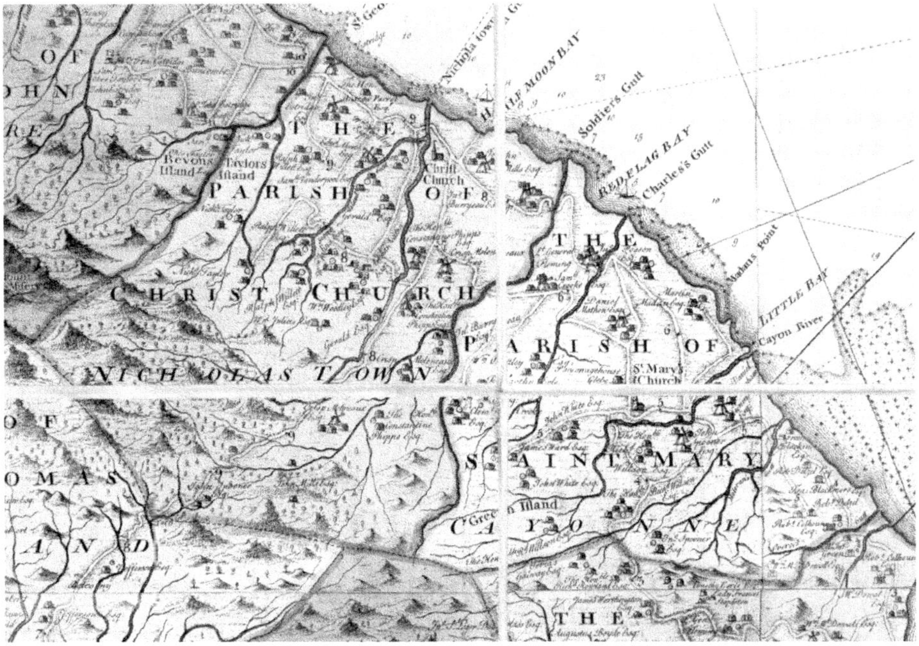

Fig. 7.3. Detail from Samuel Baker's map 'A new and exact Map of the Island of St Christopher in America', 1753 (TNA CO 700/St Christopher and Nevis 5).

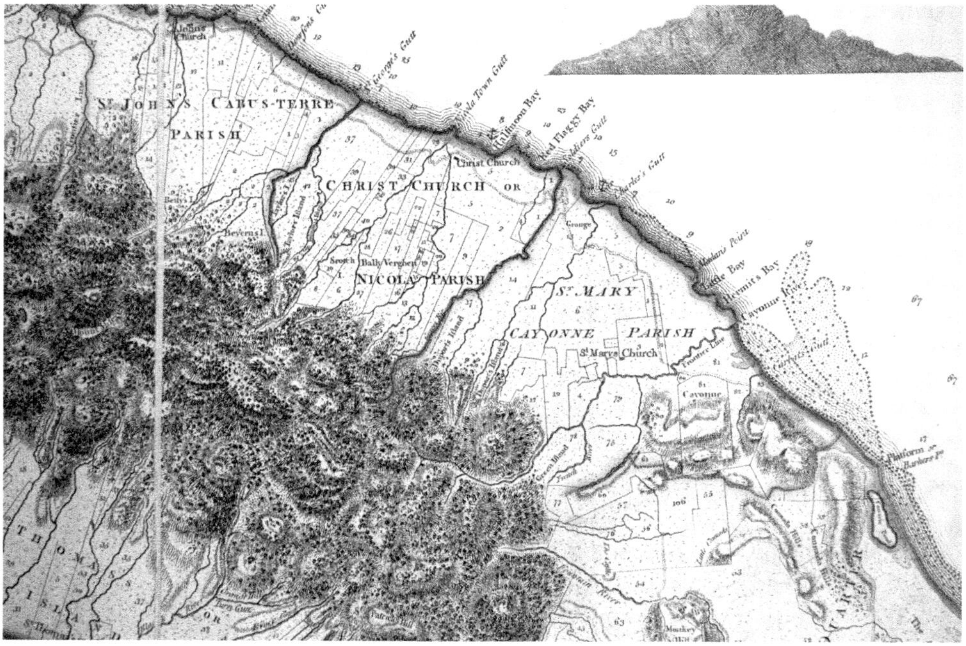

Fig. 7.4. Detail from Anthony Ravell's map 'St Christophers vulgo St Kitts' (British Library Maps 188.o.2.(2.)).

mapping using handheld Global Positioning System (GPS) technology to collect the positions of large-scale earthwork features as point data. Several of the best-preserved plantation centres were then recorded in more detail, typically topographical survey of the site using a total station theodolite, detailed descriptions, measured survey of selected buildings, and digital photography. Other plantations, where remains were either slight, poorly preserved, or inaccessible, were recorded by photography and field notes only. No artefacts were collected, apart from one case, Brighton Plantation, where the site began to be redeveloped during the survey, so a small sample of pottery was collected from disturbed contexts. A report was prepared for the St Kitts Island Authorities and St Christopher Heritage Society.[3] The overall survey would also act as a record of the physical remains of plantations within their landscape setting at a time of rapid change and development within the island and potentially as a tool for the preservation and management of these irreplaceable 'heritage assets'.

The map evidence and field observations were supplemented by historical records, including accounts of sugar cultivation and processing, travellers' or former residents' accounts, and official documents.[4] One as yet underexploited resource is the family and business papers which survive in modern archives, such as estate papers from the families of Estridge, Stapleton, Mathew, Akers, Mills, and White amongst others. Their detailed study would complement the archaeological survey and create a richer understanding of the social and economic context and development of the plantations.

Fig. 7.5. Detail of William McMahon's map 'A New Topographical map of the island of Saint Christopher in the West Indies', 1828 (TNA CO700/StChristopher8).

ST KITTS DURING THE COLONIAL PERIOD

One of the earliest settlements in the Leeward Islands, an English colony was established on St Kitts in 1624. In 1625 the French established a colony at the northern and southern ends of the island (Fig. 7.1), and it remained divided until the French surrendered their possessions in 1713 at the Treaty of Utrecht.

Early crops included tobacco, cotton, and indigo produced by the labour of indentured servants, many 'spirited' (in effect kidnapped) from the port of Bristol. Sugar was introduced in the 1640s and as elsewhere in the Caribbean, this shift to sugar production increasingly depended on the labour of enslaved Africans. But the population of St Kitts, like the political situation, was unstable. International conflict spilled over into the region with repeated French attacks which led to temporary depopulation, seizure of slaves and livestock, and damage to property, all serious setbacks to the development of stable economic production on the island.

Sugar ultimately became almost a monoculture in the island. Janet Schaw, visiting St Kitts in December 1774, was 'surprised at the complete cultivation I met every where. ... There is however a great want of shade, as every acre is under sugar'.[5] St Kitts had the reputation of producing the finest sugar in the West Indies; 'the very best soil for the production of sugar of the finest quality, and in the largest proportion, is the ashy loam of St. Christopher's'.[6] For much of the later 17th and 18th centuries sugar was a source of huge wealth. In 1770 sugar, rum, and molasses formed 92% of St Kitts's exports and much of the island had been put down to cane. However, by the later 18th century the costs of sugar production were rising, due to the increased cost of slaves resulting from competition from new English colonies in the Windward Islands, and from declining soil fertility through exhaustion from intensive cultivation.[7]

One consistent feature was the steady rise in population of enslaved Africans from the late 17th century onwards, transported to work the sugar plantations. Under the governorship of William Stapleton (1672–86) the Leeward Islands developed the sugar industry,[8] importing large numbers of enslaved Africans, no fewer than 4,000 during the 1670s into the four islands. By the late 1760s there were 46 white adult males in the parish of St Mary Cayon and just one freeholder.[9] The population of the parish in 1812, when a census was made of the whole island, was 2,316 – 9.9% of the 23,491 people on the island as a whole. This figure comprised 65 whites, 29 free coloured people and 2,222 slaves – 95% of the population of St Mary's.[10] The planters were well aware of their numerical inferiority and how potentially fragile their ability to maintain control over their slaves actually was. Increasing numbers of slaves induced a growing sense of insecurity and led colonists to demand more troops, though often without any great willingness to contribute towards the cost. Historians have found that in the Caribbean there was an inverse relationship between the numbers of troops and militia manning garrisons and the frequency of slave revolts.[11] In 1738 and 1746 the St Kitts assembly requested a regiment, and in 1770 200 men.[12] However, in 1791 at least one military opinion regarded the island as safe because the slave population was the best clothed and best treated, there were few locations for rebels to assemble, and the island was protected by a substantial fort at Brimstone Hill.[13]

The enslaved population lived in villages on the plantation. They had a six-day working week, working from sunrise to sunset with Sunday as a free day and were allowed to cultivate provision grounds, gardens or mountain land set aside for the purpose. Their produce could be sold at market which from the planters' perspective reduced costs in food rations and limited risk. However, the land given over for provision grounds and gardens was often good agricultural land and high prices for sugar inevitably put pressure for its reversion to cane cultivation, a process described by Rev. James Ramsay in the mid 18th century.[14] Food was then imported from the eastern coast of America until disruption in the 1780s.

Slavery was abolished throughout the British Empire in 1834 and brought with it a transition to wage labour for the majority of the island's population. This was a two-stage process in which the emancipation law made slaves over six years old 'apprentices' and obliged them to work for their former owners without wages for much of each week. This would last until August 1838 when full freedom was obtained. It appears that after 1838 many ex-slave families tried to employ women and children in domestic work where possible while men worked on plantations, although women remained in the plantation labour force because of a lack of alternatives.[15] Former slaves commonly remained living in the slave villages on the plantations on the condition that they were to work on the estate. Residence also involved an allowance of land to cultivate, around 10–15 acres.[16] Owners could threaten ejection as a punishment but were reportedly restrained in its use because of the fear that labourers would emigrate. Many Kittitian workers did migrate from the island to Trinidad in search of higher wages, 963 between 1839 and the first half of 1845.[17]

ORGANIZATION OF THE LANDSCAPE

The large-scale transformation of the landscape began soon after the earliest European settlement of St Kitts in 1624. According to Henry Colt writing in 1631, 'the woods are thick and mountainous and hills manye'.[18] A road was cut through the forest around the island and was found to be 32 miles in length; the French took the eight miles at either end of the island, while the British had the central section.[19] After the introduction of sugar processing in the early 1640s forest clearance proceeded more quickly and by the late 17th century the selective cutting of valuable hardwoods, lignum vitae and others, had so seriously depleted stocks that timber for building was imported from the eastern coast of America.

The laying out of the landscape for large-scale sugar cultivation took place within a hierarchy of divisions in the partition of the island. As with St Mary Cayon and Christ Church, natural topographical boundaries, notably the prominent ghuts or steep valleys which held the main watercourses, were adopted to define the extent of the parishes, as well as marking the major boundaries of the territories of the English and French. Although the English plantations for the most part respected the parish boundaries, the primary English divisions used to mark out the plantations consisted of a series of straight radial alignments perpendicular to the coastline. They were presumably marked out from the sea by compass and extended from the coast to the central upland, paying little heed to topographical features such as hills or the

Fig. 7.6. The landscape of St Kitts: the central mountain and Mansion plantation with sugar cane fields seen from Mills plantation.

steep-sided valleys, as Leech has suggested was practised in the early 17th century for neighbouring Nevis,[20] but there the single central mountain presented a more straightforward topography while the political constraints of sharing the island were also absent. On St Kitts, the compass bearings are seen at their best on the Ravell map surveyed in 1765 where plantation boundaries preserved the alignments (Fig. 7.4). The flatter lower-lying land of the coastal plain was more amenable to neat rectilinear division than the steeper mountain slopes which are cut by ghuts at increasingly close intervals higher up the slopes (Fig. 7.6).

Certainly this is the extensively partitioned landscape as captured by the earliest detailed maps in the mid 18th century. However, it is likely that this represented an 18th-century transformation and rationalization of a landscape created through initial piecemeal clearance and enclosure of small lots in the 17th century. Profitable sugar cultivation required the increased efficiency brought about by investment in larger estates, as Richard Ligon recognized in mid 17th-century Barbados.[21] On St Kitts this initial stage of small-scale landscape clearance is hard to identify but it may have resembled the small tenant plots of 10 or 20 acres recorded on an early map of 1646 at Trents in Barbados which, unusually, captures the pre-sugar plantation landscape.[22]

By the 18th century consolidation of land into larger estates created the conditions for reconfiguring the landscape, as far as the topography allowed, within the framework of the initial radial divisions. Individual plantations were laid out with coaxial field systems. Contemporary writers record that the creation of similarly sized cane 'pieces' was determined by the need to plant and ensure that the crop ripened steadily through the dry months as over-ripened cane spoilt. Each plantation's cultivable land was both demarcated and served by a rectilinear network of tracks creating a patchwork of regular cane fields, mostly in the range of 8 to 16 acres in area. Few exceeded 20 acres, while those smaller than 5 acres were usually oddly shaped plots occupying awkward situations, although occasionally individual estates, such as The Spring which lies on a sloping ridge between two deep ghuts, had consistently small fields.

However, the layout was in part also a response to aesthetic considerations. Janet Schaw records that, 'the whole Island is a garden divided into different parterres'.[23] The concept of a deliberate imposition of order on the untamed landscape was revealed by the English attitude to the newly acquired French possessions at either end of the island in 1713. The French plantations were much less regular by that time than the English. The Governor proposed in April 1716 that the surveyors should delineate two base lines north–south and east–west at 90° through the former French lands, and 'from hence all plantations might be laid out in such square tracts or quantity of acres that should be granted to by the crown to particular persons'. The reason was 'not only to make the island look like a garden but prevent in time to come any vexatious law suits or wrangling which might otherwise of necessity ensue but will prove vastly to the quieting of the inhabitants'.[24]

Within the two St Kitts parishes of St Mary Cayon and Christ Church, the result of the transformation was that each plantation was intervisible with at least two others, providing mutual protection as well as an efficient partition of the landscape. In the modern landscape the sites are connected by a network of tracks, which had

Fig. 7.7. Aerial photograph of the landscape around Hermitage (left) and Grange plantations, showing cane fields and Lodge Ghut.

already reached a highly developed form by 1828 when the McMahon map captured the detailed layout (Fig. 7.5). Some are now tarmac roads, but many remain as dirt tracks amid the cane fields, such as the landscape around the Grange and Hermitage plantations, and are likely to have early origins within a planned layout of the estates (Fig. 7.7).

THE CONSOLIDATION AND ABANDONMENT OF ESTATES

The 17th-century land holdings tended to be small and were often in the possession of former indentured servants. After the Treaty of Utrecht in 1713 there was a change in the nature of plantations. The English attempted to create a class of small yeoman planters through the sale of former French lands, offering plots of 10 acres on the poorer land but much of the newly offered land was bought up by larger planters who possessed the capital to invest in sugar production often in consortia, to buy up tracts of land.

Sugar estates were subject to a process of aggregation during the 18th century. In 1724 there were 360 plantations on the island but this had reduced to only 110 in 1783. The cost of a 300-acre estate in 1770 was estimated at £30,000, representing a threefold increase over 40 years.[25] The island was suffering a lack of soil fertility by the later 18th century and this, coupled with the ubiquity of sugar cultivation, had a significant consequence. In 1750 the island grew all its own food but by the mid-1770s was dependent on imported American provisions.[26] The Leeward Islands were not subject to the reduction in the slave workforce in the 1820s and 1830s that, after abolition of the slave trade, became so acute in some places that it led to the abandonment of some plantations, as owners of two plantations would concentrate their resources on one.[27]

The maps illustrate the reduction in the number of plantations during the 18th and early 19th century. Estates on the Baker map of 1753 no longer appear on the McMahon map less than a century later (Fig. 7.8). Some were located high up on the hill slopes, where the ground was steep and the terrain vulnerable to soil erosion and exhaustion. These were abandoned at an early date. This may have been the fate of the two upper plantations belonging to James Ward and John White above White's plantation west of Cayon village, which have left no trace evident above ground today. Within Christ Church parish the site of the estate held by William Julius in 1753 was identified on steeply sloping ground as a concentration of fragments of red earthenware sugar moulds and two terraces, which had probably once held buildings. McMahon captured the landscape in 1828 at a point when the pressure on planters had become intense from a combination of increased costs which led to mounting debts, combined with falling sugar prices, which meant that many sugar estates were becoming unprofitable and the price of estates fell dramatically.

A second change in the plantation landscape, related to the first, occurred on the lower-lying estates. For the most part sugar continued to be cultivated but the plantations underwent a process of consolidation, reducing their number as plantation centres were abandoned. Concentrating sugar processing at a single site reduced expenditure and increased efficiency. The loss of all or most of the plantation works' buildings at three sites, Earle's, Pogson's and Upper Bourryeau 1, can be seen between

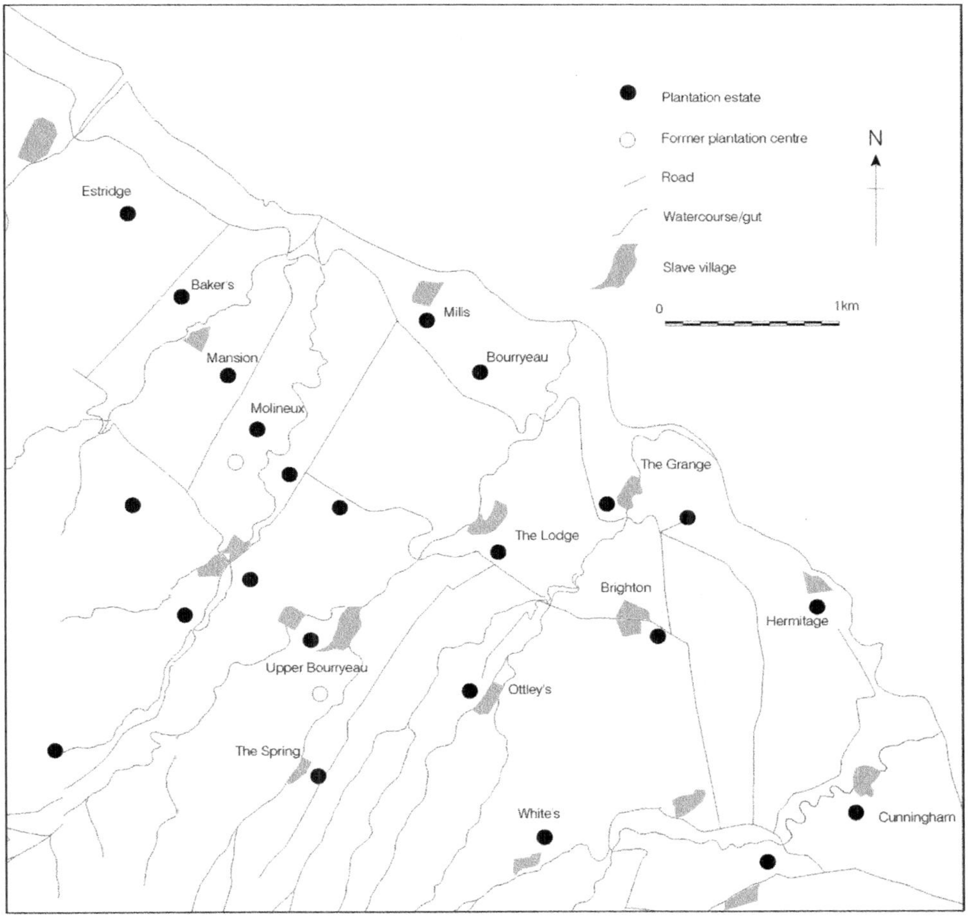

Fig. 7.8. St Kitts from the 1828 McMahon map, showing present and former plantations with sites of slave villages.

the Baker map of 1753 and the McMahon map of 1828. Furthermore, the absence from the 1828 map of plantation buildings at Upper Bourryeau 1 suggests that by this time cane was processed at the Lower Bourryeau works. A similar process may have occurred at Upper Bourryeau 2 where only a single structure is shown in 1828 and the main Molineux site downslope may have served the whole estate by this time.

PLANTATION LAYOUT AND BUILDINGS

The survey attempted to identify and record structural remains at the plantation centres in the two parishes. With the possible exception of the kitchen at The Spring, no surviving buildings could be securely assigned to the 17th century on architectural or archaeological grounds. Thus these parishes lack the early timber post-in-the-ground buildings such as the late 17th-century house at Hermitage on Nevis or the more modest, and probably earlier, examples which have been found encapsulated in stone structures at Nag's Head, St Kitts, or Fenton Hill, Nevis.[28] It may be conjectured that the latter buildings characterized the early island landscape, perhaps belonging to the early phase of smallholders or indentured servants of the mid 17th century, or the rising planter class of the late 17th century. In the two surveyed parishes that period was absent from the standing remains.

The lack of certain standing 17th-century buildings may be attributed to a series of destructive forces, both natural and human. A hurricane in 1681, for example, flattened Christopher Jeaffreson's dwelling house and outbuildings at Wingfield on the other side of St Kitts.[29] He fled and when he returned only one wall of his house remained standing. More seriously he lost most of his crop of sugar cane. He built a temporary house but six weeks later a second hurricane took off its roof. A serious earthquake in 1690 caused 9-foot wide (2.7m) cracks to open up in many places in St Kitts and threw down stone buildings.[30] The damage to buildings was not confined to the early period. A further earthquake in 1843, caused destruction or serious structural damage to numerous plantation buildings in St Kitts.[31]

The planters of St Kitts, as elsewhere in the Caribbean, had gradually by the late 17th century learnt by experience to adapt their houses to suit conditions of weather, climate, and geological instability. Hans Sloane writing of Jamaica where he was posted as physician to the governor in 1687–9, contrasts the buildings of the Spanish, which were one storey high, and 'built with posts put deep in the ground', with those of the English, 'for the most part brick, and after the English manner, which are neither cool, nor able to endure the shocks of earthquakes'.[32] In 1676 Col. William Stapleton wrote that in the Leeward Islands the hurricanes 'have taught the people to build low'.[33] The earthquake of 1690 in Nevis, St Kitts, and Antigua, which was particularly destructive of stone and brick buildings, led to a change in the types of buildings used, as jointed timber structures survived the earthquakes better.[34]

Along with earthquakes and hurricanes, planters had to contend with political instability as European wars were played out in the Caribbean. The French attacked English plantations in 1666–7, and again in 1689 and 1706. The last of these raids led to the destruction of many English plantation works, houses, and outbuildings, and the loss of slaves, cane fields, and livestock.[35] The insurance claims preserved in The National Archives, UK (TNA CO 243/2) show the extent of damage, even allowing for a degree of exaggeration. At the same time they record much valuable detail of the structures lost, the dimensions, materials and the layout of buildings which had been constructed for the most part in the latter part of the 17th century, as well as providing an insight into economic and social aspects of society at the beginning of the 18th century in St Kitts.

Daphne Hobson has undertaken an analysis of the house forms and dimensions represented in the insurance claims.[36] At the lower end of the social scale, poor planters claimed for small houses, constructed of cane and thatch and valued typically under £5. Others were partially constructed in brick or had stone ground-floor storeys and were often were roofed with pantiles. At the upper end of the scale, a wealthy planter such as John Davis of Christ Church Nichola Town claimed for a:

> dwelling house 52 ft long 16 wide 6in the wall plate the major part of the posts mastick & lignum vitae boarded round cont. vizt A hall paved with tile two chambers floored with boards a large porch paved & lofted with doors and windows to shut closed a shade paved with tile value £200; 2 slaves, livestock, goods, acreage of cane, total £806 15s.[37]

By the turn of the 18th century wealthier planters had constructed substantial timber dwelling houses in durable hardwoods such as mastic and lignum vitae. Contrary to received opinion, as Leech has observed,[38] these were neither impermanent nor insubstantial, as these timbers were highly durable and decay-resistant. Before the 1706 French raid, Oldmixon records that the English planters lived in fine houses, often of cedar, the finest in America.[39] From the point of view of building chronology, the 1706 destruction marks a watershed in the stock of surviving structures in these two English parishes. Once compensation was paid in 1711, substantial rebuilding must have occurred in the second decade of the 18th century.

The main house

From the 18th century onwards it is possible for the first time to examine surviving structures. Those in the survey have not so far been closely dated through documentary work but the great majority of surviving houses appear to date to the 18th or 19th century. They have recurrent features which show the adaptation of temperate northern hemisphere architecture to a tropical climate (e.g. Mansion, Fig. 7.9). They usually have a stone lower floor, used for storage and cellars, while the living accommodation, consisting of a main hall and bed-chambers, was provided above as a timber upper storey, entered by broad stone or tile steps to a porch. The houses were designed with wide shades and window shutters to protect against the heat of the sun, while louvres

Fig. 7.9. Mansion, the manager's house from the north.

provided ventilation to maximize air flow. The more substantial had three rooms arranged in a row, with the hall the focus of social activities. One major practical advantage in the humid tropical conditions was that the long narrow arrangement allowed the air to flow directly from window to window. The choice of appropriate materials was important, so floors of stone or earthenware tiles were preferred to keep the interior cool. Architectural features initially imported from England such as the fireplace and glazed windows were soon modified or largely dropped out of the architectural repertoire, unless with the glazed windows at Olivees consciously reinforcing ideas of elite refinement.

In the survey area, documents, historical accounts, and survey reveal that the size and status of the principal houses varied considerably. The most substantial and impressive buildings, as Leech has shown,[40] were the houses of those planters who stayed, exemplified by the early 19th-century houses of James Tobin or Huggins on Nevis, or the earlier houses at Olivees and Brighton on St Kitts. In 1774, Janet Schaw was a guest at Olivees Plantation, St Kitts, which was then occupied by William Hamilton, a lawyer and prominent member of St Kitts society, and Lady Isabella Esrkine. Schaw's description of Olivees suggests that its claim to be 'the finest house on any of the Islands' was due more to the opulence of the fittings – 'ornamented in a high degree' … 'finished in mahogany very well wrought' … mirrored panels, and chambers 'furnished in the English taste' – than the scale or distinction of its architecture, as revealed in her description of the great house:

> The great hall 'and every thing in it is superbly fine; the roof lofty, and ornamented in a high degree. It is between fifty and sixty feet long, has eight windows and three doors all glazed; it is finished in Mahogany very well wrought, and the panels finished in with mirrors. This you would believe would render the heat unsupportable, which its situation however prevents, as it stands pretty high up Mount Misery, which yields a cool and delightful shade to the back part of the house, while the front has the sea, shipping, town and a great part of the Island in prospect, and the constant sea-breeze renders it most agreeable. The drawing room and bed-chambers are entirely fitted up and furnished in the English taste, … this is esteemed the finest house on any of the Islands'.[41]

The surviving remains were planned by Leech in 2005.[42] The main dwelling he terms a 'villa', a house close to a town and standing in its own grounds, and serving as a primary residence. Leech discerns its similarity to Isaac Ware's depiction in 1758 of Clifton Hill House, the suburban house he had recently designed for Paul Fisher, a Bristol merchant. The similarities between Olivees and Clifton Hill House are several: most notably the design of the exterior stairs, the arrangement of the four flights of steps and the arched entrance to the basement, but also the dimensions of the ground floor and the provision of a hipped roof. The frontage of Olivees was finished in shingles, perhaps a substitute for the rusticated stonework of Fisher's house.

A rival for the accolade of the finest house on St Kitts may once have been Estridge (Hill Estate). This plantation, with its grand Palladian-style boiling and curing house complex, was considered in the early 19th century to stand at the apex of the social pyramid in terms of grandeur (Fig. 7.10). However, already by this time 'the ruins of

Fig. 7.10. 'View in the Island of Saint Christopher in the Parish of Nicola Town', Estridge, by J. Johnson, published 1827 (British Library 1299.m.1 pl. 4). Published just six years before the abolition of slavery, this image provides a good overview of the natural and built landscape but was itself part of the literature opposing abolition.

the proprietor's dwelling, and the forlorn and desolated spot in the vicinity of them "where once the garden smiled", exhibit the condition to which this property has fallen'.[43] The principal house had gone by the early 19th century, but the manager's house (Fig. 7.11), as large as main houses elsewhere, survives today on the edge of the plantation compound, although not accessible to survey. One aspect of the main house at Estridge is significant. As Sloane observed from his stay in Jamaica

Fig. 7.11. Estridge, the manager's house.

in 1687–9, 'the houses of considerable planters are usually removed from their sugar, or other works, that they may be free from the noise and smells of them, which are very offensive'.[44] This process had begun by the end of the 17th century but compared with many plantations, the house at Estridge lay unusually far from the sugar works, deliberately set apart from the industrial complex in a move which reinforced a physical and social separation between the estate owner and his enslaved workforce and the plantation works. The close juxtaposition of house and works, found at many plantation centres, has an English concomitant, and is noted by Leech in industrial Bristol in the 18th century,[45] and can be seen in the other main transatlantic port of Liverpool in the same century when merchants were content to live close to the docks cheek by jowl with the commercial premises which were the engine of their wealth. Increasingly by the 19th century they moved out to newly built grand classical houses in fashionable suburbs. In a Caribbean context many plantation owners exercised the ultimate separation and took themselves out of the West Indies altogether.

Other substantial houses on St Kitts included the surviving remains of the main house at Brighton which was a rebuilding of Penelope Mead's grand house (Fig. 7.2, no. 86) on one of the largest estates in Cayon. At the time of its destruction in 1706 it consisted of a large dwelling house with a hall, three chambers and porch with 'mastick' posts and boarded round, worth £280.[46] The symmetrical façade of the existing ruinous stone structure, with its three doorways and one tall window at either side, all with neatly cut voussoirs in the lintels and use of large ashlar blocks, may represent an early 18th-century rebuild of the house lost in 1706 but a later rebuild is perhaps more likely. Here too the stone ground floor supported a timber superstructure now lost due to a fire. The 1828 McMahon plan (Fig. 7.5, 'The Cayon-estate of Daniel Matthew Esq.') shows two linear features leading to the main house at Brighton from the west and south, suggesting the house was approached by imposing tree-lined avenues such as that visible on the 1827 view of Estridge (Fig. 7.10). Grainger was reminded of the 'pillars of the Temple of the Sun at Palmyra' whenever he rode 'past the charming vista of royal-palms on the Cayon-estate of Daniel Matthew Esq'.[47]

The house at the Lodge is the principal exception to construction in timber above a stone foundation, as the main house which survives largely intact is completely stone-built. On architectural grounds this was probably constructed by the mid 18th century. Termed a lodge at least by the early 19th century, it was used to entertain guests rather than at the main dwelling which may have been situated elsewhere.[48] It replaced Clement Crooke's plantation buildings which consisted of a 'framed house of 2 rooms 34 feet long and 15 broad of Leeward timber except the rafters, ends and sides boarded … worth £150, a framed room 17 by 21 feet with a porch, some part boarded, £80, and a boiling house 34 by 21 feet with Leeward posts and sides'.[49] The earliest part of the plantation house as it survives today is an Adamesque lodge or villa of rectangular plan of two storeys with a hipped roof and built in ashlar in the local volcanic stone (Fig. 7.12). There are windows on all four sides; those on the west flanking the entrance porch and steps. A plat band marks the division between the basement and ground floors; the basement floor forms one room with entrances on all four sides, all originally providing access to the garden. On the ground floor there are two rooms, the smaller being that adjacent to the entrance porch.

Fig. 7.12. The Lodge, the main house.

To the south of the lodge or villa and on the same axis is a second and detached building probably contemporary. This structure is built partly in stone and partly now in timber, and is best interpreted as the kitchen. Possibly this detached block was one of two dependencies positioned symmetrically either side of the lodge or villa.

In the later 18th century, the original architectural form of the lodge or villa was in part masked by its extension southwards to form a larger house for more permanent occupation. This larger house was built in timber and was of one floor above the basement (Fig. 7.12). The principal front of the house now faced east, first below a shade from which steps descended to the garden. A detached block was later incorporated into the main house, probably representing its change to a building for more permanent occupation. The extension was in timber, re-modelling the entrance to face east and the garden.

The Lodge is exceptional for its construction largely in stone. More typical is another large house, at Mansion, the former plantation of William Woodley MP. The main house has a timber superstructure 17m by 12m over a raised stone base, with three large rooms, in marked contrast with the much smaller overseer's house at 7.45m by 5.10m externally (Figs 7.9, 7.18).

More modest houses are indicated by surviving remains. The original house at Mills is a timber structure of three chambers, now much altered and extended, set on a stone base in which there is storage space (Fig. 7.13); the form of the timber framing suggests an 18th-century date.[50] At Ottley's the stone lower storey of the house is largely intact, where it survives with an L-shaped plan with the earliest section probably being that at right-angles to the slope. The extension to the house rendered window openings in the basement redundant. The timber superstructure, now extensively remodelled, enlarged and with an additional storey added in the late 20th century, has resulted in a considerably grander aspect than that of the 18th-century house.

Elsewhere the main house is less well preserved and in some cases the timber upper storey is lost. At White's the main house is marked by a flight of stone stairs up to a now missing first floor timber superstructure of which nothing survives. The basement level measures about 12.9m by 10m externally. However, the loss of all the facing stones means that little of the diagnostic constructional detail can be recognized. At

Fig. 7.13. Mills plantation, the main house.

The Spring a row of stone structures built against the hill slope on the higher, southern side of the compound probably represents the cellars, in one case vaulted, of the main house, while a small stone building to the east should probably be identified as a detached kitchen (Fig. 7.14). At the Hermitage the main house appears to have been completely rebuilt, probably in the early 19th century, though this requires confirmation by detailed internal survey.

This brief survey shows that the stereotype of the 'great house' or 'manor house' set at the heart of the plantation estate, which can be seen in North America and the major sugar-producing islands of the Caribbean, was largely inappropriate for St Kitts as it was also for islands such as Nevis, Dominica, and Montserrat.[51] The main house was not always large and often planters invested more in their factory buildings than their houses. A major factor in the subordination of the main house was absenteeism. By the middle of the 18th century half of the property in St Kitts was owned by

Fig. 7.14. White's plantation, detached kitchen.

absentees.[52] The legislature of the island petitioned the Crown in 1770 as 'very few of the proprietors of estates reside in this island but have retired to Europe with their families'.[53] Before the Scottish traveller Janet Schaw arrived on the island in 1774, she was told that it was 'almost abandoned to Overseers and managers, owing to the amazing fortunes that belong to Individuals, who almost all reside in England.' She saw 'several fine plantations belonging to Scotch people, who do not reside on them'.[54] Increasingly through the 18th century planters had relocated to England leaving their estates in the hands of overseers or agents. Thus, the management of the Stapleton estates in both St Kitts and Nevis was almost entirely in the hands of overseers from the early 18th century onwards.[55] Absenteeism became even more prevalent during the 19th century. In 1849 the Lieutenant-Governor of the Leeward Islands wrote that the 'number of resident proprietors in St. Kitts, superintending their estates, does not exceed eight'. Whilst Merrill considers this an exaggeration, nonetheless John Davy, writing in the 1850s, observed in St John's parish that nine of the 18 estates had given up cultivation of cane and the land had been let out to tenants to grow provisions, or abandoned, or used for pasture.[56]

Kitchens

Detached kitchens were standard at most plantations. The structure can be readily identified by a chimney and fireplace set in a stone gable wall. Hans Sloane writing in the late 17th century states 'the kitchens or cook-rooms here, are always at a small distance from their houses, because of the heat and smell, which are both noisome and troublesome'.[57] Rev. Smith on Nevis made the same point. A separate building was preferred to avoid the smell of cooking so that the plantation owner would breathe the 'pure eastern air'.[58] He goes on, 'there are no chimneys or fire-places in their houses, but in the cook-room'. The merits are obvious of separating such a potent fire-risk from the dwelling house with its timber superstructure, although the 1706 insurance claims[59] show that some 17th-century kitchens in St Kitts were in fact built in timber, but they show too that the separation of kitchen from dwelling house was already a well established practice. Hobson observes too that on the more affluent estates steward rooms and kitchens, or cook rooms, were combined under the same roof.[60] Such was probably the case at Fenton Hill, Nevis where a timber-framed house was converted to a kitchen and encased in masonry around 1700.[61]

Surviving kitchens in the study area included White's where a detached building had a large open fireplace with a stone wall extending to full gable height (Fig. 7.14). A stone building at The Spring, of random rubble construction, has a possible fireplace and an oven in the gable wall. One splayed window was evident and the structure contains thin yellow bricks, probably *klinker* bricks of Dutch origin. This small building stands apart from but close to the house, and was served by a water supply from the eponymous spring upslope. It is probably also the only structure in the survey area which may belong to the 17th century. At Brighton a detached building aligned on the main house and constructed with a gable wall to full height in stone probably served as a kitchen, though the internal details have been obscured by later modifications. At the Lodge a rectangular building may have started life as a detached kitchen before

Fig. 7.15. Mansion plantation, detached kitchen.

being incorporated into the larger house by the construction of an extension to join the two. The kitchen at Mansion in Christ Church is probably the best preserved in the study area. It stands close to the main house and is constructed of coursed blocks with a hearth set into the stone gable wall served by a brick chimney above, and an integral bread oven beside the hearth (Fig. 7.15).

Gardens

Walled gardens are present at the Hermitage and White's, though at neither site did internal features survive. On a rather grander scale is The Lodge where the plantation works are enclosed by a walled compound standing beside the ancient main road. The compound was appended to a walled garden within which the main house of the Lodge stood; a decorative pillar and finial survives at one corner of the garden, although internal features are lost. The walled enclosure, with a narrow stone tower on one corner, echoes features identified by Leech at elite merchant residences in Bristol.[62]

A formal garden survived in part at Brighton where a set of stone steps leads from the rear of the house to a central path rising up through a series of terraces retained by revetment walls. The terraces extended both in front of and behind the 18th-century main house but it is uncertain to what extent they reflect the laid gardens of the grand house depicted by Buor around 1711–13 (Fig. 7.2, no. 86) or were constructed later in the 18th century when formal gardens of Georgian style were commonly laid out to impose order and symmetry on the landscape.[63]

The plantation works buildings

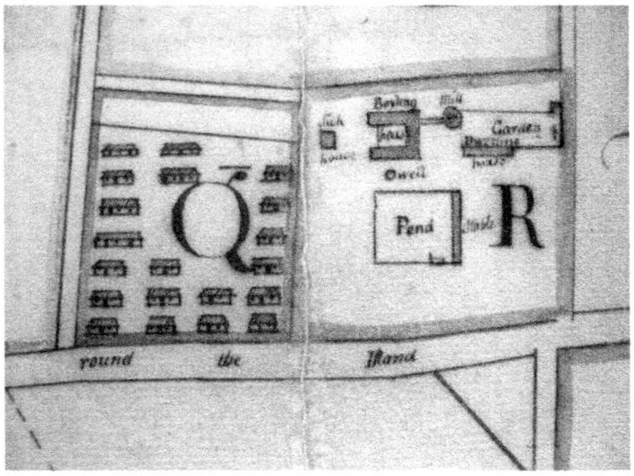

Fig. 7.16. Plan of the plantation of Abednego Mathew, 1757 (Glamorgan Archives DMW/305).

The surviving St Kitts works share many characteristics of sugar plantations elsewhere in the West Indies, which are derived ultimately from the Brazilian Pernambuco factory plantation model.[64] The consolidation of the main house and works within a single compact unit set around a central yard is a consistent feature. Not only was it intended to minimize the land removed from profitable cultivation, it also increased the efficiency of processing. The layout and constituent buildings are illustrated by one of the few detailed plans of a plantation in St Kitts, Abednego Mathew's plantation in St George Basseterre, dated 1757[65] (Fig. 7.16). The sugar works occupied a plot of just over three acres (1.2ha) and included the dwelling house, standing on one side within the compact plot. Buildings listed in the four small views on the frame of the plan are: office house, steward room, and kitchen all under the same roof; boiling house; cattle mill, garden, landry [*sic*], pigeon house, goit [small artificial channel for carrying water, here applied to a privy], 'negro houses', there was also a pond. The 'negro houses' occupy a rectangular plot immediately adjacent to the plantation works. Confirmation of the sugar works layout comes from the St Kitts sites. At Estridge, the main house stood apart, but the works buildings are arranged around an open yard (Fig. 7.19). A similar arrangement at nearby Mansion included both the overseer's and manager's houses (Fig. 7.18).

Fig. 7.17 View of works at Sandy Point Estate *c.* 1795 (photograph by R. A. Philpott of watercolour of Brimstone Hill, St Kitts by Lieut. Lees, by permission of the Scotia Bank, Basseterre, St Kitts).

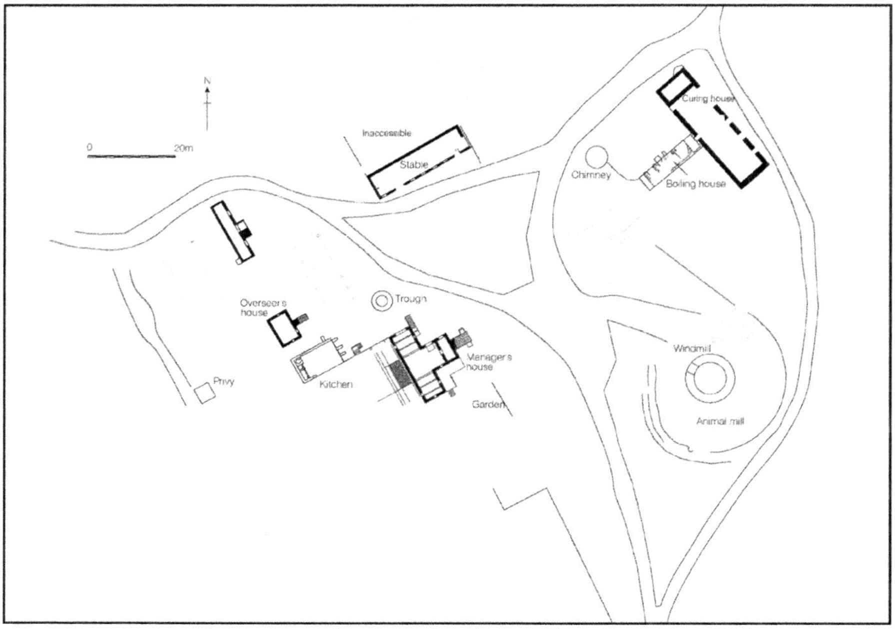

Fig. 7.18. Survey of Mansion plantation.

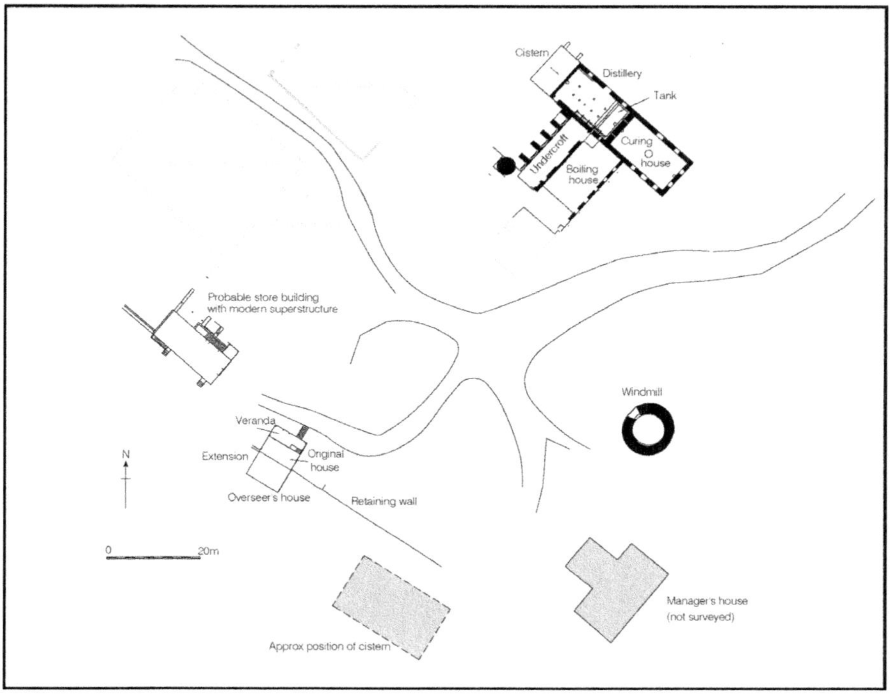

Fig. 7.19. Survey of Estridge plantation.

Occasionally traces survive of a compound boundary. At Upper Bourryeau 1 this is no more than an enclosure bank, of which part of one side and one corner remain, perhaps originally topped by a fence or hedge.

The works buildings at the plantation sites were laid out with practical considerations in mind, illustrated in a rare late 18th-century view of Sandy Point estate on the southern side of St Kitts which shows the arrangement of the sugar processing infrastructure (Fig. 7.17). The downhill flow of the sugar cane juice employed gravity through its manufacturing stages and was a determining factor in the arrangement of the works buildings. It was important to process the raw sugar cane quickly or it would spoil. Accordingly, the animal mill, and often later the windmill, where the cane was crushed to extract the juice, occupied the most elevated situation of the sequence of the processing buildings. Adjacent stood the boiling house into which the juice flowed down a channel and where the juice was poured into coppers for boiling in a series or train of coppers, before being poured into sugar cones or hogsheads for crystallizing. At a lower level stood a two-storey curing house, where the molasses dripped down into pots or directly onto the floor below for distillation into rum. The layout in terms of adjacencies and the sequence were determined by the physical constraints of the industrial process.

Boiling and curing houses

The related functions of the boiling and curing house were usually combined into a single T-shaped structure and set on a sloping site. Porter records the arrangement:

> The curing house is a large building contiguous to the boiling house, and usually built at right angles from its centre; the two forming together the shape of the letter T. The lower part of this curing house is occupied by a cavity, called the molasses cistern, which is lined … Over this cistern, and level with the floor of the boiling

Fig. 7.20. Mansion, the curing house from the NE, attached to the main structure to the right is a cistern.

Fig. 7.21. Estridge, the boiling house with chimney.

> house, is an open framework of strong joists, leaving a gangway in the middle which is boarded. The hogsheads intended to receive the sugar are ranged upright on this open floor ...[66]

At the St Kitts sites, the boiling house stood on the upslope, with stoke-holes at the rear and flues running under the floor to heat the massive metal basins or 'coppers', which were set in the boiling train within the main room. The ground floor of the boiling house connected on a level with the upper floor of the two-storey curing house, which stood at right-angles on the downslope. The curing house required a two-storey construction as it was here that crystallizing sugar was poured into hogsheads pierced with holes; these were set on uncovered close-set joists where the molasses could drip down into a tank or basin below.

With a few exceptions, White's, Mansion (Fig. 7.20), and Estridge (Fig. 7.21), boiling and curing houses have not survived well at the St Kitts plantations. None retained evidence of the settings of the boiling train in which the earlier technique of the Spanish train using multiple hearths, each heating a single copper (Spanish train) was superseded by the Jamaica train, a development from the 1680s, where the large metal basins or 'coppers' were set over a single flue (the Jamaica train) and the updraught was provided by a chimney.[67]

The importance of the boiling house is demonstrated by the valuation of Penelope Mead's property at Brighton in the insurance claim after the French raid of 1706. Valued at £450, the 60ft long boiling house, which would have included the fittings such as the coppers and clarifier, was a more valuable asset than the main dwelling house which was assessed at £280.[68] The scale of investment in plantation works buildings can be seen at its height at Estridge where a Palladian style boiling and curing house in rusticated ashlar with a steeple was constructed (Fig. 7.10), perhaps at the time of the rebuilding of the mill dated 1760. In 1834 Trelawney Wentworth described Estridge in his *West India Sketch Book I*, 'the works of this estate are of very superior construction. The boiling-house, curing-house and distillery, are all commodiously arranged under one roof, and the external appearance of the building, with its steeple, clock etc., conveys a magnificent idea of the importance of this establishment, compared with most of the works in the island.'[69] The steeple may have served to hold the bell for ringing out the divisions of daily routine – a bell tower was said to be present at Wingfield for this purpose.[70]

Estridge illustrates the form of the related functions or boiling and curing house, together with a distillery, housed within a single T-plan structure. It is built on a slope so the single-storey boiling house is integral to the two-storey curing house. The upper building – the stem of the 'T' – lacks internal details now but the arched hearths which provided heat to the boiling train remain visible. Late in the sequence the boiling house saw construction of a large 'undercroft' against the wall to shelter the hearths. The intense heat of the boiling process resulted in adoption of louvred wooden windows to allow through draught as seen surviving at Estridge. The curing house, with a pillar to support the upper floor, and a distillery marked by a large tank at one end, together form the cross bar of the 'T'. The refinement of Estridge's fine ashlar masonry, the rusticated surrounds for doors and windows, and the steeple and clocktower in the roof of the curing house and distillery, mark out the Palladian building as a high-status elite complex (Figs 7.10, 7.19).

Most boiling and curing houses are more modest structures, in both finish and scale, using the local volcanic stone and often galleted internally. The single-storey boiling house is characterized by arched window and door openings along the long façade, with recesses for shutters, as at White's and Ottley's. At White's the single-storey boiling house abuts the upper floor of the two-storey curing house owing to the strong downward slope. None of the internal fittings of the boiling house or curing house survives, though the internal walls of the curing house retain sockets for joists of the upper floor.

The use of coursed but irregular masonry may indicate an earlier date than the neatly faced work in squared blocks, which takes the form of ashlar at Estridge (Fig. 7.19) and coursed rectangular blockwork at Mansion. There is some indication that irregular galleted masonry, a style where irregular stone blocks have smaller 'chinking' stones in the mortar to fill in the corners, are found in early phases of surviving structures, and may be largely an 18th-century phenomenon.

Animal mills

The power to drive the cane-crushing machinery was derived initially from animals, oxen or mules, walking on a circular path and yoked to a rotating beam. Contemporary descriptions and views from the 17th and 18th centuries[71] show them as conical-roofed open-sided structures which protected the mill-rollers in the centre. An 18th-century view of a plantation on St Kitts shows not only a windmill but also the animal mill (Fig. 7.17), a precaution maintained by many planters to ensure cane crushing could continue if the wind dropped. Raised animal mills were a development of those set on level ground and allowed the slaves feeding the cane to the animals for crushing and

Fig. 7.22. Upper Bourryeau, remains of raised animal mill.

removing the crushed stalks interfered with the path of the animals walking the track; a raised mill allowed the cane to be fed in and waste removed with no such disruption. Raised animal mills constructed using stone retaining walls were identified from the circular platform at the Hermitage, Upper Bourryeau 1 (Fig. 7.22) and Ottley's.

Windmills

The introduction of wind power to the West Indies was an important innovation of the mid 17th century. Windmills were able to work 24 hours a day without needing rest as long as the wind held, a significant advance over animal power. Although initially Dutch in design, windmills soon took on a standardized north-west European form as found in both England and northern France. The planters of St Kitts were much slower to adopt wind power than those of Barbados, where by 1676 there were already no fewer than 400 windmills.[72] For St Kitts, the map sequence provides an index of the progress in the adoption of wind power during the 18th and early 19th century. Buor (Fig. 7.2) illustrates only two windmills in St Mary Cayon *c.* 1711–13, at the Lodge and Mathew's Brighton Plantation, and none yet in Christ Church. By 1753 Baker's map (Fig. 7.3) shows that most plantation mills across the island continued to rely on animal power, although a scatter of windmills is present, mostly in the northern part of the island. Within the study area, Baker records windmills at Mathew's (Brighton), Ottley's, the Grange, and the Lodge, while Christ Church has windmills at Akers (later Baker's), Mills, Bourryeau, and two neighbouring Estridge plantations. Thus, the Baker map provides a valuable chronological anchor for the construction of windmills, indicating that those at White's, the Spring, and the Hermitage do not pre-date 1753.

Windmills were robust constructions and survive better than many other plantation buildings. White's has the only windmill within St Mary Cayon which retains the full height of the superstructure (Fig. 7.23), though in Christ Church parish, the stone mill towers at Estridge (bearing a datestone of 1760), Mansion (dated 1764; Fig. 7.24), and Mills (undated but present by 1753) are substantially intact, enabling details of the construction to be identified. The mills conform to a standardized design with a tapering stone tower on a level circular foundation, usually with two arched entrances at ground floor level. The wider entrance was served by a ramp, defined by sloping terrace walls on either side, through which the cut cane was delivered and fed to vertical rollers inside.

Fig. 7.23. Windmill at White's plantation, St Mary Cayon.

Only at Mansion do the internal timber floors survive, consisting of four floors including the ground. Here as elsewhere the upper floors were lit by small arched windows. No machinery, sails, or caps survive on the St Kitts mills but an early 19th-century illustration of the Estridge mill shows a triangular gabled cap with subsidiary sloping roofs over the sides and a tail-pole for turning the cap and the four sails into the wind. The White's building has many features in common with the windmill at Galways, in existence

Fig. 7.24. Windmill at Mansion, Christ Church.

by 1770, on the nearby island of Montserrat in the presence of a broad entrance with ramped entrance and a narrower entrance reached by steps at 90°. Also paralleled at Galways, and at well preserved windmills in Nevis such as Spring Hill and Russell's Rest, is the series of vertical slots around the top of the interior to carry the framework supporting the rotating roof as well as the horizontal slots lower down in the interior walls to take the wooden frame for the machinery.[73]

Steam-powered mills

By 1828 McMahon's map demonstrates that most plantations still in operation had converted to wind power. However, by then a third form of motive power had already begun to make headway in the islands. Steam engines had been introduced to the Caribbean in the late 18th century,[74] and by 1825 they were in common use in the region. The famous English company of Boulton and Watt had supplied Caribbean Islands with nearly 200 steam engines designed for sugar mills between 1778 and 1825. There were said to be about half a dozen steam engines in Nevis by 1815, although Coleridge observed only two steam engines on Nevis installed in 1825.[75] The investment in steam power came at considerable cost and was not without risk since spare parts were not readily available in the islands.[76] They were only worth installing if there was a large acreage of canes to cut.[77] By 1846, 33 steam engines were in operation in St Kitts and they were beginning to take over from the windmill;[78] by 1878, the figure had risen to 73,[79] and coal was being imported as a fuel.

Although the general chronological progression is clear, it is also evident from the different development of the various sites that individual circumstances led to the adoption of new technological innovations at different times, if at all. Windmills were preferred by planters as they were faster but suffered the obvious disadvantage of being useless when the wind dropped. As a result, some planters retained animal mills as

Fig. 7.25. Upper Bourryeau, remains of steam engine dated 1889.

a back-up. In the Leeward Islands, on small relatively unproductive estates which were poorly situated to take advantage of water or wind power, cattle mills remained common.[80]

The full sequence is exemplified by the Hermitage. Here the raised cattle mill was adopted as the site of the windmill to gain extra height to catch the wind on this level coastal site. Subsequently the estate was converted to steam power, as the chimney, now reduced to its base, and associated flues as well as a large circular cistern, demonstrate. Not all sites display the sequence of all three forms of power. Upper Bourryeau 1 for example had a raised animal mill, with a stone retaining wall on the downslope, followed by a steam engine, which bears a date of 1889 (Fig. 7.25), but there is no sign of a windmill. The Spring does not appear to have ever been converted to steam power, though beside the windmill is a level area suitable for an animal mill, while White's has no extant animal mill, though both a windmill and steam engine are present. Features typical of conversion to steam power include a concrete bed to take the steam engine itself, and a nearby chimney to provide an updraught for the furnace linked by flues to the boiling house and to the steam engine. The substantial increase in demand for water in the use of steam power was met by the construction of large tanks or cisterns and there is a clear correlation between the largest cisterns and the presence of steam engines. At the Hermitage, Upper Bourryeau 2, White's, and the Grange large circular tanks stand in some cases close to the steam engines. The provision of additional water storage was taken to extreme lengths at Spring Hill on Nevis where several new tanks were created by strengthening and internally lining former plantation buildings.

Cisterns

Water was an essential commodity on the island, not only for the sustenance of the animal and human population, but also for the production of sugar and rum. Periodic droughts in the Leeward Islands caused serious losses to the sugar crop and shortages of supply. In a brief visit to Nevis in the late 1680s, Hans Sloane had noted that there were neither springs nor rivers there but rainwater was collected in cisterns.[81] Cisterns for water storage are found at most of the sites. The earlier cisterns at plantation works are small and often rectangular in plan, strongly built with thick walls and rounded internal corners, and plaster-lined internally to render them watertight. They are frequently located at the end or side of buildings where they received water channelled from the catchment of rainwater from the roofs. Thus, at The Spring a small cistern which was attached to the end of the curing house was later enlarged, while at Mansion a large cistern was incorporated in the curing house (Fig. 7.20). Isolated cisterns may on occasion provide an indication of the location of buildings of which no other surface traces remain. Their massive construction means that they often outlast the buildings whose roofs once fed them. At Pogson's a detached cistern and windmill tower are the only remains surviving above ground of that plantation, while at Upper Bourryeau 1 a cistern lay next to a terrace, now planted with cane, which may have held the main house of the plantation. An isolated circular cistern represents the only surviving remnant of the main plantation house at Estridge, which was in ruins by the early 19th century.

Waterholes

Waterholes or 'slabs' (a term which is recorded by the 18th century on Nevis, as in the 1755 map of Jessup's estate) have been noted at Upper Bourryeau 1, at the Hermitage slave village, and at the Spring slave village while a possible example is represented by a now-dry hollow at the Ottley's slave village. An important function was watering livestock, while their consistent location at slave villages suggests that the pasture grounds for animals lay close to the slave villages.

SLAVE VILLAGES

Perhaps uniquely for the West Indies, McMahon's 1828 map of St Kitts captures the entire landscape of the island. The date is critical, only six years before emancipation, and after two centuries of landscape development. The map records the position of all the slave villages in the island in their final incarnation at the end of the slavery era, and at the end of a long process of amalgamation and consolidation. As a result, the island is particularly well suited to a comparative study of the slave villages, enabling such characteristics as location, situation, and aspect to be examined, as well as internal features such as the layout and chronology of construction. In the two parishes, examination of the villages in the field has shown there are some recurrent elements in their location, not only in topography but also with respect to the other plantation buildings.

The documented amalgamation of sugar plantations on St Kitts, which it has been calculated fell from 360 in 1724 to only 110 in 1783,[82] raises the question of the reduction and amalgamation of the villages for slaves attached to the consolidated plantations. Two-thirds of the surviving plantations on the McMahon map are associated with an inhabited slave village, which are in some cases extensive. Some of these are probably aggregations out of smaller villages drawn from abandoned estate centres. If so, there may have been many more slave villages adjacent to plantation centres which had been abandoned by the time of McMahon's survey. The locational factors identified for the early 19th-century villages might therefore help to predict the location of these early otherwise unrecorded sites.

Higman has observed that the contemporary cartographic style in the depiction of slave villages on Jamaican maps usually under-represented the number of buildings.[83] The map evidence for slave houses in lines corresponded with an orderly layout on the ground, which was an indication of the direct intervention of the planter in the organization of space within the village. However, the evidence of plans from Jamaica indicates that the ordered regular or linear layouts are rare until 1790, reach a peak around 1810 and then declined after emancipation. Although some new sugar plantations were created after 1790, most of the regular layouts represent the organization of existing slave villages. He also found a correlation between the presence of the planter and the reorganization of the slave villages.[84]

A variety of factors appear to have determined the siting of the slave villages with respect to the main house, although for contemporary testimony we rely on evidence from other islands. Rev. William Smith, writing from his five-year residence on Nevis from 1716 onwards, writes; 'they live in Huts, on the Western Side of our Dwelling-Houses, so that every Plantation resembles a small Town'. The location meant that 'we breath the pure Eastern Air, without being offended with the least nauseous smell: Our Kitchens and Boyling-houses are on the same side, and for the same reason'.[85] In 1724 Labat's idealized design for an estate layout based on 12 years managing an estate on the French island of Martinique shows one or two rows of slave houses set downwind of the estate house. They are close to the animal enclosures and set below the plantation house which stands on a small hill.[86] Hans Sloane observes that the 'Negroes' houses are likewise at a distance from their master's, the context indicating that the separation was to avoid the noise and smells.[87]

Contemporary descriptions of slave villages do exist, largely of the late 18th or early 19th century, but they are cloaked in the language of the picturesque. The poem of 1764 'The Sugar Cane!' by James Grainger, a friend of the St Kitts planter John Bourryeau, romanticized the plantation landscape.

> Nor not delightful are those reed-built huts,
> On yonder hill, that front the rising sun;
> With plantanes, with banana's bosom'd deep.
> That flutter in the wind; ....[88]

Similarly, Henry Coleridge visiting the Leeward Islands in 1825 refers to 'the tall and moving windmills, the houses of the proprietors, the works and palm-thatched cottages of the negros embosomed in plantains, present the appearance, as indeed they are the substance, of so many country villages in England'.[89]

In the study area, the location of the slave villages frequently conforms to Smith's observations, being positioned downwind of the plantation house on the prevailing north-easterly trade winds. Clearly the local topography plays an important part in the precise location, but most slave villages lie within the three compass directions from north, west through to south. In the few cases where the slave village lies to the east of the plantation works and house, some are set in valleys or ghuts, as at Ottley's, though at the Grange the location of the village directly east of the house and works appears to be an exception.

The slave villages are usually close to the plantation works and they are consistently at a lower elevation than the main house or manager's house and the works. This had not only the practical motive that they could be overseen from the house and works but served too as a physical embodiment of their inferior social status. The main house at most plantations is elevated above the works, although on occasion the main house lies at some distance away, the beginnings of a move towards the deliberate social and physical separation of the planter and his enslaved workforce.

The topographical situation of the slave villages shares other common features. The sites are often on the periphery of estates and were often located so that they did not intrude into the main blocks of cane fields. Several are located on level or near level ground near the edges of the deep ravines or ghuts, such as the Grange or Upper Bourryeau 2, and in cases such as Upper Bourryeau 2 and Ottley's on tongues of land between ghuts. At the Hermitage the slave village, demarcated by a boundary bank, occupies level ground immediately adjacent to the high sea-cliff (Fig. 7.26). In some

Fig. 7.26. Slave village at Hermitage.

cases, they lie in the sloping base of valleys, such as the Spring or Ottley's, beside a much steeper-sided ghut. That the slave village sites were in some cases suitable for sugar cane production is demonstrated by those at Brighton or the Grange which were planted with cane in recent times. Areas of level ground near to the slave villages such as Hermitage may have been used as gardens or cultivable land, although pasture for animals would also have been required. The implication is that slave village sites, whilst physically inferior in situation, were not necessarily on highly marginal land unsuitable for cane production but could occupy sites on potentially productive land.

In some cases, the limits of the slave villages are demarcated by banks (The Spring and Hermitage), but often the topography imposes natural boundaries, notably on the edge of the steep ghuts.

The interiors of the slave villages preserve little evidence of their former use. The compensation claims for the damage suffered in the French raid of February 1706 indicate the flimsy construction of slave huts, with their valuation of no more than £2.[90] The archaeologically ephemeral slave houses, which may originally have been wooden or wattle and daub huts thatched with cane trash, leave few traces in the ground, and unsurprisingly not a single structure survives in any of the slave villages visited. However, traces of possible house platforms were observed at Ottley's, and possibly Hermitage within the areas shown as slave villages on the McMahon map of 1828. The slave village of Mills in Christ Church was under sugar cane cultivation when surveyed and a scatter of 18th- and 19th-century pottery was observed on the surface though none was collected. At three slave villages, Ottley's, The Spring, and the Hermitage, slabs or waterholes are present. No sign either of slave cemeteries or marked individual graves was observed in the St Kitts sites.

Plantation owners, through custom and practice, as well as self-interest, provided cultivable land to allow slaves to grow their own vegetables and fruit, at the same time reducing the planter's expenditure on food. This land was of two kinds. The

Fig. 7.27. Detail from the plan of Clarke's estate on Nevis, *c.* 1818 (NHCS Hamilton Museum, Nevis).

first consisted of land often at some distance from the plantation and slave dwellings, often mountainous or poor-quality land, set aside for the use of the slaves in their own time. Nevis provides corroborative evidence. 'Negro provision grounds' are shown on the 1755 Jessups estate map on Nevis.[91] The second type consisted of cultivated garden plots attached to the huts with the slave villages. The *c.* 1818 plan of Clarke's estate on Nevis[92] shows that seven of the 13 depicted slave huts had attached roughly rectangular plots of ground, cultivated in parallel ridges (Fig. 7.27). This may be the activity suggested by two St Kitts sites, the Spring and Upper Bourryeau 1, where low parallel ridges within the slave village indicate that the land was cultivated there, although whether these relate to the garden plots beside slave huts or cultivation after their abandonment is uncertain.

John Pinney in the 1790s stipulated two conditions in setting out a slave village at his Mountravers plantation on Nevis. Houses should be 'built at approximate distances in right lines to prevent accidents from fire and to afford each negro a proper piece of land around the house'.[93] James Grainger advocated that planters 'build thy Negroe-huts … in streets, at distance due',[94] while Beckford[95] recommended slave houses should be laid out 'in strait lines, constructed with some degree of uniformity and strength, but totally divested of trees and shrubs'.[96] The greater emphasis on increased surveillance and greater concern for regulation of slave lifestyles was part of a new concern for closely designed landscapes of the 18th century.[97] Thus, although the orderly layout within the slave village as suggested by rows of huts on the McMahon and other more detailed estate maps may be no more than cartographic convention, it may in fact reflect the actual layout.

In a series of watercolours of Brimstone Hill, St Kitts by Lieut. Lees dated to the late 18th century (in 2015 housed in the Scotia Bank, Basseterre), three separate groups of slave houses are illustrated. One, placed incidentally on the edge of the composition, is a slave village near the foot of Brimstone Hill (Fig. 7.28). A rubble stone wall encloses

Fig. 7.28. Detail from watercolour of Brimstone Hill, St Kitts *c.* 1795 (photograph by R.A. Philpott of watercolour by Lieut. Lees, by permission of the Scotia Bank, Basseterre, St Kitts).

the huts of the village, and the interior is dominated by a dense mass of bushes and trees, including at least one recognizable palm, amid the huts. Another village stands adjacent to a fenced compound, connected with the fort, but, as this slave village has tentatively been associated with the garrison of the fort,[98] it may not have been typical of villages at sugar plantations.

On other Caribbean islands slave villages are set within well-established groves of trees, as James Hakewill illustrated for Jamaican sugar plantations at Montpelier and Spring Garden.[99] Bryan Edwards, a British plantation owner in Jamaica, in the later 18th century described the slave villages familiar to him. 'They are seldom placed with much regard to order, but, being always intermingled with fruit-trees, particularly the banana, the avocado-pear, and the orange (the Negroes' own planting and property) they sometimes exhibit a pleasing and picturesque appearance'.[100] The trees served the practical functions both of providing shade as well as supplementing the slaves' diet and for the inhabitants they created areas of private space not subject to surveillance from the overseer. The frequent association of ancient mango trees with the sites of abandoned slave villages as observed today at Ottley's and Mansion, as well as Jessups on Nevis, is unlikely to be coincidence, as has been suggested through the modern survival for instance of fruit trees at slave villages sites in Jamaica.[101]

POST-EMANCIPATION VILLAGES

After emancipation in 1834, many newly freed labourers moved away from the plantations, emigrating or setting up new homes as squatters on abandoned estate land. Some slave villages were abandoned soon after emancipation, while others remained in use for the labourers who chose to stay on the plantation as paid workers and rented their house and land. The decline of the slave villages was observed by Davy who records that after emancipation the more enterprising amongst the free labourers preferred to rent plots in newly established villages away from the estates.[102]

In St Kitts, the emancipated labourers had no opportunity for squatting on public land since there was none left, which reduced the critical shortage of labour encountered on other islands.[103] Shortage of labour was experienced, however, and St Kitts saw the introduction of workers from England, Africa, Madeira, India, and China to alleviate the problem in the mid 19th century.

The first new village, Challenger's Village, on St Kitts was set up in 1840 or 1841, when a customs officer John Challenger sold or rented small lots out of a tract of land to newly free labourers.[104] Other villages were established on steep unused land, often in the deep ghuts, which were unsuitable for cultivation, such as Cayon, Ottley's, or Lodge villages in St Kitts.[105] Villages such as Leigh's, St Paul's, Parson's, Sadler's, and Tabernacle village developed, occupied entirely by black and mixed race people. 'The huts were small, mostly of wood, and thatched with sugarcane leaves'.[106] They were set on rented or purchased small plots but were intended to be easily moved should the owner decide to transfer elsewhere.

By the mid 19th century Davy observed:[107]

> And here, as there, they have been rather encouraged than checked in the forming of free villages, and in establishing themselves in dwellings of their own, either on small plots of land purchased or rented. When the latter, they have the privilege of placing dwellings of their own on them, as in Barbados, with the power of removing them, which is easily done, being altogether of wood – walls, roof, and flooring, should they chuse to change their place of abode … the most enlightened proprietors are now convinced of the advantage to be derived from the settlements, which contain an assemblage of well-disposed and industrious peasantry; while on the other hand, the old collection of negro huts, or wretched hovels, (belonging to estates, and occupied by tenants-at-will,) has too commonly since emancipation, proved a refuge and a lurking place for the indolent and profligate of the labouring class.

He describes the village of Cayon at length:

> the village of Cayon, in the district of the same name, is worth seeing, being a good example of the villages of the country which have sprung up since the abolition of slavery. It stands high, beautifully situated on the side of a deep glen, through which a rivulet finely shaded with trees flows rapidly making many pretty falls in its descent. Large and scattered, it covers a good deal of ground, land in small portions being attached to most of the cottages. Amongst its inhabitants are persons of different trades, all of the colored race, shoemakers, saddlers, masons, carpenters, wheelwrights, coopers, smiths, sempstresses.

The plantation works, boiling and curing houses were rendered redundant in St Kitts with the construction of a centralized processing sugar factory and the development of the round the island railway in 1912.[108]

THE PLANTATION LANDSCAPE TODAY

The archaeological survey in 2004 and 2005 showed that the historic plantation landscape of St Kitts was then under severe pressure from a number of directions. Damage through neglect of wooden and stone buildings with overgrowth of vegetation, particularly trees rooting in the fabric of buildings, was causing active destruction at unoccupied sites. Many of the sites had been damaged in the past by the removal of the high-quality facing stone for reuse in new buildings. Where this has occurred the long-term survival of the affected plantation buildings has been seriously compromised. The end of sugar cane production in 2005 has led to the search for alternative sources of income and pressure from development has resulted in destruction of sites. Extensive golf course developments have completely transformed historic landscapes, erasing all but the most obvious plantation buildings.

The visible plantation remains are often more obvious, the plantation centres, houses, and works, although even they can be erased from the landscape with no above ground remains to indicate their former existence. Far less visible, and therefore considerably more exposed to unwitting development, are the remains of the slave villages, their sites often still on St Kitts devoid of later development. They are the most vulnerable elements of the plantation landscape. There are implications for the preservation either physical or by record of these slave villages, which form the physical settlements of the ancestors of many Kittitians today. Although the village sites are for the most part invisible on the surface often with no physical trace of structures or boundaries, the locations can be readily identified from the 1828 McMahon map. However, so far little detailed archaeological investigation has been undertaken at any slave village in the island, apart from test-pitting at The Spring by the Digital Archaeological Archive of Comparative Slavery (DAACS) and the University of Southampton in 2008.[109] This contrasts with neighbouring Nevis where the locations of a few slave villages are known through a small number of individual estate maps, or through field survey.

Careful adaptation and interpretation of plantation remains can add significant value to any new development and, overall, has the potential to enhance the experience of visitors to St Christopher substantially. Redevelopment of sites for tourism and other purposes is likely to cause damage to these sites where it is not informed by an understanding of the nature and relative significance of the various elements. The irretrievable loss of the below-ground deposits, the archaeological sequences and material culture, and the thoughtless destruction of ephemeral structures with the early phases of settlement is an inevitable consequence of large-scale development without heritage management systems in place.

An urgent task is to take advantage of new techniques which would enable the recording of the remaining plantation buildings above ground, employing the cost-effective and highly accurate photogrammetric techniques which enable highly detailed, scaled computer models of the buildings to be created.

The internal features of the slave villages are little understood. No detailed archaeological investigation has been conducted into the villages on St Kitts, to examine their layout, the character of the buildings, and the use of space within the villages, or to investigate material aspects of the slave economy and use of material culture. Detailed intensive topographic surveys by LiDAR may reveal subtle traces of terracing, house platforms, and cultivation ridges, while shovel test pitting of the kind employed at Jessups and New River on Nevis by the joint project undertaken by DAACS, Monticello, Virginia, the University of Southampton and National Museums Liverpool in 2006 and 2008 may reveal changing patterns of use and activity through analysis of artefact distributions.[110]

The many surveys of sites in the parishes of St Mary Cayon and Christchurch Nichola Town on St Kitts and within the Mountravers landscape on Nevis, most published for the first time in this volume, reveal how many such sites remain concealed around and in the forest and scrub that has grown over the former sugar cane fields and other plantation lands, and that archaeological field survey is an effective means of rapidly identifying large numbers of sites of archaeological and historic interest.

ACKNOWLEDGEMENTS

In 2004 the project team consisted of Robert Philpott, Roger Leech, Jon Brett, Lorraine Darton, and Eleanor Leech, and in 2005 Robert Philpott, Roger Leech, and Jon Brett. The team is grateful for the help and generosity offered by many people during the course of the fieldwork. Ms June Hughes, Director of Environment (Agriculture) gave permission for the survey on behalf of the Government of St Kitts-Nevis, Mrs Jackie Armony, Director of the St Christopher Heritage Society provided invaluable support and assistance to the project, Mr Bryan Farrell, Conservation Officer at the Department of the Environment, kindly made time to take the project team to several sites. The late Vince Hubbard offered much useful advice on historical sources. Amongst the site owners Dave and Kim Lee (Lodge), Art, Ruth, and Karen Keusch and Marty and Nancy Lowell (Ottley's), and Ray and Sue Wharton (Brighton) were extremely generous in their support of the project. In the field the team received unstinting help from the people of St Kitts and we hope that the results of the research project will repay a little of their kindness. Tragically, Jon Brett died at the early age of 40 on 23 March 2007 – fittingly this [volume] is dedicated to his memory.

NOTES

1 Higman 1988, 1.
2 Berkshire Record Office D/EM P9, Z16–17 NRA 799 Morland.
3 Philpott *et al.* 2005.
4 e.g. Janet Schaw (Andrews & Andrews 1921); William Smith 1745; Davy 1854.
5 Andrews & Andrews 1921, 130–1.
6 Porter 1830, 34.
7 Johnston 1965, 191.
8 Dunn 1973, 125.
9 O'Shaughnessy 2000, 133.
10 Cox 1984, 30–1.
11 Geggus 1997.
12 O'Shaughnessy 2000, 47, 51.
13 Duffy 1997, 82.
14 Ramsay 1784.
15 Brereton 1999.
16 Select Committee 1842, 229.
17 Hall 1971, 41.
18 Harlow 1925, 87.
19 Harlow 1925, 4, fig. 1.
20 Leech 2007.
21 Ligon 1657, 86.
22 Armstrong & Reilly 2014.
23 Andrews & Andrews 1921, 130.
24 Hicks 2007, 49; Calendar State Papers S 1716–17, no. 118; cited by Niddrie 1966, 8–9.
25 O'Shaughnessy 2000, 27–8.
26 Sheridan 1976.
27 Green 1973, 449.

28 Leech 2005; Philpott *et al.* forthcoming.
29 Cited in Dunn 1973, 126, 43.
30 Oldmixon 1708, II, 249.
31 Parliamentary Papers 1843.
32 Sloane 1707, xlvii.
33 Sainsbury 1893.
34 Bridenbaugh & Bridenbaugh 1972, 189.
35 Dunn 1973, 136–9.
36 Hobson 2007.
37 TNA CO243/2 fol. 396.
38 Leech 2005.
39 Oldmixon 1708, II, 226.
40 Leech 2013, 54–6.
41 Andrews & Andrews 1921, 124.
42 Leech 2013, 53–5, fig. 4.17; Leech 2014, 362–3.
43 Wentworth 1834, 70–1.
44 Sloane 1707, xlvii.
45 Leech 2013, 48–9.
46 TNA CO243/2.
47 Grainger 1764, 196.
48 Leech 2013, 46–56; 2014, 364.
49 TNA CO243/2.
50 R. Leech pers. comm.
51 e.g. Honychurch 1975, 77; Goodwin 1987, 111.
52 Merrill 1958, 79.
53 Crist 1949, 138.
54 Andrews & Andrews 1921, 92–3, 131.
55 Johnston 1965.
56 Merrill 1958, 85.
57 Sloane 1707, xlvii.
58 Smith 1745, 225–6.
59 TNA CO243/2.
60 Hobson 2007, 194.
61 Philpott *et al.* forthcoming.
62 Leech 2013, 51–2.
63 See Deetz 1996, 62–6.
64 Watts 1987, 179–84.
65 Glamorgan Archives DMW/305.
66 Porter 1830, 86–7.
67 Hicks 2007, 47.
68 TNA CO 243/2.
69 Wentworth 1834.
70 Hicks 2007, 51.
71 e.g. de Rochefort 1665, 332; Ligon 1657, 84.
72 Watts 1987, 413.
73 Goodwin 1987, figs 5.4, 5.5.
74 Zogbaum 2002, 40.
75 Coleridge 1826, 191.
76 Davy 1854, 454.
77 Pares 1950, 363 n. 1.
78 Davy 1854, 454; Green 1973, 461.
79 Hall 1973, cited in Hicks 2007, 70.
80 Green 1973, 452.
81 Smith 1745, 218.
82 O'Shaughnessy 2000, 27.
83 Higman 1998, 127–8.
84 Higman 1998, 130–1.
85 Smith 1745, 225–6.
86 Watts 1978, 386.
87 Sloane 1707, xlvii.
88 Grainger 1764, 141.
89 Coleridge 1826, 216.
90 Dunn 1973, 139.
91 Southampton City Archives, D/MW 35/8a: a plan of Jessups plantation in 1755.
92 NHCS Hamilton Museum, Nevis.
93 Eickelmann & Small 2004, 27.
94 Grainger 1764, 160; cited in Hicks 2007, 46.
95 Beckford 1790, II, 20.
96 Hicks 2007, 46.
97 Hicks 2007, 46.
98 G. Schroedl pers. comm.
99 Hakewill 1825, pls 19, 8.
100 Edwards 1793, II, 126.
101 Higman 1998, 197.
102 Davy 1854.
103 Merrill 1958, 90.
104 Merrill 1958, 95.
105 Davy 1854, 442–3; Dyde 2005, 158–9.
106 Merrill 1958, 95.
107 Davy 1854, 442–3.
108 Hicks 2007, 71.
109 https://www.daacs.org/plantations/the-spring/.
110 https://www.daacs.org.

BIBLIOGRAPHY

Andrews, E.W. & Andrews, C.M. (eds) 1921, *Journal of a lady of quality; being the narrative of a journey from Scotland to the West Indies, North Carolina, and Portugal, in the years 1774 to 1776*, New Haven: Yale University Press.

Armstrong, D.V. & Reilly, M.C. 2014, 'The Archaeology of Settler Farms and Early Plantation Life in Seventeenth-Century Barbados', *Slavery and Abolition: A J. Slave and Post-Slave Studies* 35:3, 399–417.

Beckford, W.A. 1790, *A descriptive account of the island of Jamaica with remarks upon the cultivation of the sugar-cane* (2 vols), London: T. & J. Egerton.

Breisch, K.A. & Hoagland, A. (eds) 2005, *Building Environments: Perspectives in Vernacular Architecture* 10, Knoxville: University of Tennessee Press.

Brereton, B. 1999, 'Family Strategies, Gender and the Shift to Wage Labour in the British Caribbean', in Brereton & Yelvington (eds) 1999, 77–107.

Brereton, B. & Yelvington, K.A. (eds) 1999, *The Colonial Caribbean in Transition: Essays on Post Emancipation Social and Cultural History*, Barbados: University of the West Indies Press.

Bridenbaugh, C. & Bridenbaugh, R. 1972, *No Peace Beyond the Line: The English in the Caribbean 1624–1690*, New York: Oxford University Press.

Coleridge, H. 1826, *Six Months in the West Indies, in 1825*, London: John Murray.

Cox, E.L. 1984, *Free Coloreds in the Slave Societies of St Kitts and Grenada, 1763–1833*, Knoxville: University of Tennessee Press.

Crist, R.E. 1949, 'Static and Emerging Cultural Landscapes on the Islands of St. Kitts and Nevis, B.W.I.', *Econ. Geogr.* 25:2 (Apr. 1949), 134–45.

Davy, J. 1854, *The West Indies, before and since Slave Emancipation*, London: W. & F.G. Cash.

De Rochefort, C. 1665, *Histoire naturelle et morale des Isles Antilles de l'Amerique*, 2nd edn, Rotterdam.

Deetz, E. 1996, *In Small Things Forgotten*, 2nd edn, New York: Doubleday.

Dresser, M. & Hann, A. (eds) 2013, *Slavery and the British Country House*, Swindon: English Heritage.

Duffy, M. 1997, 'The French Revolution and British Attitudes to the West Indian Colonies', in Gaspar & Geggus (eds) 1997, 78–101.

Dunn, R.S. 1973, *Sugar and Slaves: The Rise of the Planter Class in the English West Indies, 1624–1713*, New York: W.W. Norton & Co.

Dyde, B. 2005, *Out of the Crowded Vagueness: A History of the Islands of St Kitts, Nevis & Anguilla*, Oxford: MacMillan Caribbean.

Edwards, B. 1793, *The History, Civil and Commercial of the British Colonies in the West Indies*, 2 vols, Dublin: Luke White (reprinted Arno Press, New York, 1972).

Eickelmann, C. & Small, D. 2004, *Pero. The Life of a Slave in Eighteenth-Century Bristol*, Bristol: Redcliffe Press and Bristol Museums and Art Gallery.

Farnsworth, P. (ed.) 2001, *Island Lives: Historical Archaeology of the Caribbean*, Tuscaloosa and London: University of Alabama Press.

Finch, J. & Giles, K. (eds) 2007, *Estate Landscapes: Design, Improvement and Power in the Post-Medieval Landscape*, Soc. Post-Med. Arch. Monogr. 4, Woodbridge: Boydell and Brewer.

Fryer, J. 2002, 'Post-Emancipation Life in Colonial Nevis, 1840–1880, As Reported in the Blue Books. Part 1', *Nevis Hist. Conserv. Soc. Newsl.* 63 (Feb 2002), 4–8.

Gaspar, D.B. & Geggus, D.P. (eds) 1997, *A Turbulent Time: The French Revolution and the Greater Caribbean*, Bloomington: Indiana University Press.

Geggus, D.P. 1997, 'Slavery, War, and Revolution in the Greater Caribbean, 1789–1815', in Gaspar & Geggus (eds) 1997, 1–50.

Goodwin, C.M. 1987, 'Sugar, Time and Englishmen: A Study of Management Strategies on Caribbean Plantations', unpublished PhD thesis submitted to Boston University Graduate School, USA.

Grainger, J. 1764. *The sugar-cane: a poem. In four books. With notes.*, London: R. & J. Dodsley.

Green, W.A. 1973, 'The Planter Class and British West Indian Sugar Production, Before and After Emancipation', *The Econom. Hist. Rev.*, New Series 26:3, 448–63.

Hakewill, J. 1825, *A picturesque tour of the island of Jamaica*, London (reprinted 1990, Kingston, Jamaica; Mill Press, San Francisco).
Hall, D. 1971, *Five of the Leewards, 1834–1870: The Major Problems of the Post-Emancipation Period in Antigua, Barbuda, Montserrat, Nevis and St Kitts*, St Laurence, Barbados: Caribbean Universities Press.
Harlow, V.T. 1925, *Colonising Expeditions to the West Indies and Guiana, 1623–1667*, Hakluyt Soc., 2nd ser. 56.
Hicks, D. 2007, *'The Garden of the World': A Historical Archaeology of Sugar Landscapes in the Eastern Caribbean*, Brit. Archaeol. Rep. Int. Ser. 1632, Oxford: Archaeopress.
Higman, B.W. 1988, *Jamaica Surveyed: Plantation Maps and Plans of the Eighteenth and Nineteenth Centuries*, Kingston: Institute of Jamaica Publications.
Higman, B.W. 1998, *Montpelier, Jamaica. A Plantation Community in Slavery and Freedom 1739–1912*, Kingston, Jamaica: The Press University of the West Indies.
Hobson, D.L. 2007, 'The Domestic Architecture of the Earliest British Colonies in the American Tropics: A Study of the Houses of the Caribbean 'Leeward' Islands of St. Christopher, Nevis, Antigua and Montserrat. 1624–1726', PhD Dissertation Georgia Institute of Technology.
Honychurch, L. 1975, *The Dominica Story: A History of the Island*, Oxford: Macmillan Education.
Hubbard, V.K. 2002, *A History of St Kitts: The Sweet Trade*, Oxford: Macmillan Caribbean.
Johnson, J. 1827, *A Series of Views in the West Indies: engraved from drawings taken recently in the islands*, London: Messrs. Underwood.
Johnston, J.R.V. 1965, 'The Stapleton Sugar Plantations in the Leeward Islands', *Bull. John Rylands Lib.* 48:1, 175–206.
Leech, R.H. 2005, 'Impermanent Architecture in the English Colonies of the Eastern Caribbean: New Contexts for Innovation in the Early Modern Atlantic World', in Breisch & Hoagland (eds) 2005, 155–67.
Leech, R.H. 2007, '"In What Manner Did They Devide The Land" The Early Colonial Estate Landscape of Nevis and St Kitts', in Finch & Giles (eds) 2007, 191–204.
Leech, R.H. 2013, 'Lodges, Garden Houses and Villas: The Urban Periphery in the Early Modern Atlantic World', in Dresser & Hann (eds) 2013, 46–56.
Leech, R.H. 2014, *The Town House in Medieval and Early Modern Bristol*, Swindon: English Heritage.
Ligon, R. 1657, *A True and Exact History of Barbados*, London.
Merrill, G. 1958, *The Historical Geography of St. Kitts and Nevis, the West Indies*, Mexico: Instituto Panamericano de Geografia e Historia.
Morris, E., Leech, R., Crosby, A., Machling, T., Williams, B. & Heathcote, J. 2003, *Nevis Heritage Project Interim Report 2002*, Southampton: Nevis Heritage Project, University of Southampton.
Niddrie, D.L. 1966, 'An Attempt at Planned Settlement in St Kitts in the Early 18th Century', *Carib. Stud.* 5:4, 3–11.
O'Shaughnessy, A.J. 1994, 'The Stamp Act Crisis in the British Caribbean', *William and Mary Quarterly* 51 (3rd Ser.), 203–26.
O'Shaughnessy, A.J. 2000, *An Empire Divided: The American Revolution and the British Caribbean*, Philadelphia: University of Pennsylvania Press.
Oldmixon, J. 1708, *The British Empire in America, containing the history of the discovery, settlement, progress and state of the British Colonies on the Continent and Islands of America ...*, 2 vols, London: Printed for John Nicholson at the King's Arms in Little Britain, Benjamin

Tooke at the Middle-Temple-Gate Fleet Street and Richard Parker and Ralph Smith under the Piazza at the Royal Exchange.
Pares, R. 1950, *A West-India Fortune*, London, New York and Toronto: Longman.
Parliamentary Papers 1843, *Papers relative to the Earthquake in the West Indies presented to both Houses of Parliament, Parliamentary Papers 1843*, in Accounts and Papers 4. Colonies 1843 Session 2 February 24 August 1843.
Philpott, R.A., Brett, J.R. & Leech R.H. 2005, 'Archaeological Field Survey in the Cayon Area, St Kitts: An Interim Report to the St Christopher Island Authorities and St Christopher Heritage Society', unpublished report.
Philpott, R.A. Leech, R.H. & Morris E.L. forthcoming (2020), *Searching for the 17th Century on Nevis. The Survey and Excavation of Two Early Plantation Sites*, Oxford: Archaeopress.
Porter, G.R. 1830, *The Nature and Properties of the Sugar Cane*, London: Smith, Elder, and Co.
Ramsay, J. 1784, *An Essay on the Treatment and Conversion of African Slaves in the British Sugar Colonies*, London: James Phillips.
Sainsbury, W.N. 1893, 'America and West Indies: November 16–30, 1676', *Calendar of State Papers Colonial, America and West Indies, 9, 1675–1676 and Addenda 1574–1674*, ed. W. Noel Sainsbury (London, 1893), 494–507. British History Online http://www.british-history.ac.uk/cal-state-papers/colonial/america-west-indies/vol9/pp494–507.
Sheridan, R. 1976, 'The Crisis of Slave Subsistence in the British West Indies During and After the American Revolution', *William and Mary Quarterly* 33 (3rd ser.), 615–41.
Sloane, H. 1707, *A Voyage to the Islands Madera, Barbados, Nieves, S. Christophers and Jamaica*, London.
Smith, W. 1745, *A Natural History of Nevis: and the Rest of the English Leeward Charibee Islands in America, with Many Observations on Nature and Art*, Cambridge: J. Bentham.
Watts, D. 1987, *The West Indies: Patterns of Development, Culture and Environmental Change since 1492*, Cambridge: Cambridge University Press.
Wentworth, T. 1834, *The West India Sketch Book*, 2 vols, London: Whittaker & Co.
Zogbaum, H. 2002, 'The Steam Engine in Cuba's Sugar Industry, 1794–1860', *J. Iberian Latin Am. Stud.* 8:2, December 2002, 37–59.

MAP SOURCES

Pierre Buor, undated [*c.* 1711–13] 'Plan Geometral de l'Isle de St Christophle presenté à sa Majesté par le Lieute. Collenel Pierre Buor Maior du Regt Alexandre de Garnison dans laditte isle", British Library Maps K.Top.123.79.2 TAB.
Samuel Baker, 1753 'A new and exact Map of the Island of St Christopher in America, according to an actual and accurate Survey made in the year 1753 by Samuel Baker, Lt RN. 2 inches to 1 mile' TNA CO 700 / St Christopher and Nevis 5.
Anthony Ravell, *c.* 1765 'St Christophers vulgo St Kitts. Surveyed by Anthony Ravell Esqr Surveyor General of the Islands of St Christophers, Nevis, & Montserrat. Engraved by Thomas Jeffferys [sic] Geographer to the King'. (A proof [*c.* 1765?], with MS. additions and corrections, used by the engraver of the map published by Robert Sayer in 1775.) BL Maps 188.o.2.(2.).
William McMahon, 1828 'A New Topographical map of the island of Saint Christopher in the West Indies …' TNA CO700/StChristopher8.

8

The St Kitts Scenic Train: Journey into an Island's Heritage

WILLIAM C. FOUND

SUMMARY: 350 years after the first clearing of the forest to create a classic sugar cane landscape between sea-level and the 1000-foot contour, sugar production was threatened by more efficient, large-scale production elsewhere. The year 2005 was the island's last sugar crop. The sugar railway is now used by a modern scenic train, which offers passengers an unparalleled journey into one of the Caribbean's most important heritage landscapes. The film (46 minutes) follows the train's journey, with side trips to great houses, sugar mills, and Brimstone Hill Fortress; and uses historical maps and drawings to complement the contemporary filming.

St Kitts was the last remaining small-island sugar cane landscape in the Caribbean Islands, which is the focus of a documentary film, *St Kitts Scenic Train: Journey into an Island's Heritage* (this can be viewed on YouTube: https://youtu.be/eSnMRCk-AMk; see also Found 2014). Construction of the railway, which circles the main part of the island, in the early 20th century (and accompanying construction of a large, modern sugar factory in the capital, Basseterre) allowed the island's sugar producers to compete in a rapidly changing global sugar market. Now, 350 years after the first clearing of the forest to create a classic sugar cane landscape between sea-level and the 1000-foot contour, sugar production was once again threatened by more efficient, large-scale production elsewhere. At the time of the 2005 meeting it appeared likely, and then proved to be so, that 2005 was the island's last sugar crop. The sugar railway is now used by a modern scenic train, which offers passengers an unparalleled journey into one of the Caribbean's most important heritage landscapes. The film (46 minutes) follows the train's journey, with side trips to great houses, sugar mills, and Brimstone Hill Fortress; and uses historical maps and drawings to complement the contemporary filming. It presents a view of an historic landscape which is now lost forever, and provides links to many of the papers included in this volume.

BIBLIOGRAPHY

Found, William C. 2014, 'The St Kitts Scenic Railway: A Journey into an Island's Heritage', Chapter 17 in M. Conlin and G. Bird (eds), *Railway Heritage and Tourism: Global Perspectives*, London: Channel View Publications, 247–62.

III

The Colonial Landscape of Nevis

9

Jamestown, Nevis: Fact, Fiction, and Fable

CARTER HUDGINS, ERIC KLINGELHOFER, ROGER H. LEECH, *and* DAVID HIGGINS

SUMMARY: The destruction of Jamestown, Nevis, in 1690 by a tidal wave, or tsunami, has been the subject of hurried reports in contemporary news broadsheets, Victorian romantic legend, enthusiastic local histories, and even quick assessment by reality-TV archaeologists. Documentary and archaeological research has revealed the location, extent, and details of this early English colonial settlement, which have proved to be often at odds with previous assertions and assumptions. Evidence of destruction by natural forces corroborates the story of Jamestown's fate, but exposed walls lying on the ocean floor must be dismissed as fanciful. The human tragedy of the 1690 earthquake and tsunami can now be presented as fact, stripped of fiction and fable.

This paper summarizes archaeological investigations conducted from 2003 to 2006 at the site of Jamestown, a 'lost' commercial settlement on the leeward shore of the island of Nevis.[1] According to local legend and lore, Jamestown vanished in 1690, destroyed by a tsunami. The town's end came, without warning, on April 5, 1690, 'about five of the Clock in the Afternoon,' an eyewitness would remember in a letter to a friend in London. 'We heard a rumbling Noise, like that of distant Thunder,' the eyewitness wrote, 'from the Bowels of the great Mountain, … in the very Navil of the island.' This earthquake was different from trembles that had rattled the island before. 'So strong was the Motion,' the eyewitness recounted, 'that … [a] few Moments after the Noise began, … a … Earth Quake, which shook the whole island to that degree, that all the Houses in Charles Town that were built of Brick or Stone, dropt of a sudden down from the Top to the Bottom.' The sea then suddenly receded, 'for a time forfeit the Shoar for about three quarters of a Mile together, and left a great Number of Fish of a large size to lye gaping upon the Sand, till it returned again.' This 'violent Motion of the Water' repeated 'diverse times',[2] and we can imagine that when the sea 'returned again' it lifted and then slammed mats of debris against walls, houses, and anything else that lay in its path. No other reports of this earthquake or its effects survive (Fig. 9.1).

When the earthquake of 1690 struck Nevis, the island boasted of two urbanized places, Charlestown, the island's administrative and commercial capital, and Jamestown, a smaller place where planters loaded casks of sugar for shipment to English

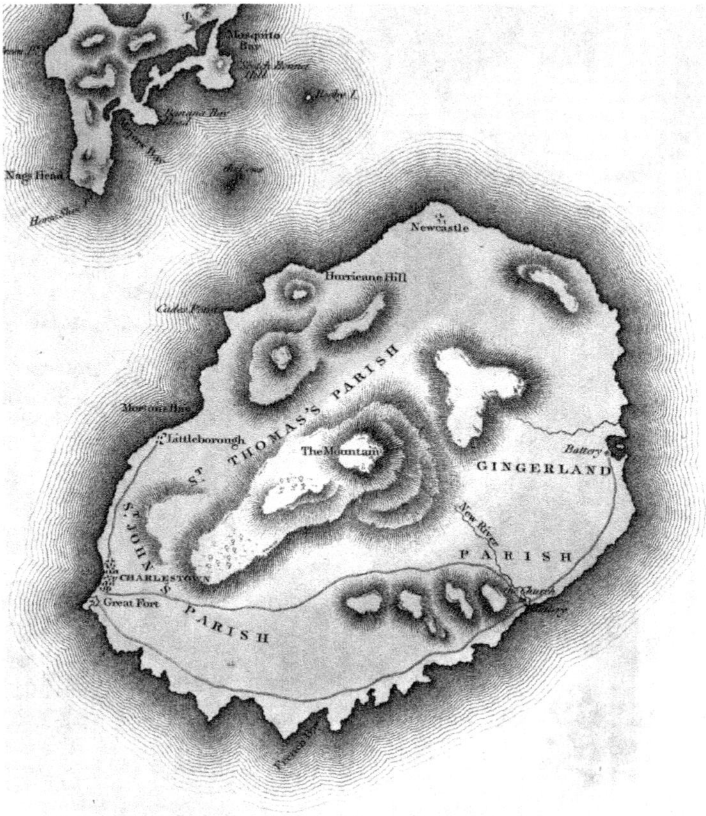

Fig. 9.1. Nevis, 1823. The site of Jamestown overlooking Morton's Bay on the western shore of the island is labeled 'Littleborough' (Source: Map of Nevis by F. Lucas, Baltimore; collection of Vince Hubbard).

ports. From what appears to have been his vantage in Charlestown, the eyewitness to the 1690 quake described extensive damage there. His account, however, says nothing about Jamestown or other places and plantations on the island. Other residents, writing long after the fact, later filled in this gap. In a fanciful history he wrote nearly two centuries after the late 17th-century shock, magistrate John Alexander Burke Iles melded historical fact with historical imagination to create a new romantic narrative for Jamestown. Iles presented Jamestown as a lost town, a settlement tumbled down by the rising sea, its residents swept away save a few who escaped to higher ground.[3] Like many inventive tales, Iles's explanation for Jamestown's destruction in his *An Account and Description of the Island of Nevis, West Indies* was a concoction spun, in part, from fact. If fact lay in late 17th-century reports, a new historical memory took root in the late 19th century, the legend of Jamestown, lost town under the sea. In a series of short field seasons, an Anglo-American archaeological team explored the site identified since the late 19th century as the location of colonial Jamestown. What were the facts behind Jamestown's legend? Was historical Jamestown located where historical memory, and fanciful tourist maps, placed it? Had a tsunami really struck the town? Did Jamestown really vanish, drowned beneath the sea like Port Royal on Jamaica? Was there more to Jamestown's story than myth?

While myths about Jamestown have proved resilient, historical records that pertain to the colonial port describe Jamestown before fiction obscured its facts. English colonists settled Nevis during the Great Migration, those decades of emigration from England to fledgling colonies as England staked more of its economy and its prestige on overseas possessions. Captain John Smith described Nevis this way: 'The air very pleasant and healthful, but exceeding hot, yet so tempered with cool breaths, it seems very temperate to them that are a little used to it; the trees being always greene, the daies and nights always very neare equal in length, always summer.'[4] Following its settlement in 1631, the island's social and economic trajectory was much like Barbados, where mixed agriculture (spices, tobacco) gave way to sugar monoculture. As part of this transition, large planters with large labor forces of enslaved Africans supplanted small independent farmers, some of whom, having sold their lands, migrated to other Caribbean islands, to South Carolina, the Chesapeake, and New England. Sugar quickly became the preferred, and most profitable, crop. Labor in the Caribbean shifted from indentured servants to a reliance on African slaves who cleared, cut, burned, terraced, planted and tended cane fields, and fueled and operated boiling houses. Analysis of the Royal African Company slave traffic for the period 1673–89 reveals that 90,000 slaves (slightly more than 5,250 per year) arrived in the English Caribbean.[5] Nevisian planters acquired nearly 20% of this stream, and by the end of the 17th century the island's population had reached 40,000, almost all of it enslaved.

By the middle of the 17th century the principal town on Nevis was Charles Town, a place one official reported was 'composed of wooden houses and huts ... surrounded by marshy ground, and stagnant water'. During his short posting to the island, George Ellwood wrote to the Royal Society in 1672 that 'the buildings [on Nevis] are poore much like to a Hogstie in England'. Ellwood descried the island's settlers as 'vulgar and illiterate'.[6] English officials showered the same kind of compliments on Virginia in the 17th century, but in the way that they very much liked the duties that flowed from Virginia tobacco, they liked sugar even more.[7] Planters and their expanding labor force of enslaved Africans quickly cleared the lower slopes of Mount Nevis for cane fields and with terracing pushed cultivation above 1,000 feet. Sugar exports rose 7,000 hogsheads annually. Forts constructed along the island's lea coast protected the island and small strategically placed ports of lading from attack.[8]

As settlement expanded and sugar exports increased, English colonists on Nevis adapted their building methods and the character of what they built to the materials they found on the island and to threats from the Caribbean's earthquakes and storms. Building materials fell into two broad categories, first, timber, albeit denser tropical woods than the timber to which settlers were accustomed, and, second, stone, all of it igneous volcanic boulders. Nevisian colonists quickly became familiar with both. Colonists had, however, little direct experience with tropical wind and/or with earthquake. John Smith reported that the Caribbean winds could come in 'great gusts and raines, and sometime a Hericano, which is an overgrown and a most violent storme'.[9] They could do great damage. In 1681 a storm that struck St Kitts and Nevis left Christopher Jeaffreson's dwelling 'miserably torn, and flat with the ground'. A great blow in 1707, still remembered as 'the Grand Storm' 70 years later, flattened many buildings.[10]

Earthquakes posed a second significant natural threat to Caribbean settlements. The Leeward Islands experienced frequent earthquakes such as the 1690 event on Nevis. A later visitor, for example, wrote that during his five-year stay on Nevis he experienced at least a dozen earthquakes.[11] Both forces, 'hericano and earth quake', would, in time, affect the way Nevisian colonists built. The first English colonists on Nevis built no better than their counterparts in Virginia. These 'poore' houses were often built of stone, a response to hurricanes that residents of the Leeward Islands had begun by the middle decades of the 17th century. Stone was stable in high winds, but building more than two stories invited catastrophe. The Rev. Robert Robertson was still advocating this advice following a 1733 hurricane, noting 'such buildings wou'd prove a better Security against Storms than we can make of timber'.[12]

Robertson argued that colonists on Nevis and St Kitts who had settled since 'the grand storm in 1707' had 'suffer'd nothing grievous from that Time by Storms'. The island's planters and merchants had, he added, become 'too easily induc'd to study Ornament and Convenience in their Buildings, rather than Safety'.[13] Rev. Robertson thought 'our Inhabitants wou'd do well to be constantly provided with strong wooden bars and Iron Hooks and Staples always ready fix'd at their Doors and Windows, into which to pin down those Bars on the Outside of the Houses'. Bolting down doors and windows provided greater security, because once a door blew open, 'the Wind enters, and fills the House, and Whirls about within it, if the Doors and Windows on the opposite Side are not set open to give instant vent, the Roof is in Danger of being carry'd off at once'. Robertson also noted that 70–80 years prior to the 1733 storm, 'our more provident Planters used to have what they call'd a Hurricane-Houses to take Refuge in, in a Storm'. He had seen the ruins of such structures and recommended that planters build them again.[14]

Colonel Sir William Stapleton, governor of the Leeward Islands, said in 1676 that in Charlestown, Nevis, 'There were good dwellings and storehouses [built with country timber], not exceeding 60 feet long and 20 broad, story and a half, the Hurri-Canes having taught the people to build low'. Houses built low and with stone could best the wind but not an earthquake. Earthquakes forced a re-consideration. In 1676 it was reported that colonists on Montserrat had previously built 'some stone buildings, but earthquakes having thrown them all done, they build with timber only except the boiling houses for sugar, which in part must be built of stone'.[15] During the 1690 Nevis earthquake, 'all the Houses in Charles Town that were made of Brick or Stone, dropt a sudden from the Top to the Bottom in perfect Ruins'.[16] Wooden houses fared better. In another account of the 1690 earthquake Lieutenant-Governor Stede reported on April 23rd to the Lords of Trade and Plantations that 'three weeks ago there were violent earthquakes in the Leeward Islands, and Antigua having many stone houses suffered much, most of the houses being either shaken down or so split and cracked that they will have to be taken down'. [17]

The buildings that coalesced at Jamestown in the second half of the 17th century bear out the process of adaptation as colonists raised buildings from local materials.

Tessa Machling, historian with the Nevis Heritage Project, has assembled documents from the National Archives in London that suggest that Jamestown's rise and fall was tied more to the fortunes of sugar than the terror of wind and wave.[18] By 1672 a town called Morton's Bay had coalesced along the shore of a shallow bay and was made a lawful port to facilitate commerce with plantations along the island's north-west coast. Four years later Jamestown was noted as the second largest town on the island. William Stapleton reported in 1676 to the Board of Trade and Plantations that although there were on Nevis 'five places for trade, there are but two considerable. First Charles Town where there are good dwellings and store houses' and 'Morton's Bay, the other place of trade where there are the like houses, but few in number because the shipps doe ride at Charleston Town and doe send their long boats to Morton's Bay to fetch their lading from thence'.[19] Subsequent acts (1682) by the island's government 'for the suppression of thatcht houses' and 'against the making of dangerous fires in Charles Town and Morton's Bay' attest to the town's growing size. Subsequent efforts to require that chimneys at Morton's Bay be built of brick or stone suggest that at least some builders relied on timber chimneys and that at least some of the houses were

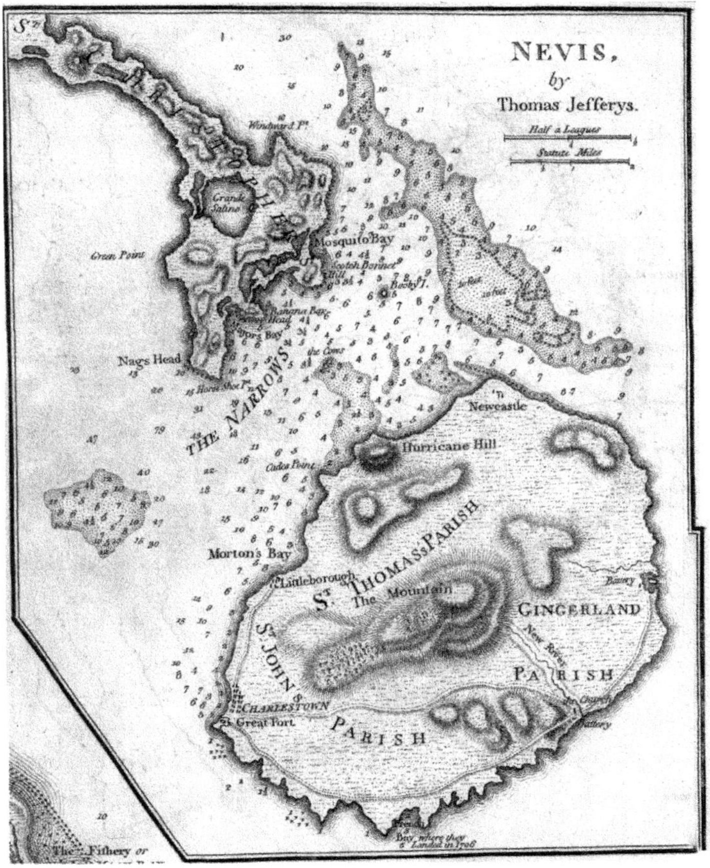

Fig. 9.2. Nevis, 1775 (Source: Map of Nevis by A. Ravell, London: R. Sayer; collection of Vince Hubbard).

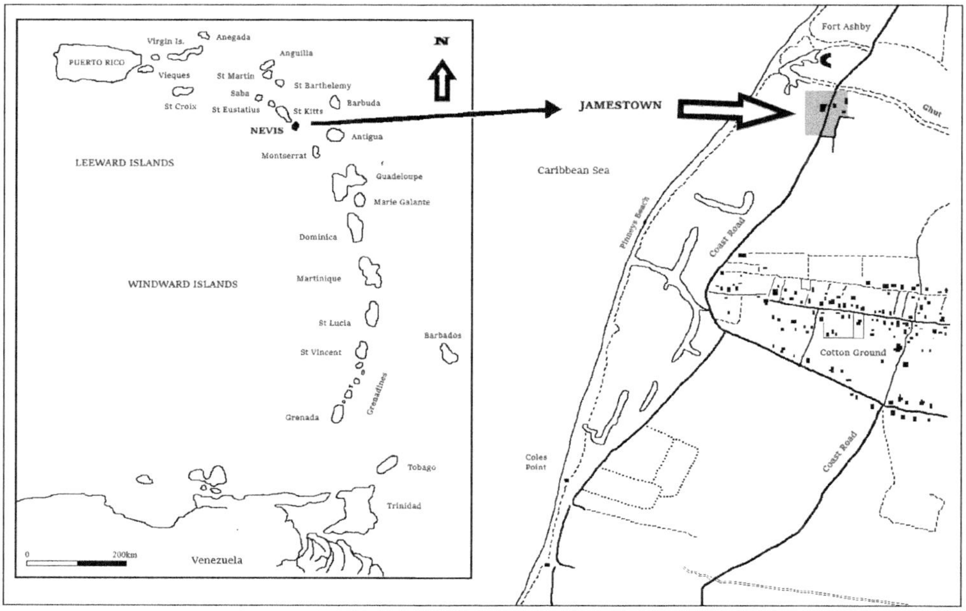

Fig. 9.3. Location of site of Jamestown, Nevis.

still relatively humble. Early maps, produced as the small settlement coalesced, label this small settlement 'Morton's Bay' (Fig. 9.2). The name 'Jamestowne' first appeared in 1684 when the settlement was listed as one of the island's 'lawful places of receiving goods'. The place name 'Morton's Bay' then disappeared, supplanted by 'Jamestown', probably to honor the future English king James II (1685–8). Maps reveal the same change in place name. Eighteenth-century maps drawn by French cartographers mark the location of the town as 'Jacqueville' or 'Petitbourg'.

Modern archaeological exploration of Jamestown began in the late 1990s. The generally accepted location of Jamestown is roughly bisected by the island's coast road, an equestrian center and old fields on its east side, a modern coconut grove to the west (Fig. 9.3). Archaeologists of the Channel 4 TV programme *Time Team* visited Nevis in 1998 and chose Jamestown for one programme. Time Team investigated a large area south of a reconstructed demi-lune battery, now called Fort Ashby, and which was thought to be located on the site of 17th-century James Fort, one of a string of batteries and fortifications that, with varying success, protected the leeward side of the island.[20] Employing a range of techniques, including geophysical survey, shovel test pits, and test trenches, the Time Team found evidence of concentrated colonial activity related to the remains of a dry laid stone wall running north–south east of the coast road. A casual search of the coconut grove also revealed building foundations. In addition to discovering locally made Afro-Caribbean wares, the Time Team recovered an assemblage of European ceramics that suggested two periods of activity at the site. The first, from *c.* 1680 to the first quarter of the 18th century, was indicated by a wide range of ceramic types typical of sites in the Atlantic world in the late 17th century. Factory-made slipwares and sponge-decorated and transfer-printed earthenwares indicated renewed activity at the site in the 19th century. This second group of artifacts presented a puzzle. Was Jamestown never really lost but just forgotten? Was it somehow reborn? Time Team, in a hurry to shoot film for its next programme, had no time to address the questions its brief investigation posed.[21]

The Nevis Heritage Project, a partnership of historians and archaeologists associated with the University of Southampton (UK) and the Nevis Historical and Conservation Society, sponsored a second investigation at Jamestown. Part of a comprehensive effort to assemble an inventory of archaeological sites on Nevis, the Jamestown Excavations Project set a number of goals for the four seasons its participants devoted to the project: (1) Delineate the boundaries of the town; (2) Date previously recorded foundations and establish an archaeological chronology for the site; (3) Retrieve evidence of recent geo-morphological change at the site; (4) Recover evidence of seismic activity. In short, this second exploration of the site set out, first, to recover, in a systematic way, evidence of the town's 17th-century rise and fall, and, second, to understand what appeared to be 19th-century building foundations visible on the ground surface at various locations, and that were, perhaps, the source of much of the romantic misunderstanding of the lost town. If these weren't evidence of Jamestown, what were they? And could they be separated from whatever survived of the 17th century?

During improvements to the coast road in 2001, Nevis Heritage Project archaeologists led by Roger Leech recorded a dry laid stone wall east of the coast road, interpreted then as part of an enclosure for the settlement. Leech also identified the stone

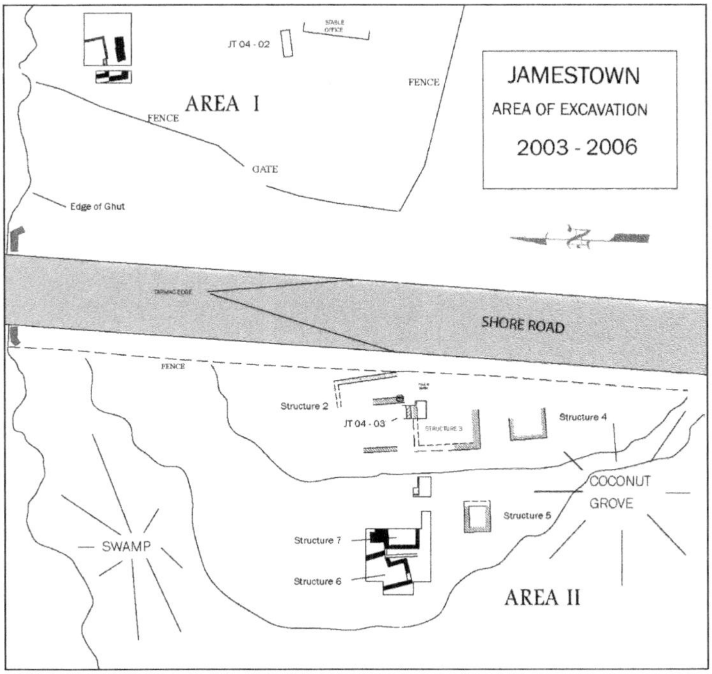

Fig. 9.4. Plan of excavations at Jamestown, 2003–6.

foundations of four buildings on the west side of the coast road. In 2003 Roger Leech was joined by American archaeologists Carter Hudgins and Eric Klingelhofer, of Mary Washington and Mercer universities, respectively, to conduct a brief examination of the coconut grove, the other area identified by Time Team as having surface evidence of Jamestown. Further geophysical testing as well as excavated test pits ascertained the extent of 17th-century occupation on the west side of the coast road. Distribution of the early artifacts from land crab burrows defined an edge of occupation running north-west to south-east from a tidal inlet fed by a fresh water ghut that drained the slopes above the site. This edge presumably represents the 17th-century shoreline of Morton's Bay. Artifacts – metropolitan slipware, Borderware milk pans, lead glass baluster-type wine glass stems, and pipe bowls – confirmed European occupation in the third quarter of the 17th century. The absence of white salt-glazed stoneware suggested that occupation here ended before 1720 (Fig. 9.4).

While artifact scatter, as revealed by both subsurface testing and land crab burrows, indicated significant activity over a broad area, the precise boundaries for the site and the relationship of stone foundations and walls to the artifacts remained undefined. Three short field seasons followed, in 2004, 2005, and 2006, during which it was determined that from its northern boundary at the ghut the town stretched at least 200m along the shore and reached inland 150m. Controlled excavations provided chronology that geophysical and surface collections could not.

A small trench was opened to examine a section of the dry-laid stone wall on the east side of the coast road identified by previous field work as a possible town enclosure. Soils were hard, compacted by horses and vehicles bringing patrons to a riding stable that occupies this portion of the site. The soils had accumulated against the wall and insinuated themselves into the small stones that comprised it. Mixed with these lenses were fragments of a broad range of ceramic and glass objects dating from the late 18th to second quarter of the 19th century. Little of the drystone wall survived. Below its lower irregular courses excavators found sherds of creamware, an indication that it was constructed no earlier than the 1760s and was thus not related to the 17th-century settlement. The slight character of this wall and its date suggested that it was a boundary wall or field enclosure.

Fig. 9.5. Wall of 17th-century structure (designated Structure 9) in Trench JT04-01 in 2004 test excavation with mortared face to left, cobbled surface to right. Archaeologist Carter C. Hudgins points to neck of *c.* 1660 bottle lodged in matrix of the wall. View faces east.

A second trench on the eastern side of the road began soon after a JCB backhoe operator, digging a utility line for the Nevis Equestrian Centre, struck a deeply buried stone. The initial exploration of this wall, of which a substantial portion survived, exposed a short section of dry-laid stone foundation oriented roughly east to west. Constructed of irregularly laid stones, it was 0.80m wide and survived to a height of 0.5m. A thick stratum

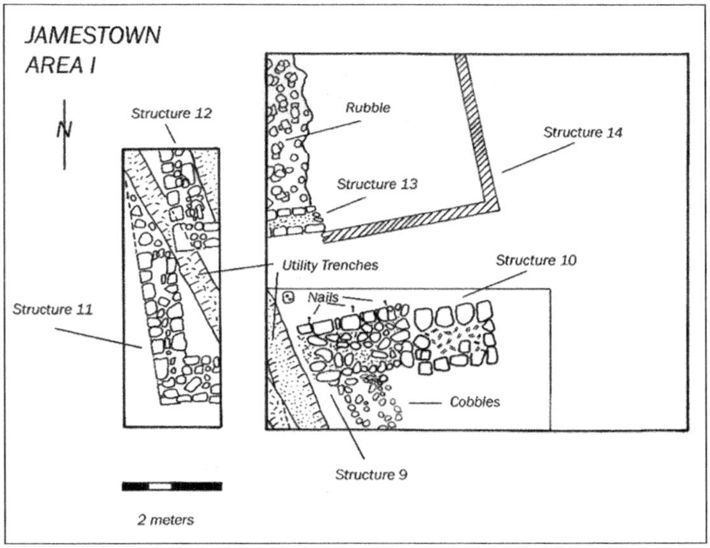

Fig. 9.6. Plan of excavations, Area I, Jamestown, Nevis.

(0.42m) of silt washed down from the lower slopes of Mount Nevis buried this section of wall and contained pipe bowls and pipe bowl fragments. This thick, homogenous stratum accumulated over the wall after the building was demolished and abandoned *c.* 1680–1720. Excavators recovered a fragment of North Devon sgraffito milk pan beneath this wall and the neck of a green glass bottle in the wall itself (Fig. 9.5). Both artifacts date from the third quarter of the 17th century. A cobbled surface abutted the base of the wall's south face, possibly indicating a pavement on the exterior of the building (Fig. 9.6).

We returned to this area in 2006 and by the end of our second season there had opened a much larger area with the intention of revealing the entire ground plan of the building we glimpsed two years before. A 2m by 6m trench and a 9m by 8m area had approximately 0.40m of overburden removed mechanically. Within it, a 3m by 6m area was excavated intensively by hand. Running through both units were the corners of not one but six buildings, each one closer to the ghut in a pattern that suggested a serial rebuilding that moved each successive structure toward the north. Each of these walls was truncated at the north and east, further evidence of abandonment and rebuilding. Unfortunately, the foundation we discovered in 2004 had been cut at both eastern and western ends so that only a stub of wall survived (Fig. 9.7).

This portion of Jamestown, located adjacent to the ghut, bears evidence of substantial occupation during the third quarter of the 17th century. Abutting the dry laid stone wall to the north, toward the ghut and into what may have been a yard, we found an extensive area of midden, trash, and debris dating to the first quarter of the 18th century that contained many thousands of artifacts. Under the midden we found more occupation layers, and, most intriguing, a post hole under both the debris and under the occupation surface, but cutting through what appeared to be an early soil layer, perhaps the ground surface when initial occupation began. The evidence

Fig. 9.7. View of Area I at end of 2006 season. View faces north. Structure 11, left foreground; Structure 12, left background; Structures 9 and 10, right foreground.

suggested that the first building in the sequence of stone walls was a domestic structure constructed during the third quarter of the 17th century. The wall's southern and northern faces differed in appearance. The northern face exhibited a more or less flat plane, and the stones here were well mortared in place. The south face, on the other hand, was roughly dressed. Three wrought nails remained in mortar, each 0.5m below the top of the surviving wall. A portion of the shank of each nail protruded beyond the mortared surface of the wall, suggesting that these nails had once held a board, perhaps wainscoting.

That building had been substantially rebuilt, with dry laid stone, and the site heavily occupied into the first quarter of the 18th century. The artifacts were diverse, with a number of high-quality glass wares, especially German and Venetian, and Italian, Dutch, and German ceramics. The absence of English white salt-glazed wares indicated that the building had been abandoned about 1720. Subsequent rebuilding raised new stone walls laid with mortar. This serial rebuilding ended with the abandonment or destruction of this portion of the settlement in the second quarter of the 19th century, a date suggested by fragments of whiteware ceramic objects and molded green glass mallet bottles.

The portion of the site that lies to the west side of the coast road proved equally complicated. We opened Trench IV, the most complex of our units at Jamestown, in 2004 and resumed work there in 2005 and 2006. Evidence for the early colonial settlement is limited here to an area wedged between a 19th-century building complex that abuts the coastal road and featureless marine sand deposits that extend some

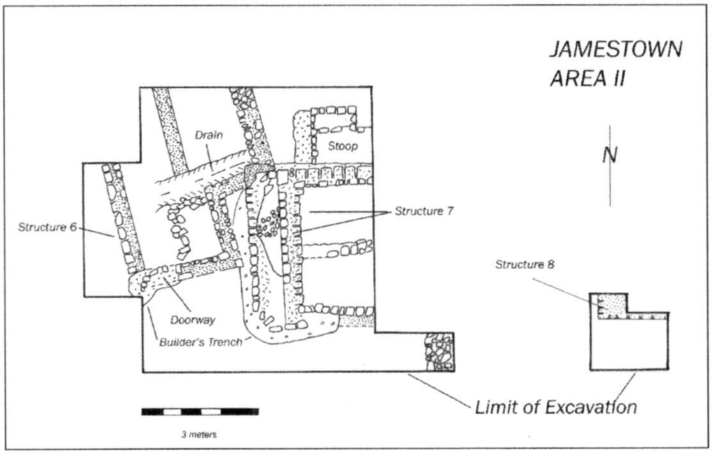

Fig. 9.8. Plan of excavations, Area II, Jamestown, Nevis.

300m to the current shoreline. Tunneling and retunneling of generations of land crabs complicated the excavation. The thorough mixing of sandy soils by this burrowing, termed 'bioturbation', had damaged, in some cases destroyed, stratigraphic evidence. We extended an initial 2m by 2m unit into a 7.5m by 6m area and excavated three additional 2m by 2m units in an attempt to recover both a more precise chronology for this portion of the site, as well as a profile of strata from the lowest portions of the site, at its western or seaward edge, to the coast road (Fig. 9.8).

Much of the unit was filled with 19th-century structural remains typified by squared stones laid in pink sandy mortar. Trench III examined structural remains lying between the coast road and the coconut grove that earlier surveys had recorded as the gable ends of two nearly abutting buildings. Excavation of this unit made it clear that the stone from one building had been used in the construction of the other, but the construction of the later building had disturbed the area so thoroughly that no strata related to construction or occupation of the earlier building survived. The presence of a few 17th-century artifacts in the destruction strata (sherds of sgraffitto, in particular) hinted that this portion of the site, like the structure discovered in Trench I and the structure in Trench IV was occupied during the third quarter of the 17th century. Far more prevalent, however, were fragments of English ceramic and glass wares that dated from the 19th century. There was an absence of those ceramic markers characteristic of occupation during the 18th century, such as white salt-glazed stonewares, cream ware, and pearl ware. It is likely that the buildings in Trench III can be associated with the 'Pleasure House' or merchant's villa noted on an 1818 map of Nevis (Fig. 9.9).

Obscured and largely destroyed by this building complex was the earlier phase of occupation, that of 17th-century Jamestown, indicated here in the form of a fragmentary structure located at the seaward edge of the site. There, we uncovered the southwest end of a stone building (Structure 6) that lay at an angle at least 10 degrees off the 19th-century orientation and lay stratigraphically beneath it. The east and south walls were approximately 0.45m wide of coursed roughly squared stone, bonded with sparing use of buff colored mortar.

Fig. 9.9. Area II, photograph of superimposed stone wall ruins Area II at end of 2006 season. View faces north-east. Structure 7 at top, right. Structure 6, left, is skewed to it. Dressed stones that frame possible door opening are visible in the center.

Fig. 9.10. Area II: Detail of mortared floor in Structure 6. Note undulating nature of mortar floor as it slopes toward wall at rear of photograph.

The upper courses of these walls had tumbled above the lower course, and both walls were cracked and displaced by as much as 100mm. The surviving end of the south wall, moreover, was canted at an angle of some 17 degrees from vertical. The most compelling evidence of seismic energy was the undulating floor and the angle at which the building pitched toward the sea. Interior features point to a doorway and a raised rubble-filled platform, perhaps the base for steps or a ramp. Stratigraphy and artifacts, no less than orientation and structural details, suggest that this building was a warehouse, part of the 17th-century waterfront tumbled in the shock of the 1690 earthquake (Fig. 9.10).

PRELIMINARY DISCUSSION OF PIPE STEMS AND PIPE BOWLS FROM JAMESTOWN

Archaeologist and pipe expert Dr David Higgins completed an analysis of kaolin pipe stems and pipe bowls excavated by Time Team in 1998 and an early reconnaissance of the Jamestown site by Nevis Heritage Project.[22] Pipe bowls and pipe stems recovered in subsequent excavations in Area II, the portion of the site closest to the modern shoreline on the west side of the coast road, provided an additional opportunity to refine the chronology of the settlement's occupation (Fig. 9.4). Higgins's analysis of 7 bowl, 53 stem and 4 mouthpiece fragments recovered from two contexts in the western portion of the site corroborated the chronology of 17th-century development and 18th-century decline indicated by ceramic evidence (Fig. 9.11).

A 1m by 1m test unit placed between the group of foundations of 19th-century buildings that lay along the coast road and the foundations of Structures 6 and 7 produced by far the largest group of pipes recovered during the excavations at Jamestown. Pipe stems and fragments of sgraffitto thrown to the surface by burrowing crabs attracted initial attention to this portion of the site. The unit excavated here located the south-west corner of a 19th-century stone foundation (Structure 8) and evidence of mid 17th-century occupation in strata at the water table encountered 1.02m. below the modern ground surface (Fig. 9.8). A total of 59 pieces of pipe were recovered from this context comprising 6 bowl, 50 stem, and 3 mouthpiece fragments. The bowl fragments all date from between about 1630 and 1690 and almost all of the stem and mouthpiece fragments would be consistent with this range, being of general 17th- or early 18th-century types. Four fragments of stem appear to date from the late 18th or 19th century. Given the degree of disturbance from burrowing crabs on this site it is quite possible that these two chronologically distinct groups of pipes represent two different phases of activity that have become intermixed in this single context.

The earlier phase of activity appears to have started at some point during the second quarter of the seventeenth century, as witnessed by a fragmentary bowl of *c.* 1630–50 (Fig. 9.11 [1]) and four decorated stems of types that were current from *c.* 1625 to 1670 (Fig. 9.11 [7–10]). This first phase of occupation continued until around 1660–90, as represented by two bowl forms of this period (Fig. 9.11 [4–5]), but there is nothing from this particular group that would suggest occupation on this part of the site immediately after 1690. There then appears to be a hiatus of activity until the later 18th or 19th century, when a much smaller number of plain stem fragments were deposited (four pieces).

Pipe stems and bowl fragments carried to the surface by crabs also drew attention to an area at the western edge of the site where excavation of an area 7.5 by 6m revealed the stone foundations of a 17th-century building overlapped by a 19th-century building (Structure 6 and 7; Fig. 9.8). A small group of just five fragments of pipe, made up of one complete bowl dating from *c.* 1650–80 (Fig. 9.11 [3]), three stem fragments, and a mouthpiece were recovered from a stratum at the water table in this unit. One of the stems is of the 17th century, but the other pieces are less easy to place, being of general late 17th- or 18th-century types. None of these pieces is marked or burnished. The bowl has a slightly uneven surface finish and is of a general south-western English

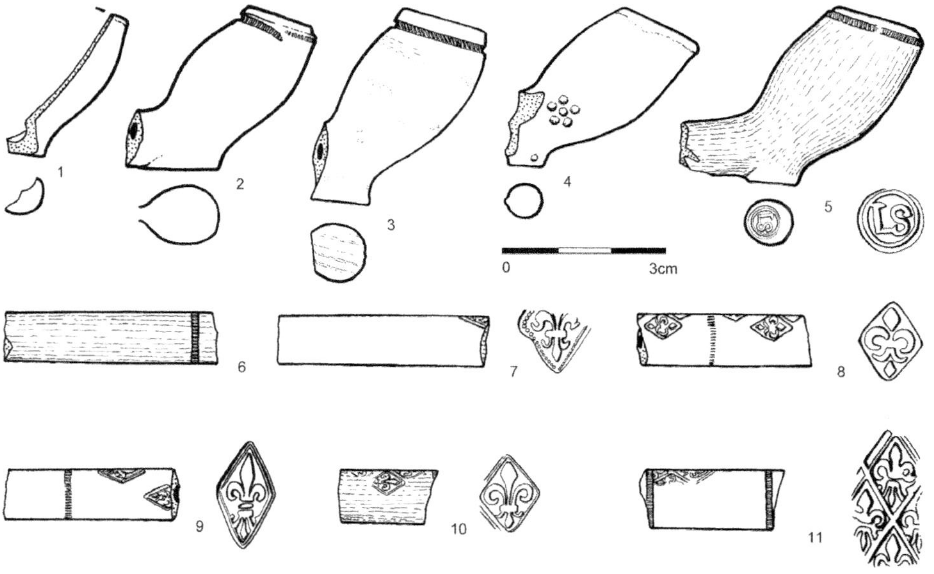

Fig. 9.11. Pipe bowls and pipe stem fragments recovered from Area II, Jamestown, Nevis.

style, perhaps from Bristol. Although too small a group to draw any firm conclusions as to dating, these fragments would fit with the previously established pattern of a mid to late-17th century phase of activity followed by some later activity on the site.

Both the general date range of the pipes as a whole and the marked two-phase depositional pattern exhibited by the first group are in keeping with the pipe finds from the 1998 excavations, which suggested a peak of activity on this site during the period *c.* 1660–1700, with a much less intense period of deposition during the later 18th or 19th century. There are three main differences, however, between the finds from the two excavation campaigns. The first is that the pipes from the western part of the site include rather earlier examples, dating from the second quarter of the 17th century, and perhaps suggesting a slightly earlier focus or start of settlement activity on this part of the site. The second is that the earlier phase of pipe activity appears to end around 1690, with no evidence of any later forms immediately after this date. Although not much different from the 1998 dating, this tends to support the argument for the first phase of settlement on the site ending a little before 1700 rather than after it. The final difference is in the nature of the finds, with a much higher percentage of Dutch material coming from the 2005 Jamestown excavations as opposed to the 1998 excavations, with a corresponding reversal in the number of Bristol products represented, as now set out.

Origin and style of the pipes

Three of the six bowl fragments from the 2005 trench (JT 05-04.05) are almost complete and two of these are certainly Dutch in origin (Fig. 9.11 [4–5]). In addition, one of the three small bowl fragments in the same context is probably of the same origin so that half of the bowl fragments recovered are probably Dutch. Furthermore, there are at least five Dutch stems marked with fleur-de-lys stamps from the same context (Fig. 9.11 [7–11]), each of which has been stamped using different dies. Each stem would have been decorated with multiple impressions of a single fleur-de-lys die and so this clearly demonstrates that at least five different Dutch pipes are represented in the context group as a whole. In contrast, the 1998 excavations produced a total of 119 fragments of pipe of which only two (one bowl and one stem) could be identified as Dutch.

A similar difference in the style and marking of the English pipes can also be observed. In 1998 the excavations produced quite a number of spurless 'export style' bowls as well as eight stamped marks, all of which are probably Bristol products. There are no export style bowls or Bristol type marks from the unit adjacent to Structure 8, which serves to reinforce the different nature of the two groups. These differences may be partly chronological and partly geographical, reflecting different supply and consumption patterns as the site developed. The slightly earlier pipes, primarily of Dutch origin and without 'export style' bowls, occur on the western part of the site, while slightly later pipes, dominated by Bristol products and including 'export style' bowls recovered by Time Team in 1998 occur elsewhere.

Burnishing and finishing

In terms of finishing techniques, there is one pipe stem from near Structure 8 that has just a single milled band around it (Fig. 9.11 [6]). Milled bands of this type were typically used on Dutch pipes to divide geometric patterns of stamped decoration and this example is probably from a Dutch pipe where it would have marked the end of a final panel of decorative stamping. There are four other examples where similar bands occur in association with fleur-de-lys stamps from this context (Fig. 9.11 [8–11]). Where more than one milled band survives these have been placed 11mm and 21mm apart (Fig. 9.11 [10–11] respectively).

Burnishing is only present on about six of the 64 fragments recovered. It is not possible to be precise because some of the fragments are very weathered, which has destroyed their original surface finish. At least six stems fall into this category of being too weathered to tell. Of the remainder, there are at least four burnished stems, two of which also have milled or stamped decoration on them and are probably Dutch (Fig. 9.11 [6], 9.11 [10]). Two of the bowl fragments are burnished and these are probably both Dutch as well (Fig. 9.11 [5] and a small rim fragment, not illustrated). The third Dutch bowl is too weathered to tell if it were burnished originally, although this style of pipe (with relief-moulded decoration) was not usually treated in this way (Fig. 9.11 [4]). The excavated evidence suggests that only a small percentage of the pipes in use, around 10%, were burnished originally and that these were primarily (if not exclusively) obtained from Dutch sources.

Moulded and stamped marks/decoration

There is one pipe fragment with moulded marks and six with stamped marks, all of which are Dutch. The moulded marks occur on a rather abraded bowl with a pattern of six relief-moulded dots on each side of the bowl, representing stylized Tudor rose motifs, and a single relief dot on the left-hand side of the heel only (Fig. 9.11 [4]). This style of decoration is common on Dutch pipes of the period and cannot be related to any particular manufacturer or production centre. There is only one actual manufacturer's mark amongst this assemblage, and that is a stamped heel mark comprising the initials LS within a simple relief border on the heel of a burnished bowl dating from *c.* 1660–90 (Fig. 9.11 [5]). This is a nicely made pipe with a finely burnished bowl and fully milled rim. The mark can be identified as that of Lambert Segertsz, a Gouda maker recorded working from 1647/53–1689.[23] Various other later makers with different family names used the uncrowned LS mark until 1847, but the date of the bowl form suggests that this example was produced in Segertsz's actual workshop.

The other five stamped marks represented all occur on the stems of pipes (Fig. 9.11 [7–11]). These are mainly individual fleur-de-lys stamps that were used to create multiple impressions on the stem, usually in the form of a lozenge design (Fig. 9.11 [8–10]). These lozenges were often carelessly formed and this style of decoration was most frequently used on Dutch pipes dating to about 1625–70. From about 1640 to 1670 larger stamps were also used comprising a quartered lozenge into which the four fleur-de-lys marks had already been engraved. One example of this style of mark was recovered from the excavations (Fig. 9.11 [11]). This type of stamp created the same effect, but with only one impression rather than four separate ones being required by the maker.

Details of the dies used on the Dutch stems are shown in Fig. 9.11 [7–11]. Although all of the same general form, the individual fleur-de-lys exhibit quite a range of detail, as do the borders that occur with some of them. These stamped marks are usually lumped together as a general class of mark and good quality drawings of the die details are rarely presented in reports. These examples show that significant variations do occur and there seems little doubt that a more detailed recording and analysis of these marks would not only refine the dating of the various styles but also enable them to be used more accurately to trace trade and marketing patterns.

This small assemblage has not only provided useful dating evidence for the excavated contexts but also raised some interesting questions about the nature of pipe supply and consumption in the Colonial Caribbean world. The finds from this site hint at a marked shift in both supply source and style from predominantly Dutch heel pipes around the middle of the 17th century to predominantly English, and specifically Bristol forms, including export styles, during the last third of the century. More detailed analysis of die types may well refine the precision with which this class of material can be used. The first priority, however, is the recording and publication of comparable 17th-century assemblages from other Caribbean sites so as to establish a better framework against which more detailed analysis and interpretation can be carried out.

Higgins's analysis of tobacco pipes bowls and stems from the western portion of the site confirms initial activity at Jamestown in the second quarter of the 17th century. Additional evidence recovered in the waning days of the excavation of the unit adjacent to Structure 8 retrieved artifacts that are perhaps related to the initial English efforts to establish a permanent presence on Nevis. Just at the water table, nearly 1.0m below the surface and under the foundation for Structure 8, we recovered, in addition to the kaolin pipe bowls Higgins dates to the second quarter of the 17th century, a charcoal layer that contained iron fragments, chain, and the priming pan of a snaphaunce firearm, evidence of still earlier settlement, perhaps the first phase of the island's colonization.

CONCLUSIONS

In conclusion, fieldwork conducted at Jamestown between 2003 and 2006 has led to several points that confirm some conclusions drawn by earlier archaeological research and correct others:

The stone wall thought to have enclosed the 17th-century settlement is, in fact, of much later date. Seventeenth-century Jamestown, rather than a walled, nucleated settlement, may have assumed an irregular plan of dwellings and commercial buildings hugging the shore of Morton's Bay and thus perhaps more like the early seaport communities of New England.

It is also clear that the town was never very big, little more than 150m by 200m, about the same size as the original 1607 Jamestown settlement in Virginia. Yet our test excavations have revealed a demonstrable change in the artifact assemblage that unlike its Virginia counterpart reflects persistence of activity into the first quarter of the 19th century.

It is now clear that that the landscape of 17th-century Jamestown and the buildings that once populated it are deeply buried across the site. Some early wall remains do lie close to the surface on the west side of the road, but both there and on the east side of the coast road, evidence of the earliest phases of settlement, both living and refuse surfaces, are buried 0.5–1m below the present ground surface.

The distribution of finds to the west of the coast road appears to represent the 17th-century shoreline of Morton's Bay. Beyond the edge of the artifacts is deep clean beach sand, evidence of the natural infilling of what was once a broader and deeper bay.

The finds recovered in the 2003–6 field seasons corroborate earlier, if unexplained, observations. Ceramics commonplace in the Atlantic world from the mid decades of the 17th century to the first quarter of the 18th century were found across the site and were associated with the walls of ruined buildings buried by a layer of homogenous water-born soils. The absence of fine salt-glazed wares in these deeply buried ruins suggests a break in occupation at the site after about 1720. Artifacts commonplace after about 1760s, creamware most telling of them, suggest a resumption of activity after that date. Artifacts associated with the construction, occupation, and destruction of stone walled buildings that rose across the site in the decades that followed the introduction of creamware indicate that there was a limited reoccupation of Jamestown, with the buildings of the 'Pleasure House' villa and its related outbuildings in the west portion of the site and small domestic buildings at the eastern edge, which remained in use until the second quarter of the 19th century.

The pipe collection has proven to be especially informative. David Higgins observed that 'the finds from this site hint at a marked shift in both supply source and style from predominately Dutch heel pipes around the middle of the 17th century to predominately English, and specifically Bristol forms, during the last third of the century'.

It is also clear that the abandoned site was reconfigured by the construction of a significant complex of buildings in the early 19th century. The foundations of structures associated with the 'Pleasure House' obscure evidence of previous activity at the site and have been the basis for conjecture and misunderstanding about the character of the 17th-century settlement.

From the excavated evidence significant structural damage can be best attributed to an earthquake and tsunami. The rebuilding observed on the east side of the coast road may represent what the eye witness account of the 1690 earthquake said about brick and stone houses in Charlestown, that they 'dropt of a sudden down from the Top to the Bottom'. Dry laid stonework would prove to be dangerously unstable in a seismic zone.

The rebuilding observed, however, suggests that Jamestown did not entirely disappear. Portions of it were repaired and re-occupied. The greater puzzle is how to explain the end of initial, intensive occupation *c.* 1720.

Jamestown in some form persisted into the 18th century. Why the town finally slipped away after about 1720 to revive toward the end of the century is now a point of conjecture. Armed conflict may explain the hiatus of activity at Jamestown. French forces captured and occupied Nevis in 1705. Before they retreated to neighboring St Kitts, the French burned the island's sugar works and absconded with most its slaves. In following years, Nevisian planters filed numerous claims for damages as the island experienced a retraction in sugar production and a decline in its status.[24]

When Magistrate John Alexander Burke Iles visited the site of Jamestown in the third quarter of the 19th century, he found only ruins. Ceramic fragments associated with the last period of occupation of the site suggest that the final abandonment of the town occurred during the social and economic changes that transformed the island post Emancipation. By that time, all the refuse that accumulated around the stone buildings east of the road was buried by deep erosional soils, deposits of topsoil washing down from cane fields on the slopes of Mount Nevis and filling in what remained of Morton's Bay after 1690. In other words, Jamestown was a buried town, lost and forgotten, even as the island's sugar economy hit its full stride. Construction of the 19th-century structures associated with the 'Pleasure House' further obscured evidence of earlier activity. Perhaps it was there, overlooking a locality once busy with trade, that in the waning days of sugar and slavery on Nevis, local stories coalesced into the tragic legend of Jamestown, the town beneath the sea.

NOTES

1 This paper complements a second account by the same authors in Ahlman and Schroedl (eds) 2020, 48–67.
2 Smith 1690.
3 Iles 1871, 8; Hubbard 1996.
4 Smith 1630.
5 Bridenbaugh & Bridenbaugh 1972, 13; Dunn 1972; Sheridan 1974, 162.
6 Stearns 1970, 229.
7 Morgan, 1975.
8 Morris *et al.* 1999; Machling 2012.
9 Smith 1630.
10 Jeafferson 1878, 2, 275–6.
11 Sloane 1725, 1, xliv.
12 Robertson 1733, 18.
13 Robertson 1733, 13–14.
14 Robertson 1733, 20–1.
15 Stapleton 1676.
16 Smith 1690.
17 Stede 1690.
18 Machling in Leech 2002, 31–8.
19 Stapleton 1676.
20 Machling 2012.
21 Taylor & Aston 1999.
22 Higgins 2002, 2006.
23 Duco 2003.
24 Three volumes with compensation claims made following the French invasion of Nevis survive: 1706 TNA Kew, CO243/2, Vol. 1/fol. 42; William Venton, CO243/2, Vol. 2/fol. 422; Mary King, CO243/2, Vol. 2/fol. 432; Thomas Joseph, CO243/2, Vol. 2/fol. 277; John Abbott, CO243/2, Vol. 3/fol. 646.

BIBLIOGRAPHY

Ahlman, T.M. & Schroedl, G.F. (eds) 2020, *Historical Archaeologies of the Caribbean: Contextualizing Sites through Colonialism, Capitalism, and Globalism*, Tuscaloosa and London: University of Alabama Press.

Bridenbaugh, C. & Bridenbaugh, R. 1972, *No Peace Beyond the Line: the English in the Caribbean, 1624–1690*, Oxford: New York.

Duco D.H. 2003, *Merken en Merkenrecht van de Pijpenmakers in Gouda*, Pijpenkabinet: Amsterdam.

Dunn, R. 1972, *Sugar and Slaves: The Rise of the Planter Class in the English West Indies, 1624–1713*, Chapel Hill: Institute of Early American History and Culture by the University of North Carolina Press.

Higgins, D.A. 2002, 'Clay Tobacco Pipes from Excavations at Jamestown, Nevis, 1998' (archive report).

Higgins, D.A. 2006, 'Clay Tobacco Pipes from Excavations at Jamestown, Nevis, 2006', Technical Report in Hudgins, Klingelhofer & Leech 2014, 60–5.

Hubbard, V. 1996, *Swords, Ships and Sugar: A History of Nevis to 1900*, Corvallis: Premiere Editions.

Hudgins, C., Klingelhofer, E. & Leech, R., 2014, *Excavations at Jamestown, Nevis, 2003–2006*, Nevis Heritage Project.

Hudgins, C.L., Klingelhofer, E. & Leech, R.H. 2020, 'Jamestown, Nevis and Urban Resilience in the Early English Caribbean', in Ahlman & Schroedl (eds) 2020, 48–67.

Iles, J. 1871, *An Account Descriptive of the Island of Nevis, West Indies*, London: Fletcher and Sons.

Jeaffreson, C. 1878, *A Young Squire of the Seventeenth Century: In the Papers of Christopher Jeafreson*, 2 vols, London: Hurst and Blackett.

Leech, R. *et al.* 2002, 'Nevis Heritage Project Interim Report 2002', Department of Archaeology, University of Southampton in cooperation with Nevis Heritage and Conservation Society.

Machling, T. 2012, *The Fortifications of Nevis, West Indies, from the 17th Century to the Present Day: Protected Interests?*, Brit. Archaeol. Rep. Int. Ser. 2349, Oxford: Archaeopress.
Morgan, E.S. 1975, *American Slavery, American Freedom: The Ordeal of Colonial Virginia.* New York: Norton.
Morris, E. *et al.* 1999, '"... the old stone fortt at Newcastle ..." The Redoubt, Nevis, eastern Caribbean', *J. Post-Med. Arch.* 33:1, 194–221.
Morris, E., Leech, R., Crosby, A., Machling, T., Williams, B. & Heathcote, J. 2003, *Nevis Heritage Project Interim Report 2002*, Southampton: Nevis Heritage Project, University of Southampton.
Robertson, R. 1733, *A Short History of the Hurricane*, London.
Sheridan, R. 1974, *Sugar and Slavery: An Economic History of the British West Indies, 1623–1775*, Baltimore: John Hopkins University Press.
Sloane, H. 1725, *A Voyage to the Islands Madera, Barbados, Nieves, S. Christophers, and Jamaica, with the natural history ... of the last of those islands; to which is prefixed an introduction wherein is an account of the inhabitants ... trade, etc.*, London: Printed for the Author.
Smith, A. 1690, *An Account of the Late Dreadful Earth-Quake in the Island of Nevis, St.*
Christophers &c, which Happened in the Beginning of April, of this present Year
1690 In a letter to a Friend in London, London: A. Smith.
Smith, J. 1630, *The true travels, adventures, and observations of Captaine Iohn Smith, in Europe, Asia, Affrica, and America from Anno Domini 1593 to 1629*, London: Printed by J.H. for Thomas Slater.
Stapleton, Sir William. 1676, Letter to Board of Trade and Plantations, 22 November 1676 TNA CO1/38/162:22/11/1676 in Morris *et al.* 2003, 31.
Stearns, R. 1970, *Science in the British Colonies of America*, Urbana: University of Illinois Press.
Stede, 1690, to Lords and Trade and Plantations, 23 April 1690, 'America and West Indies: April 1690', in CPSAWI 13, 1689–1692, ed. J W Fortescue (London, 1901), 243–55. British History Online http://www.british-history.ac.uk/cal-state-papers/colonial/america-west-indies/vol13/pp243-255 [accessed 3 May 2020].
Taylor, T. & Aston, M. 1999, *Time Team 99: The Site Reports*, London: Channel 4 Television.

10

Observations on the European Ceramics from Nevis

DAVID BARKER

SUMMARY: European ceramics recovered from excavations and fieldwalking in Nevis present a consistent picture of the wares available during the first 250 years of the island's colonial history. Earlier assemblages comprise a wide range of British and European wares of the types commonly found in colonial contexts, but by the end of the 18th century a near total reliance upon British-made goods is evident and the importance of Britain's major industrial pottery producing centres is clear.

INTRODUCTION

The writer first had the opportunity to examine ceramics from Nevis in 1998, when Channel 4's *Time Team* TV programme undertook excavations at Mountravers and test pitting at Jamestown. An initial report on the ceramics was prepared for the resulting report,[1] with a more detailed report compiled following analysis of the ceramics under more favourable conditions back in the UK.[2] Subsequent excavations at Mountravers, together with field survey at the nearby site of a slave village, directed by Roger Leech and Bruce Williams, have yielded a much larger and more varied artefact assemblage which offers fresh insights into the material culture of a plantation house, while further fieldwork and test pitting at Jamestown in 2000, 2002, and 2003 yielded further evidence for the early settlement and later activity on that site.

In addition to ceramics from Mountravers and Jamestown, material has been examined from the 2000–1 excavations in Charlestown; plantation sites at Fenton Hill,[3] Upper Rawlins,[4] and Low Ground;[5] and a post-emancipation village, Nugent's.[6] Other ceramics have been found in the island's fields during field-walking and as casual finds by local people. All seem to provide a consistent picture of the range of ceramics used on Nevis, and one which corresponds closely to that formed from the archaeological finds.

POTENTIAL OF THE CERAMIC EVIDENCE

The role of ceramics in historical archaeology is well-known and needs no reiteration here.[7] In the context of the island of Nevis, ceramics might be expected to make a particular contribution in the following areas: in providing evidence for commercial contact between Nevis and Britain, and the wider European commercial sphere within which Nevis was situated; in highlighting the economic development of the island as sugar production increased, and in determining the economic circumstances of the various sectors of the island's population; and from this it follows that we might expect ceramics to provide evidence for social hierarchies in town and country, and especially those between planter and slave.

The sample of material examined to date is sufficient to illustrate the types of ceramics available to, and in use by, the island's population from its initial settlement. However, not all periods are equally well-represented: there is comparatively little ceramic material from these sites which can be dated with any certainty to the middle of the 18th century and no 20th-century material has been examined. Otherwise, there are few surprises in the ceramic record, with a wide range of familiar British and European wares represented in all of the groups. The ceramics from Mountravers are especially important and merit further study: not only are all of the types of ceramics found on Nevis represented there, but the relationships between these can be examined within a defined chronological framework, and with the benefit of a limited body of documentary evidence.

17TH-AND EARLY 18TH-CENTURY MATERIAL

Ceramics dating to the late 17th to early 18th centuries are well represented in the assemblages from Upper Rawlins, Charlestown, Jamestown, Fenton Hill, and in the cellar contexts at Mountravers. They present a fairly consistent picture with a range of European and English wares present on all the sites. These include vessels of Rhenish stoneware, Westerwald stoneware (Fig. 10.1), North Italian marbled slipwares and sgraffito-decorated wares, while the ubiquitous English wares are jars and dishes of North Devon gravel-tempered wares (Fig. 10.2). Tin-glazed earthenwares in a range of forms, decorated and undecorated, are mostly English-made, and again are common to all sites with earlier ceramics.

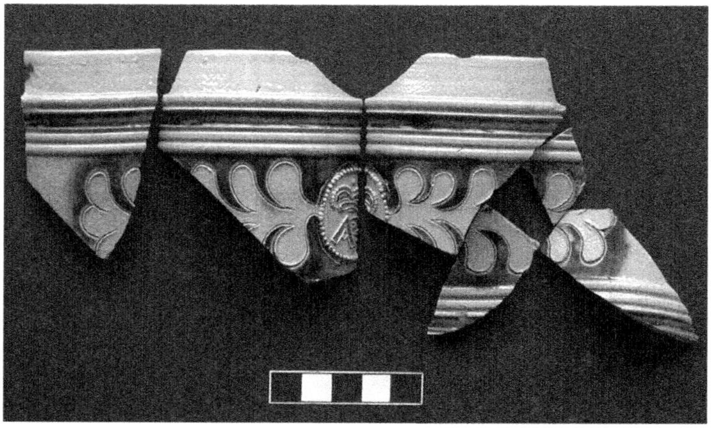

Fig. 10.1. Westerwald stoneware mug with 'A R' initials moulded in relief, Mountravers; early 18th century.

A good number of sherds of sgraffito-decorated slipware dishes from North Devon have been found (Fig. 10.3), although at neither Jamestown nor Upper Rawlins. Staffordshire- or Bristol-type slipwares – dishes and hollow wares – are found in even greater numbers but, again, not at Upper Rawlins. These slipwares, predominantly thrown cups, mugs, porringers (Fig. 10.4), and press-moulded dishes (Fig. 10.5), often decorated with trailed-and-combed or feathered slip, are widely found in the Caribbean and North America. Their source is, however, open to question, as similar wares were produced at many centres during the late 17th and 18th centuries. The products of the largest producer, the potteries of north Staffordshire, and those of Bristol, are superficially very similar in appearance and are difficult to distinguish.[8] It is probable that the products of both centres were shipped to markets in the Caribbean and North America and, indeed, Bristol was one of the ports through which Staffordshire goods were despatched before the rise of Liverpool as the port for the Atlantic trade. The full range of late 17th- and early 18th-century Staffordshire wares has not yet been found to any great extent in Nevis, with just a single sherd each of mottled ware and blackware present at Fenton Hill.[9] By contrast, several sherds of a north Staffordshire brown salt-glazed stoneware mug with rouletted decoration, dating to *c.* 1710, were found at Upper Rawlins (Fig. 10.6).[10] A similar vessel was recovered in the cellar at Mountravers.

Fig. 10.2. North Devon gravel-temper jar, Upper Rawlins; late 17th century.

Fig. 10.3. North Devon sgraffito-decorated slipware dish rim, Charlestown; late 17th – early 18th century.

The wider extent of European trade at this time is illustrated by the presence of vessels of Chinese porcelains, which are found in very small quantities in most of the excavated assemblages, although not at Upper Rawlins. Vessels are predominantly blue and white, often very fragmentary and not easily datable. The earlier cellar contexts from the Mountravers contained a small number of porcelain sherds, including a blue painted saucer (Fig. 10.7), but other sherds from Mountravers and other sites could possibly date to later in the 18th century. Many of the vessels may have been used for

Fig. 10.4. Slipware cup, Charlestown; probably Staffordshire, late 17th – early 18th century.

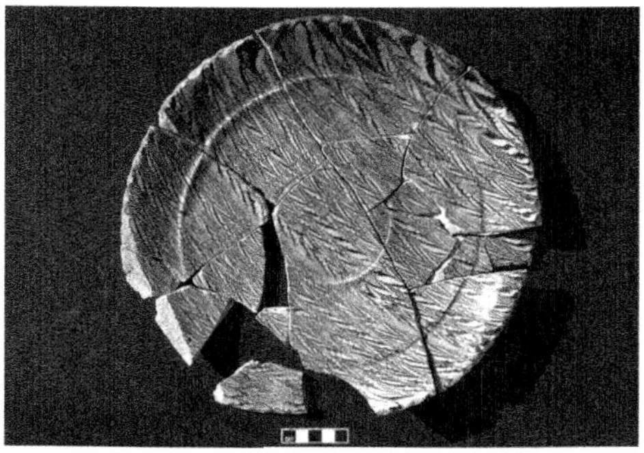

Fig. 10.5. Press-moulded slipware dish, Charlestown; late 17th – early 18th century.

Fig. 10.6. Salt-glazed stoneware mug with rouletted decoration, Upper Rawlins; probably Staffordshire, early 18th century.

tea drinking, for teabowls and saucers are common forms.

The presence of 17th- and early 18th-century material in the Mountravers cellar area contexts is no surprise, as excavated features point to the probable existence of a 17th-century timber house here. Some evidence for the degree of comfort achieved within this house may be indicated by a large number of late 17th-century Dutch tin-glazed tiles with blue-painted designs (Figs 10.8, 10.9). These may indicate the presence of a tiled fireplace or they may have adorned the walls of a small room. No two tiles seem to have the same painted design, although the 'ox head' and 'butterfly' corner motifs are used on most.

Of particular interest from the Mountravers cellar contexts is the large number of ceramic vessels associated with sugar production. These are the earthenware sugar cone moulds in which liquid sugar was crystallized to form sugar cones, and other coarse earthenware jars in which the remaining syrup from the sugar moulds was collected after the sugar had formed. Such vessels are found at other sites associated with sugar production, as well as at Charlestown and other sites on Nevis.

The sugar cone moulds are wheel-thrown, of an elongated conical form, in a buff-orange, orange, or orange-red fabric, tapering towards a narrow, pointed base where there is a small hole which was plugged during the formation of the sugar, but was subsequently unplugged to allow the remaining syrup to drain off. The vessels' rims are roughly squared-off or rounded and their interior surfaces frequently have washes of white pipe clay. The drip jars are in coarse orange or orange-red bodies, sometimes showing the effects of reduction, with patchy greenish brown internal lead glazes, which may have splashed over onto a rim or shoulder.

The range of sources must be considered for these. An examination of the 1998 Mountravers sugar cone mould sherds identified nine fabrics,[11] and subsequent thin-sectioning and microscopic analysis indicated that the majority of the vessels were probably of British origin, although an Iberian source was likely for one of the fabric types and another was potentially produced on Nevis.[12]

Other distinctive coarse earthenwares found in the cellar contexts at Mountravers have no obvious connection with sugar production. These are large jars with flattened rounded rims and a thin internal brown/black glaze over an orange-coloured fabric which are almost certainly of Mediterranean origin. Large jars, made in Montelupo, Italy, which were used for the transportation of olive oil to the Caribbean via England, have been recognized on Nevis.[13] They found subsequent use as water jars and a number of complete examples survive on the island. It is possible that the excavated coarseware jars are of Italian origin, although this remains to be confirmed.

Despite the presence of both continental and oriental wares on early colonial sites, it is British-made ceramics which predominate from the outset, and this trend was to continue. The need to tranship foreign ceramics through British ports put them at a disadvantage with British wares and when issues of quality, quantity and cost were successfully addressed by the home industries, then opportunities in the colonial markets for non-British goods were severely restricted.

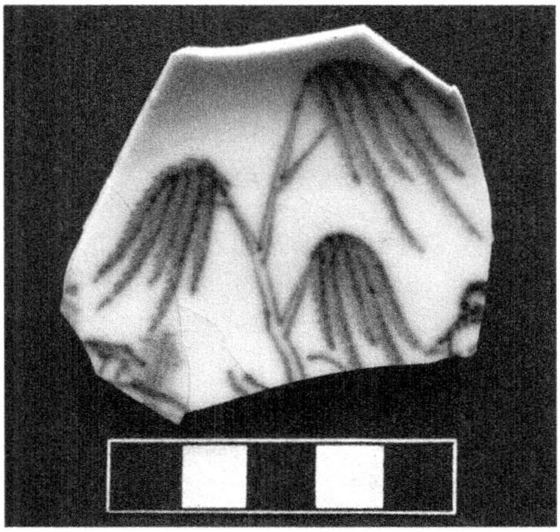

Fig. 10.7. Chinese porcelain saucer, Mountravers; early 18th century.

Fig. 10.8. Dutch tin-glazed tile, Mountravers; late 17th century.

Fig. 10.9. Dutch tin-glazed tile, Mountravers; late 17th century.

EIGHTEENTH-CENTURY DEVELOPMENTS

The ceramic evidence for the middle years of the 18th century is somewhat sparse from both Mountravers and Charlestown, and is completely absent at Jamestown. However, from what little there is points to Britain's increasing role in transatlantic trade, the growing impact of British ceramics generally, and of Staffordshire ceramics specifically. A dramatic expansion of British ceramic manufacture at this time was to a great extent driven by developments in north Staffordshire, where an industry-wide shift in production towards refined earthenwares and stonewares took place between *c.* 1720 and 1740 in what has been referred to as a 'ceramic revolution'.[14] Staffordshire manufacturers came to dominate colonial and other overseas markets with tea and table wares in these new bodies, wares which were widely emulated by most other major British pottery factories. By the second half of the 18th century Staffordshire wares had become, in effect, the industry standard and were indistinguishable from those of non-Staffordshire manufacturers.[15]

Fenton Hill is the only site whose ceramics suggest continuity throughout the 18th century.[16] While the quantity of archaeological ceramics increases overall as the century progresses, that of the Continental European wares declines; the increase in the quantity of British wares, however, is considerable. At Fenton Hill, seventeen sherds of white salt-glazed stoneware suggest mid 18th-century activity; these represent eleven vessels, including four plates, a side plate, and possible tea wares. At the Mountravers slave village, the ceramics seem to indicate an absence of activity before the 1760s, but many of the sherds recovered belong to the later 18th century. These include white salt-glazed stonewares (Fig. 10.10), some with scratch blue decoration; creamwares; a green

Fig. 10.10. White salt-glazed stoneware plate with moulded rim, Mountravers slave village; north Staffordshire, *c.* 1760–70.

Fig. 10.11. Creamware cover with over-glaze painted decoration and the Pretor-Pinney crest, Mountravers; late 18th – early 19th century.

glazed plate edge with moulded barleycorn decoration; coarse agate wares; Chinese porcelain; and even sherds of an English soft-past porcelain teabowl.

At Mountravers, excavations in the garden area yielded a very large quantity of material. Sherds from several late 17th- to early 18th-century features compare closely with those from the cellar excavation, but the majority of the ceramics recovered are of late 18th- to late 19th-century date. A wide range of wares is represented, relating not merely to the plantation house élite, but to all who lived and worked on the estate. For example, the presence of a significant quantity of hand-made Afro-Caribbean ceramics – comprising as much as 40% of the total number of sherds in the 19th-century deposits – is a reminder of the racial and social mix at this plantation, but this is a subject beyond the scope of this paper.

By contrast, some ceramics seem to provide a direct link to the plantation owner. A small number of late 18th-century creamware sherds are from a dinner service, the edges of individual vessels being decorated with an over-glaze painted maroon band. A sauce tureen cover also carries a painted eagle motif (Fig. 10.11), which is sufficiently similar to the crest of the Pretor-Pinney family as to leave little doubt that this belonged to the family prior to the sale of Mountravers in 1808.[17] A specially commissioned dinner service of this kind would have involved a considerable financial outlay, but one essential for someone of John Pinney's standing.

There is nothing else comparable within the assemblage. There are relatively few sherds of Chinese porcelain vessels which are obviously of this date, and most of these are of the less expensive blue and white variety which was a staple of the East India Company's trade for most of the 18th century. Just one porcelain plate sherd has been identified with the more expensive over-glaze painted decoration which could possibly have belonged to a dinner service of the type which would have been an appropriate possession for a plantation-owning family.

NINETEENTH-CENTURY WARES

By the early 19th century the ceramic evidence from all sites is abundant, and the picture presented by all the assemblages examined is one of the complete dominance of the market by British refined ceramics. Most of the 19th-century white earthenwares are decorated. Transfer-printed pearlwares and whitewares were the dominant ceramic type on all of the sites of this date; patterns are in a range of styles which reflect the prevalent fashion, colours, and qualities, although by the middle of the century the printed wares typically exhibit a decline in quality, perhaps reflecting a general downturn in the island's economy and prosperity.

Most of the 19th-century ceramics recovered from the 2001–4 excavations at Mountravers were British. The range of types, forms, and decoration is broadly comparable to those found at Charlestown and other island sites and many of the wares would not be out of place on any British domestic site of the period. A good number of the Mountravers printed sherds clearly belong to good quality dinner services, which are better understood by revisiting the 1998 Time Team assemblage (below). Such quality is not consistent throughout the assemblage, however, and many sherds are from plates decorated with 'Willow' and other poorer quality printed patterns. Other table wares are the ubiquitous shell edge types, with moulded and under-glazed coloured edges which occur in pearlware and whiteware. By 1810 these were the cheapest table wares available,[18] a fact which doubtless contributed to their widespread use for much of the 19th century.

Vessels with under-glaze blue painted designs in an oriental style, widely used in Britain and North America during the 1780s–1820s, do not seem to be a feature of

Fig. 10.12. White earthenware (chamber pot?) cover with under-glaze painted decoration, Charlestown; mid 19th century.

Fig. 10.13. White earthenware chamber pot cover with sponged decoration in green, Mountravers; second half of 19th century.

the Nevis assemblages, although vessels with painted polychrome floral patterns were used in Nevis during the middle to later years of the 19th century. These simple bright patterns appear mostly on bowls and are present amongst the later material from the Mountravers garden excavation and at Charlestown. A cover – possibly a chamber pot cover – from Charleston is decorated in this fashion (Fig. 10.12).

Other low-cost wares recovered from Mountravers, Charlestown, and most other sites include 'dipped' bowls and other forms, with banded and other types of slip decoration. Again, these were in widespread use during the 19th century, and from the 1790s to the 1840s were the cheapest of wares available with decoration.[19] It would appear, however, that from *c.* 1840 the cheapest of the decorated wares were those with sponged decoration.[20] These very common finds in Nevis, with few forms other than bowls, plates, chamber pots, and basins. A sponge decorated chamber pot cover from Mountravers (Fig. 10.13) is typical of this type. Sponged wares are common finds in colonial contexts, but were certainly not produced solely for export: they are frequent finds on economically marginal domestic sites in the British Isles. Did consumers express a definite preference for such brightly, but simply decorated wares, or was it simply that their functional requirements could be met at a low cost and with a range of decoration? We cannot assume a single motivating factor applied to all users of these wares across the globe.

Something not well represented in the Nevis assemblages are tea wares. Where they are found, the better quality pieces are of printed earthenware, bone china, or Chinese porcelain, and a single black basalt sherd may be from a teapot. One bone china saucer with the light blue printed pattern 'Broseley' has an impressed 'Wedgwood' mark.

Numerous vessels suggesting domestic activities not related to eating, drinking, or hygiene are also represented amongst the wares. For example, commodities such as ink and blacking were purchased in brown stoneware bottles which were probably discarded once their contents were exhausted. Several examples of these have been found.

At Mountravers, a brown stoneware ink bottle is unmarked, but a blacking bottle has an impressed mark 'BELPER & DENBY POTTERIES DERBYSHIRE / VITREOUS STONE BOTTLES & C. / J. BOURNE / PATENTEE / WARRANTED NOT TO ABSORB'. The Belper and Denby Potteries were operated simultaneously by John Bourne between 1812 and 1834, when the former factory was closed, but a post-1823 date is indicated here for in that year he took out his first patent for improvements to salt-glaze kilns.[21] Another later bottle from Charlestown bears an impressed mark of Lovatt & Lovatt of Langley Mill, Nottingham, a firm which operated from 1886 to 1931.[22] The contents of a Bristol-glazed jar from Mountravers are unknown, but it bears an impressed manufacturer's mark 'Powell / Potter / Bristol'. William Powell marketed his new liquid glazed stonewares from 1835, and although he died in 1854 the business was carried on by his sons.[23]

THE MOUNTRAVERS DINNER SERVICES

The patterns

A more focused discard event at Mountravers seems to be represented by the ceramics from Time Team's Trench 1. A sample of 1,178 sherds was recovered from what is clearly a domestic rubbish dump of some size, the contents of which date broadly to the period *c.* 1805–35. A smaller, but related group of wares – with cross-joins to Trench 1 – was excavated at the same time beneath the Counting House (Trench 3). In both of these trenches, the majority of the refined wares were good quality table wares

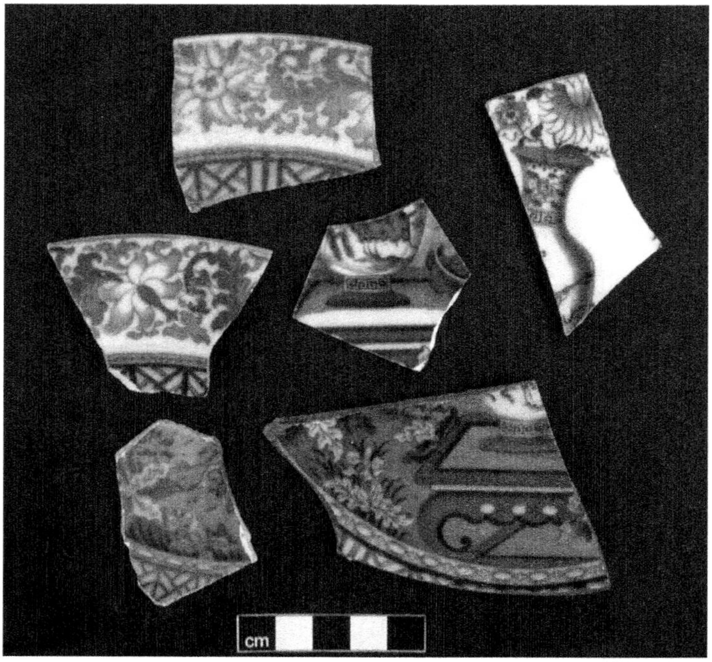

Fig. 10.14. Pearlware plate sherds with blue-printed pattern 'Chinese Vase' made by Wedgwood, Mountravers, *c.* 1805–10.

Fig. 10.15. Pearlware plate sherds with blue-printed pattern 'Chinese Flowering Pot', Mountravers, *c.* 1805–10.

of pearlware and whiteware with blue transfer-printed decoration. At least five dinner services are represented, with plates and serving dishes predominating, and smaller number of soup plates, tureens and covers, stands, vegetable dishes and covers. Tea and other wares are considerably less well-represented.

The first of the dinner service patterns is 'Chinese Vase' or 'Blue Bamboo', a chinoiserie design introduced by Wedgwood of Etruria, Stoke-on-Trent, in 1805,[24] and one of the Trench 3 sherds has an impressed 'Wedgwood' mark. The central feature of this design is a large vase bearing an image of a seated oriental figure playing a stringed instrument, with abundant bamboo, flowers, and foliage all around; there is an internal trellis border and a floral rim pattern (Fig. 10.14).

The second, known as 'Chinese Flowering Pot',[25] is also in an oriental style, but dating perhaps to the 1810s. It features a man and a boy addressing each other over a large vase with flowers, with a large building and trees behind; beyond a trellis fence is a river upon which is a small boat, while the floral border has reserves within which are two figures or exotic birds (Fig. 10.15). The manufacturer is not known. A third chinoiserie pattern is 'Flying Pennant', a Herculaneum pattern whose manufacture is dated here by the presence of a single impressed mark 'H. P, 1808'.[26]

Another pattern, again present on a large number of dinner wares, is identified by printed 'Stone China' marks bearing the name 'Morea'. This is a European romantic landscape with ruins within a floral and swag border (Fig. 10.16) and, although the marks here do not identify the manufacturer, the pattern is known to have been made by Thomas Dimmock & Co. of Hanley, Stoke-on-Trent (*c.* 1828–59).[27] Stylistically the vessels bearing this pattern probably date to *c.* 1835. There are two further Dimmock printed patterns. The first, 'Grecian Border', is identifiable by a single printed mark, but sherds with this foliate rim pattern are sufficiently numerous to indicate that a full service is represented.[28] The other is an unlisted pattern whose incomplete name, '[...] prigs', forms part of a printed Dimmock 'Stone Ware' mark.[29]

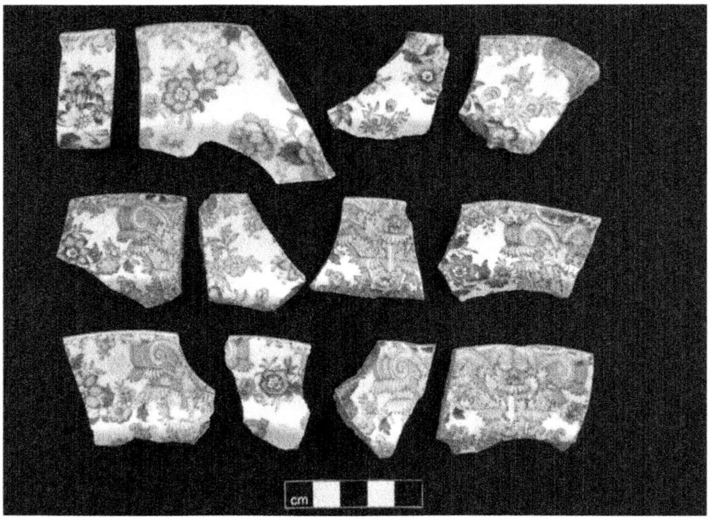

Fig. 10.16. White earthenware serving dish sherds with blue-printed pattern 'Morea' by Thomas Dimmock & Co., Mountravers, *c.* 1830–40.

The blue printed 'Willow' pattern was ubiquitous in British households during the first half of the 19th century and was the cheapest of the printed patterns.[30] It was used by almost every industrial pottery manufacturer on wares of varying qualities. At this time it was used solely on table wares and this is the case at Mountravers, although there are comparatively few sherds from the Time Team trenches. A printed mark on one serving dish identifies the manufacturer as Deakin & Bailey of the Waterloo Works, Longton, Stoke-on-Trent, a firm in business from *c.* 1828 to 1832.[31]

Not surprisingly sherds of the five main printed dinner services have also been found in the later excavation of the garden area, but the concentration of such a quantity of similar wares in Trenches 1 and 3 suggests that these related groups may well have been discarded together during some form of clearance episode, probably around 1835–40. The characteristics of a clearance group include a large number of vessels, typically with a significant proportion of larger-sized sherds with many joins, together with an absence of abrasion and little residual or intrusive material.[32] The nature of the sampling here prevents any conclusion being formed as to how complete some of the vessels might be. A suggestion that this is a clearance resulting from a natural disaster such as a hurricane seems unlikely given the limited range of material present, and a more likely explanation is that these wares were discarded simply as a result of the up-grading of the household's day-to-day table wares.

DISCUSSION

With the range of wares and ware types recovered during archaeological work across the island, a clear picture is beginning to emerge of the ceramics available to different levels of society from the 17th to late 19th centuries. In some respects, however, what is absent from an assemblage is just as important, and this is particularly true at Mountravers. Not only is there a marked lack of mid 18th-century material here, but there is clear evidence that, even for those decades for which there is an abundance of wares, we are not seeing the entire picture.

Creamware, or 'Queen's Ware', for example, is poorly represented in the Mountravers assemblage, although the notable pieces are those decorated sherds which include the Pretor-Pinney crested piece. However, Queen's Ware formed a significant part of orders for ceramics placed by John Pinney, such as that of 3 June 1776 when he ordered a range of ceramic goods from Peter Eaton of Bristol, which included a quantity of Queen's Ware (i.e. creamware) items – bowls and jugs in various sizes, six dozen shallow plates, and two dozen soup plates – as well as 'common blue and white china' (i.e. Chinese porcelain), comprising one dozen tea cups and saucers and three dozen saucers; as regards the china, 'any sort or kind will do. If they are of different patterns it is immaterial'.[33]

On 14 July of the following year, an order was placed with Nathaniel Martin for various earthenwares and, in Queen's Ware, three dozen shallow plates and four pudding dishes in two sizes.[34] Then on 18 June 1778, Pinney ordered six dozen white stone chamber pots and a Queen's Ware tureen, from Mills & Swanston of London.[35] In 1778 expenditure upon ceramics was recorded: '2 blue & wh. china Tureens w.th Covers and Dishes £6:12:0; 24 do. long China dishes different sizes £9:18:0; and 12 queen's ware Dishes 60/ 6 doz. plates 6/ £3:6:0'.[36]

The lack of creamwares amongst the Mountravers finds is surely largely an accident of archaeological survival. It is well known that a household's best, or most expensive wares, amongst which crested wares may be counted, are poorly represented in domestic groups, due to infrequent use and the level of care taken during use. Can the same be true of the blue and white porcelains, poorly represented amongst the excavated ceramics, and yet ordered in large quantities? We cannot assume that all of these wares were destined for use at Mountravers, and indeed some of the quantities involved suggest otherwise. Indeed, in a letter of 30 February 1786, Messrs Pinney & Tobin asked Messrs Akerman & Co., China Merchants of Fenchurch Street, London, to despatch a substantial quantity of china by first ship to Nevis or St Kitts. The order comprised twelve dozen meat plates, twelve dozen soup plates, twelve punch bowls (three each in three quart, two quart, and one pint sizes), three dozen cups and saucers, and six tureens, as well as two complete (dinner?) sets; all were 'to be of neat patterns and carefully put up'.[37]

By first decade of the 19th century, undecorated Queen's Ware had lost much of its appeal and status, while Chinese blue and white porcelains ceased to be imported by the East India Company by 1796. Nevertheless, the ceramics at Mountravers indicate an overwhelming preference for contemporary fashionable British wares, and for buying by brand. On 7 December 1807, for example, John Pinney and John Frederick Pinney II wrote to Mr J Goldicutt, of King Street, Covent Garden, London, about goods which had not arrived: 'We order'd sometime since a crate of Wedgwood's ware at £4. 4s od per Crate and requested it might be forwarded to the care of Mr Richard Lambert in Princes Street.'[38]

This reference is important as it belongs to the period to which no fewer than five marked Wedgwood pieces belong in the Mountravers assemblage, not to mention those wares known to have been made by Wedgwood but which are unmarked.

Wedgwood was a firm which at this date still retained something of the exclusivity achieved during the lifetime of its founder, Josiah Wedgwood I, and Pinney would certainly have been aware that to purchase wares from Wedgwood would have been to purchase quality goods. We cannot know exactly what the Wedgwood wares were that were undelivered in 1807, but by the end of the decade Wedgwood blue transfer printed wares were being used at Mountravers. At this time transfer-printed wares were the most expensive type of decorated earthenware available,[39] and the presence of at least five dinner services of this type, even if acquired over a period of 25 years or so, represents a considerable expenditure on ceramics. However, we may speculate that these printed services were not necessarily Mountravers's finest ceramics, for in a well-to-do household the blue-printed wares were more likely to have been the ceramics used on a regular, daily basis by the family and, consequently, subjected to wear and damage. Such a family's best dinner service, whether crested or not, would probably have over-glaze painted and gilded decoration. Good quality earthenwares were available, and the fine bone chinas from the leading factories would certainly have been suitable, while from 1813 polychrome painted, or printed and painted ironstone chinas were newly available and fashionable.

Some evidence of the comparative prices of blue-printed table wares can be gained from a sale of Mason's wares in 1822. A dinner set of 142 pieces of blue and white earthenware had a reserve of six guineas placed upon it, while the same reserve was placed upon a table set of only 87 pieces in blue ironstone.[40] Both are in sharp contrast to the prices for the more decorative ironstones: 25 guineas for a 142-piece set of 'Rich Old Japan', which was either printed and painted or just painted, and 35 guineas for a 142-piece set of 'Rich Old Japan, sumptuously gilt'.[41] Of course we cannot know whether anything of this sort was acquired for Mountravers.

SOURCES OF THE LATER CERAMICS

English wares

The later ceramics from all of the assemblages examined are overwhelmingly British in origin. On the basis solely of the manufacturers' marks identified, three main manufacturing centres can be seen to have been supplying Nevis with ceramics. Wares from the Herculaneum factory indicate that this Liverpool factory, well-placed for serving overseas markets, had some share of the trade with Nevis. Liverpool's importance as a port for the transatlantic trade grew during the later 18th century, but this benefited not only the local Herculaneum factory, but manufacturers in the port's industrial hinterland. Among the chief beneficiaries was the pottery industry of north Staffordshire.

Staffordshire's overseas trade, including the transatlantic trade, had been substantial, even before the completion of the Trent & Mersey Canal, with goods taking a variety of overland and riverine routes for onwards despatch from the country's main seaports, including Livepool.[42] In 1777, however, with the canal's completion, the north Staffordshire potteries achieved direct, safe, and more economical access to the ports of Liverpool and Hull, and from this time onwards these were the points of departure for all Staffordshire wares.

It is unsurprising, therefore, that Staffordshire ceramics are the dominant type in all Nevis assemblages from the late 18th century. At Mountravers, for example, the products of three Staffordshire manufacturers – Deakin & Bailey, Thomas Dimmock & Co., and Wedgwood – have been identified, and others are represented in the Charlestown assemblage. One has an impressed mark of Copeland & Garrett of Stoke-upon-Trent, together with a printed mark 'New Blanche', a name given to one of the firm's earthenware bodies.[43] Another has a printed mark of Everard, Colclough & Townsend of Longton, who were in business *c.* 1841;[44] the pattern is 'Chinese Pastime'. Other Staffordshire manufacturers include Spode of Stoke-upon-Trent and Davenport of Longport; an impressed mark of the former was excavated at Fenton Hill,[45] while the other was found at Fort Codrington.[46]

One final contributor to the trade in ceramics in the early 19th century was the Leeds Pottery, operated by Hartley Greens & Co. A single impressed mark at Mountravers is of a type which was in use from *c.* 1812 until the partnership ended in 1827.[47] Exports wares from the Leeds Pottery destined for transatlantic markets would also have passed through the port of Liverpool.

Scottish wares

During the second half of the 19th century the developing Scottish pottery industry entered the transatlantic trade and the Caribbean islands were important in this. Superficially, the products of the Scottish potteries were not dissimilar to those of other British industrial pottery-producing centres, but a number of printed patterns are indicative of Scottish manufacture. Scottish printed wares are clearly present in some of the assemblages, and other sherds may well remain unidentified. At Low Ground, for example, there are sherds of one or more plates decorated with the printed pattern 'Amboina' in green;[48] one of these bears an incomplete printed mark with the pattern name and the name of the manufacturer, J. & M.P. Bell of Glasgow. Kelly lists this amongst the patterns made at Bell's pottery[49] and suggests that the pattern was designed before 1881.[50] 'Amboina' seems to have been one of Bell's many patterns designed specifically for use on wares for export to the massive South-East Asia market; its presence in Nevis is therefore noteworthy. Another printed pattern of Scottish manufacture is present amongst the material excavated from Fenton Hill. This is a rim sherd from a plate with printed decoration showing a dolphin fountain, which is the border pattern for 'Triumphal Car'.[51] This pattern is known to have been made by J. & M.P. Bell & Co. of the Glasgow Pottery,[52] by R. Cochran & Co. of the Verreville Pottery, Glasgow,[53] and by James Jamieson of the Bo'ness Pottery.[54] A second probable Bell mark from Nugents is printed in grey, but incomplete, reading '[…] B & Co.'; surrounding foliage suggests that this was from a plate decorated with a grey printed 'sea leaf' or similar pattern, examples of which were recovered from the site.[55]

The quantities of white wares with sponged decoration found in Nevis may owe something to the increased availability of Scottish goods during second half of the 19th century. A stamped mark of Cochran & Fleming of Glasgow, found at Mountravers, dates to between 1896 and 1920, but probably belongs to a sponged vessel.[56]

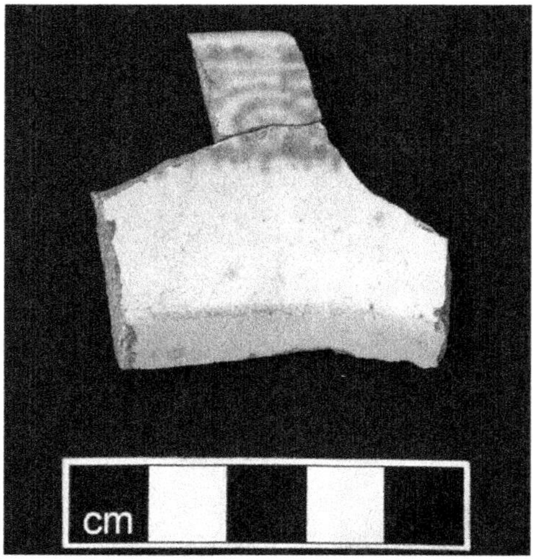

Fig. 10.17. White earthenware plate with sponged pattern 'Grecian', Jamestown; late 19th century.

Also sherds with the grey sponged pattern 'Grecian', known to have been produced by J. & M.P. Bell & Co. and other Scottish factories from *c.* 1875,[57] have been found at several sites (Fig. 10.17). Other sponged patterns are less easily attributed, but the collectors' emphasis upon the manufacture of sponged wares in Scotland has detracted from a clear appreciation of the scale of production of this type in north Staffordshire and the other British industrial potteries.[58] Factories acquired cut sponge motifs from specialist suppliers, rather than producing their own, and they are consequently not specific to any one manufacturer. In the absence of marks, therefore, it is difficult to distinguish Scottish wares from those of other British manufacturers who were also exporting vast quantities of sponged wares to the Caribbean, South America, Canada, South Africa, and the Far East.

CONCLUSION

Nevis has remained consistently British since it was first settled by Europeans. Inevitably, therefore, the ceramics present on this island reflect British commercial activity since this time and the material culture of domestic life does not differ significantly from that of the British households. Tastes were more diverse in the early years of the colony, with an abundance of Continental wares which were nevertheless far from unfamiliar in the English home, especially in the vicinity of the ports. With the rising fortunes of the colonial planter élite, however, a strict preference for, and adherence to British fashions came to prevail. In the area of ceramics, this was possible because of the changing nature of the ceramic industry at home which, for the first time, was to produce wares of the best quality and in volume. Moreover, enterprising manufacturers were able to set trends and influence consumer taste in a way that had not previously been possible, with the result that British ceramics became fashionable. Plantation owners recreated through their tea and table wares socially important and reassuringly comforting aspects of English country house or town house life, reinforcing their British identities and their place within the wider British sphere. Away from the plantation house, a British taste of sorts is still evident, albeit reflecting a different environment, both cultural and climatic, and further study in this area should be fruitful. Of particular interest would be the way in which emancipation affected the choice of ceramics and the manner of their use, and exactly how ceramics reflected the economic fortunes of the island in the post-emancipation period.

ACKNOWLEDGEMENTS

I am grateful to David Small and Christine Eickelmann for supplying information about Pinney's ceramic orders, and to Roger Leech for the identification of the Pinney crest.

NOTES

1 Bellamy, P. *et al.* 2005.
2 Barker 2001a.
3 Barker forthcoming b, 88–98.
4 Barker forthcoming c, 161–4.
5 Barker forthcoming a.
6 Barker 2006.
7 For example, Barker & Majewski 2006.
8 Barker & Dawson 1989.
9 Barker forthcoming b, 90.
10 Barker forthcoming c, 161–3.
11 Morris 2001a, 89.
12 Hardwick 2001, 89.
13 Morris 2001b, 102–3.
14 Barker 1999.
15 Barker 2001b, 78.
16 Barker forthcoming b.
17 Jack & Jack 1905, 456.
18 Miller 1991, 6.
19 Miller 1980, 34; Miller 1991, 6.
20 Miller 1991, 6.
21 Askey 1998, 143–50.
22 Askey 1998, 185–6.
23 Askey 1998, 126–7.
24 Halliday & Zeller 2018, 324.
25 R.K. Henrywood, pers. comm.
26 Hyland 2005, 42, 229.
27 Simpson *et al.* 2015, 34.
28 Transferware Database of Patterns and Sources, Pattern #13924; Simpson *et al.* 2015, 37.
29 Simpson *et al.* 2015, 36–8.
30 Miller 1980, 28; 1991, 8.
31 Hampson 1990, 59.
32 Pearce 2000, 144–5.
33 University of Bristol Special Collections, Pinney Papers, Letterbook 4: John Pinney, Nevis, to Peter Eaton, Bristol, 3 June 1776.
34 University of Bristol Special Collections, Pinney Papers, Letterbook 4: John Pinney to Nathaniel Martin, 14 July 1777.
35 University of Bristol Special Collections, Pinney Papers, Letterbook 4: John Pinney, Nevis, to Mills & Swanston, 18 June 1778.
36 University of Bristol Special Collections, Pinney Papers, Accountbook 21, Expense account 1778 (no date).
37 University of Bristol Special Collections, Pinney Papers, Letterbook 37: Messrs Pinney & Tobin to Messrs Akerman & Co., London, 30 February 1786.
38 University of Bristol Special Collections, Pinney Papers, Letterbook 46: John Pinney and John Frederick Pinney II to Mr J Goldicutt, 7 December, 1807. Richard Lambert had a warehouse by the Docks in Prices Street, Bristol.
39 Miller 1980; Miller 1991.
40 Godden 1999, 147, 116.
41 Godden 1999, 130–1.
42 Barker 2004, 211–12.
43 Coysh & Henrywood 1982, 260.
44 Henrywood 2002, 124.
45 Barker forthcoming b, 96–7.
46 Rookley 1998, 2.
47 Griffin 2005, 111.
48 Barker forthcoming a.
49 Kelly 1999, 105–6.
50 Kelly 2006, 101.
51 Barker forthcoming b, 92, 95.
52 Coysh & Henrywood 1982, 370; Kelly 1999, 103–9.
53 Kelly 1999, 189, 192.
54 Coysh & Henrywood 1982, 370; Kelly 1999, 23–7.
55 Barker 2006, 58–9.
56 Kelly 1999, 33–4.
57 Kelly *et al.* 2001, 9, 12.
58 For example, Barker 2001b, 89–90.

BIBLIOGRAPHY

Askey, D. 1998, *Stoneware Bottles 1500–1949*, Elsecar: BBR Publishing.
Barker, D. 1999, 'The Ceramic Revolution 1650–1850', in Egan & Michael 1999, 226–34.
Barker, D. 2001a, 'Analysis of the European Ceramics', in Morris *et al.* 2001, 81–4.
Barker, D. 2001b, '"The Usual Classes of Useful Articles": Staffordshire Ceramics Reconsidered', in Hunter (ed.) 2001, 72–93.
Barker, D. 2004, 'The Industrialization of the Staffordshire Potteries', in Barker & Cranstone 2004, 203–21.
Barker, D. 2006, 'The European Ceramics', in Newland *et al.* 2006, 57–65.
Barker, D. forthcoming a 'The Finds. Upper Stapleton Ceramics (US06)', in Leech & Philpott forthcoming.
Barker, D. forthcoming b, 'European and Oriental Ceramics', in Philpott *et al.* forthcoming, 88–98.
Barker, D. forthcoming c, 'European Ceramics', in Philpott *et al.* forthcoming, 161–4.
Barker, D. & Cranstone, D. 2004, *The Archaeology of Industrialization*, Soc. Post-Med. Archaeol. Monogr. 2, Leeds: Maney Publishing.
Barker, D. & Dawson, D. 1989, 'A Comparison between Staffordshire and Bristol Yellow Slipwares', unpubl.
Barker, D. & Majewski, T. 2006, 'Ceramics in Historical Archaeology', in Hicks & Beaudry 2006, 205–31.
Bellamy, P. *et al.* 2005, *Mountravers, St Thomas Lowland, Nevis: Archaeological Investigations by Time Team October 1998*, Terrain Archaeol. Rep. 5304.1.
Coysh A.W. & Henrywood R.K. 1982, *The Dictionary of Blue and White Printed Pottery 1780–1880*, Woodbridge: Antique Collectors' Club.
Egan, G. & Michael, R.L. (eds) 1999, *Old and New Worlds*, Oxford: Oxbow.
Godden, G.A. 1999, *Godden's Guide to Ironstone, Stone & Granite Wares*, Woodbridge: Antique Collectors' Club.
Griffin, J.D. 2005, *The Leeds Pottery 1770–1881*, Leeds: The Leeds Art Collections Fund.
Halliday, R. & Zeller, L.L. 2018, *Chinoiserie. British Printed Ceramics in the Chinese Style 1750–1900*, privately published.
Hampson, R. 1990, *Longton Potters 1700–1865*, Stoke-on-Trent: City Museum & Art Gallery.
Hardwick, W.A. 2001, 'The Scientific Analysis of Two Nevis Pottery Assemblages', in Morris 2001a, 89–90.
Henrywood, R.K. 2002, *Staffordshire Potters 1781–1900*, Woodbridge: Antique Collectors' Club.
Hicks, D. & Beaudry, M. 2006, *The Cambridge Companion to Historical Archaeology*, Cambridge: Cambridge University Press.
Hunter, R. (ed.) 2001, *Ceramics in America* 1, Milwaukee: The Chipstone Foundation.
Hyland, P. 2005, *The Herculaneum Pottery*, Liverpool: National Museums Liverpool and University of Liverpool Press.
Jack, T.C. & Jack, E.C. 1905, *Fairbairn's Book of Crests of the Families of Great Britain and Ireland*, 4th Edition, London; Edinburgh: T.C. & E.C. Jack.
Kelly, H.E. 1999, *Scottish Ceramics*, Atglen: Schiffer.
Kelly, H.E. 2006, *The Glasgow Pottery of John and Matthew Perston Bell, China and Earthenware Manufacturers in Glasgow*, Atglen: Schiffer.
Kelly, H.E., Kowalsky, A.A. & Kowalsky, D.E. 2001, *Spongeware 1835–1935: Makers, Marks, and Patterns*, Atglen: Schiffer.

Leech, R.H. & Philpott, R.A. forthcoming, *The Early Colonial Settlement and Landscape of Nevis and St Kitts: Studies in the Historical Archaeology of the Eastern Caribbean*, 4, *Colonial Landscapes of Nevis and St Kitts*, Oxford: Archaeopress.

Miller, G.L. 1980, 'Classification and Economic Scaling of 19th Century Ceramics', *Hist. Archaeol.* 14: 1–40.

Miller, G.L. 1991, 'A Revised Set of CC Index Values for Classification and Economic Scaling of English Ceramics from 1787 to 1880', *Hist. Archaeol.* 25:1, 1–25.

Morris, E.L. 2001a, 'Sugar-refining Ceramics', in Morris *et al.* 2001, 87–90.

Morris, E.L. 2001b, 'Theme Five: Plain Language Resources and Accessibility to Nevis Heritage', in Morris *et al.* 2001, 102–3.

Morris, E.L. *et al.* 2001, *The Nevis Heritage Project Interim Report 2001*, Southampton: The Nevis Heritage Project, University of Southampton.

Newland, C., Small, D. & Witkin, A. 2006, *Pinney's Estate, St Thomas Lowland, Nevis. Archaeological Evaluation*, Bristol: University of Bristol, Department of Archaeology and Anthropology.

Pearce, J. 2000, 'A Late 18th-Century Inn Clearance Assemblage from Uxbridge, Middlesex', *Post-Med. Archaeol.* 34, 144–86.

Philpott, R.A., Leech, R.H. & Morris, E.L. forthcoming, *Searching for the 17th Century in Nevis*, Oxford: Archaeopress Publishing Ltd.

Rookley, P. 1998, 'A Report on the Excavations at Codrington Fort during the 1997 and 1998 'Digs'', unpubl. report in author's possession.

Simpson, J., Simpson J., Smith, B. & Beardmore, B. 2015, *H. & R. Daniel Earthenwares*, Christchurch: Daniel Ceramic Circle.

11

A Caribbean Context for the World-System: A Case Study in 17th- and 18th-Century Economic and Social Interdependency

MARCO MENIKETTI

SUMMARY: Agro-industrialism in the Caribbean was a driving force in the Atlantic economy during the 17th and 18th centuries. As an institution, the sugar colonies had a far-reaching impact on the emerging world-system out of proportion to their size. Colonial landscapes from this period can be construed as landscapes of capitalism and reveal the intricate web of influences peripheral regions wielded over social and political life in the core state. Archaeological evidence from Nevis is presented to illustrate how tropical slave-based agro-industrialism propelled the evolution of capitalism. Technological and economic interdependency will be examined from an anthropological perspective fusing landscapes with material culture.

INTRODUCTION

> ... thus the land and labour [*sic*] of the country being devoted to cultivation of the sugar cane, the corn and provisions they raise are merely accidental... to the sugar cane everything is sacrificed as a trifle to the major object.[1]

Broad historical patterns are often most visible, and frequently most active, in peripheries of social systems,[2] which suggests that investigating cases of development in peripheries can lead to a more nuanced understanding of the forces structuring social systems. Caribbean frontiers are historic peripheries of the European economic and political sphere yet served as crucibles for processes stimulating the evolution of European expansion and political/economic domination in the New World. From *c.* 1600 through the mid 1800s the Caribbean was a microcosm of the socio-political transformations gripping competing imperial powers and the emerging global market. The islands were the scenes of capitalist and agro-industrial experimentation – critical arenas wherein the social relations of the modern world were forged. At the center of this tumultuous and momentous historical development was the colony of Nevis.

Archaeological research on this small yet surprisingly influential colony casts light on social dynamics in the periphery during the period of inchoate capitalism and nascent globalization. The internalization of capitalist consumer ideology can also be interpreted from archaeological remains of material culture, architecture, and use of space. The processes of socio-economic development playing out on Nevis, and subsequent landscape evolution, did so, not merely against the backdrop of capitalism's ascendancy but *integrated* and in *resonance* with its rise to dominance, perhaps contributing fundamentally to its ascendance. In peripheral outposts the transition from feudal to capitalist relations are revealed through methodological approaches grounded in landscape studies which define how colonists both, in Ortner's words, 'manipulate and are manipulated by their culture … [as they acquire] a new social repertoire'.[3] This articulation of culture is especially acute as a capitalist paradigm restructured socio-economic behaviors. It is our conjecture that these synergistic processes are found at the nexus of landscape and material culture and are explored here.

CAPITALISM AND WORLD SYSTEM

Capitalism as applied throughout this study represents a unique constellation of economic and social dependency relations; hierarchical social ordering focused on labor, and a suite of specialized institutions and behaviors reifying the social framework – the relations of production – wherein the labor of many creates wealth for the few. Capitalism did not arise simply as a means of benefiting society writ large, but as a mechanism for labor management and production control – maintaining the elite in their established positions – and creating economic stability through economic networks. Interdependencies arose as an unanticipated by-product. The archaeological record suggests that consumption itself became ideologically structured. As capitalism expanded, the cost and complexity of extricating oneself from these networked dependencies grew more expensive than that of remaining entangled.[4]

Peripheries are regions embedded in a system of commodity production and economic relations for the benefit of the metropole, and in colonial context, are dependent on the core for economic maintenance and defense – absorbing raw materials and manufactured wares, while generating specific commodities for external markets. In this model, peripheries rarely are direct beneficiaries of their own production. Sugar colonies are a prime example, where producers often were forbidden to refine and sell their product outside of restricted markets. Although integrating values and systems of the metropolis, societies in the periphery did not fully mirror the Core State. Autochthonous social development can be discerned in the conflicts that arose between peripheral colonies and the mother country as capitalism was differentially assimilated, especially apparent when we contrast Dutch, French, and British systems. Peripheries were not powerless to assert varying degrees of self-governance or to develop internally. Although functioning at the largesse of the Core State, the economic condition of a peripheral node in the world system impacted industry and commerce at the core. This is best seen in the correlation between the development of manufacturing centers, the phenomenal growth of slaving as an industry, and the rise of the shipping industry in England in response to increased trade value in sugar. The economic base of such cities as Bristol, for instance, derived from support of shipping both for sugar and slaves, but also in manufacturing related to colonial trade. Significant ancillary industries evolved to support Atlantic commerce, forming a network of relations, any one of which could be compromised by perturbations of any other. If this sounds familiar it is because our modern world is similarly structured.

The origins of capitalism's root causes, and especially its florescence in the period straddling mercantilism and industrial capitalism, sustain heated debate in the literature. Disagreement exists even as to whether we can refer to *merchant capitalism* as a distinct phase. The highly charged political nature of the arguments and the elusive character of capitalism explain to some degree why consensus among scholars should not be anticipated any time soon.

Intriguingly, scholars as diverse in perspective as Abu-Lughod, Braudel, Wallerstein, and Wolf suggest that even without an overarching political organization, capitalism developed beyond the point of economics to become a complex *social system* touching all aspects of *cultural life*.[5] If we accept the premise that capitalism arose through internal systemic developments, undirected by any governing body, we must still wonder how it came to be the dominant organizing system. What advantages were conferred and on whom? And how, as *a system*, it influenced the historical ecology and settlement dynamics of the Caribbean locally and regionally. Did the observable resulting settlement patterns stem from the systemic requirements of capitalist dynamics or were colonialists active change-agents; consciously structuring settlement – willing architects of an emergent capitalist cultural schema and its validating ideology?

Wallerstein found the roots of capitalism in a 'crisis of feudalism' transpiring in the 14th century. The need for markets was met by expansion and passage through stages of merchant capitalism, currency markets, and the evolution of peripheral regions exploited for the benefit of the Core State.[6] Critics stress that Wallerstein fails to establish a mechanism for the transition from feudalism to capitalism in his world system model, especially failing to offer an adequate explication of the dynamics of capitalism. His focus is mainly on market processes, commercial growth, and increased trade worldwide, sidestepping the Marxian insight, as Skcopol remarked, of 'paying attention to institutionalized relationships of producing and surplus-appropriating classes ...'.[7] In Wolf's view, Wallerstein collapsed capitalist world markets with capitalist modes of production. We must agree with Wolf's analysis, that capitalism was not simply a new kind of feudalism, but a 'qualitatively new phenomenon'.[8] Wolf rejects the notion of merchant capitalism, relegating such activities to simple profit driven mercantilism having a long history, preferring to cast capitalism fully in terms of modes of production, with labor transformation central to the concept. From this standpoint capitalism does not emerge until the late 18th century.[9] This is too late in my view. The archaeological record demonstrates incorporation of capitalist consumerism at least a century earlier at both ends of the production/consumer dyad. Wolf's more traditional outlook has capitalism coterminous with industrial revolution. But what made the revolution possible?

Managerial skills, which evolved in the sugar industry, may have propelled capitalism as an institution. Expansion of trade alone is insufficient to cause socio-economic metamorphoses. The ancient world engaged in trade over vast distances without arriving at capitalism as an economic base. A trading system at a global level was instrumental for incipient capitalist development. Capitalism arises out of industrial colonialism and the system of support structures that evolved in response to development in these specialized peripheral sectors. At least two economic innovations were critical in sustaining capitalism's inadvertent rise. First, new forms of credit were made available to allow initiation. Secondly, governmental encouragement through controlled markets. The resonance between global trade and new credit stimulated wider prosperity for the emergent plantocracy. Perhaps an important reality of the transition from feudalism to capitalism was that those with privileged positions in the upper echelon of the social hierarchy remained there. In the frontier social asymmetry persisted, and was even fostered. The transformation of labor into a commodity itself and the creation of a managerial class – outcomes of the sugar enterprises in the Caribbean – are among the *socio-morphs* that triggered change. New technologies also fueled change. An impetus for this evolution can be derived from the dynamics of colonialism in the frontier by conceiving of it as an *extractive periphery* – a derivative of Steffan's cosmopolitan frontier concept.[10] We can draw parallels between the island sugar industry and remote mining operations, each with an imported labor force, exported profits, and limited investment by authorities on infrastructure not directly benefiting the industry.

The case of Nevis informs on regional trends (non-Iberian) in the development of capitalism and inclusion of the Caribbean in a world-system in several interdependent ways. Colonies of the Lesser Antilles were a vital part of an interlocked system. World markets and developments on the far side of the planet influenced plantation success, ultimately affecting every colonist including slaves. Successes in sugar production by the East India Company profoundly affected industry in the Caribbean through manipulation of pricing in London markets. Trade arrangements between core states led to the irony of foreign sugar selling for less in London than that from British colonies. Revolutions by the continental colonies (with whom many Caribbean colonies sympathized), revolution in France and in Saint Domingue (the crown jewel of French sugar manufacturing), all had repercussions of social and political scope. Disruption in production influenced developments in the mother countries and the loss of a single sugar island could have damaging effects on national economies. The Caribbean periphery served both as economic zone and functioned as proxy site for warfare. Thus it is apparent the region has long been a surrogate political arena for the traditional powers of western and northern Europe. Far from being isolated, the Caribbean was incorporated into the tentative world economy at an early stage of development, and remained so into the 20th century, albeit with less economic significance.

A second regional trend for which the evidence is compelling is that of environmental degradation. Sauer was among first to recognize environment as a key component of Caribbean settlement.[11] Pulsipher's dissertation research on Montserrat, qualitatively combining landscape and ecology, foreshadowed environmental interest in the region and a trend in landscape studies.[12] Evidence of ecological transfiguration from Nevis is staggering. As one of the smallest islands in the Lesser Antilles, its problems are greatly magnified. But from this case we can recognize the pattern and the legacy of environmental neglect. Tourist brochures aside, the Caribbean is no longer an 'Eden'.

ARCHAEOLOGY, LANDSCAPE AND MATERIAL CULTURE EVIDENCE

One means of bridging the various levels of social complexity found in colonial contexts is by interpreting the modification of the natural environment resulting from colonial enterprise using a material culture framework. Spatial patterning of built landscapes are by-products of cultural behaviors. Landscapes are active and space 'in context is an artefact'.[13] Environmental transformation can be accessed and interpreted through procedures grounded in ecology, geography, anthropology, and social history.[14] Settlement and space are tightly woven together in human culture and highly revealing of social relations as many scholars have forcefully demonstrated.[15] Because empirical properties of artefacts or features and their arrangement in the archaeological record 'exhibit attributes which can inform on different phases of the artefact's life',[16] it follows that settlements will contain traces of their developmental phases accessible at different scales.

Core beliefs of colonists are fundamental in settlement systems – and represent functional relationships between sites and culture.[17] As capitalism is a social system, strong links can be inferred between the ideological underpinnings of capitalism and the physical world. The use of space – its division and partitioning between public and private, productive and non-productive, valued and marginalized – are expressions of these ideological foundations that manifest in the observable landscape. In the case of Nevis, landscape surveys reveal that roads linked plantations, centers of shipping, and estates to one another in a spidery latticework across the island (Fig. 11.1). Towns might almost be viewed as incidental. Sugar works dominated the landscape as terraces and mills defined visual and physical space, stone walls demarcated property – further dividing it between work and domicile, free and unfree – as estate houses signified authority. Terraces most especially structured space, both ordering nature and establishing labor zones. Churches were established at key crossroads appropriating intersections of private and public mobility for spiritual space. Unproductive land or marginalized sectors along ghuts on estates often was cast over to slave quarters. Because settlement was factory-focused rather than community based, no more than three towns on Nevis ever grew to significance.

In the early years of the colony European and slave populations were nearly equivalent in numbers. By the mid 18th century, however, African and creole slaves outnumbered Europeans 8:1. This demographic was brought about by increased dependence on slave-based production on ever expanding estates, consolidated and controlled by ever fewer white planter families. Labor mobility across the landscape can be interpreted as manifesting an ideology of production, through spatial management adjusted to the requirements of agro-industry. As Eric Williams boldly illustrated, slavery and capitalism are not incompatible, and although viewed as immoral, even by some of its practitioners, slavery was considered an acceptable machinery of industry in the periphery.[18] We might view it in terms of operating as the last vestige of a disintegrating feudal system, allowing maintenance of familiar hierarchical relations – slaves as surrogate peasantry, albeit with far less freedom and rights.

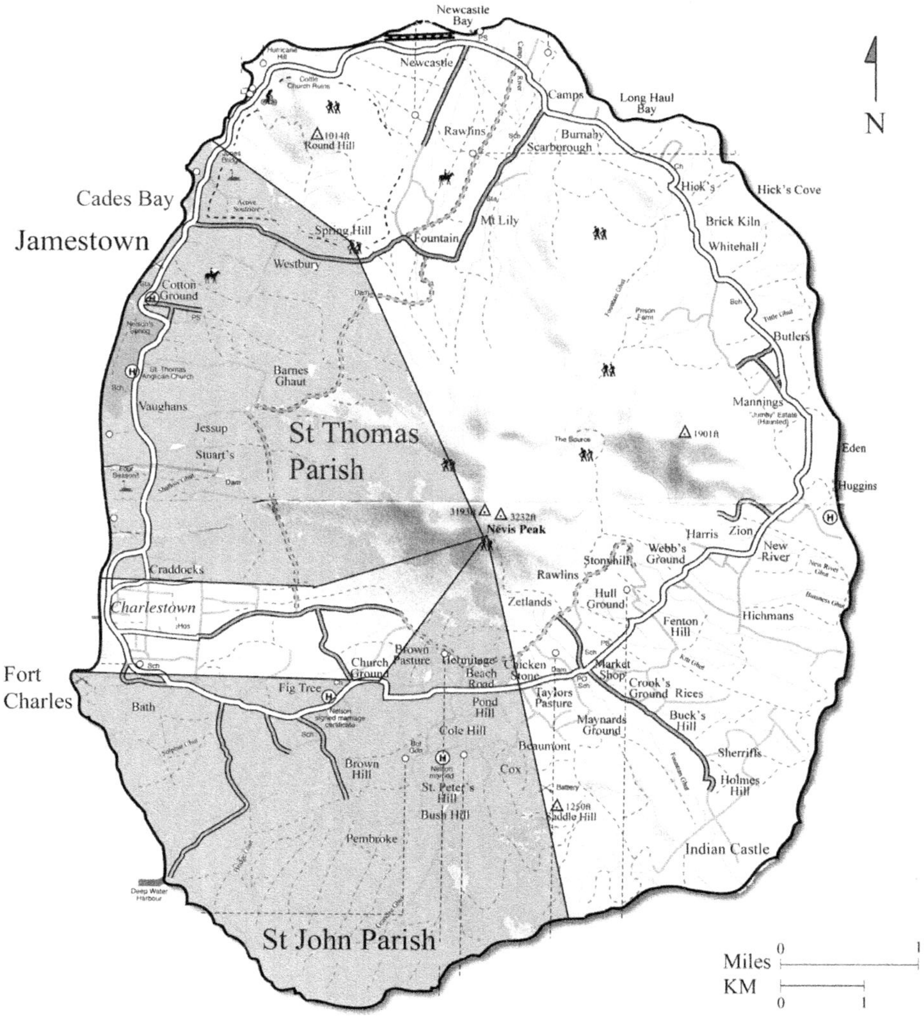

Fig. 11.1. Map of Nevis. The parishes surveyed for this study are shown shaded in gray.

MATERIAL CULTURE

While landscape may suggest social praxis, the study of material culture offers another avenue for interpreting ideology. Artefacts are symbolic expressions, and as tangible evidence of relations between core and periphery, are relevant to the world system discourse. Ceramics, for instance, can be analyzed at various scales to inform on trade networks, consumer patterns, or conceptions of social order and internal social relations that normalize behavior. Artefacts are the interface between the cognitive and physical worlds wherein objects are the symbolic carriers of values and meanings known to the contemporary user. These material correlates of social interactions bear contextual meanings, externally inscribed by culture praxis. As the 18th century progressed, new objects and commodities came into use along with new social rules. Ceramics were just one aspect of colonial incorporation into, and adoption of, the capitalist mercantilism stemming from the Atlantic economy in which peripheries aggressively participated. 'Knowing how to act was reinforced by knowing what to buy and use'.[19] The archaeological landscape on Nevis reveals immediate integration of new technology in sugar production during the 17th century, then stasis for the century that followed, with only gradual acceptance of new technologies after emancipation. As to which aspects of settlement or segments of society most reflect the integration of capitalism and adaptation to social change, the evidence at hand only reflects the attitudes of Europeans. Inadequate archaeological evidence is available for this study to address this intriguing issue among other social groups on Nevis prior to emancipation. The archaeological evidence points to reliance on externally generated consumerism and standards, internalization of culture-reinforcing behaviors associated with socially defining material culture. Artifacts clearly indicate Nevis, although a peripheral economic zone, was not a backwater. Nevisians were not the 'country cousins' of consumerism that Smart-Martin labels the frontier colonists of Virginia.[20] The constancy of shipping insured that the Caribbean colonies were unlike other frontier regions suffering more social isolation. Material culture expressions at the core found their way into Nevisian communities with minimal lag time. A simple yet revealing example can be found in tea consumption. That the preponderance of material goods are of English manufacture is a given, but the selection of specific items and the presence of exotics signifies separate agency for archaeologists to puzzle over. The very act served not only patriotic and nationalist interests, but was supported by a substantial material culture and suite of associated behaviors. Specialized industries supported the manufacture of the material component of tea, while other industries were agents in its acquisition and distribution. Patterns of behaviors surrounded consumption, which served to distinguish social sectors. Indeed, destruction of tea in the colonies could be viewed as a political act against the state through its implied subversion of established social order. At its most basic, ceramics may suggest household wealth and social activities, but can also provide useful indicators of status. But meaningful discourse concerning ideological elements of the emerging world system may also be prized from assemblages. A case in point is provided by the site of a small and relatively humble estate residence, associated with a sugar factory on a ridge below Saddle Hill, St John Parish (Fig. 11.2).

Fig. 11.2. Excavators working on the interior space of Ridge House. See Fig. 11.4 for plan details.

Based on technological, architectural, and artefactual data the industrial component of the site appears to have been operational between the late 17th until the early 19th century.[21] Archaeological evidence suggests both technological and functional modifications over two centuries. Architectural reconfigurations point to technological upgrading from Spanish train to Jamaica train and later still (possibly in the late 1800s) to a possible cotton processing facility (Fig. 11.3). The associated residential structure built on a promontory, had an adjacent garden or patio enclosed by a stacked stone wall (Fig. 11.4). A detached masonry structure down-slope some fifteen feet away was possibly a kitchen, but more analysis is needed to confirm this conjecture. The viewshed from the garden side takes in a panorama that includes Mt. Nevis to the east and St Kitts to the north-west. From the south side, Montserratt can be viewed

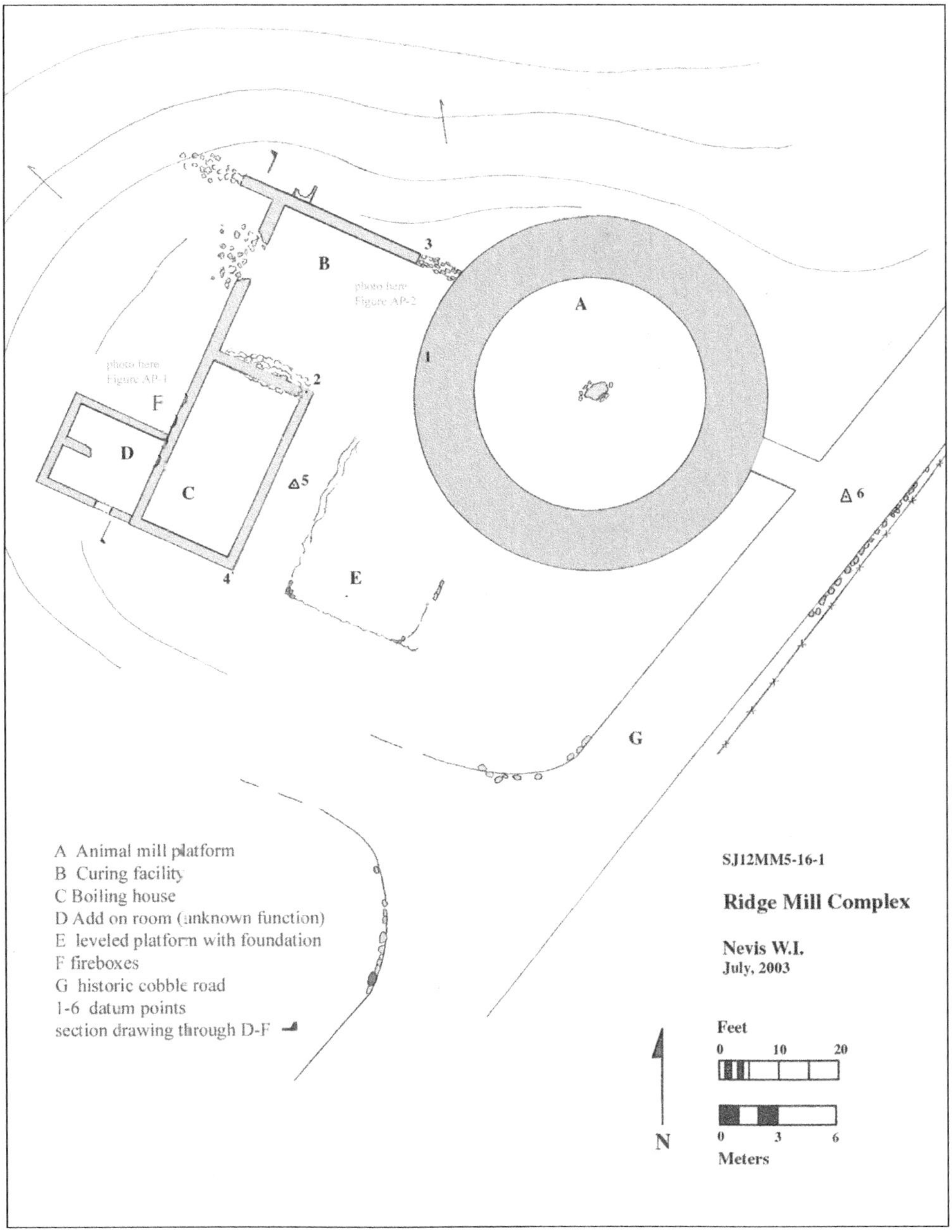

Fig. 11.3. Site plan of the mill-complex on the ridge near Saddle Hill. The room additions on the exterior western wall were built to cover or enclose fireboxes, clearly indicating changing industrial functions of the complex. These walls abut the previous structure. The interior floor of the former boiling room was modified historically by removing boiling cauldrons and the inserting a rectangular masonry trough that further blocked off firebox channels.

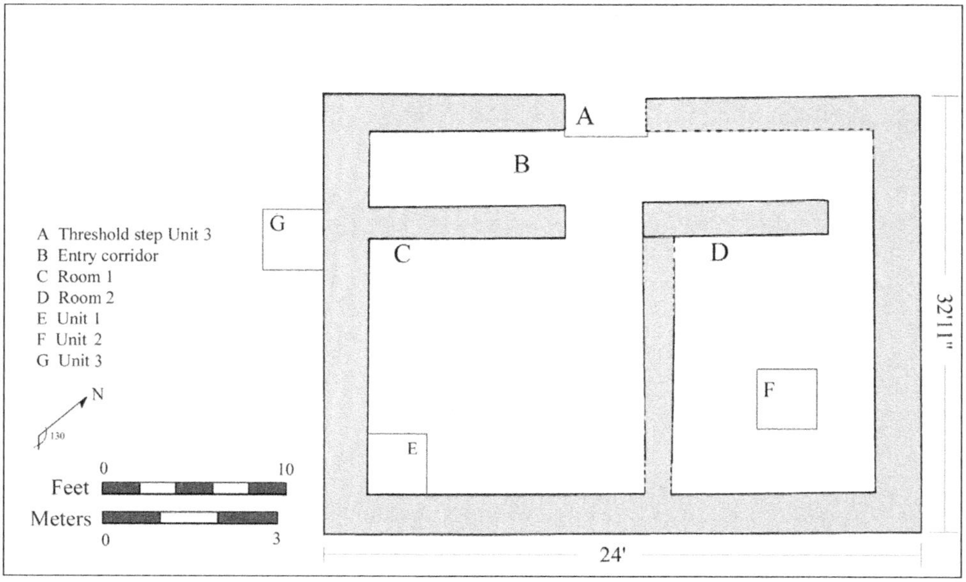

Fig. 11.4. Site plan of the residential structure on the ridge associated with the mill-complex.

on a clear day. The building was ideally situated for monitoring the approach of sail. Surveillance of the terraced slopes below would have been facilitated from this post as well, especially from a second story balcony.

The foundations of dressed stone were 24in thick with three ground floor rooms evident. Remnants of slate in the steps at the garden-side entry speak of simple elegance (Fig. 11.5). The building was not randomly placed on a flat terrace, but carefully positioned. Extensive ground preparation and fill behind robust retaining walls that

Fig. 11.5. Photograph of the north side threshold of the residential structure. Fragments of slate from the steps that escaped salvage remain in the mortar, slotted into cut stone. (Designated A in Fig. 11.4).

supported the ground floor were found during excavations, indicating a clear intent to modify, raise, and level the terrain to accommodate the house without regard to cardinal axis points or natural slope. The building was positioned with respect to the viewshed. At the south-west corner this wall stood nearly four feet. Although not a great house by any means, it was nonetheless substantial, measuring 33ft by 24ft.

Artefacts at the site were nearly all domestic in character. Close interval transects of 1m were used to achieve a total collection of surface artefacts. Although the area is heavily eroded, more than 1,700 artefacts were collected. The assemblage consisted chiefly of clay pipe stems and bowls, assorted glass (especially beverage bottles), ceramics, a single gun flint, and assorted corroded iron objects including nails. Ceramic materials found in excavation were of the same character, but were not included in the analysis presented below and comprise a separate assemblage. Ceramics were classified first by ware type, then re-categorized by use-arena, (i.e. tableware, kitchenware, storage, fine dining, day-use). These distinctions are hypothesized based on material, style, and design. The first level of analysis provided information suitable for assessing site chronology. The second level allowed for interpretation of household status, function, and consumption patterns. Material from an historic builder's trench at the base of the western exterior wall aided in corroborating site chronology. Carrying analysis one step further, ideological and cognitive frameworks of the residents emerge as expressed by the assemblage.

The ceramic assemblage included sherds of salt glazed stoneware, possibly from mugs and tankards judging by body dimensions and curvature, as well as brown and white stoneware rims and bases, and generic stonewares with brownish mottling – widely used as storage vessels. Rhenish gray stoneware body sherds and Rhenish tradition wares – deeply incised and further decorated with blue paint from both mug and jug forms, each popular from the late 17th and early 18th centuries, were recovered.[22] Plate rims and body sherds included the highly distinctive basket pattern, along with feather-edged, creamware styles (including Queen's ware). Shell-edge pearlware of varying qualities and Willow pattern plate rims in a bright blue were recorded. These patterns were produced in great quantities in English and North American pottery factories for distribution and sale to a rising middle class, eager to display hallmarks of their social attainment.[23] Fragments of lead glazed slipware were recovered in small numbers, mostly in yellow and brown slip decoration representing at least two known styles: agate and marble wares. Delft, or tin-glazed earthenware was noted but vessel forms were not identifiable from the fragments. Its popularity reached a zenith between 1720 and 1740 and was largely supplanted by finer 'soft paste' ceramics that imitated porcelain. New ware-types emerged on the market as consumer taste for coffee and tea dramatically increased after 1740. Several fragments of low-fire redware fragments from sugar cones were also scattered between the house and the mill-complex. At first thought to be roofing tiles, their actual function was confirmed by independent consultation.

Tabulation of exact numbers of ware forms from the sample along with frequency analysis of types yielded interesting percentages. The bulk, 68%, can be qualified as day ware, and 13% storage or utilitarian vessels, but 18% were fine tablewares comprised mainly of tea sets and accoutrement. Glass artefacts included bottles but also crystal, stemware, and decanters (Fig. 11.6). At this smallish residence, the finer material goods of the colonial Atlantic market were in use and on display.

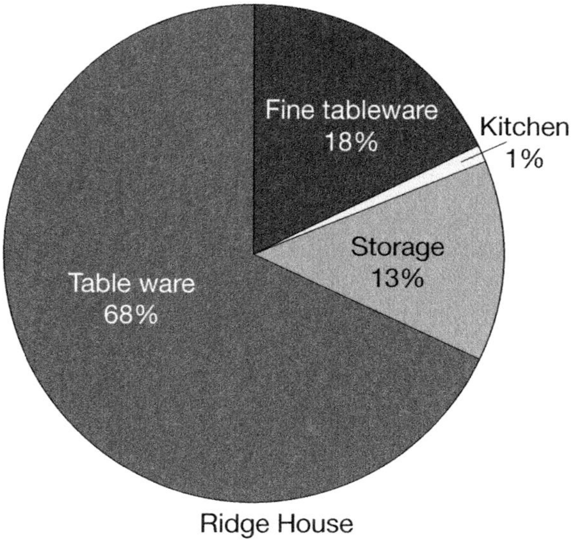

Fig. 11.6. Pie chart illustrating the percentages of various ceramic ware types according to *use-arena* and qualities at The Ridge residential structure.

Nevis was an outpost, not an entrepôt. We do not find the full range of ceramics available in England or in the Dutch freeports, yet significant variety is nonetheless evident. It is not clear whether local merchants supplied a representative sample or if planters carefully selected and imported their wares through agents, nor can we yet surmise how much lag time accrued between style introduction and adoption. Yet incorporation by members of the affluent classes of not only the latest styles but the most recent forms set standards by which attainment and position could be signified within social groups and across social divides. But the less affluent were incorporating new wares as well – evident from surveys of other house platforms. Potters in distant centers manufactured tablewares for special purposes uncommon in the centuries prior to colonization. They were both meeting a demand and creating a desire. The rising middle class in the 18th century – a product of the successful exploitation of colonial development – acquired the new and affordable markers of status as best they could, not so much displacing earlier measures of status, as adding to the litany. Matching sets became a popular innovation setting in motion a proto-modern consumerism. Because new manufacturing techniques made it possible for wares to be accessible to wider classes of consumer, traditional social distinctions based on tablewares blurred, leading to acquisition of an increasing range of wares and new table behaviors. As being a 'colonial' could hurt one's social attainment in the mother country, members of the plantocracy sought to establish themselves in the social hierarchy through established means. The adaptations that were occurring within the socialized context transformed society, but kept them connected to the evolving capitalist economy of the emerging world system.[24] Variables apparently influencing personal choice included cost, novelty, rarity, differential access, utility, but also governing social values. Use and display are simultaneous yet separate functions. Any vessel will serve for consuming a beverage, any trencher is adequate for a meal. Yet as one internalizes elements of behavior in association with specific material culture, the objects act as extensions or expressions of implied values.[25] The sheer volume and variety of tea service items from the assemblage at the Saddle Hill site suggest both adoption of the tea-complex at a material level, but also at the symbolic. Participation in the tea-complex of display and consumption directly links the consumer household in the colonial periphery to the behaviors and values of the core culture to which they aspire. It also connected the household to a world system that includes potters in England, tea plantations in the orient, shipbuilders in North America, bankers in Antwerp, sugar refiners in Europe, and a network of other commercial and social relationships.

CONCLUSION

Colonial societies are 'not autonomous social realities; they are subject to the demands and interests of the metropolis'.[26] Even those within colonial societies appearing to have complete power, namely the plantocracy, were dependent in myriad ways – economically, militarily, and above all psychologically on the mother country. Such dependency relations were exacerbated in an island context. Dependency in the psycho-social realm had far reaching influence on the decisions made by planters and colonists. Status insecurities within the plantocracy may have helped propel consumption of status trappings.

The Caribbean was not only the leading edge of European cultural expansion, but the capitalist frontier. The transition from feudal to a capitalist socio-economic system was ignited by the relations arising from the tensions of managing production and labor in peripheral colonies, and the interdependency that unintentionally crystallized between distant productive nodes. Whether driven by mercantile or capitalist mentality, a significant percentage of Europeans considered Caribbean ventures temporary, even among those who did not become wealthy and by circumstance lived out their lives on colonial islands. To paraphrase Lowenthal, people came to Nevis to make a living, not to make a life.[27] In the case of Nevis, the difficulties of finding a suitable work force and the degree of enticements necessary to attract skilled labor are revealed by historical documents. Expansion followed the demand in sugar, and profits encouraged development. Slavery tethered the periphery to the global trade system and integrated cities in the core into Atlantic commerce, much the way the need for oil links systems in the modern world system. Landscape evolved around systemic needs of production and labor management.

The sea between peripheries and core states acted not as a barrier, separating economic zones, but as a highway, fusing economies. Ships arrived at Nevis with timber from North America; corn and rice from the Carolinas; fish from the outer banks of Nova Scotia; beef from Ireland; manufactured goods from European cities, and many engaged in all manner of illicit trade. All was paid for in sugar and credit. The landscapes of capitalism were shaped by industrial needs, certainly, but also by social requirements. Estates evolved as semi-autonomous production nodes, constructed to reflect stability and strength – with rank distinctions appearing in the architecture – hallmarks of hierarchical social structuring. Several basic elements of material culture in the archaeological record can be interpreted as linking the development of Nevis to the wider Atlantic economic market and the emergent world system of the quasi-capitalist 17th and 18th centuries. Material culture from a middling planter's household on Nevis described here is representative of colonial wares found throughout the British sphere. We do not know how often these objects were on display for guests. But even if only for personal use, they nevertheless indicate a desire to obtain and display the hallmarks of status and attainment valued in the mother country – linking distant nodes across the Atlantic world.

The Caribbean during the 17th and 18th centuries was developed as a peripheral economic zone to serve the interests of traditional European powers. The timing of Caribbean colonial development coincided with nascent economic globalization and geopolitical hegemony by Europe. National interests were served but the unanticipated result was the genesis of new institutions and socio-economic systems. Over time these systems became embedded in the social and industrial fabric of the colonizing nations.

The societies that evolved among the island colonies were different in character from the mother countries even as they struggled to identify as closely as possible with society at the core. The landscapes that evolved on the island mirror the changing demands of agro-industrial outposts as the social and economic systems out of which they were born were transformed. Founded under feudalism, the island societies gradually incorporated ideological constructs of capitalism, which affected social and labor relations. Capitalism gained strength even as the system of slavery served to retain components of waning feudal hierarchy. The nexus of nascent globalization, and quasi-capitalist economics, allowed mercantile adventurism to combine with novel opportunities for investment, creating a new model for settlement and colonization founded on industrial entrepreneurial enterprise. One result was the evolution from quasi- to proto-capitalist relations, the harbinger of a modern world system.

NOTES

1 Richard Glover, 1775, a West India planter speaking before Parliament on the need for continued imports of foodstuffs from continental colonies.
2 Green & Perlman 1985, 9.
3 Ortner 1990.
4 Champion 1989.
5 Abu-Lughod 1989; Braudel 1972; Wallerstein 1974, 1980; Wolf 1982; Johnson 1999.
6 Wallerstein 1980.
7 Skcopol 1977, 1079.
8 Wolf 1982, 85.
9 Wolf 1982, 298.
10 Steffan 1980.
11 Sauer 1966.
12 Pulsipher 1977.
13 Rubertone 1989.
14 Aston & Rowley 1974; Fox 1981; Mageraue 1995; Kealhoffer 1999; Butzer & Butzer 2000; Zedeño 2000.
15 Armstrong 1990; Delle 1998; Paynter 1986; Lukezic 1994; Lewis 1984, 1999.
16 Binford & Binford 1968.
17 Parsons 1972; Wandsnider 1988.
18 Williams 1944.
19 Smart Martin 1996, 76.
20 Smart Martin 1996.
21 Meniketti 2004.
22 Identified through Noël-Hume 1974, 1985; Mayes 1972; Hughes & Hughes 1968; Sempill 1944.
23 Barker 1999.
24 For insightful analysis of agency in adapting to new systems, see Smart Martin 1996, 71.
25 Meniketti 2004.
26 Bolland 1981, 593.
27 Lowenthal 1972, 33.

BIBLIOGRAPHY

Abu-Lughod, J. 1989, *Before European Hegemony. The World System A.D. 1250–1350*, New York: Oxford University Press.

Armstrong, D. 1990, *The Old Village and Great House*, Urbana: University of Illinois Press.

Aston, M. & Rowley, T. 1974, *Landscape Archaeology*, Newton Abbot, London, and Vancouver: David and Charles.

Barker, D. 1999, 'The Ceramic Revolution 1650–1850', in Egan & Michael (eds) 1999, 226–34.

Binford, L. & Binford, S. (eds) 1968, *New Perspectives in Archaeology*, Chicago: Aldine Pub. Co.

Bolland, N. 1981, 'Systems of Domination after Slavery: The Control of Land and Labor in the British West Indies after 1838', *Comparative Stud. Soc. Hist.* 23:4, 591–619.

Braudel, F. 1972, *The Mediterranean and Mediterranean World in the Age of Phillip II*, New York: Harper.

Butzer, K. & Butzer, E. 2000, 'Domestic Architecture in Early Colonial Mexico: Material Culture as (sub) Text', in Murphy & Johnson (eds) 2000, 17–37.

Champion, T. 1989, 'Introduction', in *Centre and Periphery: Comparative Studies in Archaeology*, ed. T.C. Champion, One World Archaeology 11, 1–21, London: Unwin Hyman.

De Cunzo, L.A. & Herman B. (eds), 1996, *Historical Archaeology and the Study of American Culture*, Winterthur, DE: Henry Francis du Pont Winterthur Museum & Knoxville: Distributed by University of Tennessee Press.

Delle, J. 1998, *An Archaeology of Social Space*, New York: Plenum.

Egan, G. & Michael, R. (eds) 1999, *Old and New Worlds*, Oxford: Oxbow.

Fox, J. 1981, 'The Late Postclassic Eastern Frontier of Mesoamerica: Cultural Innovation Along the Periphery', *Curr. Anthropol.* 22:4, 321–45.

Green, S. & Perlman, S. 1985, *The Archaeology of Frontiers and Boundaries*, New York: Academic Press.

Hughes, B. & Hughes, T. 1968, *English Ceramics*, London: Abbey Library.

Johnson, M. 1999, 'Historical, Archaeology, Capitalism', in Leone & Potter (eds), 219–32.

Kealhoffer, L. 1999, 'Adding Content to Structure: Integrating Environment and Landscape', in Egan & Michael (eds) 1999, 373–89.

Leone, M. & Potter, P. (eds), 1999, *Historical Archaeologies of Capitalism*, New York: Kluwer Press.

Lewis, K. 1984, *The American Frontier: An Archaeological Study of Settlement Pattern and Process*, New York: Academic Press.

Lewis, K. 1999, 'The Metropolis and the Backcountry: The Making of a Colonial Landscape on the South Carolina Frontier', *Hist. Archaeol.* 33:3, 3–13.

Linebaugh, D. & Robinson, G. (eds), 1994, *Spatial Patterning in Historical Archaeology: Selected Studies of Settlement*, Occasional Papers in Archaeology, 2, Williamsburg: William and Mary Center for Archaeological Research.

Lowenthal, D. 1972, *West Indian Societies*, New York: Oxford University Press.

Lukezic, C. 1994, 'Colonial Site Location in Tidewater, Virginia', in Linebaugh & Robinson (eds) 1994, 13–32.

Mageraue r, R. 1995, *Interpreting Environments: Tradition, Deconstruction, Hermeneutics*, Austin: University of Texas Press.

Mayes, P. 1972, *Port Royal, Jamaica Excavations 1969–70*, Kingston: Jamaica National Trust.

Meniketti, M. 2004, 'The Historical Archaeology of Nevis, West Indies: Capitalism, Environment, and the Evolution of the Caribbean Colonial Landscape, 1625–1833', Unpublished Doctoral Dissertation, Department of Anthropology, Michigan State University, East Lansing, Michigan.

Murphy, A. & Johnson, D. (eds) 2000, *Cultural Encounters with the Environment*, Lanham, MD: Rowman & Littlefield.
Noël-Hume, I. 1974, *Historical Archaeology*, New York: Alfred Knopf.
Noël-Hume, I. 1985, *A Guide to Artifacts of Colonial America*, New York: Alfred Knopf.
Ohnuki-Tierney, E. (ed.), 1990, *Culture Through Time*, Stanford: Stanford University Press.
Ortner, S. 1990, 'Patterns of History: Cultural Schemas in the Foundings of Sherpa Religious Institutions', in Ohnuki-Tierney (ed.) 1990, 57–93.
Parsons, J. 1972, 'Archaeological Settlement Patterns', *Annual Review of Anthropology* 1:1, 127–50.
Paynter, R. 1986, *Models of Spatial Inequality: Settlement Patterns in Historical Archaeology*, New York: Academic Press.
Pulsipher, L. 1977, 'The Cultural Landscape of Montserrat, West Indies, in the Seventeenth Century: Early Environmental Consequences of British Colonial Development', Unpublished Doctoral Dissertation, Department of Geography, Southern Illinois University.
Rubertone, P. 1989, 'Landscape as Artifact: Comments on the Archaeological Use of Landscape Treatment in Social, Economic, and Ideological Analysis', *Hist. Archaeol.* 23:1, 50–4.
Sauer, C. 1966, *The Early Spanish Main*, Berkeley: University of California Press.
Schiffer, M. (ed.) 2000, *Social Theory in Archaeology*, Salt Lake City: University of Utah Press.
Sempill, C. 1944, *English Pottery and Porcelain*, London: Collins.
Skcopol, T. 1977, 'Wallerstein's World Capitalist System: A Theoretical and Historical Critique', *American Journal of Sociology* 82:5, 1075–90.
Smart Martin, A. 1996, 'Frontier Boys and Country Cousins: The Context for Choice in Eighteenth-Century Consumerism', in De Cunzo & Herman (eds) 1996, 71–102.
Steffan, J. 1980, *Comparative Frontiers: A Proposal for Studying the American West*, Norman: University of Oklahoma Press.
Sullivan III, A. (ed.) 1988, *Surface Archaeology*, Albuquerque: University of New Mexico Press.
Wallerstein, I. 1974, *The Modern World System I*, New York: Academic Press.
Wallerstein, I. 1980, *The Modern World System II*, New York: Academic Press.
Wandsnider, L. 1988, 'Landscape Configuration. Lifespace, and Occupation History: Ethnoarchaeological Observation and Archaeological Applications', in Sullivan (ed.) 1988, 21–42.
Williams, E. 1944, *Capitalism and Slavery*, Chapel Hill: University of North Carolina Press.
Wolf, E. 1982, *Europe and the People without History*, Berkeley: University of California Press.
Zedeño, M.N. 2000, 'On What People Make of Places', in Schiffer (ed.) 2000, 97–111.

12

The Colonial Landscape of Mountravers and Adjacent Plantations

ROGER H. LEECH

SUMMARY: An archaeological field survey of just over 5,000 hectares, within the parish on Nevis of St Thomas Lowland, part of a British Academy funded project undertaken by the University of Southampton and Bristol City Museums, focused on the landscape of the plantations of Mountravers and those to the south and north. Using methodologies developed in Britain for rapid archaeological field survey and historical documentation, the houses, yards, works, and sometimes gardens of at least nine plantations were identified and mapped, together with connecting roads, bridges, and a fort. Identification of slave village sites was confined to Mountravers itself. Field survey results were linked to documentary sources in both Nevis and Britain. Recommendations are then made for future preservation and presentation linked to those recently made by the UNESCO funded International Committee for Monuments and Sites (ICOMOS) to the Nevis Island Administration for the protection and preservation of the diverse culture and heritage of the island.

INTRODUCTION

A survey of the landscape of Mountravers and the plantations to north and south was the second of the two sample surveys undertaken for the British Academy funded colonial landscape project (Preface), the first being the survey of St Mary Cayon and Christchurch Nicola Town on St Kitts, already discussed by Philpott (Chapter 7). This chapter is written so as to complement rather than repeat the earlier chapters.

As on St Kitts, the survey was set within the strategic objectives set out in the Preface (p. xx), specifically here:

1 To undertake a reconnaissance survey of the 17th- and 18th-century colonial landscape of the landscape of Mountravers and the plantations to north and south
2 To identify the extent to which plantation centres have been abandoned or have changed through time, from the 17th to the 20th centuries
3 To identify the archaeological and above ground remains of the slave villages for the plantations

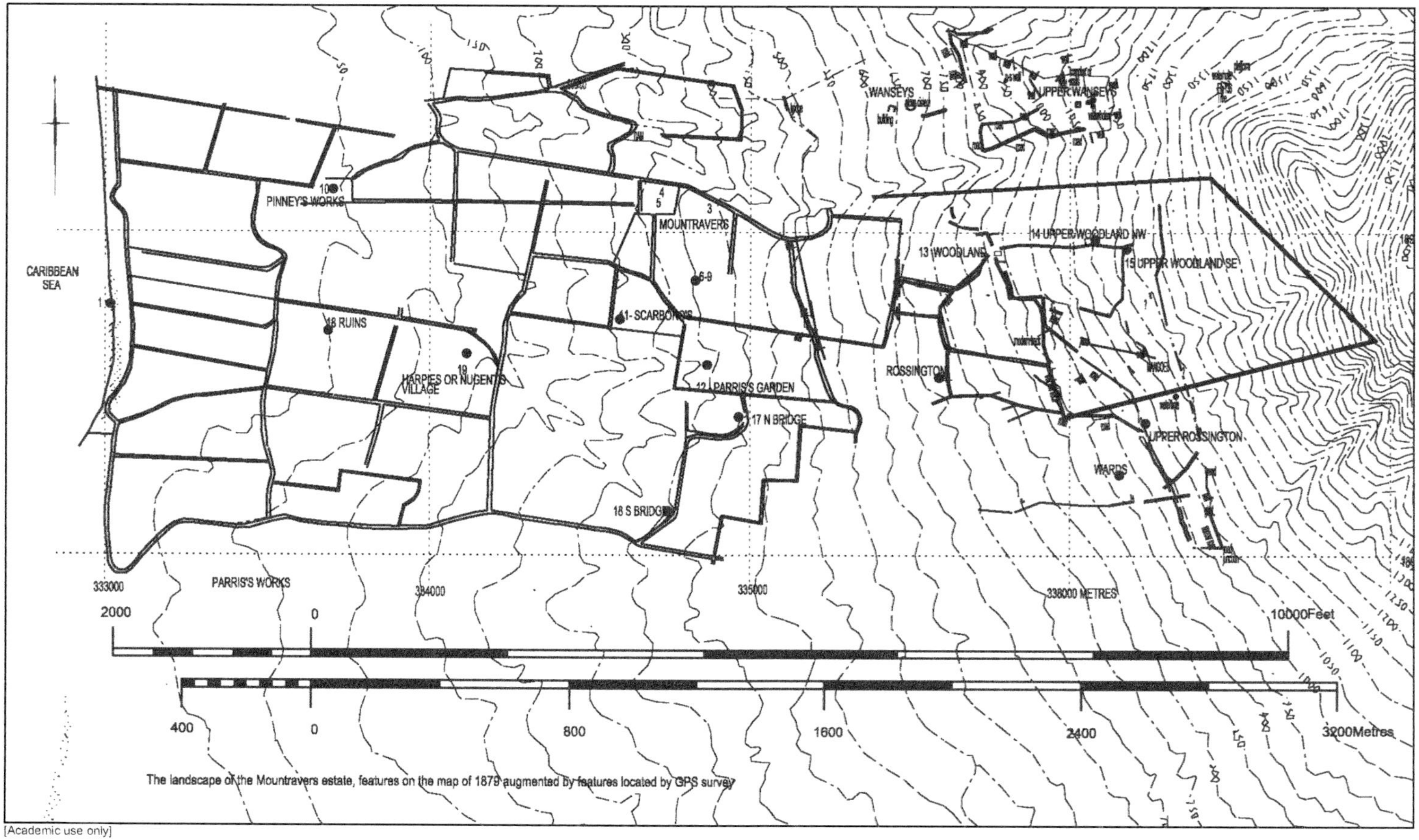

[Academic use only]

Fig. 12.1. Estate and field boundaries within and adjacent to the Mountravers Plantation, St Thomas's parish, Nevis, from documentary sources, air photographs and field survey.

The survey area (Fig. 12.1) was located within the recorded north and south boundaries of the plantations to the north and south of the Mountravers estate as defined in modern times. Chronologically, the survey concentrated on the periods up to the introduction of steam technology for sugar processing in the 19th century.

THE RECONNAISSANCE SURVEY

Preliminary research identified that the sequence of historic maps was much poorer than that for St Kitts.[1] Iles's map of 1871 (Fig. 12.2), the first to show the settlement of the island in detail, shows many plantations in what is now forest. Iles's map did not though show land divisions and boundaries, and overall the cartography is grossly inaccurate; Burdon's map of 1920 is similarly inaccurate being derived from Iles's map. The map of 1848 by Captain Barnett is much more accurate, but does not show land divisions. The earliest island-wide maps to show land divisions are of 1959 and of the

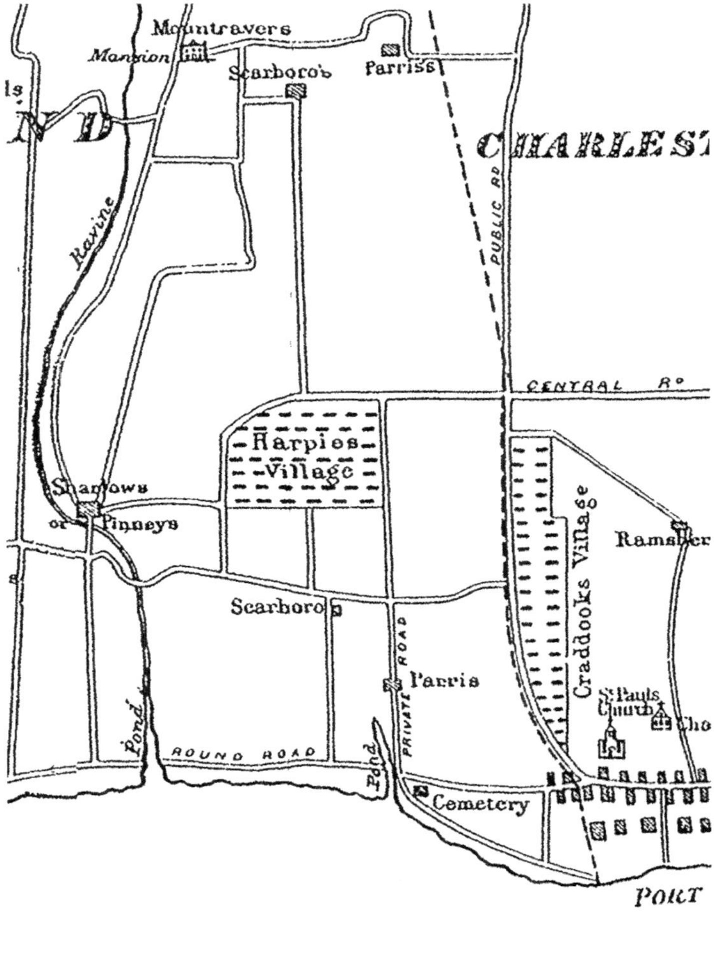

Fig. 12.2. Iles's map of 1871, the first to show the settlement of the island in detail, shows many plantations in what is now forest.

1970s, by the Directorate of Overseas Surveys (DoS). By this date forest and scrub covered much of the former plantation landscape.

However far more estate maps were identified for Nevis, though far fewer than for Jamaica where nearly 1,000 estate plans survive.[2] A further source for Nevis was the aerial photographic survey undertaken for or supplied to the DoS, held then at the Ordnance Survey in Southampton, but since relocated to the National Collection of Air Photographs (NCAP) curated by Historic Scotland in Edinburgh.

An initial assessment of the maps, particularly those of Iles and the DoS, and of the air photography, enabled the sites of the plantations named on the maps to be located on the ground. A reconnaissance visit was made to confirm the location of each site and assess the extent and survival of earthworks or structures, while intervening areas were systematically fieldwalked. Field notes and an initial digital photographic record were followed by rapid mapping using handheld Global Positioning System (GPS) technology to collect the positions of large-scale earthwork features as point data. Several of the best-preserved plantation centres were then recorded in more detail, typically topographical survey of the site using either a total station theodolite or baseline survey,[3] detailed descriptions, measured survey of selected buildings following the RCHME and later English Heritage procedures for building recording,[4] and digital photography. Some sites, where remains were either slight, poorly preserved, or inaccessible, were recorded by photography and field notes only.

As on St Kitts, the map evidence and field observations were supplemented by historical records, including accounts of the sugar cultivation and processing, travellers' or former residents' accounts, and official documents. In contrast to St Kitts, the family and business papers for the key area being studied survived in modern archives. The archives for the plantation of Mountravers are within the Pinney Papers forming part of the Special Collections of the University of Bristol, as studied by Richard Pares for his *A West-India Fortune* in 1950,[5] and more recently by D. Small and C. Eickelmann in their studies of plantation slavery on Nevis.[6] If located, the estate papers from other families settled on Nevis would further complement the archaeological survey and create a richer understanding of the social and economic context and development of the plantations. For Nevis a much more systematic search was made for relevant documentary evidence in the Common Records, held in the Court House in Charlestown, notably enrolled title deeds, mortgages, and analogous records. These records can now be linked to the University College London (UCL) Legacies of British Slave-ownership database, which usefully identifies the owners and acreage of named plantations in *c.* 1833.[7]

For Nevis it was thus possible to construct individual property histories for each plantation, modelled on the methodology developed for the author's studies of property holdings in medieval and early modern Bristol.[8]

NEVIS DURING THE COLONIAL PERIOD

The first European settlers to arrive in Nevis in 1628 were English, led by Anthony Hilton, a ship's captain and merchant from Durham with 'a considerable companie' from the newly settled neighbouring island of St Kitts.[9] As on St Kitts, early crops included tobacco, cotton, and indigo produced by the labour of indentured servants, many 'spirited' (in effect kidnapped) from the port of Bristol. Sugar was introduced in the 1640s and, as elsewhere in the Caribbean, this shift to sugar production increasingly depended on the labour of enslaved Africans. As on other islands, sugar production ultimately became central to the economy and culture of the island.

There is no record of whether they were just men or couples or families, only the likelihood that John Bourne, Mr Toby the minister to the parish of Jesus, John Young, Captain John Huddlestone, Thomas Newman, and Jenkyn Lloyd, all mentioned in the second will of John Bourne, were amongst them.[10] Within a year the new colonists on both Nevis and St Kitts suffered an attack from the Spanish in 1629, who finding only token resistance, quickly overcame the English defences, burning the newly built houses, destroying crops, and driving off many of the settlers.[11] The remaining settlers at St Kitts, who had fled to the interior rather than face deportation to England, began to rebuild. For St Kitts this was merely the first of a sequence of attacks which led to the repeated destruction of property and crops through the 17th century. The population of Nevis had been shipped to England, and only in 1630 did the settlers return under John Hilton.

When the English settlers first arrived in Nevis in 1628, the island was still cloaked in dense forest down to the water's edge, much as described by Captain John Smith after landing there in 1607 on his way to establish the colony of Jamestown in Virginia: 'It is all woddy ... in most places the wod groweth close to the water side, at a high water marke, and in some places so thicke of a soft spungy wood like a wilde figge tree, you cannot get through it, but by making your way with hatchets, or fauchions'.[12]

In time the arrival of European settlers led to changes in the vegetation of the islands. In contrast to the interior of much larger islands such as Jamaica where there were large areas of swamp or mountainous land, difficult of access, remote and inaccessible, the island of Nevis was small and was easily cleared on the coastal plain and lower hills around the large central volcanic peak. A French map of Nevis, drawn in 1630 shortly after the English settlement of the island and a year after the Spanish raid, shows the first steps in the establishment of the new colony.[13]

Within half a century of the initial settlement the island had been extensively cleared and settled. Early descriptions emphasize the extent of clearance for cultivation. For Rochefort, writing in 1658, the central high mountain of Nevis Peak was 'cover'd with great Trees up to the very top' but he could already see the progress in forest clearance, 'the Plantations are all about the Mountain, beginning from the Sea-side, till you come to the highest part of it'.[14] Governor Stapleton reported in 1676 that Nevis 'contains by computation 320,000 acres, about 7 miles in breadth and 15 miles in length, 2,000 acres patented, the whole Island settled, except the top of the mountain'.[15] Sloane made a similar observation at his visit in 1687. 'The ground is cleared almost to the top of the hill, where there remains some Wood, and where are Run-away Negros that harbour themselves in it'.[16] In 1708 Oldmixon described the landscape thus: 'There's but one Mountain, and that is in the midst of it, very high, and cover'd with great Trees to the top. The Plantations are all round the mountain, beginning from the Sea-side, and ending only at the Summet of the Mountain'.[17] By this time, cultivation for sugar occupied all the accessible land.

As on St Kitts, there was a steady rise in population of enslaved Africans from the late 17th century onwards, transported to work the sugar plantations. Under the governorship of William Stapleton (1672–86) the Leeward Islands developed the sugar industry, importing large numbers of African slaves, no fewer than 4,000 during the 1670s into the four islands.[18] One result of this was that Nevis was transformed from having the largest white population of the Leeward Islands in the 1670s to having a total white population of 1,118 against 8,380 enslaved Africans in 1756.[19]

The enslaved population lived in villages on the plantations. They had a six-day working week, working from sunrise to sunset with Sunday as a free day and were allowed to cultivate provision grounds, gardens, or mountain land set aside for the purpose. Their produce could be sold at market which from the planters' perspective reduced costs in food rations and limited risk. However, the land given over for provision grounds and gardens was often good agricultural land and high prices for sugar inevitably put pressure for its reversion to cane cultivation, a process already noted for St Kitts (p. 137). Food was then imported from the eastern coast of America until the disruption resulting from the American Revolutionary War in the 1770s and 1780s. Life on the plantations and the marketing of their produce at Charlestown have been much illuminated by Karen Fog Olwig's study, which showed how 'the West Indian community of Nevis has, since the 1600s, incorporated both African and European cultural elements into a common framework of social life'.[20]

The abolition of slavery throughout the British empire in 1834 brought with it the transition to wage labour for a majority of the island's population, already noted on St Kitts (p. 137).

ORGANIZATION OF THE LANDSCAPE

As related by Philpott (p. 137), the large-scale transformation of the landscape began soon after the earliest European settlement of St Kitts in 1624. After the introduction of sugar processing in the early 1640s forest clearance proceeded more quickly and by the late 17th century had seriously depleted the timber stocks, so that timber for building needed to be imported from the eastern coast of America.

As on St Kitts, the laying out of the landscape for large-scale sugar cultivation took place within the divisions formed in the partition of the island through the survey of a series of straight radial alignments perpendicular to the coastline and probably marked out from the sea by compass. These extended from the coast to what must initially have been a hypothetical 'centreline' (Fig. 12.3). On Nevis these compass bearings are seen at their best on the modern DoS maps, the present-day plantation boundaries preserving the alignments.[21]

As on St Kitts (p. 138), each plantation's cultivable land was both demarcated and served by a rectilinear network of tracks creating a patchwork of regular cane fields, mostly in the range of 8 to 16 acres in area. However, as on St Kitts the layout was in part a response to aesthetic considerations (p. 139).

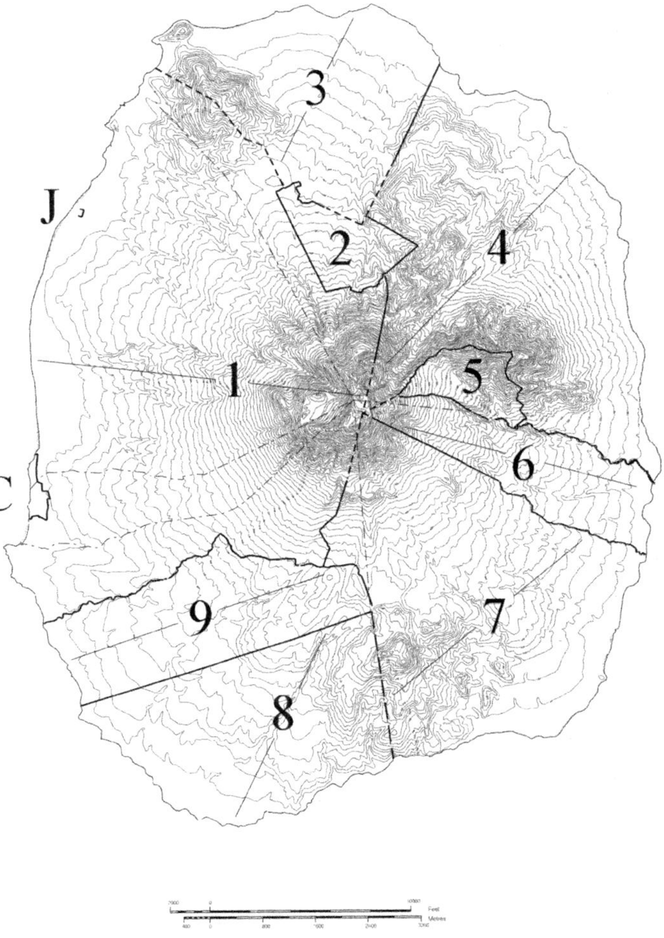

Fig. 12.3. As on St Kitts, the laying out of the landscape for large-scale sugar cultivation took place within the divisions formed in the partition of the island through the survey of a series of straight radial alignments perpendicular to the coastline and probably marked out from the sea by compass. These extended from the coast to what must initially have been a hypothetical 'centreline'.

INTERVISIBILITY AND CONNECTIONS BETWEEN PLANTATIONS IN THE LANDSCAPE OF MOUNTRAVERS

The plantations identified in St Thomas Lowland were all probably intervisible with at least two others, providing mutual protection as well as an efficient partition of the landscape. In the modern landscape the connections between plantations are somewhat obscured by the re-growth of scrub and forest, but would have been connected by a network of tracks, as on St Kitts and as shown to some extent on Iles's map of 1871 (Fig. 12.2). Iles's map shows an 'Upper Round Road' as linking many of the plantations; although in recent years cleared by the Nevis Historical and Conservation Society as a heritage walking route, the present-day archaeological evidence for its precise route could not be easily established.

THE CONSOLIDATION AND ABANDONMENT OF ESTATES

As on St Kitts, sugar estates on Nevis were subject to a process of aggregation during the 18th century, a process which continued into the 19th and 20th centuries. The evidence from Nevis comes not from maps, but through combining archaeological survey with documentary research. Pares's study of Mountravers offers hints of this process. The Pinney estate in the parish of St Thomas Lowland had as its core the estate of Charlots (also known as Sharloes and later as Pinney's Yard), acquired by Azariah Pinney through a series of complex financial and legal manoeuvres between 1704 and 1718.[22] Archaeological survey and excavation has revealed the extent of the early plantation house and works, the houses surviving only at cellar level, and the site of the boiling house hinted at by the location of the windmill, known from documentary sources to have been built by John Pinney in the 1790s.[23] All these features are considerably obscured by a 20th-century works for the production of Copra (Fig. 12.4).

The extension of this same estate eastwards towards the mountain was achieved through the marriage in 1708 of Azariah's son John to Mary Travers, a widow and the owner of the estate once known as Proctors, now appropriately renamed Mountravers and part of a larger landholding which also included an estate higher up known as

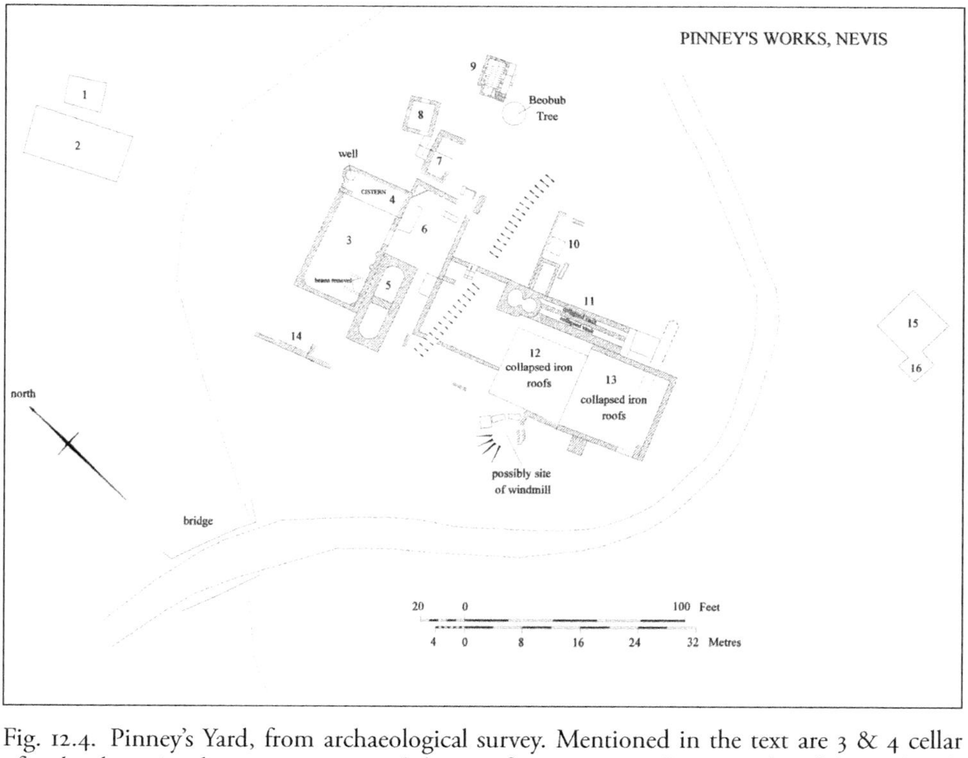

Fig. 12.4. Pinney's Yard, from archaeological survey. Mentioned in the text are 3 & 4 cellar of early plantation house, 9 – manager's house of 1818, 10–13 – Copra works of the mid 20th century, possibly incorporating an earlier boiling house.

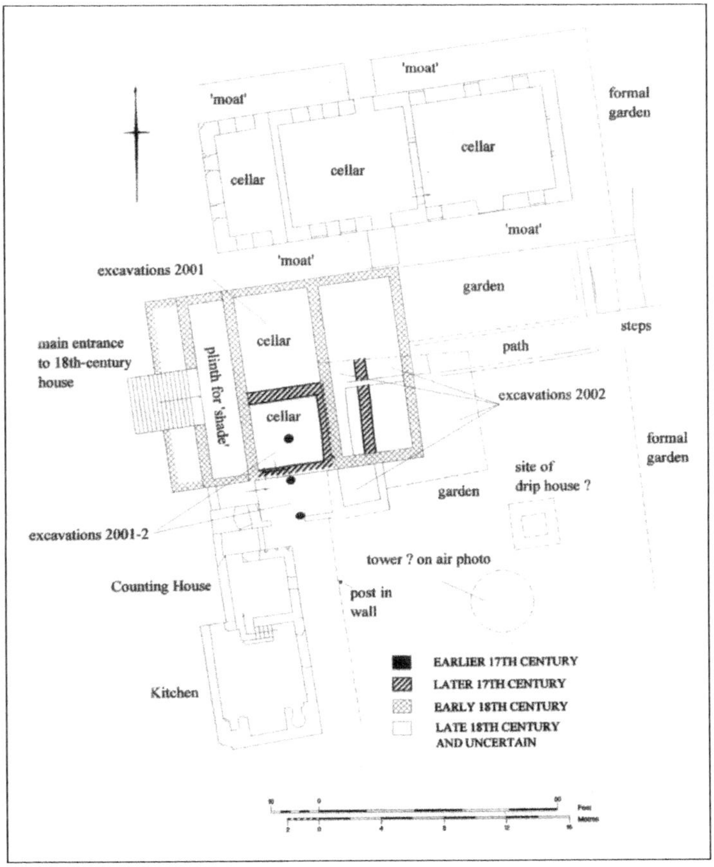

Fig. 12.5. Archaeological survey and excavation have revealed the plan and extent of the plantation house, gardens and works at Mountravers.

Mountain (later known as Governors).[24] Archaeological survey and excavation has revealed the plan and extent of the plantation house, gardens, and works at Mountravers (Fig. 12.5).

Above Mountravers, extending to the top of the mountain, was another estate known as Woodland, by the 1760s held by John Williams Sanders, a 'spendthrift'. John Pinney, the owner of Mountravers, saw in 1772 that if he could 'only take possession of his estate, which is so advantageously situated to mine, … it will make me a complete estate from sea to mountain' – which Pinney had achieved by 1778.[25] Archaeological survey identified Woodland, revealing the plan of house, garden and works (Fig. 12.6). Below Mountravers towards the sea was Scarboro's, another smaller estate, in the same ownership as Mountravers by 1833; again, fieldwork has revealed the plan of house and works (Fig. 12.7). The earliest known map of Mountravers, of 1880 and as copied into the Courthouse records in 1905, shows both Scarboro's and Woodland as part of the Mountravers estate (Fig. 12.8). Two other plantation centres or works, Upper Woodland NW and SE, are known of only from archaeological fieldwork (Figs 12.9–12.10), but were probably absorbed into the Woodland estate before

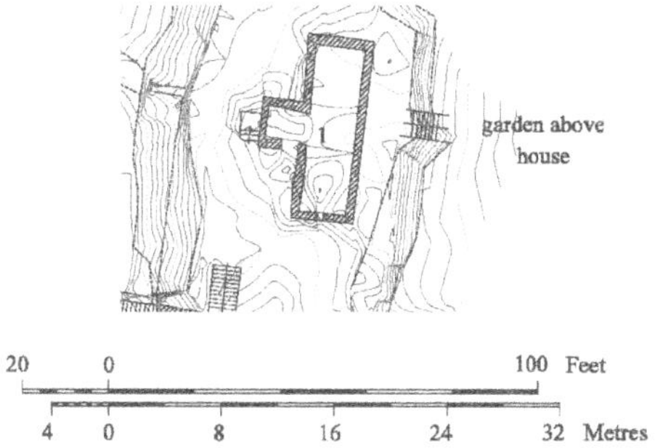

Fig. 12.6. Woodland, the plan of house and garden, from archaeological survey, see also Fig. 12.19.

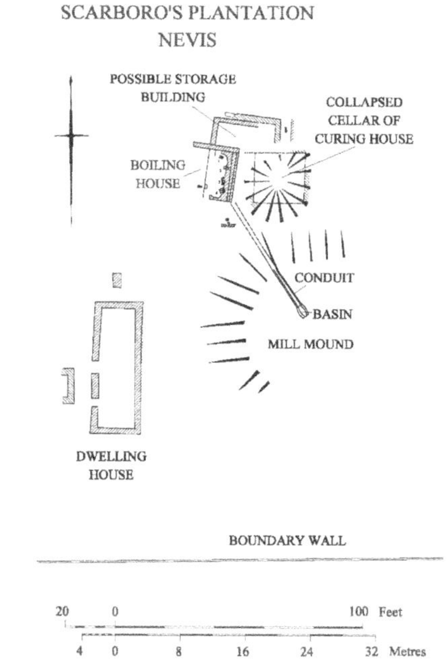

Fig. 12.7. Scarboro's, the plan of house and works, from archaeological survey.

becoming part of Mountravers. Neither are recorded on Iles's map of 1871 nor identified in any documentary source. At each was the remains of a boiling house with a train of coppers. The drains and large slab or pond at Upper Woodland SE indicate that it was also probably a site for the processing of indigo.

To the south of Mountravers, the story was more complex. The plantation known first as Mountain and later as Governors, and now heavily obscured by the growth of scrub and forest, was sold by John Pinney to Edward Brazier to become part of Brazier's in 1781.[26] Not so heavily obscured was the plantation centre recorded archaeologically and here named Upper Rossington, by 1871 probably part of the Rossington estate. Archaeological survey identified the remains of the plantation centre, not recorded on any maps, revealing the plan of the works, a platform for a cattle mill and an adjacent boiling house; no adjacent house was identified, though this could have overlain the cistern or been located in one of the enclosed areas (Fig. 12.11).

Thus, from an analysis of the archaeological and the documentary evidence, the map of Nevis illustrates a reduction in the number of plantations during the 18th and early 19th century. As on St Kitts, plantations such as Upper Rossington and Upper Woodland, were located high up on the hill slopes, where the ground was steep and the terrain vulnerable to soil erosion and exhaustion. These were abandoned at an early date. Others were amalgamated with larger plantations in the first half of the 19th century, when the pressure on planters had become intense. On the Pinney's estate at Mountravers the process was analogous to that seen on St Kitts. Sugar continued to be cultivated but the Pinney plantations underwent a

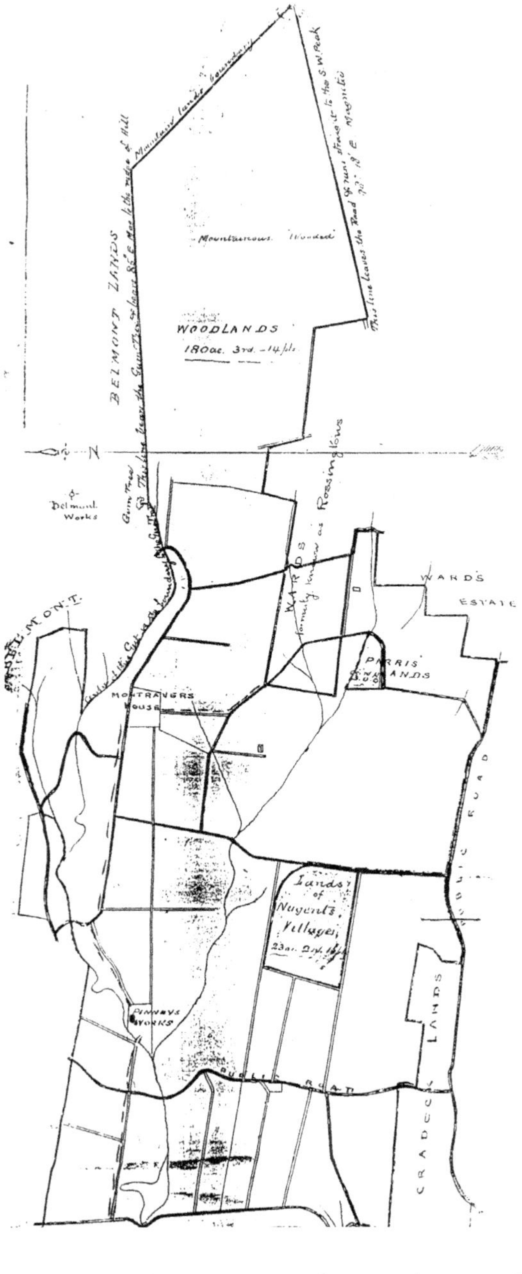

Fig. 12.8. The earliest known map of Mountravers, of 1880 and as copied into the Courthouse records in 1905, shows both Scarboro's and Woodland as part of the Mountravers estate.

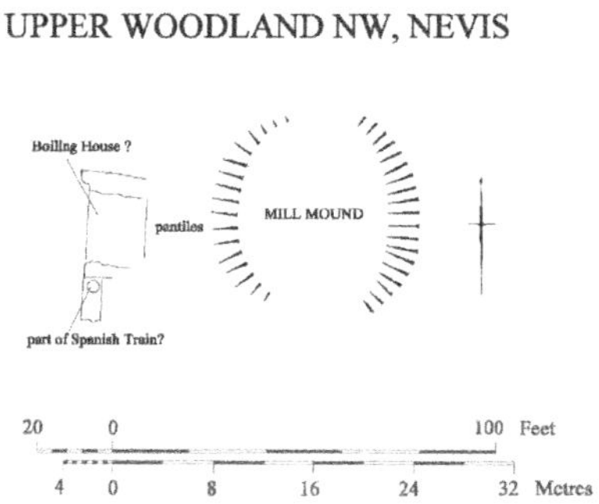

Fig. 12.9. Upper Woodland NW, plan from archaeological survey.

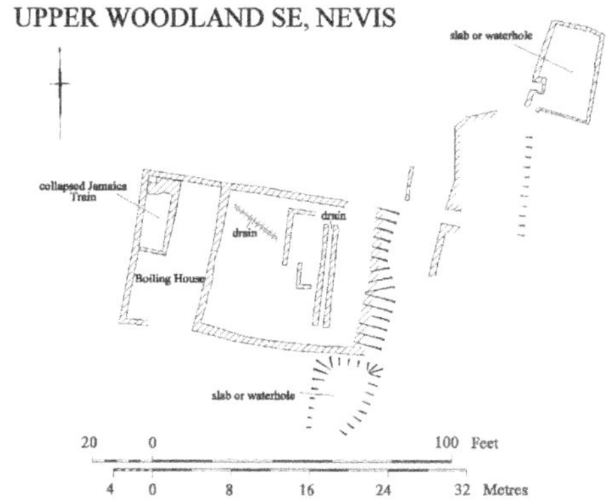

Fig. 12.10. Upper Woodland SE, plan from archaeological survey.

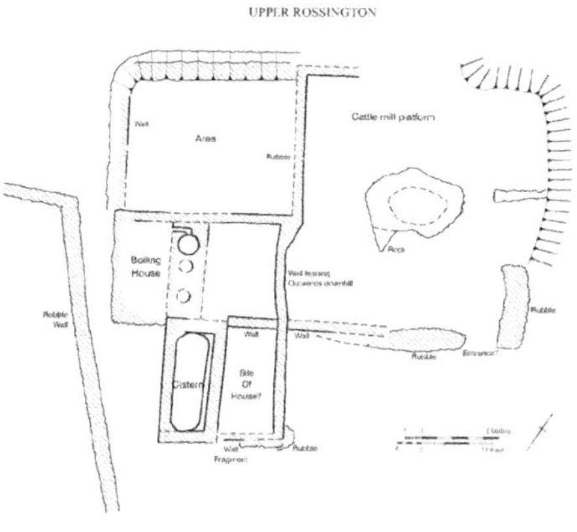

Fig. 12.11. Upper Rossington, by 1871 part of the Rossington estate. Archaeological survey identified the remains of the plantation centre, not recorded on any maps, revealing the plan of the works, a platform for a cattle mill and an adjacent boiling house; no adjacent house was identified, though this could have overlain the cistern or been located in one of the enclosed areas.

process of consolidation, reducing their number as plantation centres were abandoned. Concentrating sugar processing at a single site reduced expenditure and increased efficiency, and at Mountravers enabled the replacement of the sugar works with gardens aspiring to gentility (below p. 253). This was achieved by modernizing the works at Pinney's Yard. A new manager's house was built in 1818 (Fig. 12.12) and the works were modernized with the installation of a steam engine and mill to supplement the wind and cattle mills.[27] To the south of Mountravers similar changes were taking place in the 19th century. By 1880 the boundary with the plantation previously known as Rossington was now marked on the map of the Mountravers estate as 'Wards formerly known as Rossington' indicating that the latter had come to the end of its independent existence.

Fig. 12.12. The Manager's house at Pinney's Yard, the inscription '1818 PTH' commemorating its construction by Peter Thomas Huggins (for location see Fig. 12.4).

PLANTATION BUILDINGS AND LAYOUT

Documentation and archaeological survey

The survey of the Mountravers landscape identified and recorded the structural remains of some fifteen plantation centres, all in the parish of St Thomas Lowland. On St Kitts, a dearth of archaeological evidence for the earliest houses contrasted with the wealth of information about them in the settlers' claims for compensation after the French raid and destruction of 1705 (p. 162). More evidence for the earliest buildings, of timber post-in-the-ground or earthfast construction, such as have been more widely recorded on the east coast of mainland North America, has come from Nevis. Archaeological excavations at Mountravers and in Charlestown have revealed the plans of buildings of earthfast construction (Figs 12.13–12.14). Building surveys have also identified the Hermitage (Fig. 12.15), in the adjacent parish of St John Figtree, as one of the best such surviving buildings in the Americas.[28] As noted for St Kitts (p. 142), the relative absence of standing 17th-century buildings may be attributed to a series of destructive forces, both natural and human. For Nevis there is no set of records comparable to the insurance claims for St Kitts, though individual claims survive in collections outside the National Archives. For the Charlots estate a claim was made by Azariah Pinney and his partner Richard Mereweather for about £1,300 for losses from the French raid, including 'one dwelling house of two rooms below and above boarded and shingled and good timber ... £250 ... One boyleing house boarded and shingled ... £150 ...Three hundred pounds led being ye bed of the mill, spouts etc £7-10-0. One new still and head worme and casq ... £56'.[29] A second more detailed claim exists for the Stapleton estates in the parishes of St Paul (largely Charlestown) and St John (the Low Ground estate). Here the two large boiling houses were valued at £900,[30] a sum far in excess of the loss reported on for Charlots, but similar to the £450 valuation of Penelope Mead's boiling house on St Kitts (p. 154).

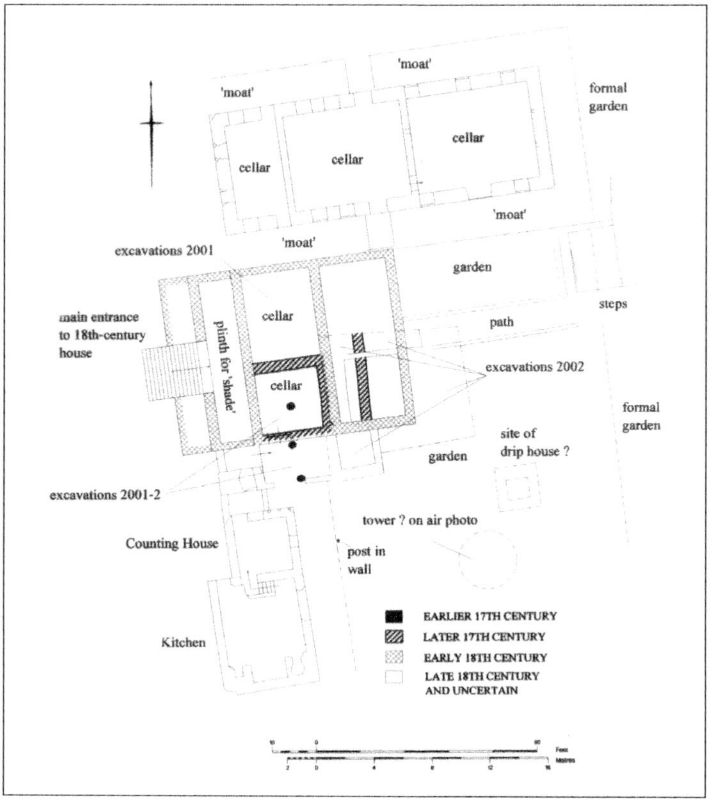

Fig. 12.13. Mountravers dwelling house complex, the earliest house evidenced by the three post holes.

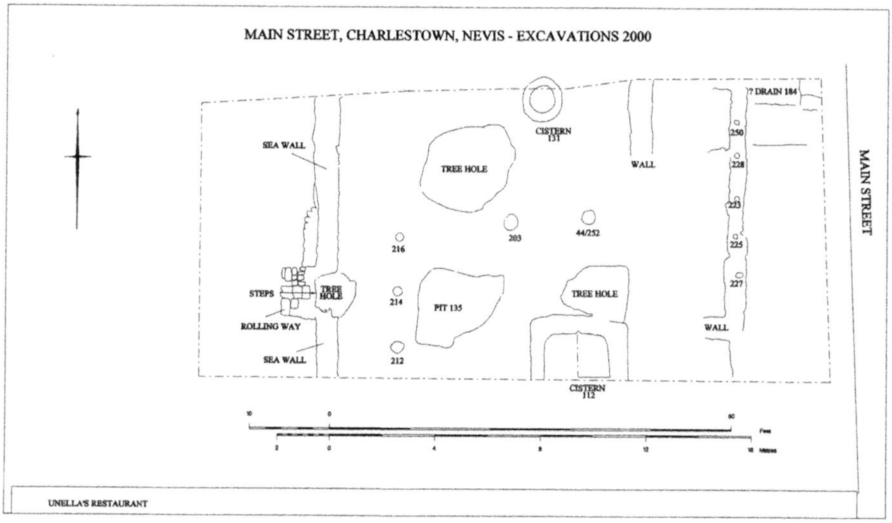

Fig. 12.14. Main Street, Charlestown, summary plan showing walls, postholes and other major features. The two tree holes are modern disturbances.

Fig. 12.15. The Hermitage, in the parish of St John Figtree, of earthfast construction and one of the best such surviving buildings in the Americas, (a–b) looking west and east, (c) plan.

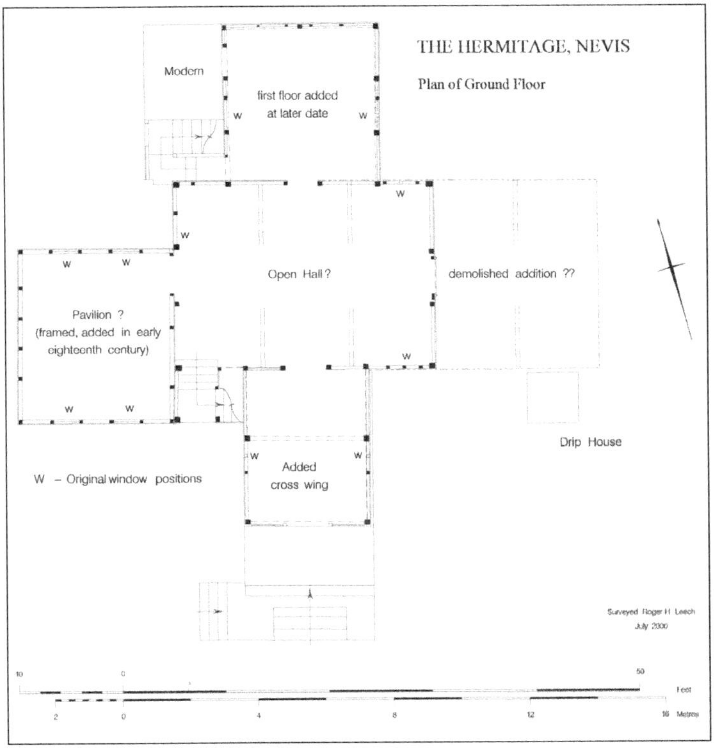

The plans of plantation dwelling houses revealed through archaeological field survey are probably of the 17th and 18th centuries. Although not closely dated they provide a useful generalized picture for the first two centuries of colonial life on Nevis. The 18th-century timber house at Mountravers succeeded the earthfast house noted above. The lowest part at basement level was built in stone, the plinth extending the length of the house possibly containing the cistern for water supply. At basement or cellar level the house was surveyed and planned through archaeological excavation, showing that the larger part was paved with bricks, the smaller part paved with stone slabs (Fig. 12.16). This division into two areas of unequal size possibly reflected the plan of the ground floor, a typical hall-parlour plan such as recorded in many houses of this period in contemporary Bristol,[31] the trading port with which Mountravers had many connections, evidenced notably for the house by the plinth above the steps being paved with Pennant Sandstone slabs from the Bristol region. However caution must here be exercised, as the planning of houses on Nevis may also have originated in the needs of lives in this tropical climate, with bed chambers placed on the ground floor for comfort or convenience. A second Pinney house will illustrate this point. In his research for *A West-India Fortune* Pares encountered the inventory of fittings

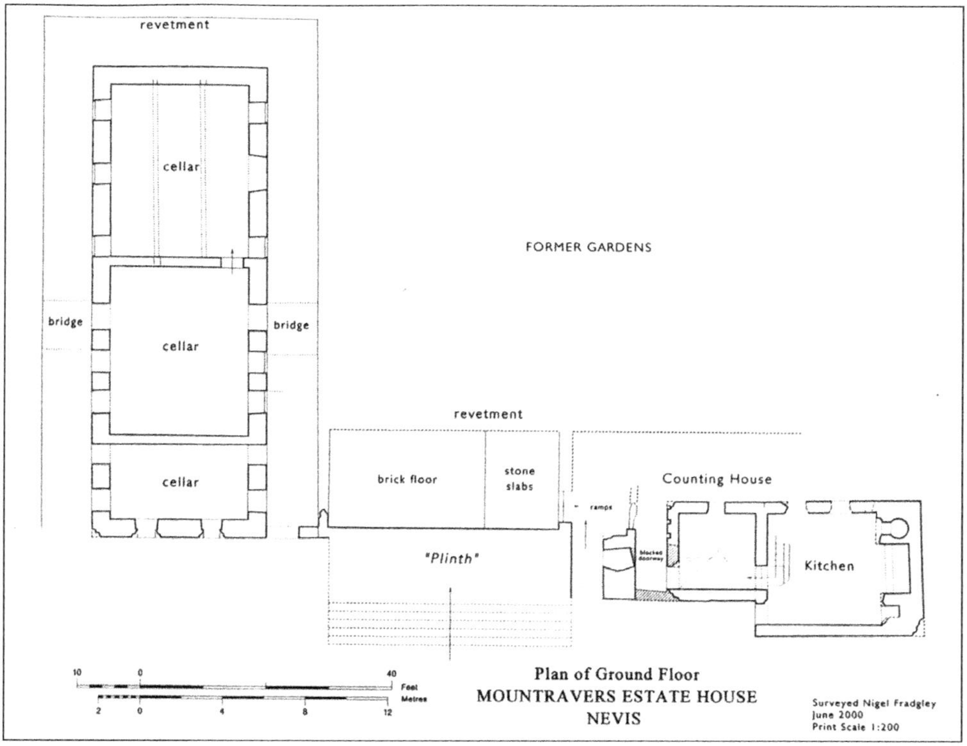

Fig. 12.16. Mountravers, at basement or cellar level the house was surveyed and planned through archaeological excavation, showing that the larger part was paved with bricks, the smaller part paved with stone slabs.

within what he described as 'The Pinney House in Nevis, 1722', leased in that year by Mary Pinney to the island council for the reception of a new governor, 'His Excellency General Hart', and identified this house as that of the 'Mountain estate also known as Governors'.[32] Located on the very edge of the Mountravers landscape as studied here (to the south of Wards on Fig. 12.1), Governors became through the sale to Edward Brazier in 1781 (above) part of the Brazier plantation and is shown as 'works' on a map of that estate; unfortunately the remains of the house and works were too overgrown by thick scrub for an overall archaeological survey to have been possible, beyond identifying the porch to the house. The need for this is however somewhat obviated by the discovery of a detailed description of this very house in the Nevis records:

> A dwelling house sixty two feet long and twenty feet wide, consisting of a hall two chambers with four closets, a pantry with three bins for grains, with proper shelves in all the closets and pantry a loft to keep liquors in and a back entry with a cupboard – four window blinds with painted canvas four good locks on the doors and a cupboard lock – 1 pair large door bolts with brass nobs and proper fastenings for all the windows and doors. The greatest part is now and the whole in very good repair a shade adjoining the south chamber in bad repair – proper and good stone steps to each of the out doors. A kitchen and steward room, built with lime and stone floored with tyles a dresser in the kitchen two windows with iron bars in the stewards room and a good lock. The whole in very good repair except the shingles on the roof which are bad: an oven at the westmost end in good order.[33]

From the inventory transcribed by Pares and the above description it can be concluded that this house was not of conventional hall-parlour plan, but rather conformed to the often later arrangement of two ground-floor rooms separated by an entrance

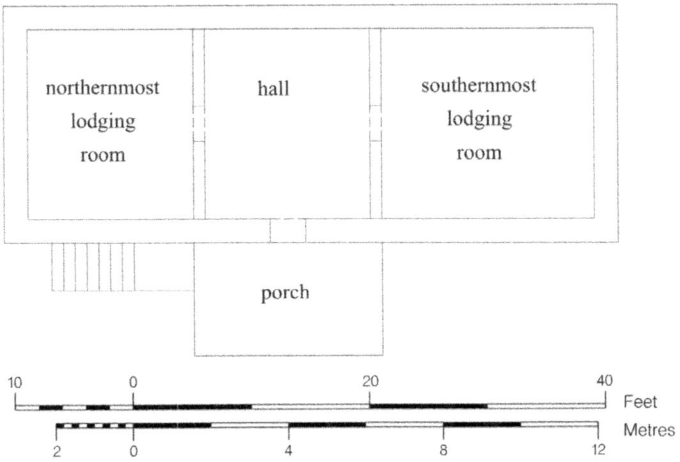

Fig. 12.17. The Pinney house at Governors, two ground-floor rooms separated by an entrance hall, in this instance both bedchambers, one 'the northernmost lodging room', the other 'the southernmost chamber designed for his Excellency's bed chamber', plan reconstructed from description of 1781, adding the porch and steps located by RHL and Mr Edward Herbert.

hall, in this instance both bedchambers, one 'the northernmost lodging room', the other 'the southernmost chamber designed for his Excellency's bed chamber' (Fig. 12.17).

This house was larger in its overall length to the other plantation houses recorded in the survey, but of similar width: Mountravers – 40ft by 18ft wide; Scarboro's – 54ft by 20ft; Woodland – 43ft by 15ft. But a distinguishing feature between these houses was the presence of a detached kitchen. These were recorded only at Governors, from the above documentary reference, and at Mountravers, both possessions of the comparatively wealthy Pinney family. Possibly this was a mark of status.

The plans of plantation yards and works (Figs 12.4–12.11)

From archaeological survey and related documentary sources, various general observations may be made. The most familiar, noted above for St Kitts (p. 140) is the siting of the sugar processing buildings. Mill and boiling house were necessarily adjacent, as at Wansey's, Pinney's Yard, Scarboro's, Woodland, Upper Woodland NW, Rossington, and Wards, enabling a swift and efficient flow of the freshly crushed sugar juice direct to the boiling house coppers. Not so easily identified was the curing house, usually a two-storey building, where the molasses dripped down into pots or directly onto the floor below for distillation into rum. This building could only readily be identified at Wansey's, Pinney's Yard, Scarboro's, Rossington, and Wards.

A second general observation arises from the above: the transition from one form of power to another, a product of the planter's search for an ever more economic and

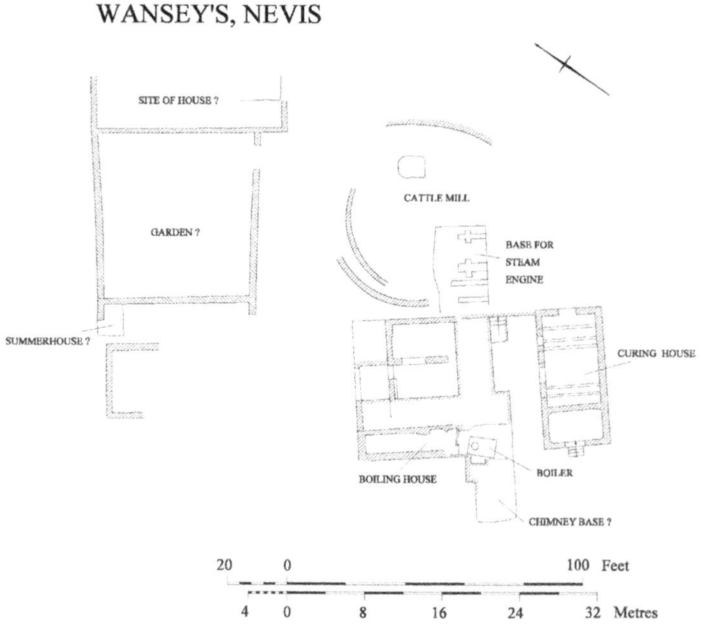

Fig. 12.18. Wansey's Plantation, plan from archaeological survey: the ruins of a cattle mill, boiling house and curing house are clearly visible, together with the remains of a steam engine denoting the later conversion of the works to steam power. Overlooking the works are the ruins of a house at least 65ft in length fronting on to a walled garden extending downhill some 55ft with towers each *c.* 10ft square at the corners away from the house.

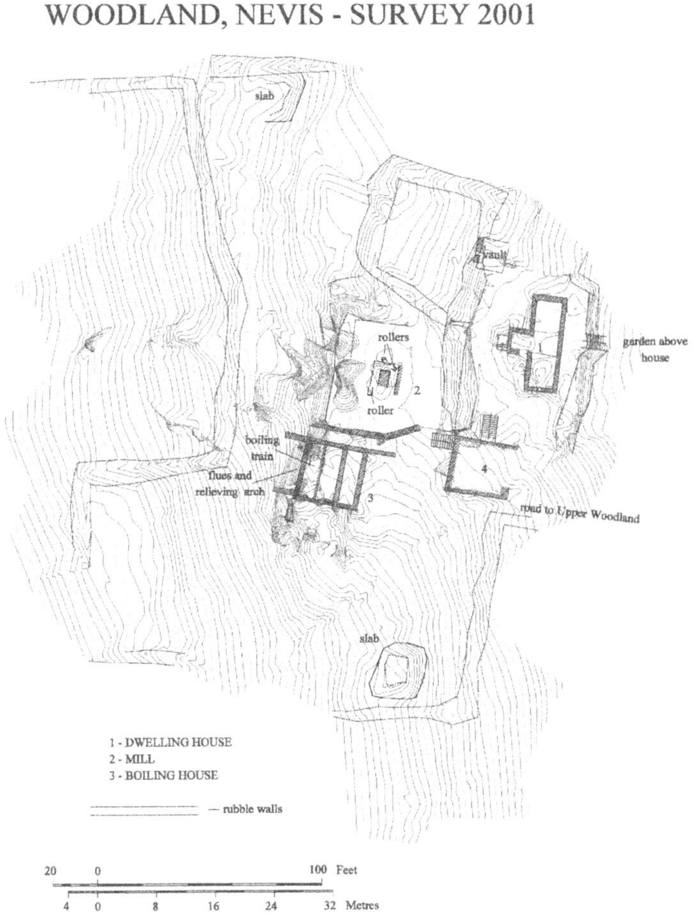

Fig. 12.19. Woodland, plan from archaeological survey: the plantation house was sited on a low eminence overlooking the mill and boiling house.

more profitable means of producing sugar. At Wansey's Plantation (Fig. 12.18) the ruins of a cattle mill are clearly visible, together with the remains of a steam engine denoting the later conversion of the works to steam power, a transition evident at Pinney's Works from the documentary evidence cited by Small.[34] As noted above by Dunning, these successive types of milling underwent many forms of technological improvement, and the presence of an animal mill as well as a windmill could also be a precaution to ensure that cane crushing could continue if the wind dropped.

A third general observation however is one of surveillance, the siting of the plantation house so as to overlook the yard with its mill and works. This was most evident at Woodland where the plantation house was sited on a low eminence overlooking the mill and boiling house (Fig. 12.19). The same pattern would have been observed in the two plantations to the south, both at Rossington (Fig. 12.20) and at Wards.

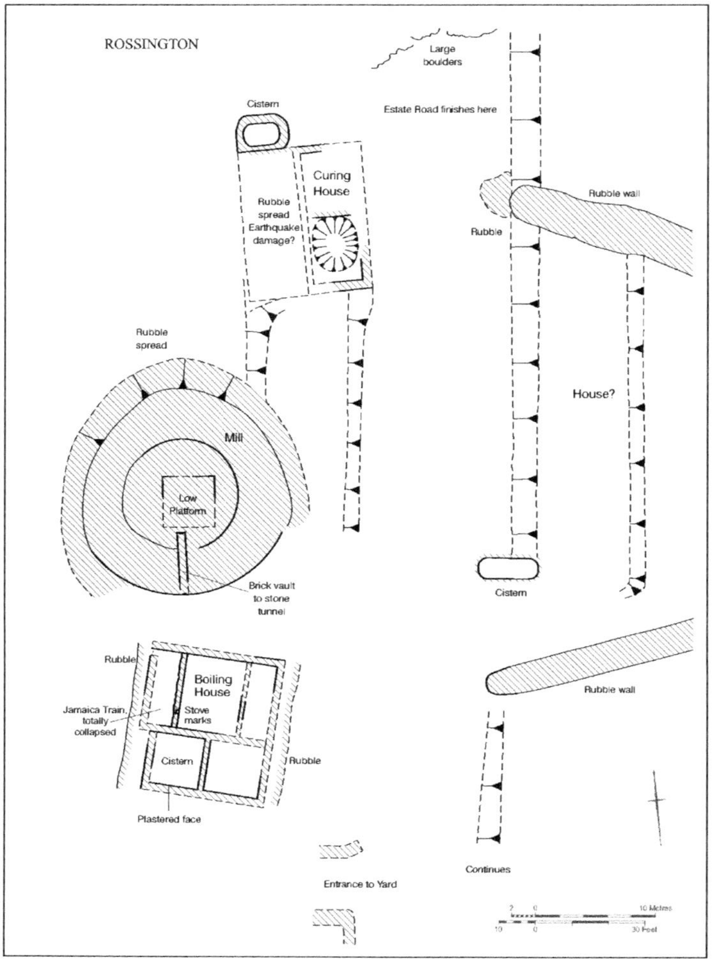

Fig. 12.20. Rossington, plan from archaeological survey, the house site similarly located to overlook the works.

Gardens

Wards Plantation (Fig. 12.21) was of especial interest, with the probable house site overlooking the cattle mill and boiling house, and itself overlooked by a series of terraced gardens accessed from paths and separate flights of steps ascending the hillside above, several pavilions or summerhouses built in stone scattered across the gardens.

Documentary research revealed that by 1759 this had been the plantation of John Ward esq., hence its name, but earlier in the century it had belonged to Ralph Payne, late Governor of the Leeward Islands. This was therefore truly an elite garden, comparable perhaps to that of the 17th-century French governor de Poincy on St Kitts.[35] On the terrace in front of the house and formal gardens, Payne, his family and guests could have sat and watched the slaves of the plantation hard at work, a juxtaposition of gentility and the slavery that supported it.[36]

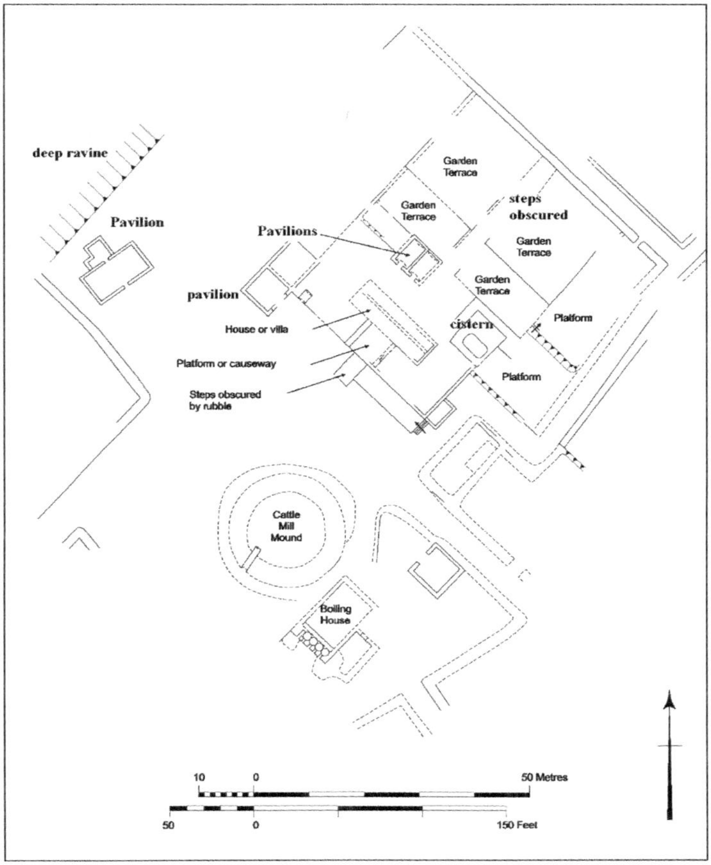

Fig. 12.21. Wards Plantation, the probable house site overlooking the cattle mill and boiling house, and itself overlooked by a series of terraced gardens accessed from paths and separate flights of steps ascending the hillside above, several pavilions or summerhouses built in stone scattered across the gardens.

Encountering gardens and associated structures deep in tropical vegetation in the course of archaeological survey was initially something of a surprise, but also provided a context and explanation for many of the features encountered by the survey of the estates immediately to the south and north of Mountravers.

At least two further gardens were still known as such by the early 20th century. A plan of the former Pinney family's Mountravers estate in 1905 shows both 'Parris's Garden' and 'Mountravers Mansion and Garden'. Parris's Garden, like that at Wards, contained both a house and a series of garden terraces, again all now enveloped in tropical vegetation (Fig. 12.22). But unlike Ward's this complex contained no sugar mill and boiling house. Iles's map of Nevis made in 1871 provides the explanation. Parris's Works was closer to Charlestown and the sea (Fig. 12.2). As around the cities of the Atlantic littoral, Parris's Garden was clearly a second residence, a place of retreat from the sugar processing works.[37]

Mountravers garden lay on the uphill or east side of the house, again consisting of a series of garden terraces with a central path leading up the hill from the centre of the house. Features within the garden included a drip house, the Caribbean substitute

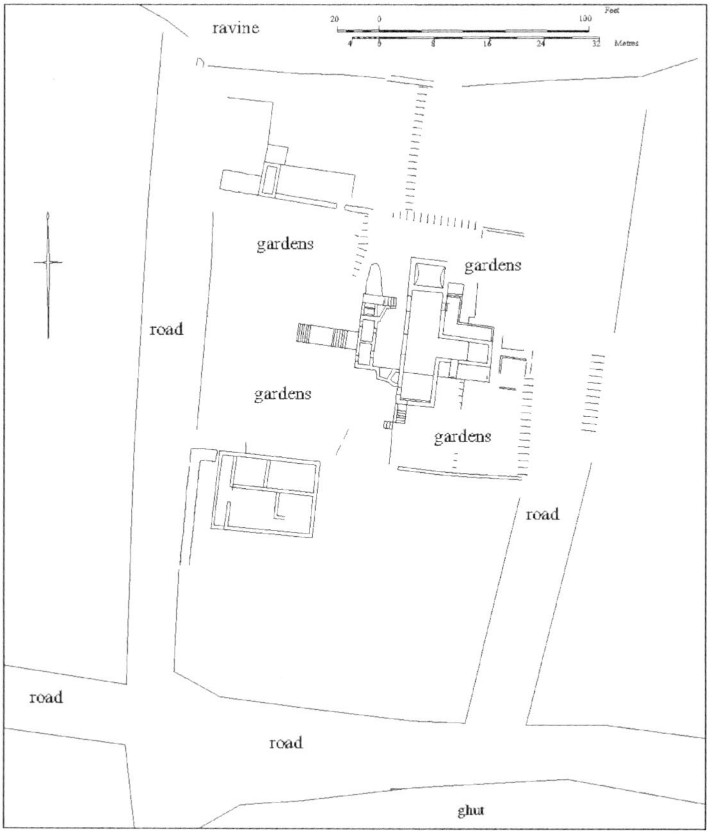

Fig. 12.22. Parris's Garden, like that at Wards, contained both a house and a series of garden terraces, again all now enveloped in tropical vegetation, plan from archaeological survey.

for an ice house, and possibly a summerhouse tower. The latter is the 'dungeon' investigated by the TV programme *Time Team*;[38] two of the pavilions at Wards were similarly first identified to the author by a slave descendant as 'slave dungeons'. With the subsequent discovery of the garden earthworks this feature is now best interpreted as a garden building. At Mountravers too there is little evidence for any sugar processing works; Mountravers Garden was probably the result of John (Pretor) Pinney concentrating the estate's sugar works at Charlots, later named Pinney's Works, and Woodland.[39] Summerhouse towers, similar in plan to the building at Mountravers previously identified as a dungeon, formed part of the design of two gardens to the north of Mountravers, one at Belmont, within a plantation earlier known as Wansey's, named after William Wansey, its merchant owner from Bristol, the other, possibly its predecessor, a garden immediately adjacent to the yard of Wansey's Plantation.

At Wansey's Plantation the ruins of a cattle mill, boiling house, and curing house are clearly visible, together with the remains of a steam engine denoting the later conversion of the works to steam power. Overlooking the works are the ruins of a house at least 65ft in length fronting on to a walled garden extending downhill some 55ft with towers each *c.* 10ft square at the corners away from the house (Fig 12.18).

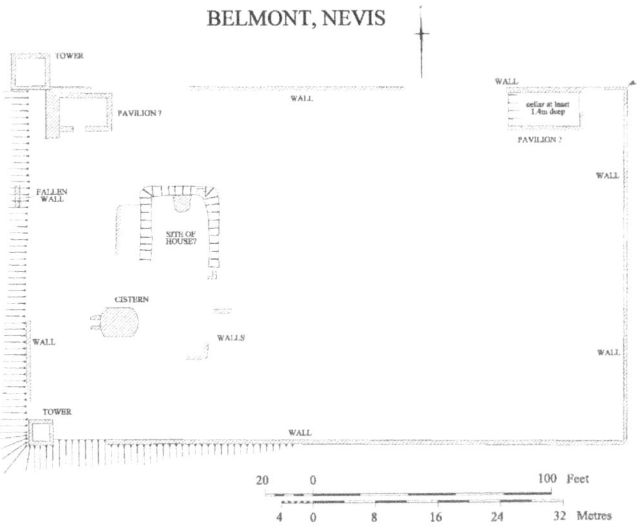

Fig. 12.23. Belmont, garden, plan from archaeological survey: on an eminence looking west towards the sea and possibly giving its name to the plantation formerly known as Wansey's.

Fig. 12.24. Belmont, garden, remains of corner tower.

To the west of the plantation is the second garden, on an eminence looking west towards the sea and possibly giving the name Belmont to the plantation formerly known as Wansey's. This garden too is now enveloped in tropical vegetation, but sufficiently clear for archaeological survey to record its overall extent, 250ft east–west in length and 150ft north–south in breadth. The interior of this garden is largely level ground, with no terracing. The only features are a building platform and adjacent cistern in the centre at the west end, overlooking the sea, and towers built in stone at three of the four corners (Figs 12.23–12.24). Two of the towers were 25ft east–west in length and 15ft north–south, one tenth of the dimensions of the garden; the tower at the south-west corner was smaller, only 10ft square.

From the presence of these two gardens on the same plantation, it could be conjectured that one succeeded the other; that William Wansey, or one of his successors, built a new garden further away from the smell and noise of the plantation yard, making use of a site which afforded views to the sea and the islands of St Kitts to the north. The idea of building garden towers could certainly have been brought by Wansey from Bristol, where similar towers existed within the garden of the house that the merchant Paul Fisher bought to demolish and rebuild as Clifton Hill House.[40]

Bridges

As surprising to the archaeological surveyor as gardens, was the discovery of well-built stone bridges taking plantation roads across ravines or ghuts, ensuring the smooth safe passage of plantation produce but also attesting to the skill of the plantation masons. All three bridges were recorded on the approach roads to gardens, perhaps underlining the wealth of these elite landscapes for visitors arriving by road from Charlestown, two on the approach to Parris's Garden, and one above the Belmont garden (Figs 12.25–12.27, Fig. 12.8 for location).

Fig. 12.25. The south bridge on the approach to Parris's Garden (Fig. 12.8 for location).

Fig. 12.26. The north bridge on the approach to Parris's Garden (Fig. 12.8 for location).

Fig. 12.27. The bridge above the Belmont garden (Fig. 12.8 for location).

FORTS

An earthwork and building on Pinney's Beach exposed by Hurricane Lennie in 1999 (Figs 12.28–12.29) was subsequently identified as Johnson's Fort, one of some twelve forts and breastworks recorded in plan and in accompanying reports by the then Lieutenant Governor of the Leeward Islands, who was responsible for overseeing their repair or construction between 1703 and 1706; the plans are numbered in a sequence that runs in a clockwise direction around the island.[41] Matching Johnson's plan of 1703–6 against the archaeological record showed it to have been a good representation of the fort as built, and indicated that the other plans were a valuable record of the forts and breastworks constructed along the coast of Nevis.

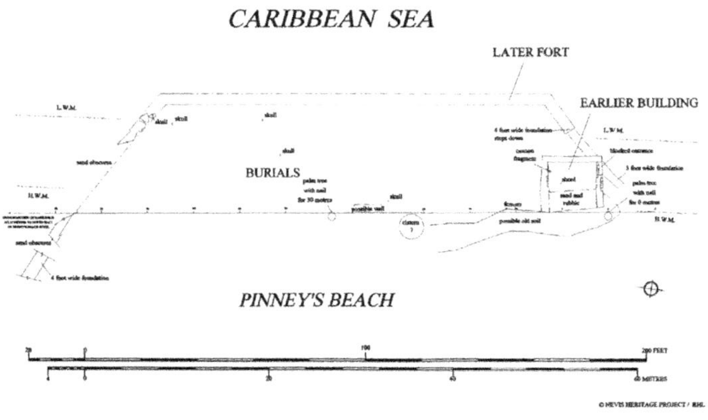

Fig. 12.28. Johnson's Fort, the earthwork and building on Pinney's Beach exposed by Hurricane Lennie in 1999, plan from archaeological survey.

Fig. 12.29. Johnson's Fort, as exposed by Hurricane Lennie in 1999.

Johnson's account added several valuable points to the archaeological survey: notably that the small stone building was a guardhouse, and that the landward side of the breastwork was protected by an earthen or 'sod' wall, all other evidence for this presumably removed by the hurricane of 1999 or earlier storms.

Further north, along the same beach, Hurricane Lennie exposed the foundations of two further forts. These were recorded in November 1999 and subsequently more fully by Tessa Machling.[42] These forts, breastworks, platforms, or batteries formed a line of defence along the west or leeward coast of Nevis. Elsewhere along the coast were gun batteries placed at strategic intervals, and one solitary larger fort at Charlestown. These were defences against principally the French, who invaded the island in both 1706 and 1782. French awareness of the existence of these defences is most evident in contemporary French maps, which show various batteries, forts, and lines of entrenchments (Fig. 12.30). The two invasions showed the ineffectiveness of this form of defence.

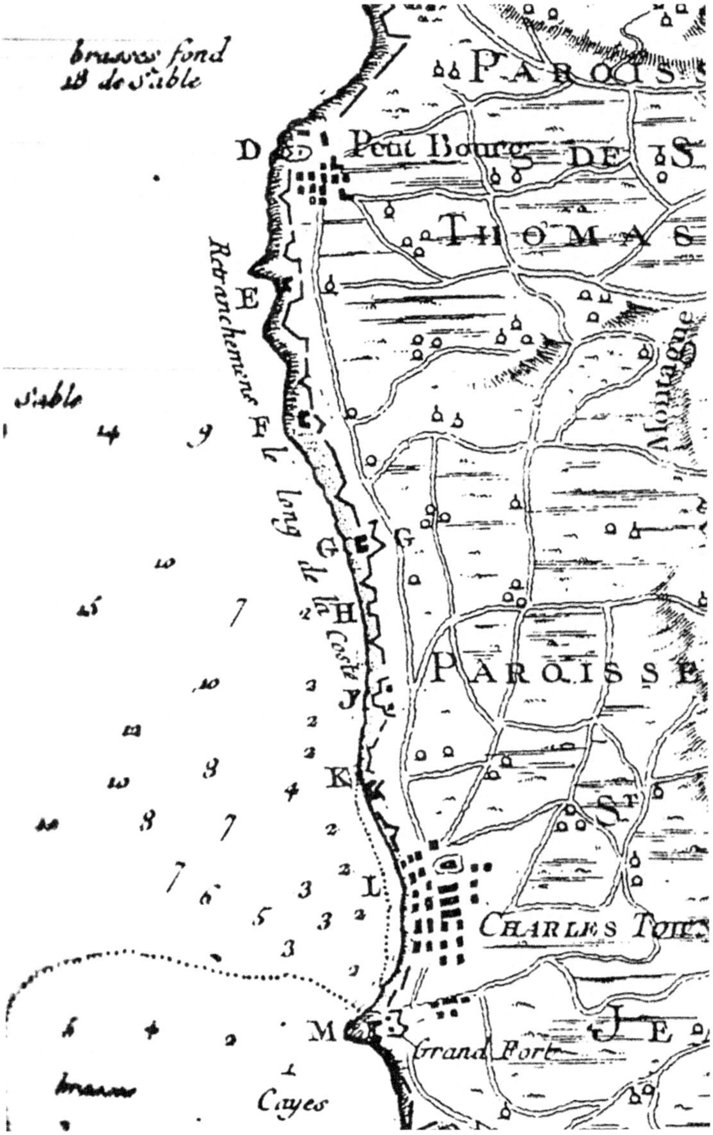

Fig. 12.30. French map of Nevis, *c.* 1758 by Bellin, probably a copy of Beauvilliers 1703, showing the linear defences and breastworks along the west coast (Oliver 1911–12, *Caribbeana*, 6–7).

SLAVE VILLAGES

In contrast to St Kitts (p. 151) there are for Nevis no general maps of the island showing the location of slave villages, and only a few plantation plans show the location of their slave villages, none of which are for the area studied here. However it was possible to examine further the location of the slave village for Mountravers as identified by Small and Eickelmann from documentary research in advance of its being investigated by the *Time Team* archaeological TV programme. The key document was a set of instructions from John Pinney, now a merchant in Bristol, written to his managers in Nevis on 8 May 1794:

> I would be no means have the negro houses removed but continue where they are and be built at proper distances in right lines to prevent accidents from fire and to afford each negro a proportion of ground around his house ... Plant a great many lemon and lime trees at the negro houses as a fence against Ward's line down to the path above Scarborough's and so on as that path runs, the width of my negro-ground and likewise at Woodland.[43]

Using these clues and with assistance from Small and Eickelmann, the archaeologists from *Time Team* then located the remains of two stone houses and other associated features.[44] In 2001 survey of the western part of the slave village site, including an adjacent slab or water hole, was completed as part of the University of Southampton

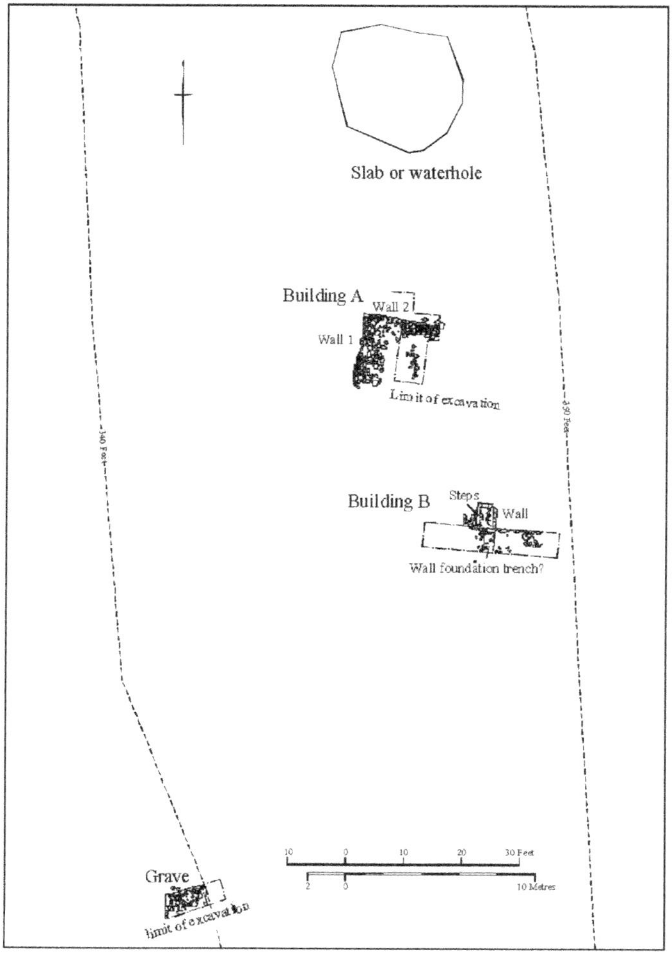

Fig. 12.31. The slave village at Mountravers, house sites, slab, and grave, plan from archaeological survey and excavations.

project. Drought conditions in June/July 2001 provided much improved visibility within the forest for field survey, and it was concluded that no further similar structures survived within this part of the forested landscape. Survey was followed by a series of evaluative excavations of the two stone structures and what had initially been identified as a further wall, but proved then to be a grave (Fig. 12.31).

The north and west walls of the northernmost building (Building A) were archaeologically recorded. Both walls, about 0.6m thick had internal and external faces of squared blocks of semi-dressed volcanic stone in regular courses, with rubble cores, bonded in very hard off-white, lime-rich mortar, surviving to a maximum height of 1.36m above present ground level. The original extent of the building could not be determined, nor whether its axis was north–south or east–west.

The southernmost building (Building B) was *c.* 7 metres to the south-east of Building A and was defined by a raised area of stone standing at least 2.5m above the immediate area to the west. What at first appeared to be the possible remains of an attached oven was shown to be a flight of steps built against the wall of the building, on a similar alignment to the north wall of Building A. The original treads to the steps had been removed revealing a cavity within the core of the structure. The sides to the steps and wall were faced in squared, semi-dressed blocks of masonry, as used for Building A, and were similarly bonded in a very hard off-white mortar. The core of the steps, however, was built using masonry and bricks, though none was complete. What was significant about the steps and wall was ribbon pointing between the stones. This form of pointing leaves the mortar standing proud of the wall, and is generally not seen on buildings in England until well into the 20th century. On Nevis however, identical pointing , apparently original, can still be seen on Cottle Church at the north end of the island, which dates from the 1820s. Sealed by a rubble spread against steps on the downhill side of the building was a deposit of African-Caribbean pottery, together with a fragment of a skillet handle carrying the letters 'HE PORE' and the date '1684'. The full inscription would have read 'PITY THE PORE'. Skillets bearing the same inscription and date were made by the foundry of John Fathers of Montacute in Somerset, *c.* 15 miles from Bettiscombe, the Dorset home of the Pinney family.[45] The context of the skillet handle within the slave village will merit further discussion: was it originally from the Pinney kitchen? Was it retained as a valuable piece of metal, or was its inscribed message of interest to a literate slave?

The interiors of the two stone structures were heavily eroded. Excavation revealed that soil erosion has reduced the present ground surface to a level below that of the floors of the buildings when in use.

A grave was located on slightly sloping ground *c.*15 m to the south of Building 2 (Fig. 12.31). The kerb of the grave, an east–west line of four semi-dressed stones, was initially thought to be a wall, identified as such by David Small with the author in 2000. Removal of the topsoil from the south side of the kerb revealed a larger stone at each end of the feature, and further stones, though much smaller and randomly placed, covering an area 2.2m east–west by 1.0m across. These stones sealed a surface of flatter, amorphous stones about 0.45 metres below the level of the kerb. At the west end of the feature a compact dark brown soil 0.5 metres in depth overlay an articulated burial, aligned east–west, head to the west, probably a Christian slave burial. The

Fig. 12.32. Wall of stone structure (Building C) exposed in construction of new road for the Newfound development, July 2008.

grave was later back-filled, with the intention that it be left as a burial monument in the landscape to be redeveloped. Survey of the area around the excavated structures revealed no further structures and indicated that beyond the area of the slave village as first identified, further remains of the same settlement will have been destroyed by sugar cultivation of the post-emancipation period.

Although this work confirmed the initial identification of the site as a slave village, no further buildings were identified through survey, until a further fragment of wall, Building C, on a similar east–west alignment to Buildings A and B was recorded some 20m to the east of Building A, when cut by a new road for the now abandoned Newfound hotel resort development (Fig. 12.32).

It can be concluded from the evidence at present available that these three buildings were amongst 'the negro-houses ... built at proper distances in right lines' by John Pinney for his slaves *c.* 1794, and that these were stone cabins similar to those recorded in many slave villages in the Tidewater states of mainland North America. A cluster of similar dwellings all ruined and roofless but standing to eaves height has been recorded above the Golden Rock plantation, possibly the best preserved such group on Nevis. It was hoped that survey of the forest and scrub landscape would identify the slave villages for the other plantations away from Mountravers itself. An exhaustive survey of the forest and scrub to the east of Mountravers failed to locate the slave village for Woodland, or similarly those for any of the other plantations recorded here.

THE PLANTATION LANDSCAPE TODAY

The archaeological surveys in 2001–4 showed that, as on St Kitts, the historic plantation landscape of Nevis was then under severe pressure from a number of directions. Damage through neglect of wooden and stone buildings with overgrowth of vegetation, particularly trees rooting in the fabric of buildings, was causing active destruction at unoccupied sites. Many of the sites had been damaged in the past by the removal of the high-quality facing stone for re-use in new buildings. Where this has occurred the long-term survival of the affected plantation buildings has been seriously compromised. Pressure from development has resulted in destruction of sites, and to the north of Mountravers extensive golf course developments have completely transformed historic landscapes, erasing all but the most obvious plantation buildings.

The visible plantation remains, the plantation centres, houses, and works, are often more obvious, although even they can be erased from the landscape with no above ground remains to indicate their former existence. Far less visible, and therefore considerably more vulnerable to unwitting development, are the remains of the slave villages, their sites on Nevis largely unidentified but also being the physical settlements of the ancestors of many Nevisians today. The only detailed archaeological investigations at any slave village in the island have been those at Jessops and New River by DAACS and the University of Southampton in 2008, in both instances where the locations of the slave villages were known through individual estate maps.[46]

Careful adaptation and interpretation of plantation remains can add significant value to any new development and, overall, has the potential to enhance the experience of visitors to Nevis substantially. Redevelopment of sites for tourism and other purposes is likely to cause damage to these sites where it is not informed by an understanding of the nature and relative significance of the various elements.

RECOMMENDATIONS FROM ICOMOS

In May 2018 the Nevis World Heritage Committee, under the aegis of the Nevis Island Administration Ministry of Culture, reported on the unsuccessful application made to designate Charlestown as a World Heritage Site,[47] and made 41 recommendations that would impact on the island and its historic plantation landscape as a whole, that 'will strengthen the protection, conservation and management of the cultural heritage of the City of Charlestown in particular and the Island of Nevis in general. These are irrespective of the World Heritage initiative and should be implemented in the interest of educating our population, informing our visitors, and to build our economic potential.' These included:

1. Continue to research and document all heritage resources and assets.
2. Identify the plantations and fortifications that have acceptable levels of integrity and authenticity and are worthy of protection and conservation. Define and declare the protected areas and surrounding buffer zones and enforce conservation regulations.
3. Treat ruins of plantations as archaeological sites, when appropriate, undertake emergency, stabilization and conservation interventions and avoid reconstructions.

The Nevis World Heritage Committee further recommended to the Cabinet of the Nevis Island Administration that

... if we really want to show ICOMOS and our people that we are serious about making good economic use of our cultural heritage, then we must establish a Department of Heritage with the mission to protect and preserve our diverse culture and heritage.

Our Cultural Heritage must be given the same level of importance as the Department of Education or Department of Tourism, or any other Government Department. This Department must operate with permanency like any other so that when there is an election and the changing of the Members of Parliament, the focus on Heritage does not go away and the mission, vision and purpose do not change. This Department should have a staff consisting of the minimum of a Director, a Secretary, a Heritage Officer, a team of trained maintenance workers and archaeological consultants. It should also have an Advisory Body made up of community members and some of the members of the present Nevis World Heritage Committee with specific skills to be able to advise the Department on the way forward.

Secondly and equally important, ICOMOS found there were no legal structures in place to protect our cultural and built heritage. We must put legislation in place that will protect our heritage. Only the Bath Hotel is mentioned by the NCEPA for protection. This must be a priority for this government and future governments in order for Nevis to be considered for any World Heritage listings now or in the future.

A strategic plan must be drawn up with action plans for each category of the ICOMOS recommendations, time frame for completion, costs, required skill sets and auditing and accountability procedures required for success.
We further proposed that we use our seat in the United Nations and on the UNESCO World Heritage Committee to lobby for funds and technical assistance from the various members who may lobby us to achieve their successes in order to successfully carry out the forty one (41) recommendations made by ICOMOS and develop this Department of Heritage.'

These are recommendations of far reaching importance for the historic environment and heritage of Nevis. It is our intention that the pilot project funded by the British Academy and reported on here should provide a springboard from which to enhance and protect further the archaeological heritage of Nevis.

The initial most obvious task for the Nevis Heritage Project is to work with other interested parties in the creation of a Historic Environment Record (HER), such as exist for all parts of the United Kingdom and many countries that have adopted the data standards set out by ICOM and the Council of Europe. Increasingly such records fulfil an educational role and provide for a community input, in England the *Bristol Know Your Place* website being a good model, from a city intimately connected with Nevis's past (Preface, Figs 0.4–0.5).

An urgent task is the recording of the remaining plantations and other sites of historic interest above ground, using LIDAR for the initial identification of sites obscured by scrub and forest, and using ground truthing survey and new rapid photogrammetric techniques which enable highly detailed scaled models of the buildings to be recorded quickly. The many surveys of St Mary Cayon on St Kitts and of the Mountravers landscape on Nevis, most published for the first time in this volume, reveal how many such sites remain concealed around and in the forest and scrub that has grown over the former sugar cane fields, and that archaeological field survey is an effective means of rapidly identifying large numbers of sites of archaeological and historic interest.

Amongst these sites, and rarely recorded on historic maps, are the former slave villages, the dwellings and burial places of many of the ancestor of people on Nevis today. Their layout, the character of their buildings and the use of space within the villages, the material aspects of the slave economy and life within these are little understood. Detailed intensive topographic surveys by LIDAR may reveal subtle traces of terracing, house platforms, and cultivation ridges, while shovel test pitting of the kind employed at Jessups and New River on Nevis by the joint project undertaken by DAACS, Monticello, Virginia, the University of Southampton, and National Museums Liverpool in 2006 and 2008[48] may reveal changing patterns of use and activity through analysis of artefact distributions.

ACKNOWLEDGEMENTS

Archaeological field survey and the associated excavations at Mountravers were undertaken between 2000 and 2005, directed by the author, with assistance from Bruce Williams of Bristol City Museum. The need for archaeological survey at Mountravers was first highlighted by and discussed with members of the *Time Team* expedition of 1999: Mick Aston, David Small, David McComish, and Peter Bellamy. Building survey at Mountravers was directed by Nigel Fradgley, my former colleague at the RCHME. The project was funded principally by the British Academy, but with much support from the late Mr Vince Hubbard, the University of Southampton, Morning Star Holdings, and the Nevis Heritage Project. The project team consisted mainly of first year students from the Department of Archaeology, University of Southampton, but also staff of Bristol City Museum, including Rachel Heaton, Andy King, and the late Dr Andrew Townsend. Archaeological fieldwork was much assisted through the local knowledge of Edward Herbert and David Rollinson, and much advice on logistical matters was provided by Ernie Dover at Morning Star Holdings. To all of these persons I am most grateful for their support.

Permission to undertake the work was given by the landowners, Mr Bill Pinney, a descendant of the Pinneys of Mountravers, and the Nevis Island Administration. The Nevis Historical and Conservation Society and its Director John Guilbert gave much support in obtaining consents and enabling use of its museum and storage facilities. Many other local people assisted, with site visits, advising and supplying accommodation and catering for the team. All are thanked for their warm support.

In the planning of the project and in the subsequent analysis of the results, I am most grateful to the following: Dr Elaine Morris for first inviting and enabling me to participate in her newly created Nevis Heritage Project, David Small of Bristol for sharing his knowledge of the history of Mountravers, the late Professor David Peacock for all his support, Russell Fox at the Ordnance Survey, Southampton for facilitating access to air photographs and maps in the now dispersed collections of the former Directorate of Overseas Surveys, Dr Rob Philpott of National Museums Liverpool for leading the analysis and reporting on of the finds, and the late Vince Hubbard, Richard Lupinacci, Ben Carr, and Martin Dalgleish for many useful discussions. Finally, I must thank my wife Pamela for reading through the manuscript and making many helpful suggestions. Any errors and omissions remain of course the responsibility of the author.

NOTES

1 References for the maps are given under Map Sources (p. 268).
2 Higman 1988, 1.
3 Ainsworth *et al.* 2007; Taylor 1974, 40–3 provides the best summary of using base line survey techniques.
4 English Heritage 2016.
5 Pares 1950.
6 Eickelmann & Small 2020; Eickelmann & Small 2004; Small 2006.
7 https://www.ucl.ac.uk/lbs/.
8 Leech 1997, 2000.
9 Harlow 1924, 14.
10 TNA PROB 11/159/624.
11 For John Hilton's account, see Harlow 1924.
12 Arber 1910, 909; Bridenbaugh & Bridenbaugh 1972, 41.
13 Bibliothèque National Paris GE D- 1541: 'Plan de l'Isle de Sainct Christophe. Plan de l'Isle Nieves' *c.* 1630.
14 De Rochefort 1665, 20.
15 'America and West Indies: November 16–30, 1676', in Calendar of State Papers Colonial, America and West Indies: Volume 9, 1675–1676 and Addenda 1574–1674, ed. W. Noel Sainsbury (London, 1893), pp. 494–507. British History Online http://www.british-history.ac.uk/cal-state-papers/colonial/america-west-indies/vol9/pp494-507 [accessed 9 April 2020]).
16 Sloane 1707, 42.
17 Oldmixon 1708, II, 195.
18 Dunn 1973, 125.
19 Pares 1950, 22.
20 Olwig 1993.
21 All discussed at greater length in Leech 2007.
22 Pares 1950, 36–9.
23 Small 2006, 7, 18.
24 Pares 1950, 50–3.
25 Pares 1950, 84–7.
26 NCHCR 1778–83, fol. 611.
27 Small 2006, 19.
28 Leech 2005.
29 Small 2006, 17; see above p. 240 and Fig. 12.4 for the plan and extent of the plantation house and works at Charlots.
30 John Ryland Library, Stapleton MSS 2/1/13/2/1 and 2.
31 Leech 2014, 214–16.
32 Pares 1950, 336–9 and 52–3.
33 NCHCR 1778–1783, fol. 610.
34 Small 2006, 19.
35 Hubbard 2002, pl. 2.
36 See Leech 2013, 47–50 for references and further discussion.
37 Leech 2009; Leech 2013, 50–1; Leech 2014, ch. 9.
38 Taylor 1999.
39 Small 2006, 17–18.
40 Leech 2013, 52–3.
41 Leech 2010, 130–5.
42 Machling 2012.
43 Small 2006, 15–16.
44 Taylor 1999.
45 Everleigh 1993–4, 12–17.
46 https://www.daacs.org/archaeological-sites-map/.
47 http://www.myvuenews.com/nevis-world-heritage-committee/.
48 See note 42.

BIBLIOGRAPHY

Ainsworth, S. *et al.* 2007, *Understanding the Archaeology of Landscapes: A Guide to Good Recording Practice*, Swindon: English Heritage.

Arber, E. 1910, *Travels and Works of Captain John Smith President of Virginia and Admiral of New England 1580–1631*, Edinburgh: John Grant.

Bridenbaugh, C. & Bridenbaugh, R. 1972, *No Peace Beyond the Line: The English in the Caribbean 1624–1690*, New York: Oxford University Press.

De Rochefort, C. 1665, *Histoire naturelle et morale des Isles Antilles de l'Amerique*, 2nd edn, Rotterdam.

Dresser, M. & Hann, A. (eds) 2013, *Slavery and the British Country House*, Swindon: English Heritage.

Dunn, R.S. 1973, *Sugar and Slaves: The Rise of the Planter Class in the English West Indies, 1624–1713*, New York: W.W. Norton and Co.

Eickelmann, C. & Small, D. 2004, *Pero. The Life of a Slave in Eighteenth-Century Bristol*, Bristol: Redcliffe Press and Bristol Museums and Art Gallery.

Eickelmann, C. & Small, D. 2020, *Mountravers Plantation (Pinney's Estate) – Nevis, West Indies and Other Work on Nevis*, https://seis.bristol.ac.uk/~emceee/otherwork.html.

English Heritage, 2016, *Understanding Historic Buildings: A Guide to Good Recording Practice*, English Heritage, Swindon.

Everleigh, D. 1993–4. 'Cooking Pots and Old Curios – the Posnet and the Skillet, *Folk Life*, 32, 7–32.

Finch, J. & Giles, K. (eds) 2007, *Estate Landscapes: Design, Improvement and Power in the Post-Medieval Landscape*, Soc. Post-Med. Archaeol. Monogr. 4, Woodbridge: Boydell and Brewer.

Harlow, V.T. (ed.) 1924, 'Colonising Expeditions to the West Indies and Guiana, 1623–1667', *Publications of the Hakluyt Soc.*, 2nd Series, LVI.

Higman, B.W. 1988, *Jamaica Surveyed: Plantation Maps and Plans of the Eighteenth and Nineteenth Centuries*, Kingston: Institute of Jamaica Publications.

Hubbard, V.K. 2002, *A History of St Kitts: the Sweet Trade*, Oxford: Macmillan Caribbean.

Klingelhofer, E. (ed.), 2010. *First Forts, Essays on the Archaeology of Proto-colonial Fortifications*, Leiden and Boston: Brill.

Leech, R.H. 1997, *The Topography of Medieval and Early Modern Bristol, Part 1: Property Holdings in the Early Walled Town and Marsh Suburb North of the Avon*, Bristol Record Soc. 48.

Leech, R.H. 2000, *The St Michael's Hill Precinct of the University of Bristol. The Topography of Medieval and Early Modern Bristol, Part 2*, Bristol Record Soc. 52.

Leech, R.H. 2005, 'Impermanent Architecture in the English Colonies of the Eastern Caribbean: New Contexts for Architectural Innovation in the Early Modern Atlantic World', *Building Environments: Perspectives in Vernac. Architect.* 10, Knoxville: University of Tennessee Press, 153–67.

Leech R.H. 2007, '"In What Manner Did They Devide The Land" The Early Colonial Estate Landscape of Nevis and St Kitts", in Finch & Giles (eds) 2007, 191–204.

Leech R.H. 2009, 'Charlestown to Charleston – Urban and Plantation Connections in an Atlantic Setting', in Shields (ed.) 2009, 170–87.

Leech, R.H. 2010, '*"Within musquett shott of Black Rock"* –Johnson's Fort and the Early Defenses of Nevis', in Klingelhofer (ed.) 2010, 127–38.

Leech, R.H. 2013, 'Lodges, Garden Houses and Villas: The Urban Periphery in the Early Modern Atlantic World', in Dresser & Hann (eds) 2013, 46–56.

Leech, R.H. 2014, *The Town House in Medieval and Early Modern Bristol*, Swindon: English Heritage.

Machling, T.C.S. 2012, *The Fortifications of Nevis, West Indies, from the 17th Century to the Present Day: Protected Interests?*, Brit. Archaeol. Rep. Int. Ser. 2349, Oxford: Archaeopress.

Oldmixon, J. 1708, *The British Empire in America, containing the history of the discovery, settlement, progress and state of the British Colonies on the Continent and Islands of America …*, 2 vols, London: Printed for John Nicholson at the King's Arms in Little Britain, Benjamin Tooke at the Middle-Temple-Gate Fleet Street and Richard Parker and Ralph Smith under the Piazza at the Royal Exchange.

Olwig, K.F. 1993, *Global Culture, Island Identity: Continuity and Change in the Afro-Caribbean Community of Nevis*, Amsterdam: Harewood Academic publishers.

Pares, R. 1950, *A West-India Fortune*, London: Longmans.

Shields, D. 2009, *Material Culture in Anglo-America, Regional Identity and Urbanity in the Tidewater, Lowcountry and Caribbean*, Charleston: College of Charleston.

Sloane, Sir Hans, 1707, *A Voyage to the Islands Madera, Barbados, Nieves, S. Christophers, and Jamaica, with the natural history ... of the last of those islands; to which is prefixed an introduction wherein is an account of the inhabitants ... trade, etc.*, London.

Small, D. 2006, 'The Modern Pinney's Estate, Nevis. An Historical Account of Seven Sites', Bristol: University of Bristol, Department of Archaeology and Anthropology, unpublished report.

Taylor, C. 1974, *Fieldwork in Medieval Archaeology*, London: Batsford.

Taylor, T. 1999, 'Nevis West Indies', in *Time Team 99 The Site Reports*, 89–102.

MAP SOURCES

Barnett, Captain E. and assistants, HMS Thunder 1848, *St Christopher and Nevis, 1:56,700*, London: Admiralty (PRO WO78/603).

Burdon, Major J.A. 1920, *Nevis, compiled and brought up to date from existing surveys by Major J.A. Burdon*, London: Geographical Section, General Staff War Office.

Iles, John Alexander Burke 1871, *An Account descriptive of the Island of Nevis, West Indies*, Norwich: Privately Printed.

Ordnance Survey 1984, *Nevis, Lesser Antilles 1:25,000*, Southampton: Ordnance Survey.

Overseas Surveys, Ordnance Survey. *Nevis 3193 [and other sheets for areas surveyed at 1:2500]*, Tolworth: Directorate of Overseas Surveys.

INDEX